PRAY BALL 2!!

PRAY

Spiritual Insights

ALL 2!!

to Sportsmanship

RABBI JAMES M. GORDON

TEAM SPIRIT PRESS

A Division of Team Spirit Institute

2018

For further information regarding this book,
please contact: www.TeamSpiritInstitute.org
or Rabbi James M. Gordon, J.D.
RabbiGordon@TeamSpiritInstitute.org

Designed by Sam Silvio, Silvio Design, Inc.
Hebrew typesetting and editing by Shikma Benmelech
Printed in Canada by Friesens Corporation

ISBN: 978-0-692-07418-3

Please treat this book as religious literature.

לזכר נשמת אבי מורי
הרב נחום חיים
בן הרב אלחנן פסח גורדון זצ״ל

Dedicated in loving memory of
my father (and) teacher
Rabbi Nathan H. Gordon (1927–2017).

Although my Dad never did get to see the
great Babe Ruth play, he was Ruthian in the impact
that he had on my life.

Praise (Prays) for *PRAY BALL 2!!*

Spiritual Insights Into Sportsmanship (from Z-A; actually Y-B)*

"Rabbi Gordon's book celebrates the capacity of sports to teach young players important values such as respect for fellow participants, optimism, and a strong work ethic . . . I gained so much from my experiences playing sports in middle school, high school and college and was glad to have a chance to read a book that frames the value of sports in a moral and Jewish context."

REBECCA YOSHOR

2014 NCAA leader (women & men) in rebounds per game; featured in *Faces In The Crowd (Sports Illustrated);* Academic All-America at Yeshiva University Stern College for Women

"Would you like to know how the competition between Maris and Mantle was like that between Hillel and Shammai on their answer to the question of whether an unattractive bride can be told she is beautiful on her wedding day? Or how it's a matter of good sportsmanship not to bring shame on a loaf of bread? You will find the answers in this delightful book about sportsmanship through the prism of Jewish teaching by Rabbi Jamie Gordon. Life lessons abound amid great sports tales."

BRUCE WOLF

Sports Journalist; Talk Radio Host

"Extensively researched and well written, *PRAY BALL 2!! Spiritual Insights Into Sportsmanship* is not only a book to be read by youth, it will serve as an excellent resource for coaches, counselors, teachers and all who are in a position to influence and develop the character of young people."

MORTON M. STEINBERG

Senior counsel, DLA Piper LLP; former President of the National Ramah Commission

"Rabbi James Gordon once again does a superior job of tying elements of sportsmanship to the *Talmud* and Jewish traditions. He uses a diversity of sports figures, ranging from Lou Gehrig to Jerry Reinsdorf, to cite vivid examples of how aspects of their lives and careers can relate to Judaism. The Rabbi's book is highly entertaining, with keen analysis and perspective.

And it teaches many important lessons that can be learned from the sports landscape."

ED SHERMAN

Author, *Babe Ruth's Called Shot: The Myth and Mystery of Baseball's Greatest Home Run;* former *Chicago Tribune* sportswriter

"In teaching and leading students who are maturing, one learns that what counts and what scores is not just what you teach, but your integrity . . . And particularly the teacher has impact by his/her deeds on the sports field, in the gym, and on the court. Rabbi Gordon has written a book . . . which hits home where people live, and particularly, where our growing children live. Rabbi Gordon is an experienced teacher who lives the integrity and the integration of values that the book brings to life."

RABBI MOSHE SIMKOVICH

Professional Development Consultant, Associated Talmud Torahs of Chicago; Founding Head of School, Kohelet Yeshiva High School (Merion, PA); beloved teacher at Maimonides School (Brookline, MA)

"Rabbi Gordon, a one-of-a-kind storyteller, recounts in *PRAY BALL 2!!* stories about the people he loves best: sports figures and rabbis. Interweaving those stories with memorable spiritual insights, he offers here a book that should inspire students of all ages. The more people who read and internalize the values taught in *PRAY BALL 2!!,* the better our world will be."

DR. JONATHAN D. SARNA

Joseph H. and Belle R. Braun Professor of American Jewish History, Brandeis University

"A wonderfully rich and invaluable resource for both teaching and learning about character development through sports. Gordon brings engaging examples and insightful observations to support his growth mindset approach to learning about character and identity. This is a must read for Jewish high school athletes, their parents and coaches."

RABBI HOWARD JACOBY RUBEN

Head of School, Jewish Community High School of the Bay (JCHS)

"Anyone who loves sports will enjoy this book. Anyone who loves Judaism will enjoy this book. And anyone who loves sports and Judaism will easily learn lessons about sportsmanship, teamwork, respect and honor that is vital to every aspect of our lives. I wish I could have read this book when I was in school!"

MARK POTASH

Chicago Sun-Times Sports Journalist

"This . . . book is uniquely insightful and . . . will inspire an extensive and diverse market of Jewish children, teens, and adults. Personally, as a child with an insatiable appetite for sports and professionally, thirty-five years later, as an executive director for organizations serving Jewish youth through camping and sports programs, I only wish this book had previously existed to both enjoy and use as an essential program resource . . . In an era when so many youth (and adults . . .) are in dire need to simply learn to act like a *mensch*, *PRAY BALL 2!!* should be viewed as a highly positive contribution toward those efforts."

MARTIN OLIFF, PH.D.

Former Executive, Jewish Community Centers

"I thoroughly enjoyed *PRAY BALL 2!!* I never had a warm, fuzzy feeling towards Jewish education . . . until this book! The comparisons that Rabbi Gordon draws from sports to the *Torah* are extremely relatable and incredibly entertaining. I found myself flipping through the book with great enjoyment . . . and I learned a lot! The teachings of our people have allowed me to thrive in college at the University of Pennsylvania and through 7 years in the NFL. This is a must read for any Jewish athlete or any athlete, for that matter."

BRENT NOVOSELSKY

Former Chicago Bear & Minnesota Viking; ChFC, VP Wealth Management

". . . Since I've known Rabbi Jamie Gordon I have always been impressed with his unique talent for blending his passion for everything sports with his deep commitment and passion for *Torah*. Readers of his new book *PRAY BALL 2!!* *Spiritual Insights Into Sportsmanship* will be treated to a fascinating adventure in sports history intertwined with valuable life lessons rooted in relevant and inspiring Jewish values."

RABBI MENACHEM LINZER

Principal, Hillel Torah North Suburban Day School (Skokie, IL)

"From the earliest age, American children are exposed to sports. Its influence on the American psyche is beyond a question of a doubt. Knowing this all too well, Rabbi James Gordon . . . has published his newest book, *PRAY BALL 2!!* *Spiritual Insights Into Sportsmanship,* using sports as a metaphor for life's lessons. In this work he teaches, without preaching, how important sportsmanship is in our daily relationships. I have no doubt that this book will influence scores of young adults for years to come."

RABBI ELAZAR MUSKIN

Senior Rabbi, Young Israel of Century City, Los Angeles; President, Rabbinical Council of America

"Rabbi Gordon takes sports stories and creates analogies to real life situations. The stories themselves are very accessible . . . as he highlights the importance of sportsmanship for those inside the game and outside the game . . . To Rabbi Gordon's credit, he has presented us with a wonderful tool to teach values . . . which are essential not only for young people, but for all people of whatever age. I recommend his work . . . to teach our youth through these sports stories . . . how to model lives of *Torah* values and proper living."

RABBI VERNON KURTZ

Senior Rabbi, North Suburban Synagogue Beth El (Highland Park, IL); Past President: Rabbinical Assembly, American Zionist Movement and Council of Religious Leaders of Metropolitan Chicago

"*PRAY BALL 2!!* *Spiritual Insights into Sportsmanship* is an extraordinary work, masterfully blending *Torah* and Jewish knowledge with American culture in an accessible manner for students of all ages."

RABBI DR. ZEV ELEFF

Associate Professor of Jewish History, Touro College and University System; Chief Academic Officer, Hebrew Theological College

"Why do we love sports? For the action. For the competition. For the stories. For the joy of rooting as a community. And also for the lessons. Games build character, and that's a lesson Rabbi James M. Gordon understands and illuminates so well in this terrific book."

JONATHAN EIG

New York Times best-selling author of *Luckiest Man, Opening Day,* and *Ali*

"This new book by Rabbi James Gordon is a worthy successor to an earlier volume with the same name. Rabbi Gordon's earlier *PRAY BALL!* had the subtitle *The Spiritual Insights of a Jewish Sports Fan* and showed how sacred precepts of Judaism can be reinforced in the proper play of major sports. By contrast, the recently published *PRAY BALL 2!!*, this time with the subtitle *Spiritual Insights Into Sportsmanship*, focuses specifically and more deeply on what eternal Judaic precepts can teach us about correct behavior on and off the athletic field. In this latest iteration of *PRAY BALL!*, as in the earlier volume, Rabbi Gordon proves to be a master teacher who shows that moral rectitude should never be subordinate to physical prowess."

DR. ERWIN H. EPSTEIN

Professor Emeritus, Center for Comparative Education, Loyola University Chicago

"Rabbi Jamie Gordon has hit a home run! . . . The chapters are filled with wonderful true stories of some present day sports celebrities and many of my heroes from years gone by. As a community based pediatrician for thirty years and former medical director of a Jewish day school and overnight camp, I have seen the need for more positive stories and mentoring. Rabbi Gordon's current work will undoubtedly resonate with athletic minded youth of all ages and talent."

DAVID DOBKIN, M.D.

President, Medical Staff, Lurie Children's Hospital; Past President, Ida Crown Jewish Academy; Past Medical Director, Camp Ramah in Wisconsin; Clinical Assistant Professor of Pediatrics, Northwestern University Feinberg School of Medicine

". . . The media exposes our children to numerous negative role models in college and professional sports. *PRAY BALL 2!!* can counter these stories with its examples of Jewish male and female sports figures who exemplify *derech eretz* and *kavod*. . . ."

Thank you Rabbi Gordon for providing such an important tool to build passion in our students for the Jewish values associated with sportsmanship."

MARCI DICKMAN

Director of Lifelong Learning, Beth Emet The Free Synagogue (Evanston, IL); Former Head of School, Sager Solomon Schechter Day School (IL)

"Youth very readily identify with sports heroes but often fail to see how their significant acts reflect ancient truths. . . . There is no question that Rabbi Gordon has identified an important educational opportunity heretofore unrecognized, and has effectively provided the tools with which to take advantage of this opportunity."

RABBI DR. BURTON I. COHEN

Former National Director of the Ramah Camps and Israel Programs; Associate Professor Emeritus and former Chair, Department of Education, Jewish Theological Seminary of America

"Rabbi Gordon . . . has the unique ability to see vital lessons in what may seem like ordinary stories . . . He makes the almost seamless connection to Jewish sources, and Jewish values. In a unique twist, Rabbi Gordon has brought sport to the day school/yeshiva, and has brought the day school/yeshiva to sport. . . . The book is an eye-opener."

RABBI DR. REUVEN P. BULKA, C.M.

Rabbi, writer, broadcaster and activist in Ottawa, Ontario, Canada; former co-president of the Canadian Jewish Congress

*Growing up I always felt bad for the kids whose last names began with the letter Z. Since names were listed alphabetically, the Zimmermans and Zuckers always went last. In a book about sportsmanship, it only seems right that the Z, Y & Xs should (finally) go first!

For the unabridged texts of these blurbs/letters of endorsement see www.TeamSpiritInstitute.org.

Some Additional Words of Praise (*Prays*) – for the original *PRAY BALL! The Spiritual Insights of a Jewish Sports Fan* (in the order they appear on the backcover of the book)

"Jewish tradition teaches: 'In all of your ways shall you attempt to know (and love) Him (G-d).' The glory of our tradition is that we never separated the physical and the spiritual; it has always been our goal to elevate every aspect of the physical in order to bring the religious and the secular together. From this perspective Rabbi Gordon's most exciting and relevant book *PRAY BALL!* is a worthy addition to anyone's Judaica library."
RABBI DR. SHLOMO RISKIN
Chancellor and Founder, Ohr Torah Stone; Chief Rabbi of Efrat

"This is a fascinating book for people who love sports – but also realize that there is something far deeper and more meaningful in life beyond sports. To present both worlds simultaneously and to tie them together so scucessfully is quite a feat."
RABBI PINCHAS STOLPER
Founding Director of NCSY; Former Executive Vice President of the Orthodox Union

"*PRAY BALL!* is recreation for the soul. Rabbi Gordon puts us through our paces in seeing deeper messages behind athletic heroics in an inviting, engrossing and delightful manner. *PRAY BALL!* is the perfect Bar or Bat Mitzvah gift for young sportst enthusiasts which will also be read cover-to-cover by their parents."
RABBI DANNY LANDES
Former Director, Pardes Institute of Jewish Studies, Jerusalem

"Through the archway of sports, Rabbi Gordon leads us into an arena of fascinating events and remarkably relevant spiritual teaching, where we discover practical advice gleaned from the exciting endeavor of sports combined with the divine guidance of *Torah* which can help us find our way through life's complexities . . . Youth and adults alike will return again and again to this book to find delight and inspiration."
RABBI HERBERT BRONSTEIN
Past President of the Chicago Board of Rabbi and the Association of Reform Rabbis.

"How does the coaching genius of Phil Jackson teach the Jewish concept of Family Harmony (*Shalom Bayit*)? What moral responsibility, as 'my brother's keeper,' does a sports agent have to his client? How does the relationship between Tiger Woods and his father reflect Jewish values? What do we learn about *teshuva* – repentance – from Dennis Rodman? . . . *PRAY BALL!* combines the best of both the sports and Jewish worlds."
LOU WEISBACH
Entrepeneur and Former High School Basketball Coach
LEIGH STEINBERG
Prominent Sports Agent

"For all those who miss Michael Jordan and the Championship Bulls, here's your opportunity to reminisce. And while you're reminiscing, you'll receive the added bonus of learning more about Judaism in the process."
TAL BRODY
Former Captain, Israel National Team; Captain, 1977 Maccabee Tel-Aviv European Basketball Champions

Contents

Preface
by Zev Eleff

In November 1909, the editors of a New York weekly published a humorous editorial about "College Foot-Ball." The *Hebrew Standard* joked about a college classroom scene, of a professor lecturing to a room-full of empty chairs. The absences could be explained by a single clause: "The Foot-Ball Season Begins." Back then, Jews of all stripes—and Americans of all kinds—worried about the strange interaction between athletics and education. Neither, it seemed, wanted to complement the other. Instead, sports and education challenged one another for the attention of American youth.

We have come a long way. For decades, educators have made use of sports as a teaching tool; educating children through competition and games or utilizing athletics as a frame of reference, a metaphor, really. Few, however, have managed to synthesize moral education with sports as well as Rabbi James Gordon. He is an accomplished author and educator, whose earlier writings have already started this trailblazing endeavor to harmonize the crucial life-lessons that Judaism and sports offer.

PRAY BALL 2!! *Spiritual Insights into Sportsmanship* is an extraordinary work, masterfully blending *Torah* and Jewish knowledge with American culture in an accessible manner for students of all ages. Beginning with the opening anecdote about Michael Jordan, this book engages a sports culture that is both compelling and educative. The many anecdotes in this volume are presented in a clear form, and will garner appreciation from diehard, casual and uninitiated fans.

The colorful vignettes are intentional, strategic even. Rabbi Gordon uses them as a portal of entry to readers, beyond the deep *Torah* traditions that accompany each section and chapter.

The wisdom and lessons found within its pages are deep and inspiring. All too often, authors of educational works compromise on content to increase readability. Not so in this book. Rabbi Gordon lucidly tackles many core Jewish principles relating to interpersonal relations and contextualizes them within the sophisticated tradition of biblical and rabbinic literature. What is more, he draws important teachings from figures like Anne Frank, Elijah the Prophet and *Reish Lakish* in a way that is both relatable and ensures that these personalities retain their ultimate dignity and unparalleled legacy.

Finally, and perhaps most impressive of all, we are all in Rabbi Gordon's debt for furnishing a work that has no age limits. Parents, children, teachers and students of all ages will appreciate the book. While I am sure that middle school educators will take the most advantage of this volume, I am confident that *PRAY BALL 2!!* will find its way into rabbinical sermons, summer camp programs, adult education and outreach classes and even in high school classrooms. Unlike back in the early twentieth century, instructors will have little trouble competing with sports. Rabbi Gordon has ensured that the two can go hand in hand.

Rabbi Dr. Zev Eleff is an Associate Professor of Jewish History, Touro College and University System; and Chief Academic Officer, Hebrew Theological College.

Foreword
by Jonathan Eig

Jackie Robinson was an extraordinary teammate on a squad that didn't want him. Lou Gehrig was the most valuable member of a team to which he never felt like he truly belonged. Muhammad Ali chose boxing, in part, because he couldn't bear the thought of playing for any team; he preferred to go it alone.

I've spent years getting to know and writing about these three extraordinary athletes. Their stories teach us a great deal about what it means to be an athlete, a teammate, a human being. In history, we can learn as much from the good examples as the bad.

Consider Robinson first. When he joined the Brooklyn Dodgers in 1947, he was the only black man in the major leagues. His presence was not a milestone – not at first, anyway; it was an experiment, one that most people expected to fail. Robinson and millions of black fans cheering him hoped and believed that team spirit and talent would prove more powerful than prejudice. While remaining mostly silent, Robinson played his way onto the Dodgers and earned the respect of fans. Has there ever been a better example of the American Dream played out on a sporting field? Give a man a chance to work hard and show his stuff, and watch him change the world. The more the Dodgers won, the more racism faded, even among his most virulent opponents. Bobby Bragan, one of Robinson's teammates, told me he was dead-set against playing with a black man. Bragan was raised in the South and taught to believe that black people were inherently inferior to white. He thought nothing would ever shake that belief – until Robinson joined his team and the Dodgers went to the World Series and the earth neither cracked open nor did hell freeze over. That's the power of sports.

Sports helped Lou Gehrig overcome his crippling shyness. He would never be wild or outspoken enough to pal around with a gregarious, man's man like Babe Ruth. But he could play ball with him, and that was enough. Gehrig slowly grew into one of the most courageous men ever to swing a baseball bat – so courageous that when he was struck with the tragic news of his illness, he stood before 60,000 fans, overcame his shyness, and gave the greatest speech in the history of professional sports, saying that while he might have been dealt a bad hand by illness, he would always consider himself lucky to have lived such a beautiful life and to have made such glorious friends. What could be more heroic than that?

Finally, there's Muhammad Ali, who knew at the age of 12 that he preferred not to share the spotlight. No football or basketball for him. Too many rules. Too many teammates. Ali did not exhibit good sportsmanship. He belittled his opponents. He gloated. Some of his behavior was inexcusable, but his misdeeds were offset in years to come by his courage, by his willingness to sacrifice for his beliefs. Remarkably, despite his more than healthy ego, Ali remained humble. He never refused an autograph. He performed countless unseen acts of charity. He was the rare athlete who may have behaved better privately than publicly.

Why do we care about how these and other athletes behave? Do we really need them to be our role models? Don't we have parents and teachers and others to inspire us? Yes, we do. But great athletes inspire us, too, with their grace and strength and determination, and sometimes with their character, too. Jackie Robinson teaches us courage and sacrifice. Lou Gehrig teaches us to be grateful and unselfish. Muhammad Ali teaches us stand up for our beliefs. None of these men is perfect, but I'd gladly have any of them on my team.

Jonathan Eig is the *New York Times* bestselling author of five books, including *Ali, Luckiest Man,* and *Opening Day.*

Introduction
A Parent's Love of the Game

It was a meeting in which we were both in the same place for the same reason. We were on equal footing, so to speak. The venue was a small gymnasium in a high-class, quaint suburb of Chicago. The reason why Michael Jordan and I were there was to watch our daughters, both junior high students, play basketball. That day, I saw MJ in a totally new light, which earned him even greater respect in my eyes.

For years, it was rumored that Michael Jordan, on occasion, would show up at games when his sons and daughter played against the Jewish parochial school that my children attended. As a superstar who cherished his privacy, it was known to all that Jordan followed a certain protocol as a sports parent. His modus operandi included arriving late and leaving early. This, of course, sent the message to those in attendance that Mr. Jordan did not want to draw any attention away from his children. Like the other proud parents, MJ was there strictly to show support for his child.

I also have a tendency of running late (and sometimes leaving early), but clearly for other reasons. That evening happened to be one of those times. Arriving about five minutes after tipoff, before I could enter the gym, I was greeted by my father, a proud grandfather of one of the players on the visiting team, who told me excitedly in simple, clear Hebrew: **!מִיכָאֵל פֹּה**/*Mikhael po!* – **"Michael is here!"** I did not immediately comprehend about which "Michael" my dad was referring until I entered the gym and sat in the seat which my parents saved for me in the second row of the bleachers. Sitting directly in front of me was the legend. But today he was just one of the dads.

Squeezed into the tight space in the bleachers, I was so close to the greatest hoopster in the history of basketball that I could almost see my reflection in MJ's cleanly shaven bald head. Although it was tempting to ask him for an autograph or engage him in simple "fan's conversation," I respected Mr. Jordan's privacy and vowed that any exchanges that I would have would be strictly in my capacity as a father of one of the players.

My daughter, Rita, who wore jersey #33 and was our team's point guard, knew who Jasmine's father was, but treated him like any other parent. When she needed to inbound the ball, Rita simply stood in front of Mr. Jordan, pretending that he was just another anonymous parent in the stands, who had to move his feet so that she could stand out-of-bounds and pass the ball to a teammate.

When Jasmine Jordan, went to the free-throw line and missed a shot, instead of showing disappointment or dismay, her dad had a big smile on his face laughing with (NOT at) his daughter who appeared, that day, not to be playing at the top of her game.

Towards the end of the game, I finally broke my silence and said to Michael Jordan, "Your daughter and her team played a good game." Without missing a beat, Mr. Jordan responded, "So long as they have fun." Rita, who happened to play her best game at the junior high level that day, received the ultimate compliment when the legendary Michael Jordan told her "Great game, 33!"

Although Rita's basketball career continued for nearly an additional decade, as she played varsity high school and NCAA Division III ball, the greatest compliment that she ever received from any coach, fan or parent, was when she was in eighth grade. It came from the world's all-time greatest basketball player.

Michael Jordan is known for many things, including his passion for the game of basketball and his fiercely competitive spirit. When it comes to being a sports parent, Mr. Jordan showed me that he was on par with the best of dads. The great Michael Jordan realized that, at that level of youth sports, being competitive meant encouraging your child to enjoy the game for the sake of the joy of the game itself.

One of the main goals of this publication is to teach and, hopefully, inspire the reader to incorporate – through the medium of sports (as both participant and spectator) – more and more of the **values** (מִדּוֹת/מִדָּה – *Midot/Midah* – singular) that are presented in this book. Similarly, it is my objective to inspire Jewish educators (rabbis, other teachers, camp counselors, coaches, etc.) to use this book as an important resource to connect sports-minded youth with some of the many rich practices of the Jewish tradition, so that sports can be used – even more than it already is – to build character.

"The Second City" Influence

Also known as "the Second City," Chicago is second to none when it comes to being a sports town. Naturally, as a huge sports fan and native Chicagoan, I have a particular affinity towards Chicago teams. While I have included numerous amazing stories of acts of sportsmanship performed by members of the professional and school teams of many different cities, naturally, the reader will find a "home team bias," in that there is a relative abundance of stories involving Chicago sports teams and figures. All of the stories in this book are timeless and transcend geographic boundaries.

Going forward, it is my intention to provide additional, supplementary stories to appeal even more to readers from other sports cities who may feel somewhat "shortchanged."

The inspiration for the title of this book originates from my first book, **PRAY BALL!** *The Spiritual Insights of a Jewish Sports Fan*. Published in 1999, it was my intention that the original **PRAY BALL!** would formally introduce readers and educators to the concept of using sports to teach Jewish values, history and traditions. Since then, I have written numerous drafts focused on using sports to teach specific values. These drafts have been successfully piloted in multiple

Does Participating in Sports Build Character?

In their book *Character Development and Physical Activity,* Professors David Lyle Light Shields and Brenda Jo Light Bredemeier present both sides of this issue. In short, they conclude that if the proper culture is developed under the direction of appropriate coaches, administrators and parents, participation in youth sports can be a most positive medium to build good character. However, if a suitable environment is not fostered, then the sporting experience can be damaging to the moral development of the youth participants.

The authors credit Greek philosopher Plato (428–348 BCE), as being the first known thinker to acknowledge the close connection between a person's moral and physical fitness. The first "modern style" school system to incorporate sports as a character-building medium was in 19th century England. In fact, in 1864, the Royal Commission on Public Schools stated: "The cricket and football fields . . . are not merely places of exercise or amusement; they help to form some of the most valuable social qualities . . ., and they hold, like the classroom and the boarding house, a distinct and important place in Public School education." In the English system, the students themselves administered these youth sports systems. So, in addition to all of the lessons learned on the field, the student-athletes learned valuable teachings in self-governance.

Using sports to build character spread to schools in the United States in the late 1800s. Unlike the British system, where the focus was on students at elite boarding schools, who also governed the sports system, in the US the school administrators managed the sports education. Also, schools whose student bodies were comprised of youth from many different socio-economic backgrounds were fortunate to be a part of this new type of education. In fact, sports proved to be a valuable way for immigrant youth to become more fully integrated in and familiar with American values and culture.

Youth sports are another fertile medium to teach what has been referred to as moral development or values clarification. The early pioneers in this field include German psychiatrist Dr. Sigmund Freud, Swiss psychologist and scientist Dr. Jean Piaget, and American psychologists Dr. Hugh Hartshorne and Dr. Mark A. May. Perhaps the modern day scholar who was the most involved in this field is Dr. Lawrence Kohlberg (1927–1987) who is best remembered for developing a six-stage theory of moral development. His work has been carried on and further developed by his many scions.

In Hebrew the word מִדָּה/מִדּוֹת – *Midah* (singular) *Midot* (plural), is defined many times as ***character trait(s)/types(s)***. Sharing the same root as the word meaning "measurement(s)," *Midot*, in effect, are the traits that measure a person's character. Colloquioly, *Midot* refers to positive character traits. In fact, a בַּעַל מִדּוֹת/*Ba-ahl Midot* describes an ***upstanding person, one who possesses many fine character traits***.

Although there has been extensive research, as well as books written and videos produced regarding teaching moral development in public and other secular schools through the medium of sports (see Jennifer Beller's *Positive Character*

Development in School Sport Programs, and the extensive bibliography it contains, as well as the bibliography in *Shields and Bredemeier*), very little has been produced in this area in Jewish formal and informal education.

As noted in detail in this book's introduction, the ultimate source of all **Jewish values/מִדּוֹת** (*Midot*) is the *Torah*. The Sages teach that there are 613 **Commandments in the Torah**. In Hebrew these commandments are called מִצְווֹת *Mitzvot* (plural)/מִצְוָה *Mitzvah* (singular).

What is Sportsmanship?: The Four Levels of Sportsmanship

What is Sportsmanship?

Good question. Believe it or not, there is no adequate Hebrew word to describe sportsmanship.

Does that mean that Israelis or other Hebrew speaking Jews do not engage in acts of sportsmanship? Of course they do. Then why isn't there a mainstream Hebrew word? My own hypothesis is that, because the definition of sportsmanship varies according to whom you ask, it is difficult to articulate a precise term for it.

The Hebrew term that I feel best represents what sportsmanship is all about is דֶּרֶךְ אֶרֶץ וְכָבוֹד/*Derekh Eretz v'Khavod* – **Respect and Honor**. A somewhat comparable *Yiddish* term is *Menschlikhkite* (roughly, acts performed by a *Mensch* – i.e., respectful/honorable acts); after all a *Mensch* – literally a "man," but figuratively a unisex term – is a person who exhibits *Derekh Eretz v'Khavod* – Respect and Honor, in all areas of his/her life.

So what is sportsmanship? It is the way that people who are involved in sports show respect to the other participants, and thus bring honor to the games themselves and the important life lessons they can teach.

In Jewish tradition, there are many famous individuals who championed the importance of always practicing דֶּרֶךְ אֶרֶץ וְכָבוֹד/*Derekh Eretz v'Khavod* – **Respect and Honor**. One of the better-known scholars who promoted these values was the Sage Hillel. The *Talmud* (*Shabbat* 31a) relates the famous story of a person – with great *Chutzpa* (**audacity**) – who demanded that Hillel teach him the entire *Torah* (i.e., all about Judaism) while standing on one foot.

The Sage Hillel took the challenge and responded:
דַּעֲלָךְ סְנֵי, לְחַבְרָךְ לֹא תַעֲבֵיד.
זוֹ הִיא כָּל הַתּוֹרָה כּוּלָה,
וְאִידָךְ פֵּירוּשָׁה הוּא; זִיל גְּמוֹר!
Da-alakh s'nei, l'chavrakh lo ta-aveid. Zo he kol HaTorah kula, v'idakh perusha hu; zil g'mor!
"That which is hateful to you, do not do onto others. This is the entire Torah, and the rest is its commentary; [now], go [and] study!"

According to Hillel's spontaneous response to this loaded and, may I add, deep philosophical question, the essence of Judaism is that we treat others with proper דֶּרֶךְ אֶרֶץ וְכָבוֹד/*Derekh Eretz v'Khavod* (***Respect and Honor***); that is, in the same manner that anybody would like others to treat him/her. Ultimately this is the purpose of the *Torah's* 613 *Mitzvot* (***Commandments***). When we treat the Almighty and His creations in the proper manner, we, in turn, will be treated well, and our actions will help fill the world with peace and harmony.

We need to look at sports in a similar manner. If we follow the parameters (written & unwritten rules) of sportsmanship, the sporting experience will be a positive one for all involved, and can lead to teaching and learning valuable life lessons which can be applied to our experiences, both inside and outside, the confines of sports venues.

Although sportsmanship begins with simply following the rules of the game ("Level I"), it goes way over and beyond this clearly articulated baseline. Sometimes, for example, we witness a player extending a helping hand to a fallen opponent and other acts of expected good sportsmanship ("Level II"). On less frequent occasions we even see such extraordinary acts of sportsmanship, such as a conscientious tennis player overruling an incorrect call by a line judge and sacrificing his own victory as a result! ("Level III"). Ideally a participant will internalize the acts of sportsmanship s/he exhibits on the field/court and translate these behaviors into acts of Respect and Honor in settings outside of their sport ("Level IV").

Who must exhibit sportsmanship?

All who are involved in the sporting experience at any level (i.e., youth, high school, college, professional, adult recreational, etc.). This includes players, coaches, referees and all officials, fans, cheerleaders, parents, administrators, executives, the media, and even public address announcers. When fully embraced by participants, sportsmanship should lead to respectful and honorable behavior both on and off the sports fields and courts. Sportsmanship should transcend the sporting venue and manifest itself in the way a person interacts in their home, social, school and work environments.

Just as all of Judaism flows from דֶּרֶךְ אֶרֶץ וְכָבוֹד/*Derekh Eretz v'Khavod* (***Respect and Honor***), all of sports' positive values emanate from sportsmanship. To be a successful coach or team captain, a sports leader must act in a sportsmanlike manner towards one's players/teammates, opponents, umpires, fans and all others involved. To be a valuable teammate, not only must a player be at the top of his/her game, but they also must be an exemplar of sportsmanship.

The Four Levels of Sportsmanship: A Spiritual Insight

The Book of *Deuteronomy*, the fifth and final book of the *Torah*, is comprised in large part of a lengthy monologue that Moses delivers to the new generation of the Children of Israel. Born and raised in the desert, these Israelites are set to enter *Eretz Yisrael*, the Promised Land. There are three main components to Moses's speech: (1) a reiteration of key historical events in the 40-year journey in the wilderness; (2) *Mussar* (**moral teachings**); & (3) the introduction of (and in some instances, a repetition of) especially essential *Mitzvot*.

A *sidra* (**weekly portion**) that highlights the latter component is *Parashat VaEtchanan* (*Deuteronomy* 3:23–7:11). This portion contains the restatement of the *Aseret HaDibrot* (**Ten Statements/Commandment**s or **Decalogue** – 5:6–18) and the first paragraph of the *Sh'ma* (6:4–9). In many ways these two paragraphs represent a microcosm of the entire *Torah*. While the *Decalogue* includes key *Mitzvot* on how we must interact, both with God as well as with fellow human beings, the first paragraph of the *Sh'ma* delineates *Mitzvot* regarding the usage of certain religious objects (i.e., *T'fillin* and *M'zuzot*), whose purpose is to remind and inspire Jews to perform the Commandments. The Fifth Commandment, Honoring Parents, combined with the *Mitzvah* of *Talmud Torah* (**Jewish education**) found in the *Sh'ma*, are reminders to parents that their primary duty is to ensure that their children receive a proper Jewish education.

After the presentation of these two powerful paragraphs, Moses instructs the new generation of Israelites (6:17–18):

שָׁמוֹר תִּשְׁמְרוּן אֶת־מִצְוֹת ה' אֱלֹקֵיכֶם
וְעֵדֹתָיו וְחֻקָּיו אֲשֶׁר צִוָּךְ:
וְעָשִׂיתָ הַיָּשָׁר וְהַטּוֹב בְּעֵינֵי ה' ־לְמַעַן יִיטַב לָךְ
וּבָאתָ וְיָרַשְׁתָּ אֶת־הָאָרֶץ הַטֹּבָה אֲשֶׁר־נִשְׁבַּע ה' לַאֲבֹתֶיךָ:

Shamor tishm'roon et Mitzvot HaShem Elokeikhem, v'edotav v'chukav asher tzivakh.
V'asita HaYashar v'HaTov b'einei HaShem l'ma-ahn yitav lakh, u-vata v'yarashta et HaAretz HaTova asher nishba HaShem la-avotekha.

You must observe diligently HaShem your God's Commandments, and His ordinances and statutes which He has commanded.
And you shall do that which is straight [fair] and good in the eyes of HaShem, so that it will be good for you, and you may come into and possess the good Land [of Israel] that HaShem has sworn to your forefathers.

The *Decalogue* and *Sh'ma* paragraphs represent the supreme importance of following the 613 *Mitzvot* as presented in the *Torah* and further elucidated by our Sages. In that way, it can represent what I term **Level I of Sportsmanship** (i.e., following the rules).

The concept of וְעָשִׂיתָ הַיָּשָׁר וְהַטּוֹב בְּעֵינֵי ה'/*V'asita HaYashar v'HaTov b'einei HaShem* (**And you shall do that which is straight [fair] and good in the eyes of HaShem**), represent what I call **Levels II and III of Sportsmanship. Level IV of Sportsmanship** is when a person takes Levels I, II & III and incorporates it in and applies it to their daily (off-the-field/court) life, by treating others with the utmost honor and respect (*Derekh Eretz v'Khavod*).

The *Ramban*/Nachmanides (1194–1270) in his commentary on verse 18, states that the phrase ***do that which is straight [fair] and good***, refers to how to handle situations for which the *Torah* does not delineate a specific *Mitzvah*. While the *Torah* specifies such *Mitzvot* as honoring elders/scholars, not to take revenge or bear a grudge, and not stand by idly while a fellow Jew is in distress, it cannot provide instruction for every life event. According to Nachmanides, this phrase "fills in the blanks," so to speak; it advises every Jew to handle similar matters in a sensitive, compassionate way without forgoing a person's physical and financial survival.

Rashi (1040–1105), on the other hand, tells us that the words וְעָשִׂיתָ הַיָּשָׁר וְהַטּוֹב בְּעֵינֵי ה'/*V'asita HaYashar v'HaTov b'einei HaShem* (***And you shall do that which is straight [fair] and good in the eyes of HaShem***) refer to *p'shara* (**compromise**) and *Lifnim MiShurat HaDin* (***going over and beyond the letter of the law***).

When a *Bet Din* (**Jewish court**) renders a decision, it should consider issues beyond the strict letter of the law, such as maintaining a peaceful relationship between the parties, especially when a future relationship is inevitable.

Now what does all of this have to do with sportsmanship? In my *Torah* sports-minded approach, it is analogous to my four levels of sportsmanship. The *Decalogue* and *Sh'ma* remind us, first and foremost, to observe the *Mitzvot*. The 613 Commandments are spelled out by the *Torah* with further elucidation provided by the Sages in the *Mishna, Gemara*, Codes and ***Responsa literature*** (*Sh'elot u-T'shuvot*). **Level I of Sportsmanship is simply to follow the rules of the game.**

Level II of Sportsmanship is to do acts that, although not specifically delineated in the rules, a conscientious person can figure out. For example, when you see an opponent on the ground, although there is no written rule that you must extend a helping hand, nonetheless, it is a matter of common decency (sportsmanship) to do so. This is analogous to the interpretation of Nachmanides (cited above).

Rashi's interpretation of וְעָשִׂיתָ הַיָּשָׁר וְהַטּוֹב בְּעֵינֵי ה'/*V'asita HaYashar v'HaTov b'einei HaShem* (***And you shall do that which is straight [fair] and good in the eyes of HaShem***) tells the sportsman/woman that when there is an opportunity, one should strongly consider performing **extraordinary (Level III) acts of Sportsmanship (i.e., go over and beyond what the rules of sportsmanship dictate).**

A person displays **Level IV of Sportsmanship when s/he has internalized Levels I, II and III, and then manifests honor and respect in all facets of their life.**

Chapter 2
Basic
Sportsmanship

Sportsmanship Level 1:
Following the Rules

Following the Rules

So you want to be a good sport? Start by following the rules. Every sport has rules. Study them. Learn them. And then respect them by following them.

Players and coaches who are caught breaking rules are penalized. Inevitably, their indiscretions hurt the entire team and their chances of winning. While avoiding fouls in basketball is a key to winning the game, once fouled, it is critical that the team that incurred the foul takes advantage of the foul. In most cases, this means hitting your free throws. In football, penalties are recognized by moving the line of scrimmage back five or fifteen yards giving the aggrieved team better playing position. In hockey, the offending player is removed from the game for a number of minutes (usually two), isolated in the penalty box, and his team is forced to play with one less skater for the duration of the penalty or until the team with the power play advantage scores.

What follows are stories of gifted athletes who were especially known for following the rules in hockey, basketball and swimming.

No one followed the rules better than Stan Mikita. Along with his stellar play, this hockey superstar was rewarded for his playing by the rules by being awarded the NHL's sportsmanship award – the Lady Byng Memorial Trophy – twice.

The Transformation of Stan Mikita

Parents refer to it as a time-out, while teachers call it detention. In hockey it is known simply as a penalty, with the punishment being served in the penalty box. Out of all the major American sports, ice hockey is the only sport where a player who is cited for an infraction of the rules, is not only removed from the game, forcing his team to play shorthanded, but is required to sit by himself in a secluded area until his penalty time has lapsed. I like to think that the rationale for originally implementing this rather peculiar practice is one in the same with why a parent gives a child a time-out; that is, to provide the offender the opportunity to cool down and ponder what he did wrong, with the hope that he will reform his ways.

One of the greatest hockey players of all-time was Chicago Blackhawks legend Stan Mikita. Having moved to Canada at age eight from his native Czechoslovakia, the relatively diminutive, five-foot-nine inch Mikita is remembered during his twenty-two-year NHL/Blackhawks career for his artistic stick handling, deft skating, and prolific scoring. Although he retired after the 1979–1980 season, Mikita still remains the all-time assists and points leader in Blackhawks history.

Awarded the prestigious Lady Byng Memorial Trophy, which is presented annually to the player who best displays a combination of "gentlemanly conduct" with playing skill, Mikita is also recognized for his sportsmanship and the relatively few minutes he spent in the penalty box. However, such was not the case during the first chapter of his playing career. From his rookie season in 1959–1960 through the

1964–1965 campaign, Mikita actually averaged more than 100 penalty minutes per season. During this six-year span, with the exception of one season, #21 had more penalties in minutes than points.

After 1965 though, something drastic changed in Stan Mikita's life and game.

The story is told that one day, one of Stan's young daughters inquired innocently why Dad spent so much time sitting by himself during a Blackhawks game. Apparently inspired to set a more favorable example, Mikita learned how to better control his temper. The result was an almost 180-degree change in his game and contribution to his team's success. For the balance of his career, from the 1965–1966 season to his final season in 1979–1980, #21's collective point total cast a giant shadow over his collective total penalty minutes. In fact, Stan Mikita became the first player to win all three of the most prestigious NHL awards in back-to-back years when he led the league in scoring (Art Ross Trophy) and was the league's MVP (Hart Trophy). The third award was for his exemplary display of sportsmanship (Lady Byng Memorial Trophy).

DIDJA KNOW
that Wilt "The Big Dipper" Chamberlain never fouled out of an NBA game? Chamberlain played in more than 1,200 NBA (regular season and playoff) games, and is best remembered for such NBA records as scoring 100 points in a single game, averaging 50.4 points in the 1961 – 1962 season, grabbing 55 rebounds in one game, and scoring 50 or more points in 118 games. It is incredible that this super-competitive superstar never fouled out. Over a 14-year Hall of Fame career, Chamberlain played for four NBA teams, winning championships with the Philadelphia 76ers (1966–1967) and the Los Angeles Lakers (1971–1972).

Not only did Stan Mikita help his Blackhawks to a Stanley Cup championship (1961) and to multiple winning seasons, but he is also credited with inventing the curved blade stick. This helped increase scoring. He is also the first star to wear a protective helmet, inspiring many other players to start wearing this headgear, which now is a mandatory part of the hockey uniform. A great example of how important it is to manage one's temper, Stan Mikita shows that a highly skilled player can contribute far more to the success of his team, while on the ice and not in the penalty box. From learning how to manage his temper – inspired by the words of a child – emerged one of hockey's greatest, most exciting, and sportsmanlike players.

Honesty is the Best Policy

In the world of Olympic swimming, the U.S. athletes best remembered for their championship feats include Mark Spitz (seven gold medals in 1972), Michael Phelps (23 gold medals in 2004, 2008, 2012, and 2016), and Katie Ledecky (five gold medals in 2012 and 2016). These are household names who then leveraged their Olympic fame to earn fortunes in endorsements, motivational speaking, and other commercial activities.

A name that should also be included on this list is Shirley Babashoff. Unfortunately, instead of being a household name, Babashoff lived her post-Olympic life as a shunned athlete.

During the 1976 Olympic Games held in Montreal, Shirley Babashoff, who won one gold medal as a member of the US relay team, should have won an additional four individual golds. Instead, she had to settle for four second-place silver medals.

Blunt about her runner-up status, Babashoff articulated to the media and others that she had strong suspicions that her East German opponents who were awarded the gold medals in these four competititons benefited from banned performance enhancing drugs. Instead of being taken seriously, Babashoff was shunned by the swimming world and members of the media, viewed as a bad sport. Needless to say, this hurt her image needed to land lucrative endorsements and speaking engagements.

There is a statement that "time heals all wounds." Sometimes wounds heal faster when information surfaces that vindicates the wrongly accused/convicted. After the fall of the Berlin Wall in 1989, it was reported that documents were discovered which revealed that members of the East German swim teams (men and women) were given anabolic steroids as a part of a doping program that was under the perview of the East German government's Ministry for State Security.

Although Shirley Babashoff was vindicated, and her raising issues of possible usage of prohibited PEDs led to a more effective system of Olympic drug-testing, she and her teammates have not been awarded duplicate awards for the medals that they, in great likelihood, would have won had Babashoff been taken seriously over 40 years ago.

Unfortunately, an athlete is not always properly rewarded for playing by the rules. Slowly, but surely (Shirley), this may just change.

Following the Rules: Spiritual Insights

Reish Lakish: From Captain of Thieves to Leader of Scholars

The *Talmud* (*Bava M'tzia* 84a) relates that one day, while at the shores of the Jordan River, *Reish Lakish* (*Shimon ben Lakish*), an infamous leader of a band of robbers, noticed that someone was swimming in the river. Apparently with the intent to stir up trouble – after all, that's what criminals do – *Reish Lakish* jumped into the Jordan to pursue the swimmer. The unknown swimmer happened to be the great *Talmudic* sage and very handsome *Rahbi Yochanan*. When seeing the bandit's extraordinary, Olympic-level diving skills, the venerable sage remarked: חֵילָךְ לְאוֹרַיְיתָא/ *Cheilakh L'Orai'ta* – "**Your strength to [i.e., should be used for] Torah!**" Not missing a beat, *Reish Lakish* retorted: שׁוּפְרָךְ לְנָשֵׁי/*Shuf'rakh L'Nashei* – "**Your beauty belongs to women.**"

Rahbi Yochanan then made the following offer to *Reish Lakish* – contingent, of course, on the approval of his sister. *Rahbi Yochanan* said to the leader of the band of highway bandits that, if *Reish Lakish* would abandon his criminal ways and instead devote his many great skills (i.e., strength, leadership, intellect) to repent/ perform *T'shuva* (**Repentance**; i.e., the study and practice of *Torah*), *Rahbi Yochanan*

DIDJA KNOW
that because
of his striking
appearance,
Rahbi Yochanan
was referred to by
the Aramaic term
שׁוּפְרָא/*Shufra*
[*beautiful/
handsome man*]
(*B'rakhot* 5b)?

DIDJA KNOW
that the woman's
name *Shifra*
(שִׁפְרָה) is
derived from the
same root
as שׁוּפְרָא/ *Shufra?*

would do all that he could to convince his sister – also known for her beauty – to marry *Reish Lakish*. This was an offer that *Shimon ben Lakish* simply could not refuse.

Reish Lakish did indeed repent, as he channeled all of his leadership, intellectual, and physical skills to the study of *Torah*, emerging as a scholar par excellence, at the level of his teacher and now brother-in-law *Rahbi Yochanan*.

Because a great sage took an interest in and made an irrefusable offer to a misdirected criminal, this highway robber was able to channel his skills for the benefit of the Jewish people. The first level of *Derckh Eretz v'Khavod* (**Respect and Honor**) is to **not** harm the person and property of others. While *Rahbi Yochanan*'s efforts led to *Reish Lakish* attaining this level, it also was the impetus for *Rahbi Shimon ben Lakish* to perform and teach others to perform many *Mitzvot* that manifest *Derekh Eretz v'Khavo*d.

THE BOX SCORE

Level I of Sportsmanship is simply to follow the rules. NBA superstar Wilt Chamberlain is an example of an athlete who played by the rules, as he never fouled out of a single NBA game. Shirley Babashoff trained and swam in accordance with Olympic rules and regulations. Unfortunately, it took more than a decade for Babashoff to be vindicated for openly raising questions about competitors who she suspected did not adhere to the rules.

It took the innocence of the young daughter of one of hockey's greatest players, Stan Mikita, to transform him from a player who committed many penalties to a skater who won multiple awards for sportsmanship and high level of play. Like Stan Mikita in his early days, *Reish Lakish* was a man who also did not follow the rules. In fact, he did not even respect other people and their property until *Rahbi Yochanan* changed his life for the better.

Chapter 3
Sportsmanship "Selfies:" Acts of Sportsmanship towards Oneself

Sportsmanship Level II: Chapters 3–12

Level II of Sportsmanship is to do acts that, although not specifically delineated in the rules, a conscientious person would automatically perform.

Acts of Sportsmanship for those Inside the Game: Chapters 3–7

Maximizing Potential

Sports are all about competition; mainly competition against opponents (individuals and teams) for victory, as well as competition against potential teammates for limited spots on the squad and playing time. For many, the fiercer the competition, the greater challenge there is to act in a sportsmanlike manner.

When it comes to learning life lessons – especially in youth sports – the most valuable competition is when a participant competes against oneself or, more specifically, against one's potential.

Carmen Salvino: The Best Never Let it Rest

"Good, better, best, never let it rest, until the good is better and the better is best." This adage reminds us that it is vital that a person tries to do their very best in every endeavor that s/he undertakes.

For a team or individual to be credited with a victory, all they have to do is amass a better – usually higher – score. Credit is not given for effort. However, in terms of learning rich life lessons, the greatest victory is achieved when an individual tries his or her hardest to reach their greatest potential. Sometimes people who try their best defeat their opponents, while other times they do not.

The sports that best prepare us for the "game of life" are ones in which we can go out each and every time and try to compete for our own "PR," or personal record.

In this regard, my favorite organized youth sport is cross country running. Traditionally, it is a "no-cut" sport – at least, for many schools, through the high school level. While the objective is to finish with fewer total points, ultimately each team's score is comprised of the sum total of the top five individual runners' times. Every time a runner competes, s/he begins the race aware of their PR in that particular event and tries to beat it. Regardless of the outcome of the meet, every team member is able to evaluate their own progress and contribution to their team's standing. In that way, cross country is probably the purest team endeavor in terms of competition and has the greatest potential to demonstrate the highest consistent level of sportsmanship. (Ironically, it is also a sport in which a parent cannot complain about their child's "playing time." After all, the less talented the runner, the more playing time s/he gets [i.e., it takes longer to finish a particular event].)

Some other sports in which the player competes against their PR every time they participate include other track and field events, swimming, skating (figure and speed), golf, and bowling.

One of the all-time greats in the sport of bowling is Carmen Salvino. Smitten by the bowling bug at the age of 12 when he worked at a Chicago bowling center as a pin-setter, young Carmen constantly worked to perfect his game so that he could be the best that he could be. When he was 17, he became the youngest bowler to compete in the Chicago Classic League; appropriately he earned the nickname "Chicago's Boy Wonder." In 1958, Salvino was one of the founders of the Professional

Bowlers Association (PBA). With the birth of the PBA, bowling took off and became a very popular professional and amateur/recreational sport in the United States. In the 1960s, Salvino won an amazing ten PBA tournaments and travelled the world competing and as an ambassador of the sport.

As he got older and began to realize that his game was beginning to slip, Carmen Salvino sought the counsel of an unlikely person: rather than a professional bowling mentor, he asked for the advice of a friend, Hank Lahr, an engineer who also happened to be a very good bowler. Lahr helped Salvino see the game through the eyes of an engineer/scientist and taught him all about such topics as translational motion, rotational vectors, and friction. This tutelage helped Salvino realize that he needed to make adjustments to his game, which he did, thus prolonging his career. It also inspired Carmen to expand his involvement in the sport of bowling to include the development of new bowling equipment.

Even when competing in "PR sports," such as bowling, which depend ultimately on achieving your best score and hoping that it is the highest among all competitors for that match, sportsmanship comes into play. The temptation of winning at all costs has sometimes led athletes in various sports to use anabolic steroids and other prohibited performance enhancing drugs to boost their physical abilities. And there are other examples, such as in baseball, some pitchers have applied foreign substances to the balls to make it harder for a batter to connect, and in some other cases, professional hitters have tried to sneak cork into their bats for more pop.

Yet Carmen Salvino is an exemplar of an athlete who acts in an honest, sportsman-like manner when looking to prolong his career and better his game. By his own admission, over time he also mellowed, and became an even more likeable opponent and teammate. Mr. Salvino is a marvelous role model for the adage: "Good, better, best, never let it rest, until the good is better and the better is best."

Maximizing Potential: A Spritual Insight

"Why weren't you like Zusya?"

A story that illustrates this category of competition is an account told about a *Chasidic* leader by the name of Rabbi Zusya of Hanipoli, who lived in the 1700s.

When *Rav Zusya* was in the end stages of his life, the venerable Sage became very introspective about his mortality. One day, noticing that he was unusually despondent, his students tried reassuring their beloved *Rebbe* that he had earned a secure place in the **World to Come** (עוֹלָם הַבָּא/Olam HaBa).

"*Rebbe*, you shouldn't be concerned," his students told him. "After all, you have the patience of Hillel, the wisdom of King Solomon, the kindness of Abraham, and the humility of Moses."

Rabbi Zusya replied, "I am not worried about how I will respond when confronted by the angels of the Almighty and asked, 'Why weren't you like Hillel? Why weren't you like King Solomon, Abraham or Moses?' But, I am concerned as to how I will respond when asked the ultimate question: 'Why weren't you like Zusya?'"

Why weren't you like (*fill-in your own name*)?

This is the main question that a person must consider whenever they take upon themselves any challenge in life. So long as a person is honest and tries their hardest, that person will always be a winner.

Trying one's hardest – what I refer to as "The Rabbi Zusya Principle" – and then accepting the results is the ultimate form of sportsmanship towards oneself. After all, what better way is there to show oneself self-respect and honor?

THE BOX SCORE

From bowling legend Carmen Salvino we are inspired to "never let it rest until the good is better and the better is best."

From Rabbi Zusya of Hanipoli we are taught that the only person against whom we should compete is ourselves (i.e., our own potential). This is especially true with our own מִדּוֹת / *Midot* (**character traits**).

Optimism: The Significant Role of a Positive Attitude

Ernie Banks: The Ambassador of Eternal Optimism
"Wait until next year!"

In many sports towns this is a familiar lament.

From October 14, 1908, until the day that the Cubs won the World Series on November 2, 2016, this woeful exclamation was especially popular among Chicago Cubs fans. After all, before defeating the Cleveland Indians in 10 innings in Game Seven of the 2016 Fall Classic, the Cubs had last won the Series in 1908. Yet, each season during this 108-year drought, Cubs fans remained loyal and optimistic, hopeful that their favorite team would finally win – again.

An important element of sportsmanship is being able to accept defeat graciously, while ideally maintaining and displaying a realistic level of optimism. A contagious trait, optimism can even lift the spirits of fans who are tired of losing, while keeping them loyal to their beloved team during their losing seasons.

In a city where Cubs losses had been painfully accepted until recent times, fans look for players who can help ensure that the flame of hope is never extinguished. The sports figure that best illustrates this optimism is the late "Mr. Cub," Ernie Banks (1931 – 2015).

The first African-American ball player in Cubs history, Banks was warmly embraced by many fans, independent of race. Eventually, number 14 became the jersey of choice for many young baseball players in the city, as well as middle-aged softball players, whether they were rich or poor, black or white, Christian or Jewish. Not only did Ernie always grant a request for an autograph, but he enjoyed speaking with fans and learning more about their lives.

Don't mistake Ernie for loving losing. He didn't. A passionate competitor, instead of manifesting his great disappointment with anger or demanding that he be traded to a contender, Ernie transformed his dismay into optimism. "Mr. Cub" approached each game with a positive attitude summarized by such statements as: "It's a beautiful day for baseball! Let's play two!" Before each season, Banks, the player, always hopeful and optimistic, predicted that the Cubs would succeed in the upcoming season: "This is the year of the little bear." Before the 1965 season, he predicted: "The Cubbies will come alive in '65." In 1968, Banks proclaimed: "Things look great in '68."

Unfortunately, each year the Cubs fell far short of Ernie's bright predictions. Then before the 1969 season, Banks, who was now surrounded by other top players and led by fiery manager Leo "The Lip" Durocher, boldly proclaimed: "The Cubs will shine in '69!"

And shine they did, at least for most of the season. The Cubs opened the '69 campaign winning nine of their first 10 games. Historic Wrigley Field was transformed into a "field of – dreams" being fulfilled. The "Bleacher Bums" were led by relief pitcher Dick Selma, Ron Santo clicked his heels after each victory, and Ken Holtzman threw a no-hitter against the mighty Atlanta Braves. The Cubs carried a nine and one-half game lead over the New York Mets into mid-August. As predicted by Ernie Banks, they were indeed shining. Then, suddenly, the Cubs' fortune soured as they began losing and the Mets began winning. A seven-game Met winning streak coincided with an eight-game Cub losing streak. The "Miracle Mets" ended up winning the division by eight games and went on to win the World Series.

The collapse of what many consider the best Cubs team of all-time caused tremendous sadness and consternation among players and fans. In spite of it all, one person remained hopeful – Ernie Banks. While others mourned, Ernie stated with great optimism and hope: "It was just not meant to be. But things will be heavenly in 1970!"

Sadly, Ernie never had the opportunity to play on or even witness a Cubs World Series Championship team during his lifetime. Nonetheless, he was a true champion when it came to sportsmanship. By treating fans and others in a golden fashion, accepting defeat graciously, and brightening up each day with his glowing optimism, Mr. Cub taught sports fans that sometimes it is, indeed, worth it to be patient and "wait until next year!"

Optimism in Jewish Tradition: A Spiritual Insight

HaTikva, Anne Frank & Nachum Ish Gahmzu

To succeed in life's endeavors, it is important to have hope. While approaching life with a realistic attitude, it can only help if one is optimistic. The Hebrew word for **hope** is תִּקְוָה/*tikvah*. Most appropriately, Israel's national anthem is known as the *HaTikvah* (**The Hope**).

Throughout history, there have been many people whose optimism has inspired hope among the Jewish people. When Moses agreed to send 12 leaders (one from each tribe) to evaluate the Children of Israel's prospects of conquering the Land of Israel, the only two spies who brought back an optimistic, hopeful report were Joshua and Caleb. In about 1880, Naphtali Herz Imber composed the lyrics to – what later became Israel's national anthem – the *HaTikvah*. Originally called *Tikvatenu* (**Our Hope**), this song has instilled hope in millions of Jews. After the Holocaust, the world was introduced to the optimism and hope of Anne Frank, a teenager who, before her death, recorded her accounts and feelings in a personal diary while hiding in Nazi-occupied Amsterdam during World War II. At the end of every Passover *Seder*, the participants express their hopeful optimism when they proclaim: לְשָׁנָה הַבָּאָה בִּירוּשָׁלַיִם/*L'Shana ha-ba-ah BiYrushalayim!* – "*Next year in Jerusalem!*"

In *Talmudic* literature, the sage who is best remembered for instilling optimism and hope in others is *Nachum Ish Gahmzu* (**Nachum of Gahmzu**). Although *Nachum*, in great likelihood, was from *Gimzo*, a city in ancient Israel (*II Chronicles* 28:18), he received the name *Gahmzu*, because of his sunny, positive approach towards life. No matter how bad things were, he would proclaim: גַּם זוּ לְטוֹבָה/*Gahm zu l'tova!* – "**This too is for the good!**"

The *Talmud* (*Taanit* 21a) relates a story about *Nachum Ish Gahmzu* that reinforces the lesson that those who approach life with an optimistic, hopeful attitude eventually will be rewarded for their efforts. As a representative of the Jewish community, *Nachum* was chosen to deliver a gift of precious jewels to the Roman Emperor. The journey necessitated an overnight stay at an inn. That night, thieves stole the jewels from his pouch and replaced them with dirt.

After *Nachum* arrived at the palace, he presented the Emperor with the pouch that, unbeknownst to him, now contained earth. When the King opened the bag and found the dirt, he threatened to kill all the Jews of his Kingdom since he felt that they were mocking him. *Nachum* then invoked his famous saying: *Gahm zuh l'tova!* inspiring the miraculous arrival of the

Prophet Elijah. Elijah convinced the Emperor that this earth was holy and could help the King defeat his enemies in war. This proved to be correct, as the earth helped the Romans capture a certain city that before they were unable to conquer. Not only were *Nachum Ish Gahmzu* and the Jewish people of the kingdom spared, but they were also rewarded with precious jewels, and in time, the robbers were punished.

THE BOX SCORE

We learn from the optimistic approaches of "Mr. Cub," Ernie Banks, and – the sage Nachum of Gahmzu (and Naphtali Herz Imber and Anne Frank), that no matter how bad things may be, it is always important to have hope.

When we play sports, we must remain optimistic of our chances of winning or succeeding in other ways. An important ingredient of sportsmanship, optimism, helps in how we treat players, fans, umpires, and the press, and how we deal with losing. We learn this all from Ernie Banks.

Hope of peace, better times, and the arrival of the *Mashiach* (**Messiah**) continue to hearten and inspire the Jewish people to move forward after personal and national tragedies. Being optimistic, but realistic, makes it easier not only to succeed in all of our endeavors, but to be received pleasantly by others, since we – inevitably – will treat other people with more **Respect and Honor** (דֶּרֶךְ אֶרֶץ וְכָבוֹד /*Derekh Eretz v'Khavod*).

Losing Graciously

An important component of sportsmanship is knowing how to lose graciously, whether it be the final outcome of a game or simply an individual play.

No one knows what that's like better than Indianapolis Colts quarterback Andrew Luck. The successor to future Hall of Famer Peyton Manning, Luck threw for more yards in his first three seasons than any other quarterback in NFL history. He led his team to the playoffs during each of these campaigns.

Though he seldom loses a game, he oftentimes is knocked down or tackled by opposing linebackers. Instead of showing anger or displeasure, many times, Luck compliments the opposing player by shouting out such remarks as: "what a hit!" or "great job!" While some feel that this may be Luck's form of trash talking and getting into the heads of his opponents, teammates feel that the main reason behind all of these compliments is simply because Andrew is a real nice guy. According to Andrew's father Oliver, a former NFL quarterback, "My wife and I raised all four of our kids with appropriate values, with respect for other people and to be kind and generous and I guess that carried over to the football field."

While his win-loss record and passing statistics may be close to the best in the NFL, his grace even in defeat can be appropriately termed: "The Best of (Andrew) Luck."

Losing Graciously: Spiritual Insights

Rabban Gamliel & His Challenges as Nasi

After the destruction of *Beit HaMikdash HaSheni* (**The Second Holy Temple**) in 70 CE, the center of *Torah* Judaism shifted from Jerusalem to Yavneh. The *Metivta* (**Academy**) of *Yavneh* succeeded the *Sanhedrin* as the primary *Halakhic* institution (court and school) of the Jewish people. This august body was headed by the *Nasi*. Second in-command was the *Av Bet Din*. The first to serve in these positions at *Yavneh* were *Rabban Gamliel* (*Nasi*) and *Rabban Yochanan ben Zakkai* (*Av Bet Di*n). After *Rabban Yochanan ben Zakkai* passed away, *Rahbi Yehoshua* was appointed as his successor.

Both brilliant scholars and *poskim* (**renderers of Jewish law**), *Rabban Gamliel* and *Rahbi Yehoshua* did not always concur on *Halakhic* decisions. With the full intent of acting in the best interests of unifying a people that was devastated by the destruction of the *Beit HaMikdash*, *Rabban Gamliel* ruled with an iron fist, sometimes to such an extreme that some deemed it as being over-the-top. In fact, on several occasions, *Rabban Gamliel* publicly challenged *Rahbi Yehoshua*, and in doing so, unfortunately, shamed him.

On the final occasion (*B'rakhot* 27b-28a), when publicly calling out *Rahbi Yehoshua* regarding whether **Maariv** (the **evening service**) was obligatory or optional, a group of sages felt that *Rabban Gamliel* had gone too far, and that he now had to be removed from office. After a lengthy discussion as to who was best qualified to succeed him, the Sages appointed *Rahbi Elazar ben Azaria* to the post. Accepting his loss with grace and dignity, *Rabban Gamliel* continued attending and learning at the *Metivta*. Slowly, he began to realize that he had acted too harshly with *Rahbi Yehoshua* and others.

After coming to this realization, *Rabban Gamliel* went to the home of *Rahbi Yehoshua* and apologized. Upon learning of the reconciliation between these two great *Torah* scholars, the Sages who had deposed him felt that *Rabban Gamliel* was indeed remorseful and that it was appropriate to reinstate him to the exalted position of *Nasi*. However, it was not so simple since *Rahbi Elazar ben Azaria* had already started his duties, and it would not be just to remove him from his new position.

The *Talmud* goes on to tell us that a compromise arrangement was made where *Rabban Gamliel* would serve as *Nasi* for three weeks, and then *Rahbi Elazar ben Azaria* would serve for one week. Because the Sages saw that *Rabban Gamliel's* intentions were sincere in trying to protect the integrity of the *Metivta*, and that he sincerely apologized to *Rahbi Yehoshua*, they felt that he was worthy once again to lead.

THE BOX SCORE

In sports competitions and life in general, we experience victories and other successes in between many defeats. We learn from Indianapolis Colts Pro Bowl quarterback Andrew Luck the importance of losing graciously. Like Luck, when we get knocked down we should bounce back in a dignified manner.

Rabban Gamliel showed that, even when losing, in this case, the highest Rabbinic/leadership position in Israel of the time, it should be handled with grace and humility, דֶּרֶךְ אֶרֶץ וְכָבוֹד /Derekh Eretz v'Khavod (**Respect and Honor**).

Chapter 4
Brother vs. Brother/Sister vs. Sister: Acts of Sportsmanship towards Teammates

Competition for Playing Time: Gale Sayers and Brian Piccolo

Because there are a limited number of spots on team rosters at all levels of competition, players must compete against one another just to make the squad. Once on the team, teammates must compete for playing time. Although such competitions can, and at times indeed do, result in bad feelings, sometimes they help bring teammates closer.

For many, the first word that comes to mind when remembering Brian Piccolo is "courage." After all, in his short life of only 26 years, Brian exhibited indomitable courage in refusing to allow cancer to define him. In spite of his battle against the disease to which he eventually succumbed, Piccolo was able to raise a young family, carve a solid NFL career, and leave a lasting, loving legacy.

In Brian's memory, after every season, the Chicago Bears, who retired Piccolo's #41 jersey, present a veteran and rookie with the Brian Piccolo Award. In addition to exhibiting courage, the recipients must show dedication, loyalty, teamwork, and a sense of humor as did the late running back.

Brian also established himself as a role model for an important manifestation of sportsmanship: generosity and decency when competing against his teammates. Like all players, he competed for a place on the team's roster and then for playing time. Unlike most players, Piccolo's main opponent for playing time was a future Hall of Famer – Gale Sayers.

Following the 1964 NCAA football season, Gale Sayers, a phenomenal running back out of the University of Kansas, was selected in the first round of the NFL draft by the Chicago Bears. Known as "The Kansas Comet," Sayers did not lead the NCAA in yards rushed that season. Actually this feat was accomplished by a far less heralded player from Wake Forest University named Brian Piccolo.

NFL draft day came and went for Piccolo without his receiving a call from a team. Determined to sign as an undrafted free agent, Piccolo caught the eye of several NFL scouts and coaches, including NFL founding father and Chicago Bears owner and coach George Halas. In the final days of 1964, Brian signed a contract with the Bears. Injured in pre-season, Piccolo was placed on the Bears' taxi squad.

Realizing that the best way to suit up with the team the following season would be to try to play alongside Sayers as a fullback – as opposed to competing against him for the starting halfback position – Piccolo's plans were put on hold as Bears running back Jon Arnett, who had earlier announced his retirement, changed his mind and "unretired." Now the best opportunity for Brian to be a "Monster of the Midway" was as a member of the Bears special teams.

During the 1967 season and the first eight games of 1968, Brian complemented Gale Sayers by substituting for him when he needed a breather, and, at times, playing alongside him. But during 1968's ninth game, Sayers went down with a serious knee injury. The "next man up" was Piccolo, who stepped in and starred as the team's starting halfback.

Back then, with knee surgery and physical therapy far less advanced than it is today, there was a good chance that Sayers would not be able to return at close to the same level of play that he possessed before his injury. Instead of taking advantage of this reality, which would enhance his opportunity of playing more and perhaps even lead to starting as halfback in 1969, Piccolo emerged as Sayers's number one fan and aide in ensuring his return to top form. A team player, Piccolo worked with and challenged Sayers during his lengthy and most challenging rehab. The next season, Sayers returned at a high level, rushing for more than 1,000 yards, though his knee would never be the same.

Sayers, the superstar African-American halfback from Kansas University known for his blazing speed and deft running ability, and Piccolo – the white upstart, a running back from Wake Forest with only average speed, also made news off the field as they became the first inter-racial roommates in NFL history.

Sadly, in the fall of 1969, Brian Piccolo was diagnosed with a rare form of cancer. While the aggressive, state-of-the-art medical treatment that Brian received was accompanied by an outpouring of love from his family, friends, and fans, one of his biggest cheerleaders and supporters turned out to be his teammate, Gale Sayers.

In the end, instead of letting competition lead them to become adversaries, Brian Piccolo and Gale Sayers chose to help each other both on and off the field. This special bond of friendship, competition, and sportsmanship is the foundation – and indeed, was even glorified – in the 1971 movie, *Brian's Song.*

Tragically, despite his immense courage and all of the love and support he received, Brian Piccolo succumbed to cancer on June 16, 1970. His legacy continues through the labors of his widow Joy, three daughters Lori, Traci, and Kristi, numerous grandchildren and other loving family members, friends, and fans in the work of the Brian Piccolo Cancer Research Fund.

Chasing a Record: Maris and Mantle and the Quest for 61

1961 is a season well-remembered by baseball fans and documented by many historians.

For almost the entire season, two New York Yankee teammates, Mickey Mantle and Roger Maris, competed with (not against) each other attempting to break, what at that time, was a "sacred" record. For 34 years, the most home runs hit in a single season were 60 by Yankee legend Babe Ruth. Many fans cheered for Mantle to break the record, since he was regarded as the top Yankee slugger and heir apparent to the legacies of Babe Ruth, Lou Gehrig, and Joe DiMaggio. As much as fans were comfortable seeing Mantle set a new record, they did not want Maris to break Ruth's record since they felt that Maris was an "upstart" not worthy of holding such a coveted title.

In the final game of the 1961 season Maris hit his 61st round-tripper, establishing a benchmark that lasted until 1998 when St. Louis Cardinal slugger Mark McGwire broke it after his own rivalry that season with Sammy Sosa of the Chicago Cubs. (McGwire later admitted to taking performance enhancing drugs and Sosa was also accused of it, though he has denied it repeatedly. Later, after Barry Bonds also broke Maris' record, he was also tainted by years of scandals involving PEDs.) Mantle's 1961 total was 54. Although they competed for the same record, Roger Maris's and Mickey Mantle were close friends and roommates during that famed season, exhibiting sportsmanlike behavior towards each other, even in the heat of competition.

Their amicable competition is so beloved, that it was depicted in comedian/actor/huge sports fan Billy Crystal's production of the movie *61*.*

Competition for Playing Time: A Spiritual Insight

Hillel vs. Shammai ·

Two of the greatest scholars in Jewish history, *Hillel* and *Shammai*, lived around the turn of the millennium. The last of the *Zugot* (**Pairs** [of Rabbinic scholars who led the Jewish people living in Israel]) and the first of the *Tannaim* (**the Sages who contributed to the Mishna**), these two venerable sages shared duties in administering the *Sanhedrin* (**the highest Jewish court of law**). *Hillel* served as the *Nasi* (**president**), while *Shammai* was the *Av Bet Din* (literally, *"the father of the Jewish Court"*; i.e., second in command).

These two esteemed scholars and the students of their *y'shivot* (**academies**) *Beit Hillel* (**the House/School of Hillel**) and *Beit Shammai* (**the House/School of Shammai**) agreed in, perhaps, 99.9 % of matters regarding Jewish law. On rare occasion, however, they disagreed on finer details. Even though their disputes may have resembled competitions, the *Talmud* (*Ethics of Our Father* 5:20) considered them to be constructive (i.e., לְשֵׁם שָׁמַיִם/*l'shem Shamayim* [**for the sake of Heaven**]). After all, the main purpose of these disagreements was not to satisfy the egos of the disputants, but rather to clarify the law so that more Jews could observe the tradition in a more precise manner. In that way, their disputes were similar to teammates sharing the same goal.

With rare exception, in a "competition" (i.e., מַחֲלוֹקֶת/*machaloket* [**dispute/disagreement**]) between *Hillel* and *Shammai*, the law went in accordance with *Beit Hillel*. As explained in the *Talmud* (*Eruvin* 13b):

יָצְאָה בַּת קוֹל וְאָמְרָה: אֵלּוּ וְאֵלּוּ דִּבְרֵי אֱלֹקִים חַיִּים הֵן, וַהֲלָכָה כְּבֵית־הִלֵּל.

Yahtz'a Bat Kol v'am'ra: Ehlu v'ehlu Divrei Elokim Chayim hehn, v'Halakha k'Veit Hillel.

A Bat Kol [Divine Voice] came forth and said: "These and those [Beit Hillel and Beit Shammai's opinions] are both the words of the Living God, but the law [when there is a difference in opinion] goes according to Beit Hillel."

Having been raised in abject poverty (see *Yoma* 35b), *Hillel* was an extraordinarily patient man who could empathize, oftentimes, with the underdog.

One classic *machaloket* between the students of these two prodigious Sages is found in *K'tubot* 16b–17a regarding whether a person can bend the truth in order to save someone from embarrassment and tell an unattractive bride on her wedding day that she is beautiful. While *Beit Shammai* prohibited such behavior, *Beit Hillel* allowed it.

When competitors' primary skills are essentially equivalent, we then use additional criteria as the tie breaker. In sports, it may be the person to whom teammates respond better. In the case of Jewish leadership, we learn from *Hillel* that being gentler and more patient are extremely important traits to inspire others to observe Jewish tradition.

THE BOX SCORE

While teammates have the same goal of putting the best interests of the team before their own personal accomplishments, inevitably, a competition exists. When competing for a place on the roster, playing time, or a record, it should be done in a fair and friendly way in the same manner as done by Gale Sayers and Brian Piccolo or Mickey Mantle and Roger Maris. These are important expressions of sportsmanship.

Rabbis (and other *Torah* teachers) are also "teammates" in that they all have the same common goal of transmitting *Torah* to others. Accordingly, when they compete, it should be strictly *I'shem Shamayim* – **for the sake of Heaven** (*Pirkei Avot* 5:20). The "competing" students of *Torah* should be sure to express only great *Derekh Eretz v'Khavod* to one another. We should take a lesson from the *Tannaim Hillel* and *Shammai* and their students who engaged in *machalokot* (**disputes/ disagreements**) only in order to elucidate the *Halakha* in select situations for the benefit of all Jews.

Chapter 5
Education in Sports: Acts of Sportsmanship between Coach and Player

The Mentors

A Coach Is a Teacher

The ideal coach not only teaches his/her players the fundamentals of the particular sport, but also remains a mentor or parent figure long after the player's athletic career has ended.

Teacher and Student: John Wooden and Bill Walton

In 1997, while watching a Chicago Bulls game on TV with my oldest child Max, then four years old, I pointed to Coach Phil "the Zen Master" Jackson, and asked Max if he knew what a coach was. Without contemplating too deeply, my son responded: "A coach is a teacher."

While successful coaches, like Phil Jackson, must perform many different roles, the most important quality that a coach must possess is that of being an outstanding teacher. Being an effective, patient educator/mentor is critical to succeed at any level of coaching, especially when dealing with student athletes.

In my opinion, one which is shared by many others, the greatest coach in sports history – when combining both winning percentage and life lessons conveyed to players – is the late, great John Robert Wooden (1910–2010).

Wooden is best remembered for his success as the coach of the University of California at Los Angeles (UCLA) men's basketball team. During his 29-year tenure as a college head coach, 27 at UCLA (1948–1975), the "Wizard of Westwood" amassed an amazing .804 winning percentage. Incredibly, in a 12-year span, Wooden's Bruin teams won an unprecedented 10 NCAA championships, including seven consecutive titles (1967–1973).

The first of only four men to be inducted into the James Naismith Basketball Hall of Fame as both a player (1960) and coach (1973), not only was Wooden a talented player and a brilliant leader, but an outstanding student as well. As a Purdue Boilermaker star guard and team captain, Wooden was awarded the Big Ten Award for Proficiency and Athletics. Upon his graduation, John Wooden viewed the chance to coach young men as a golden opportunity to mentor not just winning basketball players, but also future leaders and upstanding citizens. Beginning his professional career as a high school coach and English teacher (his college major was English), Wooden was able to launch a career intertwining his passion for sports and education.

Upon his retirement from college coaching in 1975, Wooden remained active until his death at age 99, by continuing to teach and inspire through his writings, speaking, and by remaining a visible, influential presence in the lives of many of his former players by whom he was regarded as both a basketball coach and a life mentor. The author or co-author of over a dozen books (including children's books), Wooden, the educator, is perhaps best remembered for his "Pyramid of Success," a teaching tool comprised of 15 values (the "building blocks" of the pyramid) by which to lead one's life. Appropriately, on his website, he is identified as "John Wooden Coach & Teacher."

Regarded as an impeccably honest and fair man, Wooden was also known to be a strict disciplinarian who, early on each season, earned the respect of all of his players. Although he was relatively straight-laced in his philosophical views, Coach Wooden garnered the support of his players even during the tumultuous 1960s. Perhaps the player that presented the most challenges to him in this regard was Bill Walton.

By chance, I had the opportunity to enjoy a quality 15-minute private conversation with Walton. In 2006, while waiting for a flight to Los Angeles, I saw the Hall of Famer also waiting to board the same plane. Already a well-known basketball analyst for ESPN, somehow the six-foot-eleven giant of a man went unnoticed, or at least was left alone, by other passengers – except for my children and me.

Once my kids received autographs and our "team photographer" (my wife Marilyn) took photos with the former NCAA and NBA Champion hoopster (see this book's photo-insert), I found myself asking the question most on my mind: "Are you still in contact with Coach Wooden?" Walton replied that he was and that, in fact, he was meeting his former coach for breakfast the very next day. After the chance meeting, I learned that Walton also regarded Coach Wooden as his mentor, teacher, and friend. He even ensured that his children (all boys) got to spend time with and learn directly from the "Wizard of Westwood," as well.

Not only did Bill Walton attract media attention for his stellar play at UCLA (leading the Bruins to their sixth and seventh consecutive NCAA titles in 1972 and 1973), but he was also known for being involved in liberal political causes that were not ones embraced by his coach. Nonetheless, in spite of their different outlooks on life, from his freshman year at UCLA until Coach Wooden's passing, the player had the utmost respect for his beloved coach and teacher.

In a tribute, Walton writes a touching message on his website about his mentor. It is striking from that blog post that the most significant impact Wooden had on Walton was in his role as a teacher of both basketball and life lessons:

● "John Wooden teaches by example."
● "He taught us how to practice against an imaginary, ideal opponent so as not to waste time and effort. He taught us to find a source of motivation to inspire us to ever higher levels of preparation and work. . . . He taught us that confidence is an integral part of achieving peak performance, but that confidence must come from a lifetime of preparation that ensures deliverance to the championship level."
● "I thank John Wooden every day for all his selfless gifts, his lessons, his time, his vision and especially his patience. That is why we call him coach."

After all, a coach is a teacher. Thanks, Max.

DIDJA KNOW
that besides John Wooden, the three other men to be inducted into the Naismith Memorial Basketball Hall of Fame as both a player and coach are Lenny Wilkens, Bill Sharman and Tom Heinsohn? Unlike these three men, Wooden never played or coached in the NBA.

The Mentors: Spiritual Insights

יְהוֹשֻׁעַ בֶּן פְּרַחְיָה וְנִתַּאי הָאַרְבֵּלִי קִבְּלוּ מֵהֶם.
יְהוֹשֻׁעַ בֶּן פְּרַחְיָה אוֹמֵר: עֲשֵׂה לְךָ רַב.

Yehoshua ben P'rachaya v'Nitai HaArbeli kib'lu m'hem.
Yehoshua ben P'rachaya omer: Ahseh l'kha Rav.

Yehoshua the son of P'rachya and Nitai from Arabel received [the tradition]
from them [i.e., Rabbi Yosse ben Yoezer and Rabbi Yosse ben Yochanan].
Yehoshua the son of P'rachya says: "Provide for yourself a rabbi [teacher]"
(Ethics of our Fathers 1:6).

One of the key ingredients of success, according to the Sage *Yehoshua ben P'rachaya*, is to have a relationship with a teacher who can help guide you through life. Rabbi *Yehoshua's* teachers were his rabbis, who are mentioned in an earlier *Mishna* (*Pirkei Avot* 1:4) – Rabbi *Yosse ben Yoezer* and Rabbi *Yosse ben Yochanan*.

Committed Jews do not fly solo in life. Rather, they have an inner-circle of support. Along with one's parents, spouse, and other family members, some of the key members of this "advisory council" are rabbis, professors, and other teachers. For many, their teacher/mentor is the rabbi of their synagogue who has officiated at all of their family's life cycle events. They have been there to teach, inspire, and guide them through the highs, lows, and "routine" days of life. For others, their mentor is a beloved teacher (not always an ordained rabbi) with whom they feel a special connection.

In addition to inspiring through *Torah* education, the ideal rabbi/teacher, is one who can also serve as a mentor. This mentor should be a person who can provide comfort, support, direction, and inspiration on how to lead a productive, meaningful Jewish life.

Throughout history, there have been many famous rabbi/teacher-student combos which can also be classified as mentor-mentee(s).

Here are a few:

● **Moses and Joshua.** Known as מֹשֶׁה רַבֵּנוּ/*Moshe Rabbenu* (***Moses our Rabbi/Teacher***), Moses was the Rabbi to two generations of Israelites and to all Jews throughout history. His most famous student was Joshua, who succeeded him in his role as the leader of the Israelites.

● *Rabban Yochanan ben Zakkai* (30 BCE–90 CE) **and Five Students in Particular**. As cited in (*Pirkei Avot* 2:10) these students were: *Rahbi Eliezer ben Hyrcanus, Rahbi Yehoshua ben Chananya, Rahbi Yosse HaKohen, Rahbi Shimon ben N'tanel,* and *Rahbi Elazar ben Arakh.* In the very next *Mishnh, Rabban Yochanan ben Zakkai* sings the praises of each one of these elite disciples.

A famous story (*Gittin* 56a–b) about *Rabban Yochanan ben Zakkai* is that, realizing that the destruction of the Second Temple by the Romans was imminent, he asked his students to take him from Jerusalem via a coffin, as this was the only way that a Jew could leave (i.e., dead, to be buried outside of Jerusalem). Once outside of the walls of the holy city, *Rabban Yochanan ben Zakkai* was able to meet with the Roman General Vespasian from whom he requested: תֵּן לִי יַבְנֶה וַחֲכָמֶיהָ/ *Ten li Yavneh vaCha-kha-meh-ha* – *"[Just] give me Yavneh and its scholars!"* His request was granted to establish a new *Torah* center in *Yavneh*, paving the way for the spiritual survival of the Jewish people post-destruction.

● *Rahbi Akiva* **and Seven Students in Particular.** Along with Moses, *Rahbi Yochanan ben Zakkai* and Hillel the Elder, it is believed that *Rahbi Akiva* also lived until the ripe old age of 120. After the death of his 24,000 students who did not treat each other with proper respect – שֶׁלֹּא נָהֲגוּ כָּבוֹד זֶה לָזֶה/*Shehlo nahagu kavod zeh la-zeh* – *Because they did not treat each other honorably* (*Y'vamot* 62b), the *Midrash* (*B'reisheet Rabba* 61:3) states that *Rahbi Akiva* then taught seven of his students who had survived. He prepared them to become the educational/spiritual leaders of the surviving and future generations. *Rahbi Akiva* strongly cautioned his new students to learn from his earlier students' mistakes of not treating each other well (i.e., acting jealous towards each other – *Sh'hayta einehem tzara ehlu l'ehlu* – literally, *because their eyes were narrow towards one another*), and then stated: עָמְדוּ וּמִלְאוּ כֹּל אֶרֶץ יִשְׂרָאֵל תּוֹרָה/*Ahm'du u-milu kol Eretz Yisrael Torah* –

"Stand up and fill the entire Land of Israel with [the study and performance of acts of] Torah."

The 20th century witnessed the birth, brilliance, and deaths of many prominent *Torah* scholars. Perhaps the two most prominent – both of whom had students/followers of all backgrounds, including non-Jews – were Rabbi Menachem Mendel Schneerson and Professor Nechama Leibowitz. Both of these luminaries had thousands of students who, although they could not have "private time" with their beloved teacher/mentor every day, were inspired by their teachings, scholarship, and exemplary acts of kindness.

The Rebbe to Jews Worldwide

Rabbi Menachem Mendel Schneerson – *ZTz"L*/*Of Blessed Memory* (1902–1994) was born in the Ukraine and passed away in New York. The seventh leader in the history of the *Chabad-Lubavitch Chasidic* sect, "the *Rebbe*," as he was affectionately known, was considered to be a child prodigy. In addition to his high levels of *Torah* scholarship, he also studied science and mathematics at the University of Berlin and the *Sorbonne* in Paris.

Having fled Paris after the Nazis' occupation in 1941, the *Rebbe* and his wife *Rebbetzin Chaya Mushka "Moussia" Schneershon*, settled in New York where he was appointed to head the social service, educational, and publication branches of *Chabad* by his father-in-law, Rabbi *Yosef Yitzchak* Schneershon (a distant cousin), who was the leader of Chabad at that time. About a year or so after his father-in-law's death in 1950, Rabbi Menachem Mendel Schneerson became the new leader.

During the more than forty years of his leadership, the *Rebbe* took a relatively small number of followers (the vast majority were murdered in Europe during the Holocaust) and created a community that today is estimated to be in excess of 200,000. The *Rebbe* instilled in his followers the lessons that every Jew is important and that it was Chabad's mission ***to reach out and bring every Jew closer to Judaism*** (קֵרוּב/*Keiruv*). If all Jews were to perform *Mitzvot*, it would hasten the arrival of the ***Messiah*** (מָשִׁיחַ/*Mashiach*).

A master teacher and writer, the *Rebbe* spent many Sundays in his Crown Heights Brooklyn home meeting one-on-one with Jews and some non-Jews who were seeking the *Rebbe's* advice, guidance, blessing, and support. He was famous for promoting the act of צְדָקָה/*Tz'daka* (**charity**) by handing out dollar bills to each person with whom he met, with the request that they give this money, and additional funds going forward, to ***charity*** (*Tz'daka*).

Largely because of the *Rebbe's* influence, according to chabad.org there are now over 3,500 *Chabad* institutions in over 85 countries in the world. During his lifetime, Rabbi Schneerson taught hundreds of thousands of students through his lectures, writings and conversations. His followers have ensured that the *Rebbe's* legacy continues by reaching out to more and more Jews and bringing them closer to Jewish tradition.

Rabbi Schneerson offered advice or counsel to many well-known world citizens, including internationally acclaimed scholars Israeli Rabbi Adin Steinsaltz and former Chief Rabbi of the United Hebrew Congregations of the Commonwealth in England, Rabbi Lord Jonathan Sacks, musician Bob Dylan, former Israeli prime ministers Menachem Begin and Yitzhak Rabin, and former US president Ronald Reagan.

Shortly after Rabbi Menachem Mendel Schneerson died, he received posthumously the Congressional Gold Medal honoring the *Rebbe* for his "outstanding and lasting contributions toward improvements in world education, morality, and acts of charity."

Although the *Rebbe* and his *Rebbetzin Chaya Mushka* were not blessed with any biological children, they had thousands of "children" who lived in all corners of the world, since Jewish

DIDJA KNOW
that there is life on Mars? How did I reach that conclusion? Well, on a recent space mission the astronauts found two things: a can of Coca-Cola and a Chabad center. Of course this is a joke. While one may get a chuckle when hearing it, the greater message is a tribute to the *Rebbe*, his mission, and the great respect that his students had for him (i.e., that Lubavitch-Chabad will go to [almost] any place in the world [or universe] so long as at least one Jew resides there).

tradition equates students with children (*B'rakhot* 64a).

People treated the *Rebbe* with the utmost **Derekh Eretz v'Khavod** (**Respect and Honor**) both during and after his lifetime through their actions and words. Rabbi Schneerson's myriad number of students act as his agents by doing *Kiruv* (**outreach**) work and conveying his *Divrei Torah* (**words of Torah**) to others. It is also common for *Chabad-Lubavitch* families to name a son *Menachem Mendel* and a daughter *Chaya Mushka*, in memory of their beloved teachers.

Nechama Leibowitz Morah (Teacher)

נחמה ליבוביץ
מורה

Per her request, this three-word Hebrew inscription is the epithet on the מַצֵּבָה/ *Matzevah* (**tombstone**) of Professor Nechama Leibowitz.

Like Rabbi Menachem Mendel Schneerson, Professor Leibowitz did not have any biological children. Like the *Rebbe*, however, she also had thousands of children (students) worldwide.

A woman who did not align herself with the feminist movement, Nechama Leibowitz was a leading scholar and teacher of the *Torah* in its literal sense (i.e., the *Five Books of Moses*) who also happened to be a woman. An extremely humble person, she did not claim to be an innovator, rather a teacher who taught the *Pentateuch* with the classical traditional commentaries that included *Rashi, Ramban* (*Nachmanides*), *Ibn Ezra*, and *S'forno*. Occasionally she would mix the works of modern and classical authors and philosophers in to her interactive exchanges with her students and writings.

With an unending zeal and passion to disseminate *Torah*, Dr. Leibowitz traveled all over Israel (in large part by taxi) to teach in such venues as *Y'shivot*, women seminaries and world-renown universities like Jerusalem's Hebrew University. On her way, oftentimes Professor Leibowitz would learn with the taxi drivers, many of whom were fairly well-versed in *Torah*.

Professor Leibowitz was a beloved mentor to many of her students, who would visit with her even when they were not formally enrolled in any of her courses. A teacher who demanded a lot from her students, she was honest and fair with them. While she positively reinforced the attentiveness and scholarship of her serious students, she had a low tolerance for students who took Jewish learning lightly.

Several decades before the internet, Nechama Leibowitz connected with her students from around Israel and the world by mailing to them her famous handouts. Known as *Gilyonot* (**study sheets**), to inspire thinking, questioning, and exploration, the professor composed questions based upon each *Torah* portion and certain of its themes. These were so popular that she had a countless number of students who would complete them and return them by (snail) mail to Professor

Leibowitz who would grade and return each one to the student who sent it. These *Gilyonot* led to the publication of her famous compendiums known as *Studies in the Book of Genesis, Exodus, Leviticus, Numbers and Deuteronomy*. In these books, Dr. Leibowitz includes thematic essays highlighting many traditional and some modern commentators. At the end of each essay, she posed a series of questions.

In addition to the **Respect and Honor**/*Derekh Eretz v'Khavod* that her students gave her during her lifetime, as a tribute to Nechama Leibowitz's scholarship, some of her top students have published (posthumously) some of her teachings. These books include a Passover *Haggadah* named *Studies on the Haggadah from the Teachings of Nechama Leibowitz*. Her *Gilyonot* are accessible to all current and future students at: **http://www.nechama.org.il**

Although she never sought greatness, Professor Nechama Leibowitz was and continues to be the teacher of myriads of students. She leaves a lasting impression as a scholar and mentor to future generations of *Torah* students, teachers, and scholars.

In Jewish tradition, teachers are agents of parents in the awesome obligation of teaching and instilling in their children *Torah* values. Just as we are commanded to honor and revere parents, we must honor and respect teachers in a similar manner.

THE BOX SCORE

"A coach is a teacher." The ideal teacher of sports or any secular discipline should be able to instill in his/her students, not only the specific subject matter, but also important life lessons.

An important expression of sportsmanship is that players treat coaches with the proper respect and honor that their position brings. If the relationship was a positive one, oftentimes, it will continue long after the player no longer plays for the coach.

A critical expression of דֶּרֶךְ אֶרֶץ וְכָבוֹד/*Derekh Eretz v'Khavod* is that we treat teachers with proper **Honor and Respect**. After revered rabbis and teachers have passed away, we continue to honor them by studying their writings and retelling their inspiring *Divrei* (**words of**) *Torah*. Sometimes we even name children after them to further honor their memories.

Making Each Team Member Feel Important

One of the functions of a successful coach is to serve as a pseudo-psychologist and make every member of the team feel appreciated. While nearly all players would like to play as much as possible, this is simply impossible. A coach must inspire every team member to put their own desires and egos secondary to the needs of the team.

Send Me in Coach!

"Hey, Coach, why aren't you playing my son more? Can't you give him some more 'tick?' He's a great player!"

Often, in youth leagues and on school teams, parents are more concerned with the amount of time their child plays than they are with the best interests of the team overall. One quality of a successful youth coach is if they are able to give every player the opportunity (even if it is minimal) to play in game situations – and still win. Youth leagues – and many pre-high school teams – often have minimum requirements as to how much time each player must play. But in high school, college – and in the pros – there are no such rules. Yet, a coach must be mindful of keeping each player fresh and ready to contribute by instilling in each and every team member the feeling that they are unique and contribute in their own special way to the success of the team as a whole. Some reserve players might get to participate in every game. Others do not.

For some, their greatest contribution to the team is made during practices when they serve as members of the "scout team," helping to hone the skills of the starters by challenging them, and recreating game time situations.

Over the years, the value of the reserve bench player has been elevated, as more and more specialists are emerging in the different sports. In basketball, for example, there are three-point specialists who can be called upon at the end of a game when a three-pointer will tie or win the contest. The NBA's *Sixth Man Award* is given to the reserve player who has contributed the most to his team. In baseball, we have defensive specialists, pinch runners, and many "flavors" of relief pitchers: long relievers, middle relievers, set-up men and, of course, the closer ("lights out") who comes in to try and save the game.

One of the team sports that takes the greatest physical toll on the players is football. Until 1937, very few substitutions were done in this sport. Called, "single platoon," the same 11 men who played offense would also play defense, playing the entire game, unless they were injured. When legendary college Coach Herbert "Fritz" Crisler began coaching at the University of Michigan in 1938, after stints at his alma mater, the University of Chicago, the University of Minnesota, and Princeton, he started implementing distinct offensive and defensive units, as is universally done today in football at the high school, college, and professional levels. Regarded as a football luminary, it is believed by some that Coach Crisler was inspired to adopt this specialized system through late night/early morning conversations that he had with renowned author F. Scott Fitzgerald on the eve of games Crisler coached at Princeton.

Having attended Princeton, and trying out for and being cut by the national champion Tigers (at the first session), Fitzgerald was a loyal Princeton fan as well as a self-proclaimed expert on football. In a 1956 interview later published in the University of Michigan's *Michigan Daily*, Coach Crisler revealed to a graduate student named Donald A. Yates that, during his tenure as Princeton's head football coach, Fitzgerald would recommend new plays or strategies to him.

One such piece of advice was, apparently, the inspiration to establish distinct offensive and defensive units on the same team. According to a 1958 article in the *Quarterly Review* of the *Michigan Alumnus*, Coach Crisler said that Fitzgerald "came up with a scheme for a whole new offense. Something that involved a two-platoon system." Crisler was later widely credited with instituting two-platoon football.

"Send me in, Coach." Not only is this a plea uttered by many eager players wanting more game-time opportunities, but it is also the name of a short play by F. Scott Fitzgerald. While every American high school graduate knows the author because of his classic, *The Great Gatsby*, every football fan should also know him as the possible "author" of the multiple unit football strategy. Along with Fritz Crisler, Fitzgerald should be widely credited for creating more opportunities for football coaches to respond to players: "Kid, go in and play!"

As the decades passed and the two-platoon system became the accepted tradition at all levels of football, in time, a third distinct crew within the teams evolved. Not only were the punter and the kicker members of this third unit, but shortly after, regular position players mainly entered the game on kick-offs, punts, and field goal/extra point attempts. Known as the "Special Teams," these units have their own assistant coaches. "Special Teamers," as they are called, are also recognized for their contributions and, each year, exceptional players are elected to the NFL Pro Bowl exclusively for their special team contributions. In most cases, professional special teamers have been either offensive or defensive stars in college. Many of them realize that, to make it in the NFL, they need to check their egos at the door and accept a new, less glamorous role as a blocker or tackler on the special team's unit.

DIDJA KNOW that during his tenure with the Chicago Bears, Brent Novoselsky wore jersey #89, the same number worn by "Da Coach," Mike Ditka, when he played tight end for the Bears? On December 9, 2013 the Chicago Bears officially retired jersey #89.

One player who fits this mold is retired NFL player Brent Novoselsky. A tight end at the University of Pennsylvania and graduate of its prestigious Wharton School of Business, Novoselsky was not drafted by any NFL team following his 1988 graduation. The native of Skokie, Illinois, a Chicago suburb, was offered a tryout by his home team, the Chicago Bears. Novoselsky made the final cut as a free agent, which launched a seven-year NFL career. After his rookie season, Brent moved on to the Minnesota Vikings where he excelled as a special teams player credited with more than 100 career tackles, and retired after he was forced to do so because of a serious injury.

Making Each Team Member Feel Important: Spiritual Insights

Oskar Schindler: The Unique Value of Every Human Being

Oskar Schindler was an anomaly.

A war-profiteer, gambler, and a man who enjoyed living the high life, he was awarded posthumously the great distinction of being "Righteous Among the Nations" by Jerusalem's Holocaust memorial center, Yad Vashem, and was also awarded the U.S. Holocaust Museum's Medal of Remembrance, as well. Schindler is credited for saving the lives of more than 1,000 Jews during the Holocaust.

Born and raised in the Sudetenland, located in today's Czech Republic, Schindler became a member of the Nazi party in 1939 when this region was annexed by Germany.

About a month after the German invasion of Poland, which marked the formal beginning of World War II, Schindler took control of a Jewish-owned enamelware factory located in Poland, not too far from the Auschwitz concentration camp. Out to make a fortune, Schindler quickly achieved his goal. Counseled by Itzhak Stern, a Polish-Jewish accountant, after securing contracts from the German army for kitchenware, Emalia – as this modest factory was known – expanded vastly. By 1942, Schindler's factory employed about 800 workers, almost half of whom were Jews living in the nearby Krakow Ghetto. In 1944, at its peak, this factory employed more than 1,000 Jewish forced laborers. In addition to enamelware, Schindler's operation also began to manufacture ammunition used by the Germans.

What separated Oskar Schindler from other opportunistic war-profiteers was the relatively humane way that he treated his workers. After a while, Schindler's priority in managing his business shifted from making money to saving Jews. The once hedonistic Schindler matured into a caring humanitarian, a man who refused to tolerate the senseless brutal treatment and slaughter of the Jews.

Oskar Schindler and his wife Emilie risked their own lives and spent their fortune on efforts to save Jews. Using the official commercial status as a "business essential to the war effort," he was able to claim exemptions for Jews who were threatened with deportation to Auschwitz claiming that, without utilizing their unique skills in his factory, the German war effort would be compromised. If a Jew was on "Schindler's List," his/her chances to survive the war were almost guaranteed.

Having consumed all of his financial resources saving the lives of his workers, after the war, Jewish relief organizations and groups of survivors supported Oskar and Emilie Schindler. From the end of World War II until his death in 1974, Oskar Schindler split his remaining years living in Germany and Argentinia. After he died in Germany, a group of "Schindler Jews" brought his remains to Israel, where he was laid to rest in the Catholic cemetery on Mount Zion in Jerusalem.

Oskar Schindler's story became known to the world largely because of the movie *Schindler's List* for which famed Jewish director Steven Spielberg received an

Academy Award. In this most inspirational film, a quote from the
Talmud (Sanhedrin 4:5) is used as a prevailing expression of the humanity
displayed by Schindler:

וְכָל הַמְקַיֵּם נֶפֶשׁ אַחַת מִיִּשְׂרָאֵל, מַעֲלֶה עָלָיו הַכָּתוּב כְּאִלּוּ קִיֵּם עוֹלָם מָלֵא.

V'Khawl ha-m'kayem nefesh ahchat miYisrael, ma-ah-leh ahlahv HaKatuv k'ihlu
kiyem olam maleh.

**Anyone who saves a single soul from Israel, the Torah regards as if he
saved an entire world.**

Powerful in its own right, this quote is a part of a larger text that deals
with the importance and uniqueness of every single human being. In this *Mishna*,
the Sages discuss the interrogation of and warnings given to all potential witnesses
in capital punishment cases. The court wanted to make sure that the witnesses fully
and clearly understood that their testimony could lead to the putting to death of
the alleged perpetrator. In addition to reminding the witnesses that every human
being can create his/her own world, so to speak, through their children and future
generations, the court also expressed the uniqueness of every human being:

שֶׁאָדָם טוֹבֵעַ כַּמָּה מַטְבְּעוֹת בְּחוֹתָם אֶחָד
וְכֻלָּן דּוֹמִין זֶה לָזֶה,
וּמֶלֶךְ מַלְכֵי הַמְּלָכִים הַקָּדוֹשׁ בָּרוּךְ הוּא
טָבַע כָּל אָדָם בְּחוֹתָמוֹ שֶׁל אָדָם הָרִאשׁוֹן
וְאֵין אֶחָד מֵהֶן דּוֹמֶה לַחֲבֵרוֹ.

Sheh-ahdahm toveh-ah kama mahtb'ot b'chotahm echad v'khulan
domin zeh la-zeh, u-Melekh Malkhei HaM'lakhim HaKadosh
Barukh Hu tavah kol ahdahm b'chotamo shel Ahdam HaRishon v'ein echad
meh-hen domeh la-chavero.

**. . . For a person casts several [i.e., numerous] coins from one mold
and they all are [turn out to be] identical to one another, but the
King of Kings the Holy One Blessed Be He casts each human being in the
mold of Adam and no human being is identical to the next.**

In Hebrew we refer to the individuality of each and every human
being as עֶרְכּוֹ שֶׁל הַיָּחִיד/*ehrko shel ha-yachid – the [unique] value of
the individual.* Not only did Oskar Schindler understand that every
human life was precious, but he also comprehended how every person was
special and that their unique skill set contributed to the success
of his business.

שֶׁלֹא לַעֲמֹד עַל דַּם רֵעִים

Shehlo LaAhmod Ahl Dahm Rei-ihm

Not to Stand By Idly While Someone's Blood is Shed
Sefer HaChinukh #237; Sefer HaMitzvot,
LT #297

Based upon the words: לֹא תַעֲמֹד עַל דַּם רֵעֶךָ/
*Lo Tahahmod ahl Dahm Reiehkha - **Do not
stand idly by when someone's blood is shed***
(*Leviticus* 19:16), a Jew is commanded to do all
they can (without putting their own life in peril)
to save the life of a fellow Jew. From this verse we
are also commanded not to withhold evidence
when that information can help a fellow Jew
by saving their life or from incurring a financial
loss. The Modern State of Israel extends the
practice of this *Mitzvah* to all people (Jews and
non-Jews) by being on the frontlines in offering
medical and other types of aid when other
countries are in the midst of a crisis. Oskar and
Emilie Schindler earned their places as Righteous
Among the Nations for not standing by idly while
the blood of fellow human beings was being shed.

THE BOX SCORE

An integral ingredient of a successful team is the ability
of every member (and with youth sports, every parent as
well) to suppress his/her egos; players must accept
their specific roles with the team and still play their very best,
no matter how celebrated or invisible. Although a star
tight end in college, Brent Novoselsky accepted a less flashy
role and played in the NFL as a prominent member of the
special teams. A top-notch coach is able to make every
member of the team feel that they are contributing uniquely
to the wellbeing of the squad. These are special expressions
of sportsmanship.

The concept of *Ehrko Shel HaYachid* teaches that every
person is unique and special. We are reminded by the
Talmudic maxim, "Anyone who saves a single soul from
Israel, the *Torah* regards as if he saved an entire world"
(*Sanhedrin* 4:5) along with the extraordinary efforts of
Oskar Schindler, of the value and uniqueness of each and
every human being. When we keep this in mind and
treat people with the respect that they deserve, we are
exhibiting an important manifestation of דֶּרֶךְ אֶרֶץ וְכָבוֹד /
Derekh Eretz v'Khavod (***Repect and Honor***).

Chapter 6
Thou Shalt Not Shame! Acts of Sportsmanship between Opponents

Winning with Humility

As stated earlier, Level II of Sportsmanship is analogous to Nachmanides's interpretation of וְעָשִׂיתָ הַיָּשָׁר וְהַטּוֹב בְּעֵינֵי ה'/V'asita HaYashar v'HaTov b'einei HaShem – **And you shall do that which is straight [fair] and good in the eyes of HaShem** (Deuteronomy 6:18). Level II is comprised of acts of sportsmanship that, although not specifically mandated, we should expect sports participants to perform, because, simply put, it's the right thing to do. For example, at the conclusion of an NHL playoff series, it is customary for members of both teams to form congratulatory lines and participate in wishing their opponents well. This has become a standard practice after each game in many youth and pre-college school leagues.

While often times we put a premium on learning how to deal with rejection, failure and loss, it is easy to overlook the important role that sportsmanship plays in properly handling victory and success.

Winning Like Bobby Orr

Robert Gordon Orr, was perhaps the greatest defenseman in the history of the NHL. Not only did he fiercely protect his goalie from offensive attackers, but Bobby Orr was the offensive quarterback/point guard of his team. Having won the coveted Art Ross Trophy twice for leading the NHL in scoring, he is the only defenseman in the history of the league to win this award. During his 12-season career, nine with the Boston Bruins, Orr was voted the Rookie of the Year, the NHL's best defenseman for eight seasons, and the NHL's Most Valuable Player three times. He also played on eight All-Star teams and led his Boston Bruins teams to two Stanley Cups. Knee injuries caused him to retire prematurely and, at age 31, he was the youngest person voted into the Hockey Hall of Fame.

In spite of all of his incredible accomplishments, Bobby Orr is known to be an exceptionally humble man both on and off the ice. Unlike most players who openly celebrate scoring a goal, Orr was known for usually skating with his head down after he scored, so he would not shame the opposing players.

DIDJA KNOW that before June 1, 1979, incoming NHL players did not have to wear helmets? Provided they signed a waiver, veteran players were still permitted to play helmetless. St. Louis Blues center Craig MacTavish was the last player to play in an NHL game without wearing a helmet in the 1996–1997 season.

It is told that one day after a game at the old Boston Garden, a fan's car got stuck in the snow. A young man approached the distressed driver and instructed him to steer as he pushed. After the car was removed, the driver went to thank this anonymous stranger. This do-gooder turned out to be none other than Bobby Orr.

In a 2013 article in the *Boston Globe* titled "At 65, Bobby Orr is Focused on Doing Good – Quietly," Bob Hohler describes numerous acts of kindness performed by Orr. They include such noble deeds as turning his home into a hospice unit so that John "Frosty" Forristall a former Bruins trainer could die in dignity, rescuing a former Bruins teammate from alcohol and drug abuse, and numerous inspirational visits to sick or injured youth.

Nearing the end of his career, Orr played two seasons for the Chicago Blackhawks. Since injuries and multiple orthopedic surgeries forced him to play far below his high standards, the *New York Times* reported that Orr refused to cash a paycheck from the Hawks, saying that he did not earn them.

Winning with Humility: A Spiritual insight

The Most Humble Person in the History of the World

וְהָאִישׁ מֹשֶׁה עָנָו מְאֹד
מִכֹּל הָאָדָם אֲשֶׁר עַל פְּנֵי הָאֲדָמָה:

V'ha-ish Moshe anav m'od, mi-kol ha-ahdahm asher ahl p'nei ha-ahdahma.

And the man Moses was extremely humble, more than any person on the face of the earth (*Numbers* 12:3).

Why did Moses earn this accolade?

Some say that his self-effacing manner is what qualified him. After all, when the Almighty chose him to lead the Israelites out of Egypt, Moses did all that he could to get out of this assignment. Moses claimed that he had certain shortcomings, including an apparent speech impediment, that he felt should disqualify him from this position of responsibility (*Exodus* 3:1–17).

Some contend that self-deprecation is not an essential element of humility. In words attributed to authors Rick Warren or Rich Howard and Jamie Lash (and, at times, misattributed to CS Lewis): "Humility is not thinking less of yourself, it's thinking of yourself less."

Although Moses is introduced in the second chapter of the *Book of Exodus* and is the *Torah*'s leading character until his death, as recorded in the final chapter of *Deuteronomy*, his exemplary level of humility is not mentioned until the middle of the *Book of Numbers*. Specifically it is introduced after Moses's decision not to respond in a defensive or combative manner to a negative, albeit well-intended, statement made about him by his sister Miriam with the support of his older brother Aaron.

In fact, when the Almighty punished Miriam for speaking *Lashon HaRah* (**true, but negative language which did not need to be uttered**) and inflicted her with the dermatological (spiritual) disease known as *Tzarah-aht* (*VaYikra Rabba* 16:1) which forced her to be secluded outside of the Camp of Israel, Moses prayed for her healing:

קֵל נָא רְפָא נָא לָה

Kel na r'fa na la

"Lord please, please heal her [Miriam now]" (*Numbers* 12:13).

Instead of thinking about himself and any hurt that he may have experienced, Moses was more concerned about the wellbeing of his beloved sister.

The only reference in the *Talmud* to *Numbers* 12:3 depicting Moses and his humility is found in *N'darim* 38a cited in the name of *Rahbi Yochanan*:

Ein HaKadosh Barukh Hu mashreh Sh'khinato elah ahl Gibor, Ahshir, Chakham v'Anav.

"The Holy One Blessed Be He rests His Sh'khina [Divine Presence] only on one [i.e., a prophet] who is mighty, wealthy, wise and humble."

This *Talmudic* passage teaches another important reason why Moses was considered the most humble man in world history. To truly test a person's humility, the more talented they are, the more challenging it is to remain humble. Moses, who possessed many fine qualities that earned him respect from people of all walks of life, was humble in spite of being mighty, wealthy, and wise.

Humility is an important trait for all people to possess. While we strive for success in all ways, it is important to appreciate the greatness of others as well as that of the Almighty.

Celebration vs. Taunting

Unlike the unusually unpretentious Bobby Orr, many players do not hide their exuberance and sense of triumph when they score a goal, hit a home run or score a touchdown. When is celebrating a great play acceptable, and when does it cross the line and considered unsportsmanlike?

The Ickey Shuffle

In his brief NFL career (1988–1991), Cincinnati Bengals running back Elbert "Ickey" Woods is probably best remembered for his touchdown celebration. Known as the "Ickey Shuffle," Woods's joyous expression is still recalled fondly today and was part of a 2014 television commercial for the GEICO insurance company.

Throughout the history of the NFL, there have been many signature celebrations. They include the *Lambeau Leap* in Green Bay and the Denver Broncos' *Mile High Salute*. While the NFL permits certain touchdown celebrations, the league sets limits on these displays of revelry.

In a letter to fans dated May, 2017, outlining certain relaxations in the rules guiding touchdown celebrations, NFL Commissioner Roger Goodell stated in part:

"In my conversations with NFL players, it was also clear how much our players care about sportsmanship, clean competition, and setting good examples for young athletes. That is why offensive demonstrations, celebrations that are prolonged and delay the game, and those directed at an opponent, will still be penalized."

Celebration vs. Taunting: A Spiritual Insight

King Solomon: The Man Who (Just May Have) Inspired the NFL Rule Making Committee

When a person hears the name "King Solomon," they associate it with many different achievements, including: the builder of the (first) בֵּית-הַמִּקְדָּשׁ/ Beit HaMikdash (**Holy Temple**), the husband of many wives, the father of numerous children, and a very wise man.

One of Solomon's books of wisdom is the **Book of Proverbs** (סֵפֶר מִשְׁלֵי/Sefer Mishlei). A famous piece of King Solomon's sage advice is:

בִּנְפֹל אוֹיִבְךָ אַל-תִּשְׂמָח וּבִכָּשְׁלוֹ אַל-יָגֵל לִבֶּךָ:

Binfol o-yivkha ahl tismach u-vi-kahsh'lo ahl yagel libehkha.

When your enemy falls do not rejoice and when he stumbles do not be glad of heart (*Proverbs* 24:17).

When the Israelites miraculously crossed the Sea of Reeds (Red Sea), the angels wanted to sing praise to God, but the Holy One Blessed Be He insisted that they not proceed:

אָמַר הַקְבָּ"ה: מַעֲשֵׂה יָדַי טוֹבְעִין בַּיָּם וְאַתֶּם אוֹמְרִים שִׁירָה?

Amar HaKB"H: Ma-aseh yadai tov'in ba-yam v'atem om'rim Shira?

The Holy One Blessed Be He said: "The creations of My Hands are drowning in the Sea [of Reeds] and you [want to] recite a Song [of praises]?" (*M'gilla* 10b).

Based upon these texts, as we recite the Ten Plagues during the Passover *Seder*, it is a custom to spill out drops of wine from our (second of four) wine cup. After all, a full cup of wine symbolizes joy. How can we rejoice when we are recalling the downfall of the Almighty's creations? No matter how sinister the Egyptians may have been, they were still created by the Almighty in His image.

Public Shaming
Running Up the Score

In November 2010, a Pikeville, Kentucky middle school basketball team defeated another local team by a score of 100–2. The lopsided game even garnered some national attention, and media outlets, bloggers, and residents questioned the results. Upon further investigation, it was reported that the winning coach – apparently seeing that his team of middle-schoolers was vastly superior to the opponents – pulled his starters from the game after the first few minutes and ordered his players to stop playing defense, giving the opponent the best opportunity to score and compete. Unfortunately, the teams were so poorly matched that such an unbalanced score could not be prevented even with such concessions. What responsibility do league schedulers have in matching competitions, so as not to embarrass the less talented team? Who's at fault? The winning coach or the commissioner?

THE BOX SCORE

Everybody likes to win and celebrate. Good sportsmanship directs a winner to celebrate in a humble fashion that does not taunt the opposition. Bobby Orr, one of hockey's greatest alltime players, was a role model for humility.

In Jewish history, the greatest exemplar of humility was Moses. We learn from King Solomon that, while we can celebrate our victories, our celebrations should focus on ou accomplishments (and the Almighty's role), and not on the downfall and misery of our enemies.

Winning graciously is an important expression of *Dereckh Eretz v'Khavod* (**Respect and Honor**) and can translate into success both on and off the court/field.

DIDJA KNOW
that in high school and college, teams are divided into levels and leagues in part based upon their anticipated skill levels? For example, in collegiate sports competitions, the most talented (usually, larger) schools are in NCAA Division I. Oftentimes universities with a smaller student population are placed in Division III.

Public Shaming: A Spiritual Insight

Better to Cast Oneself into a Furnace than Publicly Shame Another

A seminal *Mitzvah* is not to shame anybody publicly.

נוֹחַ לוֹ לְאָדָם שֶׁיַּפִּיל עַצְמוֹ
לְתוֹךְ כִּבְשַׁן הָאֵשׁ, וְאַל יַלְבִּין פְּנֵי חֲבֵרוֹ בְּרַבִּים.

Noach lo l'ahdahm sh'yapil ahtzmo l'tokh kivshan ha-esh, v'ahl yalbin p'nei chavero b'rahbim.

"It is better for a person to cast himself into a fiery furnace rather than publicly shame another person" (Stated by *Rahbi Shimon bar/ben Yochai* in B'rakhot 43b; Sotah 10b; and *Bava M'tzia* 59a).

Two of the major proponents of this *Mitzvah* were the *Tanna Rahbi Shimon bar Yochai (RaShBY* – 2nd century CE) and *Rabbenu Yona* of Gerondi (1200-1263). Although they lived about 1000 years apart and in different regions of the world – *RaShBY* in Israel and *Rabbenu Yona* in France and later Spain – they both felt that it was necessary to stress the importance of this rather sensible law. Having each committed an act of publicly embarrassing another person or their memory, both of these esteemed scholars apparently felt great remorse, changed their ways, and preached to others the importance of this *Mitzvah*.

Here are their stories . . .

Rahbi Shimon bar Yochai was one of the most colorful people in Jewish history. The student of *Rahbi Akiva* and teacher of Rabbi Judah the Prince (the redactor of the *Mishna*), *RaShBy* was a revered scholar who was a foremost contributor to the *Mishna* and other classic Jewish texts. Regarding his scholarship, he is, perhaps, best remembered as being the scholar to whom Jewish tradition attributes the authorship of the *Zohar*, the main text for the study of *Kabbala*.

An outspoken critic of the Roman government that ruled Israel at that time, *Rahbi Shimon's* criticism triggered the Romans to issue a death warrant against him. This forced *RaShBY* and his son *Elazar* to flee and hide in a cave. During this time, the father-and-son scholarship tandem studied all day and was miraculously sustained by the fruit of a carob tree that grew near the cave. After 12 years of isolation, the Prophet Elijah came to the cave and informed them that the Roman emperor had died and that it was now safe for them to emerge and integrate back into society.

Unfortunately, the two were so affected by their isolation and immersion in such a holy lifestyle, that they could not accept the fact that most of the members of the Jewish community had to work to support themselves instead of engaging fulltime in *Torah* study and being supported by the Almighty. Upon seeing a Jewish farmer at work, they criticized him for what they perceived was his choice of forsaking a life anchored by the study of *Torah* to perform manual labor. Because of this, *RaShBY* and son were Divinely punished and forced to retreat back to the cave for an additional 12 months of isolation.

This time, when they re-emerged, upon seeing a non-scholarly Jew who was engaged in a simple act of preparing for the Sabbath, they came to the realization that this man was representative of many dedicated, observant, well-intended Jews who worshiped the Almighty largely through their performance of religious acts. *Rahbi Shimon* praised his actions, unlike his response in the earlier situation.

Detailed in the *Talmud* (*Shabbat* 33b), some argue that this episode was caused by *RaShBY's* lengthy isolation from the Jewish community, and is an aberration from his sterling character. After all, *Rahbi Shimon* was known for being an ardent advocate for the dignified treatment of others, as exemplified by his statement articulated earlier.

Rabbi Jonah ben Abraham Gerondi was a pious scholar and community leader. As a student of Rabbi Solomon ben Abraham of Montpellier (*Reb Shlomo Min HaHar*) he also was an adherent of his הַשְׁקָפָה/*hashkafa* (*religious outlook*) that the philosophical works of Maimonides were heretical. This led *Rabbenu Yona* to support the burning of volumes of the works of the RaMBaM (*Maimonides*) by Christian authorities in Paris in 1233.

About seven years later, the Christian authorities decided that it was now time to burn – in the very same town square – wagons filled with *Talmudic* tractates. *Rabbenu Yona* interpreted this as direct Divine retribution for his acts of publicly shaming the memory of Maimonides. This prompted *Rabbenu Yona* to repent and document his insights regarding repentance in a tome that remains highly popular to this day, *Sefer Shaarei Teshuva* (**The Book of the Gates of Repentance**). In this book, the author explains how we should equate public embarrassment to murder. *Rabbenu Yona* articulates that when we shame someone publicly, the ruddiness in their face disappears and is replaced by whiteness that he compares with the whiteness of death:

וְהִנֵּה אָבָק הָרְצִיחָה הַלְבָּנַת פָּנִים.

V'hineh ahvahk ha-rtzicha halbanat panim.

"And behold the dust of murder is [equivalent to] the whiteness of a person's face [who was publicly shamed]."

We learn from these two world-class Jewish scholars that, while it is human to err, it is also human to repent; that is, learn from and correct our own mistakes, and then, going forward, to do all that we can to prevent ourselves and others from committing such egregious sins as shaming someone in public.

Public Shaming (Part Two)

The Sad Downfall of the Jackie Robinson West All-Stars

"43–2"

While this numerical combination may refer to a verse from Isaiah or the citation of an Alabama, Colorado and Indiana statute, it also was the score of a recent Little League baseball game. The Jackie Robinson West All-Stars (JRW), a team from the South Side of Chicago, scored 43 runs against a suburban opponent's 2. This 2014 victory led the JRW All-Stars to their

THE BOX SCORE

Not shaming others is a most important expression of *Derekh Eretz v'Khavod* as well as sportsmanship.

In youth sports it is very important for administrators to ensure that games should only be scheduled between teams that can play competitively against one another, so not to publicly shame any of the participants. If coaches see at the outset that there is a mismatch, they should make sure that they allow all of the members of their squad to play and not do things that will unnecessarily embarrass the other side. In professional sports, we have amateur drafts wherein the poorer performing teams pick prior to the better teams. There is also an exemption to anti-trust laws, restricting players from moving freely from team to team. These measures are taken in order to ensure a more even level of competition among all league teams.

Sometimes while trying to do the right thing, we end-up unnecessarily shaming someone else. When *RaShBY* and his son emerged from the cave, they possessed a certain arrogance caused by being out of circulation in the mainstream world for so many years. Rabbi Yona of Gerondi did not properly think through his decision to participate in the public burning of the works of the *Rambam* (**Maimonides**).

Both luminaries/leaders learned from their mistakes of how one must be extremely careful in not shaming others in public.

eventual U.S. Little League World Series Championship later that year.

My hunch is that losing 43 – 2 is also the event that drove at least one adult leader from the losing team to complain to the officials of Little League International (LLI). The complaint triggered an investigation, leading to findings of alleged rule infractions by JRW of recruiting out-of-district players, and the eventual stripping of JRW's World Series Championship.

My life experiences tell me that a contest between children should never be allowed to reach such an outrageously large discrepancy in score. Although, per LLI rules, the game was shortened to four innings ("The Slaughter Rule"), it should have been tactfully ended at a much earlier point. In other words, LLI rules should be changed so that blowouts of this magnitude can never occur in the future. No matter how resilient we may claim kids are, there is nothing gained in doing something that can shame another human being of any age.

Public Shaming (Part Two): Spiritual Insights

What's in a Name?
When I read of this lopsided score (43–2) that, at first glance, I thought was the final tally of a football game, I was reminded of the passage from the *Talmud* (*Gittin* 55b–56a) that discusses one of the main reasons cited for the destruction of the Second Temple:

אַקַמְצָא וּבַר קַמְצָא חָרוּב יְרוּשָׁלַיִם.

AhKamtza u-Var Kamtaz charuv Y'rushalayim.

On account of [the episode involving] Kamtza and Bar Kamtza Jerusalem [i.e., the Second Temple] was destroyed.

Referred to as שִׂנְאַת חִנָּם (*sinat chinam/**unwarranted hatred***), this passage tells the story of a heinous public humiliation, and how it caused one of the greatest tragedies in Jewish history. In this text we are told about a man who had a friend named *Kamtza* and an enemy named *Bar Kamtza*. This unnamed man once threw a party and, by mistake, his servant invited *Bar Kamtza* to the party instead of *Kamtza*. The host was so upset that *Bar Kamtza* was in his home, that, in the presence of his guests that included prominent community leaders who did nothing to stop it, he embarrassed this uninvited guest and evicted him from his house.

Publicly humiliated, *Bar Kamtza*, in a deceitful manner, convinced the Roman government that the Jews were going to rebel. This eventually led to the destruction of the Temple.

73

that The Eight Levels of Charitable Giving, as codified by Maimonides is designed to provide financial relief to an impoverished Jew, while causing him/her the least amount of shame?

The highest level is creating an opportunity for being self-supportive by providing the person in need with an interest-free loan, a job, business partnership, etc.

While the next seven levels deal with giving a gift to the poor person, the highest of these seven levels is when the gift is given without the benefactor knowing the identity of the beneficiary and vice a versa.

(*For further details see* Maimonides, *Mishneh Torah, Mat'not Aniyim* 10:7-14).

that not shaming others is so important in Jewish law, that we reinforce this directive through the personification of various inanimate objects used in Jewish life?

Here are two examples:

● It is common practice to cover the *Challot* ([two] *special loaves of bread*) on the *Shabbat* (and *Yom Tov*) table. One of the reasons why we do so (*Tur Shulchan Arukh Orach Chayim* 271 quoting the *Talmud Y'rushalmi*) is because we are sensitive and do not want to cause any "embarrassment" to the *Challot*, since during the rest of the week we commence our meals by reciting the *HaMotzih* (*blessing over the bread*). At our Friday night and Saturday afternoon meals, we first bless the wine when we recite *Kiddush*, and only after this do we uncover the

Challot and recite the *HaMotzih*.

● *Parashat Yitro* (*Exodus* 18-20) contains two of the most important passages in the *Torah*: the basis for the creation of multi-tiered judicial systems and the (first rendition of the) *Decalogue* (*Aseret HaDibrot/ Ten Commandments*). The *Sidra* (*Torah Portion*) ends with the Almighty commanding the *Kohanim* (*priests*) not to use steps when ascending to the Altar:

וְלֹא תַעֲלֶה בְמַעֲלֹת
עַל־מִזְבְּחִי אֲשֶׁר לֹא
תִגָּלֶה עֶרְוָתְךָ עָלָיו:

V'lo tah-ah-leh v'mah-ahlot ahl mizb'chi asher lo tigaleh ervat'kha ahlahv.

"And do not climb the stairs of my altar; in order that your nakedness will not become exposed on it" (*Exodus* 20:23).

Because of this command, a ramp was installed in the place of stairs for the *Kohanim* to ascend.

It seems rather peculiar that we are concerned that inanimate stone from which the stairs were crafted would "see" the undergarments of the priests as they lifted their legs while climbing the stairs. After all, stone can't see?

Rashi, based upon the *Midrash M'khilta*, teaches that the purpose of this command, (just as the tradition of covering the *Challot* while reciting *Kiddush*), is to further reinforce the importance of not causing any shame or embarrassment to any human being. After all, if we are so concerned that stone (or bread) may be publicly shamed, how much more so should we be careful not to shame fellow human beings?

Chapter 7
In the Public Arena: Acts of Sportsmanship involving Game Officials

Agree to Disagree

Nice Guys (Can and Sometimes Do) Finish First

"Nice guys finish last."

Attributed to fiery former MLB player and manager, Leo Durocher (1905-1991), over the years many sportsmen, including players and coaches, have proved Mr. Durocher's proclamation wrong.

Remembered as one of the most colorful personalities in baseball history, Durocher earned a place in baseball's Hall of Fame primarily for his accomplishments as a manager. As a player he was a sure-handed fielding, weak-hitting shortstop, most famously referred to by his New York Yankee teammate, Babe Ruth, as "the All-American out." After playing three years with the New York Yankees, Durocher moved to the National League where he played for the St. Louis Cardinals, Cincinnati Reds, and Brooklyn Dodgers. As captain of the St. Louis Cardinals' "Gashouse Gang," Durocher led the Redbirds to the 1934 World Series Championship.

Recognized for his exceptional leadership skills, in 1939, Durocher expanded his role from simply player to the player-manager of the Brooklyn Dodgers a position that he held intermittently through the 1945 season. He then fully retired as a player and remained the Dodgers manager through the beginning of the 1948 campaign when he left to become the manager of the crosstown rival New York Giants, the team to which he once referred to as "nice guys."

When he left the Giants after the 1955 season to become a color commentator on NBC baseball telecasts, Durocher's résumé as an MLB skipper included three National League Pennants and one World Series Championship. Durocher then took an 11-year hiatus from the dugout, which he snapped when he became the manager of the Chicago Cubs in 1966. Durocher retired as a manager in 1973, after spending one-and-a-half seasons as skipper of the Houston Astros.

Although Durocher retired as the manager with the fifth most wins in MLB history with 2,008 career victories, he is probably best remembered for his tirades against umpires. Nicknamed "Leo the Lip," for his infamous verbal exchanges with umpires, players, and executives, Durocher retired in second place for career total ejections as a manager, behind the legendary John McGraw.

Even though Leo Durocher was of the opinion that "nice guys finish last," I think that even he would agree that there are indeed exceptions to this rule.

One exception to this rule is retired high school baseball coach Gene Etter. During his long, distinguished managing career, Etter was never thrown out of a game.

Gene Etter served as the coach of the Baylor High School baseball team for over 40 years. Having played football at the University of Tennessee, Etter also played minor league baseball in the Chicago Cubs organization. The coach with the second-highest number of wins in Tennessee history, Etter led his Baylor teams to about 850 career victories.

Though Etter would, in great likelihood, qualify as a "nice guy" by Durocher's standards, the Baylor coach was known to be highly competitive and did not always agree with the umpires' calls. However, instead of arguing, he engaged umpires in constructive conversations. In fact, another Tennessee high school baseball coach, Steve Garland commented to the *Chattanooga Times Free Press*, "I've never seen him argue – discuss or question, yes, but never argue – and I've never even seen him be demonstrative when asking about an umpire's call."

As a high school mathematics teacher and baseball coach, Gene Etter earned the nickname the "gentleman genius," a moniker that he truly earned. After all, during the course of his 40-plus years as a high school coach and educator, Coach Etter positively impacted upon the lives of thousands of youth teaching many important life lessons, including how to disagree in a sportsmanlike (i.e., respectful) manner.

Agree to Disagree: Spiritual Insights

DIDJA KNOW
that – according to Shane Tourtellotte in his article *You're Outta Here!* (*Part One*) – in MLB history, beginning from 1889 when umpires were first allowed to eject managers, there have been nine managers (who managed at least 500 games) who were never ejected? At the top of this list is Frank Selee. During his career (1890-1905), he managed the most games (2,180) and had the highest winning percentage (.598). The "Splendid Splinter," the great Ted Williams, is also on this illustrious list. In the 637 games that he managed the Washington Senators/ Texas Rangers (1969-1972), Williams was never tossed from a single game.

A Failure to Communicate

In the *Talmud* (*Bava M'tzia* 33a), we are taught how important it is for a student to articulate a question to their rabbi in a most sensitive, respectful manner. *Rav Chisda* was a top student of *Rav Huna*, who may have even surpassed his revered teacher in *Torah* knowledge. When studying together the laws regarding the *Mitzvah* of הֲשָׁבַת אֲבֵדָה / *Hashavat Aveida* (**returning lost items**), they encountered the situation where a person comes across – at the same time – the lost items of his father and rabbi, and is only able to retrieve one of these items. While the law is that the person must return his rabbi's item before his father's, provided that his father is not at a comparable level of *Torah* study as is his teacher, *Rav Chisda* asked:

תַּלְמִיד וְצָרִיךְ לוֹ רַבּוֹ, מַאי?
Talmid v'tzarikh lo Rabo, mahy?

What [is the law regarding whether to retrieve a father or a rabbi's belongings first], in the case of a student that the rabbi needs [i.e., the student is one from whom the teacher is able to sharpen his learning]?

Although *Rav Chisda* was asking a hypothetical question, *Rav Huna* misunderstood him as referring to him (i.e., that *Rav Chisda* was such a student, and that he therefore could retrieve his father's belongings first).

This miscommunication triggered a 40-year estrangement between these two great sages. Based upon the verse: *VaOlekh . . . "And I [Moses] led you through the desert for forty years . . ."* (*Deuteronomy* 29:4), the *Talmud* (*Avoda Zara* 5b) teaches further the significance of 40 years. In addition to being the number of years that the Israelites travelled in the desert, for some of the Israelites, this is the amount of time that it took them to fully comprehend the teachings of Moses. Likewise for many students, perhaps *Rav Chisda* counting as one of these, it can also take up to 40 years for a student to fully comprehend the teachings of his rabbi.

NAME THAT *MITZVAH!*

The above encounter between *Rav Chisda* and *Rav Huna* is an illustration of

מִצְוַת כִּבּוּד חֲכָמִים
Mitzvat Kibbud Chakhamim

The Mitzvah of Honoring Sages (and Elders)

Sefer HaChinukh #257; Sefer HaMitzvot, Ahseh #209

A similar *Mitzvah* of מִצְוַת יִרְאַת אָב וָאֵם / *Mitzvat Yirat Av VaEm – The Mitzvah of Revering Parents* [*Sefer HaChinukh #212; Sefer HaMitzvot, Ahseh #211*], teaches that a child of any age should avoid correcting or contradicting his/her parents. An exception to this rule is when the difference in understanding is in regard to matters of *Torah*. In such cases, according to many *Poskim* (**Halakhic authorities**), a child may correct the parent, but must do so in a very sensitive, respectful, and – ideally – indirect way. For example, if the parent inadvertently said something erroneously, the child should say something to the effect of:

אַבָּא, כָּתוּב בַּתּוֹרָה כָּךְ וְכָךְ . . ./*Abba katuv BaTorah kakh v'khakh – "Father, it is written in the Torah as such . . ."* It is also permissible for a child to engage in the give-and-take (*Shakla V'Tarya*) with his father that is a normal part of the *Torah* learning process between study partners (*Chavrutot*) and teacher and student. A child must honor and revere his/her parents in a similar manner to the way that all Jews must show honor and reverence to the Almighty.

Since the honor/respect/reverence that a student must show his teacher is based upon the parent-child relationship, I think that it is reasonable to conclude that the above-cited exceptions hold true also in regard to a teacher. [For further details regarding the variance of opinions and serious nature of this issue, see *Arukh HaShulchan* 240:12 *and* 33; Maimonides, *Mishneh Torah, Hilkhot Sh'chita* 11:10; *Tur Shulchan Arukh* 240; and *Shulchan Arukh, Yoreh Deah* 240:2. For an extensive discussion and analysis of primary sources, please see: Rabbi Moshe Lieber's *The Fifth Commandment* (Artscroll Series), pp. 95-98 and 104-106].

THE BOX SCORE

Sometimes in the heat of competition we forget our manners. When we protest, question, or dispute a decision, we must try our hardest to do so in respectful fashion. This especially holds true when a person's fellow disputant is a person of authority. Disagreeing in a courteous manner is an important expression of sportsmanship.

We learn from the positive example set by legendary high school baseball coach Gene Etter of how a successful sports coach can politely engage in a disagreement with an umpire.

We learn from the great sage *Rav Chisda* and from the *Mitzvot* of honoring and revering teachers and parents how a student – no matter how learned s/he may be – must be especially sensitive in the manner that they raise questions when studying with their teacher.

Chapter 8
"Who's In Charge Here?!" Acts of Sportsmanship by Parents

Acts of Sportsmanship for those Outside the Game: Chapters 8-12

Helicopter Parents

"Mother hovers over me like a helicopter . . ."

When it comes to accounts of "sports parents," unfortunately, we have become accustomed to hearing mainly horror stories. These tales include that of the frustrated mother who lives vicariously through her daughter, trying to achieve what she herself was unable; the father who storms the court to confront a referee whose call he disputes; and the parents of players on opposing teams whose argument in the stands escalate into full blown fisticuffs. On rare occasions, you hear about feel-good moments, like the one involving Michael Jordan and "#33," described in the introduction of this book.

A popular term describing parents who are over-involved in their children's lives is "helicopter parents." The term was first introduced by Israeli-born psychologist Dr. Haim Ginott (1922–1973) in his 1969 book *Between Parent and Teenager*. In this bestseller, Dr. Ginott quotes a patient of his describing their overbearing mother: "Mother hovers over me like a helicopter and I'm fed up with her noise and hot air . . . I'm entitled to sneeze without an explanation."

Real Simple magazine reported that even before the end of 2013, in that year the term "helicopter parent" registered nearly 20 million hits on Google.

While it is good for parents to be involved in their children's lives, there is a point where it can become detrimental.

With this background in mind, consider the following: Ought a parent of a player be allowed to interact, if ever, with: his/her child, the coach, or referees during games or practices – without being considered a helicopter parent?

Helicopter Parents: A Spiritual Insight

Biblical Helicopter Parents?

In reviewing parent-child relationships in Jewish history, one finds many instances where, on the surface, it may appear that the mother or father is acting like a helicopter parent; that is, getting involved in their children's (some of whom are adults) lives more than what is helpful.

In all of the following seven cases, traditional interpretors suggest that the parent (and in one case each, grandparent and parent-in-law) did the right thing, not just for the child's sake but also for the welfare of the Jewish people.

Here are my *Top Seven* (one for each day of the week) *Biblical Helicopter Parent Stories:*

(7) **Jacob-Joseph**. Jacob spent more time with Joseph when they both lived in Israel than he did with any of his other sons. While it may appear that Jacob doted on Joseph because he was the son of Rachel, Jacob's favorite wife, upon closer

examination, one can conclude that Joseph was the son who honored his father the most by studying (pre-Sinai) *Torah* with him regularly.

Regarding their close relationship the *Torah* states:

וְיִשְׂרָאֵל אָהַב אֶת־יוֹסֵף מִכָּל־בָּנָיו כִּי־בֶן־זְקֻנִים הוּא לוֹ וְעָשָׂה לוֹ כְּתֹנֶת פַּסִּים:

V'Yisrael ahav et Yoseph mi-kol banav ki-ven-z'kunim hu lo v'asah lo k'tonet pasim.

And Israel loved Joseph more than all of his sons because he was a child born to him at an old age; and he made him [Joseph] a fancy woolen coat (Genesis 37:3).

Ben z'kunim literally means a **son of old age**. *Onkelos* (1st Century CE) and other commentators interpret this term as meaning that Joseph was a *wise son* (*Bar Chaki*m), having gained much of his wisdom by studying regularly with Jacob who had accumulated great knowledge during his 14 years of study in the (pre-Sinai) *y'shivot* of *Shem* and *Ever*.

Because Joseph chose to do so, while the other brothers apparently declined the same opportunity, Jacob rewarded Joseph by giving him the striped, multi-colored tunic symbolizing leadership. While Jacob may have done the right thing by being involved in Joseph's life to the extent that he was, and justly rewarding him for learning and preparing himself to be able to survive in a highly-assimilated society, unfortunately, the other brothers, especially Leah's sons, could not deal with it, and became insanely jealous. This led to the sale of Joseph into slavery in Egypt. And the rest, of course, is history.

Result: Although Jacob's more favorable treatment of Joseph led to the hardship of separation for over 20 years, in the big picture, this time investment paid off in a big way as it prepared Joseph to become a prodigious world leader who was firmly grounded in Jewish tradition and who refused to allow himself and his sons to assimilate.

(6) **Jacob-*Ephraim*/Joseph-*Menashe***. When Jacob migrated to Egypt to weather the famine in Israel, he established a relationship with his grandson *Ephraim*, the younger brother of *Menashe*, which was similar to his relationship with Joseph. This helped *Ephraim* develop into a great (pre-Sinai) *Torah* scholar. When Jacob dispensed blessings to his sons and grandsons, *Ephraim* and *Menashe*, he once again favored a younger (grand)son over the older one, by blessing *Ephraim* before *Menashe* (Genesis 48:20). With the parenting of Joseph, though, *Menashe* did not feel jealous, and understood that a *Torah* scholar is more worthy to lead the Children of Israel, and therefore should be accorded the blessing that usually goes to the *b'khor* (**first born**). As Joseph's top political aide, *Menashe* was secure in how his father regarded him and the tremendous mutual respect that they had for one another.

Result: In this case, even though it may appear that Jacob was over-involved in *Ephraim*'s life, it all worked out, as *Menashe* accepted the second blessing without any objection. Since the first time that Jacob blessed his grandsons, *Ephraim* and *Menashe*, fathers around the globe bless their sons on Friday night and other special occasions that they should aspire to be like these two brothers, who got along famously.

(5) **Hanna-Samuel.** One can make the case that Hanna was the opposite of a helicopter parent. After all, she so desperately wanted a son, that she made a vow with Eli the Kohen in Shilo that, if the Almighty blessed her with a pregnancy, she would lend her son to serve God (I *Samuel* 1:11). Soon after making this vow, Hanna gave birth to Samuel, and then fulfilled her pledge.
Result: Even though Hanna did not actively parent her son when he was young, her willingness to keep her word ensured the development of one of the most influential Hebrew prophets in Jewish history.

(4) *Bat-Sheva*/**Solomon**. It is said that Solomon had about 700 wives and 300 concubines. *Bat-Sheva*, Solomon's mother, was very involved in both Solomon's childhood as well as adulthood. Prenatally, *Bat-Sheva* did whatever she could to ensure that her son, and not any of his half-brothers, would succeed their father David, and become King (*Sanhedrin* 70b). Even after he was married for the first time and later became King, *Bat-Sheva* involved herself in Solomon's life, when necessary. After building the Temple and abstaining from drinking wine for seven years, one day, Solomon drank excessively. Terribly upset by this reckless behavior, his mother, the widowed queen, admonished him severely (*Mishlei* 31:1–9; *Sanhedrin* 70b; *Leviticus Rabba* 12:5) by reminding him that a king should not engage in such unseemly behavior. The *Midrash Tanchuma* (*Exodus* 1) credits this maternal rebuke as the reason why Solomon became the wisest man in the world.
Result: Although far from perfect, Solomon is remembered for many important traits and accomplishments, including his wisdom and for building the First Holy Temple in Jerusalem (*Bet HaMikdash HaRishon*). His mother, *Bat-Sheva*, played a major role in his becoming a successful leader.

(3) **Jethro-Moses/***Yocheved*. It is well-known that the way to succeed as a parent-in-law is not to meddle in your children's business. There are exceptions to almost all rules. Such was the case with Jethro. As a caring father, father-in-law, and grandfather, Jethro was concerned that the demands of Moses's job were causing undue strain on his relationship with his wife and children. In the portion that bears his name, פָּרָשַׁת יִתְרוֹ/*Parashat Yitro*, Jethro observes "a day in the life of Moses." After watching Moses arbitrate disputes from morning until evening, Jethro who, according to the *Talmud* (*Sanhedrin* 106a), had served as an advisor to Pharaoh, remarked to his son-in-law:

לֹא־טוֹב הַדָּבָר אֲשֶׁר אַתָּה עֹשֶׂה:
נָבֹל תִּבֹּל גַּם אַתָּה גַּם הָעָם הַזֶּה אֲשֶׁר עִמָּךְ
כִּי־כָבֵד מִמְּךָ הַדָּבָר לֹא תוּכַל עֲשֹׂהוּ לְבַדֶּךָ:

*Lo tov ha-davar asher ata oseh. Navol tibol gahm ata gahm ha-ahm ha-zeh asher
imakh, ki-khaved mim'kha ha-davar lo tukhal ahsohu l'vadekha.*

**"This matter that you are handling is not good; you, along with this people who
are with you, will surely burn out, because this matter is too heavy for you
[to do without assistance]; you cannot accomplish it alone"** (*Exodus* 18:17-18).

Jethro then recommended that Moses institute a multi-tiered judicial system.
The easier cases would be handled by others who were qualified to do so.
Only the most difficult cases would be heard by Moses.
Result: Jethro's involvement not only brought some much needed relief and
work-life balance to Moses (and subsequently to his daughter and grandchildren),
but he introduced to the world the multi-tiered judicial system, employed
today in such democratic countries as Israel and the United States.

(2) **Sara-Isaac.** The first matriarch, Sara, made one of the boldest moves ever
performed by a parent in the history of parenthood. Concerned that her one and only
son Isaac, the heir apparent to the role of Patriarch of the Jewish people, would
become morally compromised growing up in the same household as his half-brother
Ishmael, infamously known for his delinquency (see *Rashi Genesis* 21:9), Sara
demanded that her husband Abraham evict Ishmael and his mother Hagar from their
household. Feeling very torn and not knowing what to do, Abraham consults
with the Almighty who advises him to listen to his wife, and He would ensure the
well-being of Ishmael and Hagar.
Result: Because of Sara's temerity, a corrupt influence was removed from the
patriarchal and matriarchal household, and Isaac was given the opportunity
to mature into a soft-spoken righteous leader of the Israelites. Ishmael and Hagar
also fared well, not just by surviving but with Ishmael becoming the progenitor
of the Arab people.

(1) **Rebecca-Jacob.** The #1 example of a parent who acted in a manner that today
may be labeled as "helicopter parenting" but which history has proven was critical
and completely necessary, was when Rebecca orchestrated a scheme to ensure that
the leadership of the Jewish people was passed to Jacob and not to Esau. Although
similar to the actions of her predecessor Sara, as well as devious to boot, I rank
Rebecca's action ahead of her mother-in-law's because she was selecting one of her
own sons over another.

Although I'm certain that Rebecca knew that Jacob's life would be in peril, she thought about the "big-picture," realizing that the Jewish people would only have a chance to survive and thrive with Jacob as its leader. Had the right to lead been given to Esau, there is no way that the Israelites would have been able to go forward and accomplish its holy mission. As a matriarch, wife, and mother, Rebecca made a most difficult decision under extreme pressure; that is, to have Jacob deceive his blind (physically, spiritually, and cognitively) father, Isaac, into thinking that Jacob was Esau and then bestowing the blessing of the *b'khor* (**first born**) upon him. **Result:** Jacob got the blessing of the *b'khor*, had to flee to escape from the anger of his brother Esau, and be separated from his family for over 30 years (see *B'reisheet Rabba* 68:5). After many struggles with a deceitful father-in-law/uncle (Laban) and having to wrestle with the Angel of Esau, Jacob emerged as the third patriarch, and with the additional (spiritual) name of *Yisrael*/**Israel**:

כִּי־שָׂרִיתָ עִם־אֱלֹקִים וְעִם־אֲנָשִׁים וַתּוּכָל

Ki-sarita ihm Elokim v'ihm anashim va-tukhal

"Because you have struggled with Elokim [the God of Justice] and men, and you have prevailed" (Genesis 32:29).

Going forward, in Jacob's merit, the Jewish people were named: *B'nei Yisrael – the Children of Israel*.

THE BOX SCORE

The world's most difficult job is being a parent. Anyone who disputes this is simply wrong.

At times, in sports and other disciplines, parents use their children to try to achieve what they were unable to accomplish. When a parent is over-involved in their children's lives, they are sometimes referred to as a "helicopter parent." Many times we find supportive parents who use sports and other experiences to teach their children valuable life lessons.

In Jewish tradition, a father (parent) has many obligations in properly raising his son (child). There are many examples in Jewish history where a parent, who at first blush, may appear to be too involved in their child's life, actually proves to be acting in a proper manner.

Chapter 9
What is Acceptable Behavior? Acts of Sportsmanship by Fans

According to one theory, the word "fan" is a shortened version of "fanatic." What is a fanatic? The *Merriam-Webster Online Dictionary* defines a fanatic as a person who is "marked by excessive enthusiasm and often intense uncritical devotion." Although this definition seems to imply that fans can engage in unrestrained behavior, this, of course, is not the case. While fans should enthusiastically support their team, they also must act in a sportsmanlike manner. Although we may have different standards of what constitutes acceptable fan behavior depending on the level of sports competition and culture, at all levels and cultures, the fan is an important player in influencing the game environment and must act in an appropriate manner.

The Fans: What is Acceptable Behavior?

Home Field Advantage

July 9, 2002 is an historic day in Major League Baseball. On that date, for the first time ever in an MLB All-Star game, both the American and National League squads had exhausted their supply of pitchers. With the score deadlocked after 11 innings, there were no fresh arms left. Unlike the other major American team sports (i.e., basketball, football, and hockey), in baseball, free substitution is not allowed.

Who was going to pitch in the 12th inning and beyond?

This quandary needed immediate resolution. What better person was there to make this decision than MLB's #1 Fan, Commissioner Bud Selig, who was present at the Midsummer Classic which also happened to be hosted at Miller Park where his beloved Brewers played?

Selig had several options: (1) "amend" existing rules in this one instance, and allow pitchers to re-enter the game; (2) insist that position players pitch; or simply (3) allow the game to end and be recorded as a tie score. The Commissioner chose the third alternative and, for the second time ever, the All-Star game ended with no victor. Because of this embarrassing outcome, going forward, MLB All-Star teams were allowed to add two more players (presumably pitchers) to their squads. As an added incentive for players and managers to compete at a more serious level, the winning team's league would be granted the home field advantage in the World Series. This practice ended after the 2016 Midsummer Classic as a part of a new Collective Bargaining Agreement.

Why was this such a significant incentive?

Over the course of the last century-plus, statistics have shown that, in every major sport, the home team has consistently won at a higher rate than the visiting opponents. Known, as the "home field advantage," some of the reasons behind this phenomenon have been attributed to such factors as supportive fans make players feel good and thus help enhance the performance of the home team, familiarity/

comfort with the home field/stadium by the members of the home team, and the opportunity of sleeping in your own bed (and not in a hotel) the previous night. While these factors are often helpful to the home team players, they are not the main ingredients that drive home field advantage.

Surprisingly, an academic study done by Yale finance professor, Dr. Tobias J. Moskowitz has shown that the people who are impacted upon the most by a home field crowd are not the players (or coaches), but rather, the men and women who serve as the games' judges (i.e., umpires, officials, and referees). The results of this study are documented in Moskowitz's book *Scorecasting*, co-written with *Sports Illustrated* journalist, L. Jon Wertheim. Presuming that game officials are honest, what the professor's study has borne out is that referees are merely human, and are influenced by social pressure, conformity, and the desire to please others.

According to Moskowitz and Wertheim, there is a referee bias against the visiting team and in favor of the hosts. The larger (louder and closer to the playing venue) the home crowd, the more profound the referee bias.

In the authors' own words: ". . . psychology suggests that the larger and more passionate the crowd is, and the more ambiguous the situation is, the greater the home favoritism should be." So, for example, in tight games, the extra strikeouts called on the visiting team and the extra walks called on home team batters occur mainly in games with large crowds. At NBA games with large crowds, the discrepancy in the rate of calling travelling violations on the home team compared to the visiting team rises from 15 percent to 28 percent. The authors conclude: "In virtually every sport the home advantage is significantly larger when the crowd is bigger.

Every city boasts that it has the world's best sports fans. If cities had to vote for the city, other than their own, with the best (i.e., most influential) fans Seattle would, probably win for the support of their gridiron warriors.

Because of the physical and vocal support of their adored Seahawks, the home fans have been referred to as "The 12th Man." Due to their deafening noise level, the NFL initiated a noise rule in 1989. In spite of this rule, according to the *Guinness World Records*, on December 2, 2013, the 12th Man registered what was at that time the *"Loudest roar at a sports stadium,"* a deafening 137.6 decibels.

Recognizing the contribution of their fans to their team's success, the Seahawks honor the 12th Man before each home kickoff by having different fans raise the specially designed "12th Man Flag." To show even greater appreciation to the contribution made by the Seattle fans, on December 15, 1984, Seahawks home jersey #12 was officially retired by the team.

Opening Days

Archrivals. This is an over-the-top, but common, sports term that a team and its fan base may use when describing the opponent in a heated rivalry. The opposing teams usually have a long and colorful history of competition between each other. Some of the major pro sports rivalries that fit in this category include the Chicago Bears vs. the Green Bay Packers, New York Yankees vs. Boston Red Sox, and New York Knicks vs. Boston Celtics. In the college football ranks, historic rivalries include Michigan vs. Ohio State and Army vs. Navy. Almost every high school team also has an archrival.

While most of these rivalries are carried out in competition and in fun, on occasion, they can get out of hand. This is especially true when alcohol is involved. When going to an archrival's home stadium, unfortunately, opposing fans can, at times, become verbally abusive. In fact, in recent years, increasing numbers of violent, physical fights have been reported in a variety of sporting venues between fans of opposing teams.

Rivalries also remain alive and well in cities with two professional franchises in the same league. Instead of providing two teams to cheer for, it seems that most fans feel that you must pick and choose. Cheer for your team and boo the archrival.

Sportsmanship, in this case between fellow fans, teaches that, while it is okay to have and support these rivalries, we must make sure that we do not interject intolerance or anger into these "sporting emotions." While it may be acceptable to "razz" a fan cheering for the opposing team, it is not acceptable to be verbally abusive or, heaven forbid, physically destructive in our behavior. Instead of adopting the attitude that so many Chicagoans have towards their baseball teams, that is, you must root against all teams with the exception of "your" team, we must adopt a new perspective of respecting all teams. In the world of Chicago baseball, just because you are a Cubs fan doesn't mean that you can't cheer for the Sox; and just because you are a White Sox fan, doesn't mean that you can't root for the Cubbies!

Another example of unacceptable behavior: During the 2015 NHL playoffs, it came to light that the Tampa Bay Lightning had a policy restricting fans seated in two luxury club seating areas (about 1,400 seats) from wearing apparel of the opposing team. When a Chicago Blackhawks fan tried to purchase tickets through a major ticket broker, their credit card was rejected because it was registered to a person who lived outside of Florida (i.e., with a non-Florida zip code). According to Lightning Communications VP Bill Wickett, "During the playoff run, we've done everything we can to make Amalie Arena a great home environment for our team and our fans. We're going to keep doing that and we hope people understand."

Although this may be done in Tampa Bay and, perhaps, by other cities' professional sports franchises, in the "City of Big Shoulders," this is totally unacceptable. Although Chicagoans want to do all they can to give their teams a home field/court/ice advantage, they will not do so at the expense of fans from the opposing team. For example, while requiring each league team to make tickets available for purchase by fans of the opposing team, the Chicago Fire soccer club goes beyond this policy of Major League Soccer by also dedicating a tailgating area in their parking lot for fans of the visiting team.

In response to the Lightning's restrictive policy, which may even be in violation of the First Amendment's allowances for free speech, the Blackhawks number one fan, Chicago Mayor Rahm Emanuel, released the following statement: "Chicago Blackhawks supporters are known to be among the best in the NHL, and certainly we wish the Tampa Bay Lightning management would welcome Chicago fans to their city and not be afraid to let them into their arena for the Stanley Cup finals. As Mayor of Chicago, I welcome Tampa fans – and hockey fans from around the country – to fly to Chicago and enjoy our world class hotels, restaurants, cultural attractions, and then go watch Stanley Cup hockey in Chicago. It doesn't get any better than that."

The Mayor knew what he was talking about when he said that "it doesn't get any better than that." After all, the Blackhawks won the Stanley Cup, beating the Lightning 2-0 in Game Six, on home ice, at Chicago's United Center.

Fans play an important role at every sporting event at all levels of competition. While it is expected that a crowd should be more supportive of the home team than the opponent, there are parameters as to what is acceptable in treating fans of the opposing team, as well as fans who support the archrival. How fans act towards other fans, the opposing team, and referees/umpires is an important aspect of sportsmanship.

The Fans: What is Acceptable Behavior? Spiritual Insights

Ushpizin

Leading off for the *Ushpizin* . . .

An important part of the festival of *Sukkot*, and for all Jewish holidays, is to invite guests into our homes. In fact, regarding someone who does not open up his/her home, Maimonides (*Mishneh Torah Hilkhot Sh'vitat Yom Tov* 6:18) states:

אֲבָל מִי שֶׁנּוֹעֵל דַּלְתוֹת חֲצֵרוֹ
וְאוֹכֵל וְשׁוֹתֶה הוּא וּבָנָיו וְאִשְׁתּוֹ,
וְאֵינוּ מַאֲכִיל וּמַשְׁקֶה לַעֲנִיִּים וּלְמָרֵי נֶפֶשׁ,
אֵין זוֹ שִׂמְחַת מִצְוָה, אֶלָּא שִׂמְחַת כְּרֵסוֹ.

Aval mi sheh-noel daltot chatzero v'okhel v'shoteh hu u-vanav v'ishto, v'eino mahahkhil u-mashkeh la-aniyim u-l'marei nefesh, ein zo simchat Mitzvah, elah simchat k'reso.

However, anyone who locks the doors of his courtyard [on Yom Tov] and eats and drinks only with his children and wife, and does not feed or give drink to the poor or embittered souls [i.e., those in need] – this is not the joy of [performing] a Mitzvah, rather – the joy of his belly.

On *Sukkot* we have a special custom based upon *Kabbala* known as *Ushpizin* (**Exalted, Holy Guests**). On each of the seven nights of the holiday, we invite a group of seven *Biblical* heroes (Abraham, Isaac, Jacob, Moses, Aaron, Joseph, and David) into our *Sukkah*. For each of these exalted guests there is a corresponding **Kabbalistic emanation** (*s'fira*). The emanation for Abraham is **Kindness** (*Chesed*). It is traditional to recite this special invitation before we bless our food and can serve as a way to welcome our contemporary guests as well.

It makes sense that Abraham leads off in this distinguished lineup of Exalted Guests. After all, he was the first person to introduce the world to the *Mitzvah* of *Hakhnasat Orchim* (**Welcoming in Guests**). The *Torah* (*Genesis* 18:1-8) along with the *Midrash* teach that, while recuperating from his *bris* (at age 99), Abraham spotted three "men" walking and invited them into his tent. Without knowing their identity, Abraham, with the assistance of Sara, gave them water to wash their feet, a place to rest, and a gourmet meal. It turns out that these three "men" were actually messengers (angels) of the Almighty.

Described in greater detail in the NAME THAT *MITZVAH!* section that follows, the *Mitzvah* of *Hakhnasat Orchim* is an extraordinarily important *Mitzvah* and one with which the Jewish people can collectively empathize, as we were **strangers in the Land of Egypt** (כִּי־גֵרִים הֱיִיתֶם בְּאֶרֶץ מִצְרָיִם – *Ki Gerim hehyitem b'Eretz Mitzrayim – Exodus* 23:9) .

NAME THAT *MITZVAH!*

Being a Good Host – הַכְנָסַת אוֹרְחִים
Hakhnasat Orchim

Although it is universally understood that
Hakhnasat Orchim is a *Mitzvah*, it is not one that
is specifically listed in either *Sefer HaChinukh* or
Sefer HaMitzvot. It is a **Rabbinic Commandment**
(*Mitzvah D'Rabbanan*). The Sages agree that
by properly inviting and caring for guests, one
performs an important act of *Chesed* (**Kindness**).
There are different opinions among *Chazal* (**the
Sages**) as to which *Torah*-ordained Commandment
acts of *Chesed* belong.

As stated by Maimonides (*Mishneh Torah, Hilkhot
Avel* 14:1), *Hakhnasat Orchim* is an expression of:
מִצְוַת אַהֲבַת יִשְׂרָאֵל
Mitzvat Ahavat Yisrael

The Mitzvah of Loving Your Fellow Jew
Sefer HaChinukh #243; *Sefer HaMitzvot,
Ahseh* #206

Just as a person enjoys being graciously
welcomed into someone's home as a guest, we
must do the same to others.

The *Talmud* (*Shabbat* 133b) interprets the phrase
Zeh Keli v'Ahnvehu – **This is my God and I will
glorify Him** (*Exodus* 15:2) – to mean that we
are supposed to incorporate into our lives such
Divine character traits as being *Rachum*
(**Compassionate**) and *Chanun* (**Gracious**).
In *Sotah* (14a), the *Talmud* lists different acts of
Chesed that *HaShem* performed with the directive
that we too should perform these acts. In this list,
one of the acts that is mentioned is when

HaShem performed the *Mitzvah* of *Bikur Cholim*
(**Visiting the Sick**) when He visited
(through angels) Abraham after his *B'rit Mila*
(**bris; ritual circumcision**).

This visit provided Abraham and Sara with
the opportunity to perform the *Mitzvah*
of *Hakhnasat Orchim* which they passionately
seized by welcoming in to their tent
(home) the three angels and caring for them
(*Genesis* 18).

These passages suggest, perhaps, that the
Rabbinic Commandment of *Hakhnasat Orchim*
can be derived from:

לָלֶכֶת וּלְהִדַּמּוֹת בְּדַרְכֵי הַשֵּׁם יִתְבָּרַךְ
*LaLekhet U-Lhidamot B'Darkhei
HaShem Yitbarakh*

**To Follow and Imitate the Ways of
HaShem the Blessed**
Sefer HaChinukh #611;
Sefer HaMitzvot, Ahseh #8

According to the venerable Rabbi Yisrael
Meir Kagan of Radin (a/k/a the *Chofetz
Chaim* [**pronounced: Chayim**] – 1838–1933) in his
book *Ahavat Chesed* (*Chelek* 3: *Chapter* 2), from
the actions of Abraham and Sara, we learn that
the *Mitzvah* of *Hakhnasat Orchim* entails
providing guests with the opportunity to bathe,
eat, drink, and sleep. When the guests leave,
in a gesture of hospitality and safety, we
are supposed to **walk with them for a short
distance, pointing them in the right direction**
(לְוָיָה /*l'vaya*). Whatever we do to welcome
our guests, it should be done with grace and
a smile on our face.

Bullying and Scapegoating

The Scapegoating of Steve Bartman

Ever since my first outing to an MLB (Chicago White Sox) game at age five, one of my dreams was to catch a live game ball (either a home run or foul ball). For many years I was meticulous in making sure that I brought my baseball glove to every game and that I sat either in the bleachers or in an area that was not protected by a screen. Although I did catch (on the fly in my glove) a batting practice home run ball hit by a Montreal Expos player into the Wrigley Field bleachers in 1970 – and kept the ball in spite of threats by the Bleacher Bums to throw me over the wall – that still did not satisfy my dream. Nor did having my children when they were kids give me the balls that they coaxed from players – by acting cute and adorable (which they still are) – extinguish this insatiable desire of mine.

The barometer of whether I had fulfilled my dream was when I would no longer experience a recurring Freudian nightmare that I had from time to time. I knew that I was dealing with challenging moments in my life when I would dream that a home run ball was flying my way while sitting in the packed Comiskey Park bleachers and then dropping the ball in front of thousands of fans.

This persistent nightmare finally stopped playing at my "theatre of dreams" in 2007. While sitting next to my father – my then-teenaged son and his friend went to sit in the bleachers, hoping to catch a home run ball on the right field line of what is now called Guarenteed Rate Field – a screaming line-drive off the bat of 2005 World Series MVP Jermaine Dye came flying in our direction. At the crack of the bat, my attention was fully directed to the flight of that ball. The ball landed about 10 rows behind us and began to bounce eluding the grasps of about five fans. Then, all of a sudden, the ball bounced towards where I was seated (or at this point standing). I angled my body perfectly to block out others (including my own dad!) and then, with the sleight of my right hand, grabbed the ball from midair. In order to ensure that no over-zealous fan would steal it from me, like a football cornerback who just intercepted a pass sealing a Super Bowl triumph, I brought my prized possession towards my belly and cradled it. After all of my competitors conceded defeat, I proudly proclaimed victory by raising my right hand with the ball firmly held in it and waved it towards any television cameras that were interested.

Through sheer perseverance (and a favor from a friend), I secured the autograph of Jermaine Dye. Every day when I glance at my prized piece of sports memorabilia, not only am I reminded that one can achieve (almost) any dream that they pursue – with, of course, a bit of luck – but a person can also eliminate certain nightmares by catching a foul ball.

Also, on that day in September 2007, I finally understood fully how wrong baseball fans were and still are for blaming Steve Bartman for the demise of the Chicago Cubs in 2003.

As baseball fans know, the Cubs were five outs away from winning the National League Pennant and advancing to the World Series for the first time in over 50 years. Then a Florida Marlins player hit a ball barely over the wall separating the fans from the foul territory on the left field line. As Cubs left fielder Moises Alou was reaching in to the stands trying to catch the ball, a group of fans started competing with him to catch the ball.

The fans were doing what all serious fans do; that is, trying to fulfill the dream of catching a game ball. As what happened to me, it is common to block out what is transpiring in the game and one's life in general, as catching a ball requires full focus and concentration. A slightly-built man in his twenties wearing earphones, eye glasses, and a Cubs hat, was the unfortunate fan who touched the ball first, "officially" preventing Alou from making the catch.

Realizing that the foul ball could have been the second out in the eighth inning of Game Six of the National League Championship Series with the Cubs leading 3-0, Alou – joined by thousands of Cub fans in the stands that day, and millions watching on TV – took their frustrations out on Mr. Bartman, who did absolutely nothing wrong. What happened since that fateful moment has amounted to using Steve Bartman as a scapegoat for the Cubs losing Game Six of the National League Championship Series.

While making Bartman the scapegoat – replacing the infamous Curse of the Billy Goat (1945) and the New York black cat (1969) – many Cub fans, some members of the media and others committed clear acts of what we refer to today as "bullying."

The official U.S. government website against bullying youth – stopbullying.gov – defines "bullying" as: ". . . unwanted, aggressive behavior among school aged children that involves a real or perceived power imbalance. The behavior is repeated, or has the potential to be repeated, over time. . ."

You don't have to be a kid to be a bully or to be bullied; it happens at every age. In Bartman's case, the repeated, aggressive behavior included things like verbal harassment at the game by fellow fans, such as, "We're going to kill you!" and angry fans throwing objects directly at him. Immediately after this incident, Mr. Bartman had to be whisked away to an unknown place just to survive the irrational, over-the-top behavior of Cub fans. Unfortunately, the bullying did not end there. The next day, Mr. Bartman's identity was disclosed in the media, and members of the press and others began to harass him outside of his home and work.

With the original scapegoat being an actual goat upon which all of the sins of the Israelites were cast (*Leviticus* 16), the definition has remained that a scapegoat is an innocent person who is blamed by others for something that they did not do.

Although the Chicago Cubs organization made attempts to clarify that Mr. Bartman was not at fault, as he – and other fans – were reaching for a ball that was not in play – the stigma of causing the collapse of the 2003 Cubs remains affixed to the unfortunate Steve Bartman, at least by some fans. (If there was anyone to blame for the Cubbies' unraveling in Game Six, it would be the Cubs shortstop, whose bobble prevented an inning ending double play or the Cubs manager and pitching coach for not handling their pitchers better, or the ownership/ management for not providing the best players and coaches, etc.)

Bartman has been offered thousands of dollars to share his story in documentaries, books, and talk shows, yet he has refused to benefit in any way from an act – obviously not his fault – but for which he apologized anyway. Some fans have opined that the only way Mr. Bartman can be exonerated was for the Cubs to win the World Series, and for Bartman to be officially welcomed back to Wrigley Field.

Well that day has finally arrived, as the Chicago Cubs ended a 108-year streak of futility when they captured the 2016 World Series championship. Led by owner Tom Ricketts, the Cubs extended an invitation to Mr. Bartman to return to Wrigley Field, the home of his beloved Cubs. On Monday, July 31, 2017, Steve Bartman accepted the invitation when he met with Ricketts and Cubs Presidents Theo Epstein and Crane Kenney in the owner's office where he was given a World Series ring with the name "BARTMAN" on it. Ricketts then led Bartman through Wrigley Field pointing out the new renovations, and how the park has been upgraded since that infamous day in 2003.

This is – in part – what Steve Bartman said in the July 31st press release:

"I humbly receive the ring not only as a symbol of one of the most historic achievements in sports, but as an important reminder for how we should treat each other in today's society. My hope is that we all can learn from my experience to view sports as entertainment and prevent harsh scapegoating, . . ."

From the nasty acts of bullying done by fans, ball players, members of the media and others, we learn from the unfortunate case of diehard Cubs fan Steve Bartman that sportsmanship includes taking responsibility for one's own mistakes and not using innocent others as scapegoats (i.e., not blaming others for wrongs that they did not commit).

Bullying and Scapegoating: Spiritual Insights

Captain Alfred Dreyfus

The original scapegoat was an integral figure of the *Yom Kippur* service in the *Beit HaMikdash* (**Holy Temple**). As described in the *Torah* (*Leviticus* 16), Aaron designated two identical he-goats. One was sacrificed to the Almighty, while upon the second one, Aaron confessed all of the sins of the Children of Israel. This goat (הַשָּׂעִיר לַעֲזָאזֵל/*HaSa-ihr LaAzazel* – **The Scapegoat**) was then dispatched to the desert where it later died.

Just as the original scapegoat was used to carry away the sins of the Israelites, a post-*Biblical* scapegoat is an entity used to absorb the blame of catastrophes caused and crimes perpetrated by others. When something goes wrong, and those responsible for the failure refuse to assume responsibility, then people often will look for someone vulnerable to blame. In many instances in history, the Jews have been the scapegoats, as anti-Semites "justify" initiating pogroms, blood libels, expulsion from towns and countries, and the *Shoah* (**Holocaust**) by blaming all their problems, economic or related to the cultural or moral degradation of their society, etc., on one group of people. Instead of refuting and suppressing the false accusations, in many instances, the masses have followed their evil leaders.

One of the more notorious cases of scapegoating in history happened in the aftermath of France's crushing defeat to the Germans in the Franco-Prussian War in 1871.

In 1894, a French intelligence officer doubling as a cleaning woman assigned to the German embassy in Paris, found in a wastepaper basket a shredded, but easy to reassemble, *note* (*bordereau*) offering to sell the Germans secret information about a new French ammunition. The French Minister of War was alerted that there was a traitor in his ranks.

The task of finding the traitor was assigned to Major Armand Mercier du Paty de Clam, an amateur graphologist and a known anti-Semite. Du Paty de Clam identified Captain Alfred Dreyfus, a 35-year-old married father of two, as the prime suspect. With no credible evidence, what led to Dreyfus's indictment – in great likelihood – was that he was a Jew, albeit a highly assimilated one. Dreyfus was the only Jew on the French Army's General Staff at that time.

With the corrupt support and pressure from the army, press, and many others, the French Minister of War – although he knew that there was no way that Dreyfus could have done what he was accused of – allowed the charade against Dreyfus to go to trial. Although the "evidence" (all concocted) still added up to an extremely weak case against Alfred Dreyfus, he was convicted of treason in 1894 and sentenced to imprisonment at the infamous penal colony of Devil's Island where he was expected to die within a short time.

Before being sent off to Devil's Island in French Guyana, Captain Alfred Dreyfus was subjected to a public humiliation and degradation where he was stripped of his buttons and badges. His sword was then broken over the warrant-officer's knee. During this public humiliation, mobs of anti-Semites along with French patriots angrily shouted at Dreyfus such statements as "Down with the Jews! Death to the traitor!" Dreyfus proclaimed his innocence by proclaiming *"Vive la France!* You have degraded an innocent man. I swear that I am innocent."

What became known as the "Dreyfus Affair" began to divide France into two main groups, the Dreyfusards and the anti-Semites. In addition to his wife Lucie and brother Mathieu, Alfred Dreyfus attracted other prominent Frenchmen who proclaimed his innocence. Among those was Lieutenant Colonel Georges Picquart who, in his capacity as head of French counter-intelligence, discovered the identity of the real traitor who wrote the *bordereau*, Major Fendinand Walsin Esterhazy. Known to be both honest and an anti-Semite (an oxymoron?), Picquart's honesty and conscience outweighed his hatred for and bias against Jews. Esterhazy was later found to be not guilty – by a corrupt tribunal, and Picquart was reassigned to Tunisia, a danger zone.

Triggered by the court-martial of Esterhazy, beloved French novelist and social critic Emile Zola, in an impassioned essay in the form of a letter to France's president, *J'Accuse* (*I Accuse*), blasted the Dreyfus conviction and its associated anti-Semitism, declared his innocence, and attacked the then-recent court martial and acquittal of Esterhazy, calling it a sham. His fiery essay – calling on French society and its government to right the wrongs done to Dreyfus – caused non-Jewish Zola to be charged and later convicted of criminal libel. But because of the support of Zola, Alfred's wealthy and politically sophisticated brother Mathieu and others, Dreyfus was eventually re-tried. Unfortunately, in spite of the weak fabricated evidence against him, once again, Dreyfus was found guilty of treason. Because of public pressure, instead of sentencing Dreyfus to additional years of imprisonment, he was sentenced to time already served.

It wasn't until 1906 – 12 years after his first trial – that a military commission officially exonerated Alfred Dreyfus. In addition to restoring his rank, he was promoted to the rank of Major and given all back pay.

Though the story had a relatively positive ending, the virulent anti-Semitism would follow Dreyfus: in 1908, while attending Zola's funeral, he was victim of an assassination attempt. His favorite granddaughter was deported by the Vichy state and died at Auschwitz. And, anti-Semitism and anti-"other" sentiments continue to exist, in pockets of France and other countries.

Not only did the Dreyfus Affair expose the horrors of anti-Semitism and scapegoating and how the Jewish people have and continue to be the targets of blame when those who are actually responsible refuse to accept responsibility, but it turned out to be an event in history that helped inspire Theodore Herzl to revive Zionism. Herzl, while covering the Dreyfus Affair as a journalist for a Viennese newspaper, witnessed the public degradation of Dreyfus. Herzl concluded that the best way to defeat anti-Semitism was by creating a Jewish homeland. Although both Dreyfus and Herzl died before 1948, they turned out to be key players in the creation of modern day Zionism and the establishment of the State of Israel.

Accepting Responsibility in Jewish Tradition

חֵטְא חָטְאָה יְרוּשָׁלַם עַל־כֵּן לְנִידָה הָיָתָה

Chet chat'a Y'rushalyim ahl-ken l'nida hayata

Jerusalem sinned [an egregious] sin; therefore, she has become a wanderer (*Lamentations* 1:8).

In the aftermath of the destruction of the first Holy Temple, the author of the **Book of Lamentations** (*M'gilat Eikha*/מְגִילַת אֵיכָה) – believed to be Jeremiah the Prophet – attributes the commission of sins by the Jewish people as the spiritual cause of the national catastrophe that had just occurred.

This verse sets the tone for one of the most important lessons in Jewish history; that is, before we blame others for our misfortunes, we first must examine our own acts which may have led to such disasters. While many times we are not to blame, at times, it is indeed our fault. The way we rectify the wrong is by performing *T'shuva* (**repentance**). Important elements of *T'shuva* are accepting responsibility for our sins, showing remorse, apologizing to the wronged party, and then asking for forgiveness both to the aggrieved person and to the Almighty.

It has been suggested (see NJOP's Jewish Treats referenced in SOURCES) that this was the purpose of the *Biblically* mandated he-goat, which was designated for and sacrificed to God: "Perhaps this goat was meant to remind the people of their own personal sin offerings and their own personal repentance. No sin can be wiped away blaming others. Only by turning directly to God and asking for His forgiveness can sin be expiated."

This is indeed the Jewish way.

NAME THAT *MITZVAH!*

According to the *Torah* (*Exodus* 22:20-23), we must be especially sensitive to the needs of people who can easily be taken advantage of and bullied. The *Torah* specifies three potentially defenseless groups in particular: the *widow* (אַלְמָנָה /Ahlmana), *orphan* (יָתוֹם/Yatom), and *convert to Judaism* (גֵּר/Ger). While the term *Ger* is commonly used to refer to a convert to Judaism, it also means "a stranger." After all, a convert must embrace a new religion, culture and history, experiences that are new and "strange" to him/her. Not only can we be sympathetic to those who are most vulnerable, but we can and must be empathetic. After all, we know what being "bullied" is all about; our ancestors were slaves in Egypt and were oppressed:

כִּי־גֵרִים הֱיִיתֶם בְּאֶרֶץ מִצְרַיִם

Ki Gerim hehyitem b'Eretz Mitzrayim

Because you were strangers in the Land of Egypt. From this passage and other sources, various *Mitzvot* are derived. They include:

שֶׁלֹּא לְהוֹנוֹת הַגֵּר בִּדְבָרִים

Shehlo L'honot HaGer BiDvarim

Not to Verbally Wrong a Convert to Judaism
Sefer HaChinukh #63;
Sefer HaMitzvot, LT #252

שֶׁלֹּא לְהוֹנוֹת הַגֵּר בְּמָמוֹן

Shehlo L'honot HaGer B'Mamon

Not to Financially Wrong a Convert to Judaism
Sefer HaChinukh #64; Sefer HaMitzvot, LT #253

שֶׁלֹּא לְעַנּוֹת יָתוֹם וְאַלְמָנָה

Shehlo L'anot Yatom V'Ahlmana

Not to Oppress an Orphan and Widow
Sefer HaChinukh #65; Sefer HaMitzvot, LT #256

THE BOX SCORE

Scapegoating is a form of bullying.

We learn from the unfortunate case of Chicago Cubs
fan Steve Bartman - who did what most passionate
fans would do at the ballpark - that bullies come in all shapes,
forms, and ages. It is an activity that is not restricted
to children.

Jewish tradition has various *Mitzvot* prohibiting the abuse
of the most vulnerable members of society. Anti-Semitism
is one of the most egregious forms of bullying/scapegoating.
The Dreyfus Affair inspired secular Jewish Austrian
lawyer/journalist Theodore Herzl to re-vitalize Zionism.

The Zionist dream was finally realized in 1948 with the
establishment of the modern State of Israel - only after the
Holocaust (i.e., the largest perpetration of bullying in
world history). *M'dinat Yisrael* (the **modern State of Israel**)
provides a homeland for all Jews to seek haven –
especially those who are targets of anti-Semitism
(i.e., bullying/scapegoating).

Chapter 10
Calling the Shots: Acts of Sportsmanship by the PA Announcer

The PA Announcer

We are a product of our environment. An important person who influences fan and player behavior is the public address (PA) announcer. This individual sets the tone of the event and the mood/reactions of the fan. While we often do not see the PA announcer, s/he can be very influential in promoting sportsmanship.

The Role of the PA Announcer: Entertainer, Communicator or Both?

What is the role of the public address announcer? Is s/he an entertainer, an informer (i.e., provider of information), or both?

As the voice of the home/host team, the PA announcer serves both functions. The balance of informer vs. entertainer depends upon the level of competition.

At the professional sports level, while this announcer is primarily an informer, s/he also serves as a bit of an entertainer, as well as a cheerleader. Just think of the introductions of the starting lineups in the NBA. While informing the audience who will be starting and providing important information like their jersey numbers and where they played college ball, the introduction of the home team players is far more emotionally-charged than for the visitors. By performing the job in this manner, the announcer gets the crowd pumped up and creates a more favorable environment for the home team.

A good example is found at Chicago's United Center, where the six-time NBA champion Bulls host their games. If and when a player from the visiting team commits his sixth foul and is forced to leave the game, Ray Charles's smash hit song, *Hit the Road Jack*, is blasted for all to hear – even if the player's name isn't Jack. On the other hand, when a home team player fouls out, no such accompanying music is played.

The role of the PA announcer at high school sporting events is much different. While still providing some amusement, ideally the role of this voice-behind-the-scenes (often a high school student) is almost exclusively informer. While states provide diverse guidelines – one example is the Michigan High School Athletic Association (MHSAA) where the announcer is an important contributor to ensuring that sports events have an educational component – in addition to accurately articulating the names, numbers, and statistics of players on both teams, in many instances, the PA announcer also provides regular "infomercials" that promote important values for all high school students. The wide variety of educational info could include concussion awareness, details about scholar-athlete awards, patriotism, how to become a game official, and the importance of sportsmanship.

Here are two such messages from the MHSAA, both entitled *It's All About Sportsmanship*:

- "There are more ways in life, and in sports, to be connected than ever before. And while many things around us change in school sports, one thing doesn't – sportsmanship. Whether you're texting or tweeting or looking someone eye-to-eye, good sportsmanship should always prevail. Remember, when the game is on the line, it's all about sportsmanship."

- "School sports are about producing championship-caliber people, not championships. A true champion treats everyone with respect, win or lose. When we do that, every young person is a trophy kid, and isn't that more important than handing a kid a trophy? Remember when the game is on the line, it's all about sportsmanship."

John Johnson, MHSAA communications director, puts out an internal template that guides announcers on how to work the game/match. One of his suggestions is: "Don't be a homer: Maintain the same delivery pitch for announcements involving the visiting team as well as your own. A 'homer' literally creates at times an advantage for one team by unnerving the other, and sometimes disturbs the home team as well. Don't cheerlead on the public address system, and never make editorial comments about officiating."

The NCAA provides its participating schools with templates for PA announcers to follow in the various sports, with some specific announcements pertinent only to a particular division. In addition to a script on how to introduce the starting line-ups, many sample messages are included promoting the importance of such values as sportsmanship, honoring members of the U.S. Armed Forces, thanking corporate sponsors and opposing sports wagering. (For further details, please see **http://www.ncaa.org/sites/default/files/2016-17DIIIMBB_ PrelimRd_PA_Script_20170214.pdf.**)

One of the best known public address announcers in the United States is Gene Honda. Having attended the University of Illinois, Honda is the PA Announcer for Illini football. He has also served as the announcer for the Chicago White Sox for more than 30 years as well as for the Chicago Blackhawks for about half of that time. Additionally, Gene's voice is widely recognized by a countless number of NCAA March Madness fans. As the official PA announcer for the DePaul Blue Demons and the Big Ten tournament, Gene has also earned the honor of serving as one of the announcers in the Final Four.

While the role of players, coaches, and fans is more readily discernible in promoting sportsmanship, we learn that it is also important to give a shout-out to all PA announcers, at any level, who help promote sportsmanship among all of the participants.

"And now for today's starting line-ups . . ."

The PA Announcer: Spiritual Insights

Honoring the Bride and Groom, While Respecting and Informing the Guests

The wedding announcer, a Jewish version of the sports PA announcer, is a significant participant in Orthodox Jewish weddings. A role traditionally given to the eldest brother of the bride and/or groom, his job is to make sure that all those who are participating in the ceremony are respectfully introduced and that all the guests in the "audience" are properly informed as to the proper order of the ceremony. To ensure that all the guests are fully educated regarding all of the components of the wedding ceremony and the reasons behind the traditions, often, the couple provides their version of a "scorecard" or "program," that is, a personalized pamphlet which explains these customs as well as includes the names of all members of the wedding party (i.e., the "starting lineup").

While marriage is the most serious commitment that a couple will make to one another, the wedding master of ceremonies at times will inject a lighter tone to help make sure that the couple and all others are relaxed. An effective wedding PA announcer will also remind the guests right before the ceremony to shut off their phones and any other devices that may distract others and threaten the integrity of the ceremony.

Realizing that names of individuals and institutions may be pronounced differently than in the manner written, the wedding PA announcer who does his

---

DIDJA KNOW that after the destruction of the First Temple (586 BCE), a profession known as a *M'turg'mahn/ Turg'mahn* (תּוּרְגְּמָן/מְתוּרְגְּמָן) became fairly common? Various translations have been attributed to this position, as, depending on the situation, the *m'turg'mahn* assumed different roles. The translations include translator, interpreter, elucidator, or announcer. As a translator, the *m'turg'mahn* would translate the lecture/ lesson of a rabbi from the original language to the vernacular. Still today, in some Yemenite synagogues, a *m'turg'mahn* recites the *Targum Onkelos* (an Aramaic translation/ commentary) of each verse of the *Torah* after it is read. In his role as an interpreter or elucidator, the *m'turg'mahn* would provide a translation that better explained the teachings of the lecturer. Finally, in his role as an announcer, the *m'turg'mahn* amplified the teaching of the rabbi, enabling the masses of students in the room to clearly hear (and comprehend) the teacher's lessons.

The teacher would speak in a relatively soft voice, intended primarily for only the *m'turg'mahn* and all those students seated nearby to hear. Because the role of the *m'turg'mahn* often required him to quickly understand and immediately articulate complex subjects to the students in a comprehensible manner, the *m'turg'mahn* himself had to be a scholar. He was a lot more than simply an ancient form of a microphone. Perhaps the most famous of all the *m'turg'mahnim* (plural) was *Rahbi Chutzpit HaM'turg'mahn*. He is known to almost all Jews, as he is included as one of the **Ten Martyrs** (עֲשָׂרָה הֲרוּגֵי מַלְכוּת) /*Ahsara Harugei Malkhut*) – about whose tragic deaths we read during the *Yom Kippur Musaf* service. He was sentenced to death by the Roman ruler Hadrian, because he defied the Hadrianic Decree of teaching *Torah* (about 130 CE). A brilliant scholar, *Rahbi Chutzpit* was fluent in 70 languages (*Otzar Midrashim* [Eisenstein] *Ahsara Harugei Malkhut*).

homework will make sure that he knows how to pronounce all of these names properly. He will also have consulted with those who have an honor under the *Chupah* (**marriage canopy**) as to the title (professional or personal) by which they wish to be introduced.

The wedding PA announcer is one of the unsung heroes of a Jewish wedding. While wedding singers and crashers have received their due in Hollywood, it is finally time to recognize the wedding PA announcers for all that they do in launching the Jewish marriage.

DIDJA KNOW that an essential trait that a qualified *m'turg'mahn* had to possess was דֶּרֶךְ אֶרֶץ וְכָבוֹד/ *Derekh Eretz v'Khavod*. He needed to have proper respect for the Almighty, the *Torah*, the rabbi whose lectures he was enhancing, and for all the students at each class session. *Chutzpit* did indeed possess these traits. It is related (*B'rakhot* 27b) that one day, *Chutzpit* was caught in a "crossfire" between *Rabban Gamliel* (the *Nasi* whose teachings *Chutzpit* was broadcasting), Rabbi Joshua, and the rabbis. When those in attendance felt that the well intended *Rabban Gamliel* was going too far in publicly chastising Rabbi Joshua, they shouted out for *Chutzpit* to stop the lesson. Out of respect to Rabbi Joshua and the masses, *Rahbi Chutzpit* stopped. This incident led to the temporary deposing of *Rabban Gamliel* as *Nasi*, his sincere apology to Rabbi Joshua, and then his subsequent reinstatement to the top post in the Sanhedrin. This event resulted in various reforms in the Sanhedrin allowing more Jews access to the highest level of Jewish scholarship. Sentenced to death one day shy of his 130th birthday, *Chutzpit* implored of Hadrian to delay his execution by one day, allowing him to recite the *Sh'ma* two more times. Instead of honoring his wish, the cruel emperor tortured this handsome, erudite scholar/orator (*Otzar Midrashim* [*Eisenstein*] *Ahsara Harugei Malkhut*; see also *Chullin* 142a).

NAME THAT *MITZVAH!*

From the modern day PA announcer, we are reminded of the following two *Mitzvot*:

Being a Good Host – הַכְנָסַת אוֹרְחִים/
Hakhnasat Orchim
(Please see the section earlier in this book titled *The Fans: What is Acceptable Behavior? Spiritual Insights.*)

Laws Regarding Proper Speech –
שְׁמִירַת הַלָּשׁוֹן/*Sh'mirat HaLashon*
We are taught by our Sages (including *Maimonides, Mishneh Torah, Hilkhot Deot* 7:1) that there are three basic categories of prohibited speech:

(1) מוֹצִיא שֵׁם רַע/*Motzih Shem Rah* – **Causing Someone a Bad Name** – articulating untruths about a person (in American law – defamation: slander in the verbal form and libel when committed to writing);

(2) לָשׁוֹן הָרַע/*Lashon HaRah* – **Truthful, but negative things about a person.** With limited exceptions (i.e., when it absolutely must be said) this speech is prohibited;

(3) Even sharing [*seemingly innocent truthful pieces of gossip*] (רְכִילוּת/*R'khilut* – **Tale Bearing**) about another person is contrary to Jewish law, as this may lead to telling harmful gossip.

The most prolific author on prohibited speech was Rabbi Israel Meir Kagan. Known as the *Chofetz Chaim*, he earned this pen name because of his most famous publication by the same name taken from *Psalms* 34:13. In his book *Sefer Chofetz*

Chaim Sh'mirat HaLashon (***The Book of the Chafetz Chaim Guarding One's Tongue/ Language***), Rabbi Kagan goes into great depth describing the many laws regarding prohibited speech. The *Chofetz Chaim* brought to the fore of the Jewish community the importance of proper speech in everyday life. Leading an observant Jewish life begins with what we say and how we communicate with others.

The *Sefer HaChinukh* and *Sefer HaMitzvot* list a series of (*Torah*-ordained) *Mitzvot* regarding prohibited speech. They include:

שֶׁלֹּא לְרַגֵּל
Shehlo L'ragel
Not to Gossip
Sefer HaChinukh #236; Sefer HaMitzvot, LT #301

שֶׁלֹּא לְהוֹנוֹת אֶחָד מִיִּשְׂרָאֵל בִּדְבָרִים
Shehlo L'honot Echad M'Yisrael BiDvarim
Not to Verbally Wrong a Fellow Jew
Sefer HaChinukh #338; Sefer HaMitzvot, LT #251

שֶׁלֹּא לְהוֹנוֹת הַגֵּר בִּדְבָרִים
Shehlo L'honot HaGer BiDvarim
Not to Verbally Wrong a Convert to Judaism
Sefer HaChinukh #63; Sefer HaMitzvot, LT #252

שֶׁלֹּא לְהַכְשִׁיל תָּם בַּדֶּרֶךְ
Shehlo L'hakhshil Tahm BaDerekh
Not to Mislead an Unsuspecting Person
Sefer HaChinukh #232; Sefer HaMitzvot, LT #299

Why must we be so careful in what we say and how we say it? Because once a person's reputation has been damaged, it is almost impossible to fully repair it.

Chapter 11
Executive Treatment: Acts of Sportsmanship by Team Executives

The Front Office: What Makes a Good Team Leader?

There are individuals in every team who perform tasks that, although not publicly recognized, are still essential for the success of the team. In top-level professional sports teams, there can be in excess of one hundred people who work in or for the front office alone. Departments include marketing, financial, legal, ticketing, security, plus media and community relations. As with all businesses with more than one employee, there is a hierarchy: everyone has a boss. For a team to succeed both on and off the field, not only must the employees show respect to their bosses, but the opposite holds true as well.

In sports, the team's ownership, as manifested by all of its employees, from top executives to members of the grounds crew, must also treat the fans with respect. After all, the fans are the customers of the business. Without customers, a business would not be able to survive. It can also be considered fine "sportsmanship" for employers to treat employees, colleagues, customers (fans), and all others with respect, honor, and dignity.

Jerry Reinsdorf: The Chicago Bull Who Wears White Sox

I like "doing business" with Jerry Reinsdorf.

The principal owner of the Chicago White Sox and Chicago Bulls, from 1990-2005 he won more championships than any of the other owners of the four major professional sports leagues (MLB, NBA, NFL, and NHL).

In addition to shooting the cover and author's photos in the United Center for this book, the only other time that I "did business" with Mr. Reinsdorf was when I did an eight-hour photo shoot at what was then known as "The New Comiskey Park" in search of the perfect cover and author's photos for my first book *PRAY BALL! The Spiritual Insights of a Jewish Sports Fan*. I wanted to use the park as a backdrop for my cover and I was graciously granted access to the park.

Perhaps Chairman Reinsdorf mulled in his own mind that since *PRAY BALL!* was written for a worthy cause – Jewish education – this would be his way of contributing to the project.

The day of the photo shoot in June 1999 was one of the most enjoyable, fun, and memorable days in my life. Before I entered the park, I happened to run into one of the better-known White Sox employees – the chairman himself – Jerry Reinsdorf. When I introduced myself and thanked him for the opportunity, he was very gracious and wished me success. I received similar kindness after I sent him a gift copy of *Pray Ball!* Not only did Mr. Reinsdorf send me a handwritten note thanking me for the book, but he also sent a special White Sox hat, one with the team's name written in Hebrew letters: סקאָס טיייװ/*Vite Sox*.

I learned from my experiences with Jerry Reinsdorf and his representatives that successful sports executives can, and oftentimes do, display acts of "off-the-field" sportsmanship. As a self-proclaimed student of the business of sports, I have observed, mainly through the lens of the media, Mr. Reinsdorf in action since he led a group of investors – in the syndicated purchase of the ChiSox – back in 1981. Jerry Reinsdorf was one of the first MLB owners to set-up a limited partnership that purchased their team's ball park. During the 30+ years since purchasing the team, I have seen, on many occasions, how Mr. Reinsdorf uses the same traits in his interactions with employees and others that he showed towards me in my two transactions with him. These traits include patience, an open mind to creativity, honesty, respecting delegation of authority/boundaries, willingness to take risks while managing it as best as possible, kindness, and loyalty.

Here are some examples:

- **Honesty and Loyalty:** It was reported that, back in 1991 Chicago Bulls star Scottie Pippen wanted a long-term contract to ensure his financial stability. Despite warnings from Mr. Reinsdorf that Pippen would regret signing such a deal since he would be bound by this contract, and very likely be paid less than market value towards the end of the term of the agreement, Pippen insisted on going forward with the deal. Later, when Pippen's star rose and he was being paid a smaller amount than less talented players, he requested that Mr. Reinsdorf renegotiate his contract. Mr. Reinsdorf refused to do so, as his word was golden. Although a strained relationship apparently emerged from this incident, eventually Scottie Pippen came back to the Bulls. After stints with the Houston Rockets and Portland Trailblazers, he returned to Chicago so that he could retire from his playing career as a Chicago Bull. Pippen later assumed such roles as a team ambassador and special advisor to the president and COO. His jersey (#33) is only one of a handful of Bulls jerseys retired by the organization.

Michael Jordan also signed a similar type of long-term deal. Although Mr. Jordan did not complain about being locked in, at the end of the contract, very generously, Jerry Reinsdorf rewarded MJ for his loyalty (and not complaining) by paying him a "balloon"-type payment of a reported 30 million dollars for his final season as a Chicago Bull.

The chairman acted in a similar fashion with White Sox legend Paul Konerko. After presenting Mr. Reinsdorf with the ball that was used for the final out sealing the 2005 World Series Championship, Jerry Reinsdorf was instrumental in making sure that Konerko, who became a free agent after that championship season, would return and eventually, after the 2014 season retire as a White Sox player. In his final season as a player, Konerko was a part-time player and an unofficial, full-time mentor/coach, who participated in a farewell tour on many road trips. In 2015, the White Sox retired jersey #14, the number that "Paulie" wore with the team, and honored their loyal player with "Paul Konerko Day" at the ballpark.

● **Delegating authority while maintaining control.** Mr. Reinsdorf has proven to be very successful in delegating authority while ensuring that he maintains control. For starters, he assembled a group of high-powered, sports-fan business people to invest money first in the White Sox and later the Bulls. While the group of owners is not identical for the two corporations, there is an overlap. For both corporations, Reinsdorf is the chairman and controlling partner.

When it comes to hiring, Mr. Reinsdorf is careful in delegating authority and not meddling in the "professional" turfs of his employees. Unlike certain owners, Reinsdorf does not micromanage. His respecting the delegation of authority can, at times, hurt him and the team. Most notably, after listening to White Sox broadcaster Ken "Hawk" Harrelson's suggestions on how to best run the team, in 1986, he offered the Hawk the opportunity to move from the broadcast booth and become the general manager of the team. As GM, one of the first big moves Harrelson made was dismissing a young Tony La Russa as Sox manager. As it is well-known, La Russa became a Hall of Fame manager, winning over 2,700 games and piloting teams in both the American and National Leagues (the Oakland A's and St. Louis Cardinals) to World Series Championships. Although Jerry Reinsdorf regretted allowing La Russa to get away, he remained close with him. After one year as Sox GM, the Hawk returned to his perch in the White Sox broadcast booth.

● **Diversity in Hiring.** Under Chairman Reinsdorf's guidance, the White Sox and Bulls have been leaders in ensuring a diverse work force. Mr. Reinsdorf has been honored for these efforts and for his commitment to giving back to society through the charitable and other initiatives of his two professional sports franchises.

● **Providing Opportunity.** Believing in the importance of giving people the opportunity to better themselves, Jerry Reinsdorf has gone above and beyond in this area. Perhaps his greatest success story is offering Bulls legend Bob Love the opportunity to serve as a representative of the Bulls organization more than 20 years ago. The third-leading scorer in Bulls history (behind MJ and Pippen), after his playing career ended, Love experienced hard times. Although he had a college degree, he was not able to find suitable employment because he had a profound speech impediment. Working as a busboy for Nordstrom's, a major department store in Seattle, where he ended his playing career as a Supersonic, company management there stepped-up and facilitated his speech therapy. Today, Bob Love, in his capacity as Bulls director of community affairs and team ambassador, gives about 300 speeches per year to community groups.

While ultimately the goal in business is to make money for the owners and investors, Jerry Reinsdorf has shown through his actions that this goal can be achieved in a respectful, honorable, and dignified manner. Yes, one can operate at the highest level of sportsmanship and still be a huge winner!

The Front Office: A Spiritual Insight

NAME THAT *MITZVAH!*

As described in the story above, Jerry Reinsdorf is known for treating his employees and customers fairly and respectfully. What follows is a list and brief description of some of the *Mitzvot* that deal with employment and labor. The reader will be able to readily see how connected Chairman Reinsdorf is to these commandments (some more directly than others).

Honoring a Person's "Turf"

שֶׁלֹּא לְהַסִּיג גְּבוּל

Shehlo L'hasig G'vul

Not to Encroach a Border

Sefer HaChinukh #522; Sefer HaMitzvot, LT #246

Recognizing the important value of a person's property, Rabbi HaLevy cites a unique *Mitzvah* that prohibits a Jew from encroaching upon someone else's property boundaries. In the area of economics, this principle has been interpreted as placing limitations on competition when it could adversely affect the ability of a person to make a living. In an employment situation, it could also refer to an employer respecting his employees' decision-making jurisdiction and not unnecessarily meddling in.

Treat Those Who Work For You with Respect

In Jewish tradition, not only is every day Mother's Day and Father's Day, but Labor Day, as well. After all, just as we are commanded to treat our parents with proper *Derekh Eretz* and *Kavod* on a daily basis, we are also commanded to treat those who work for us with the appropriate dignity. There is a series of *Mitzvot* on how to properly treat those who work for us.

לָתֵת שְׂכַר שָׂכִיר בְּיוֹמוֹ (1)

Latet S'khar Sakhir B'Yomo

To Compensate a Laborer for his Labor on the Same Day (that he Works)

Sefer HaChinukh #588; *Sefer HaMitzvot, Ahseh* #200;
see also *Sefer HaMitzvot, LT* #238
An employer is obligated to pay one who performs work for him/her promptly.

(2) לְהַנִּיחַ לַשָׂכִיר לֶאֱכֹל מֵהַמְּחֻבָּר שֶׁעוֹשֶׂה בּוֹ

L'haniach LaSakhir Leh-ekhol MehHaM'chubar SheOseh Bo

To Allow a Laborer to Eat from Produce Still Attached to the Ground While Working
Sefer HaChinukh #576; *Sefer HaMitzvot, Ahseh* #201

With the intent of showing compassion towards workers and gratitude to the Almighty for His bounty, this *Mitzvah* commands the employer to allow his worker to eat produce that he his harvesting while it is still attached to the ground. While looking out for the wellbeing of the worker, this *Mitzvah* – along with *Sefer HaChinukh Mitzvot* #577 and #578 – ensures that the worker does not exploit this benefit, restricting him from taking more than he can eat at that time, and requiring that he not eat while he is actually working.

(3) Severance Pay

שֶׁלֹּא לְשַׁלֵּחַ עֶבֶד עִבְרִי רֵיקָם

Shehlo Li-Shloach Eved Ivri Reikam

Not to Emancipate a Hebrew Slave Empty-Handed
Sefer HaChinukh #481; *Sefer HaMitzvot, LT* #233; **and**

לְהַעֲנִיק לוֹ בְּצֵאתוֹ לַחָפְשִׁי

L'ha-anik Lo B'tzeto LaChawfshi

To Provide (a Hebrew Slave) with Provisions When he is Emancipated
Sefer HaChinukh #482; see also *Sefer HaMitzvot, LT* #233

A Hebrew only became a slave when dire financial circumstances forced him to sell himself into slavery. Given a special status (*Eved Ivri*), the *Torah*, as detailed in the *Sefer HaChinukh* #42 and *Sefer HaMitzvot* (*Ahseh* #232), teaches that we must treat Hebrew slaves with dignity. In fact, they were protected so well by the laws of the *Torah* that the Sages remarked: כָּל הַקּוֹנֶה עֶבֶד עִבְרִי כְּקוֹנֶה אָדוֹן לְעַצְמוֹ / *Kol ha-koneh Eved Ivri k'koneh adon l'ahtzmo* – "Anyone who acquires a Hebrew slave, it is as if he has acquired a master for himself" (*Kiddushin* 22a). Some of our modern day labor laws in the United States and in other legal systems have similar provisions that – I am certain – are based upon these *Torah* laws. Common in many legal systems (see Israel's *Severance Pay Law*) is the concept of severance. When an employer parts ways with an employee, it is a common practice (and a matter of common sense and – just plain decency) to provide him/her with a financial package. While being an expression of gratitude for their service, in many cases, it also helps the employee care for his/her family while looking for new employment opportunities. In Hebrew, this concept is known as הַעֲנָקָה/ Ha-ahnaka, and is based upon: *Deuteronomy* 15:12-14:

כִּי יִמָּכֵר לְךָ אָחִיךָ הָעִבְרִי אוֹ הָעִבְרִיָּה
וַעֲבָדְךָ שֵׁשׁ שָׁנִים וּבַשָּׁנָה הַשְּׁבִיעִת תְּשַׁלְּחֶנּוּ חָפְשִׁי מֵעִמָּךְ:
וְכִי תְשַׁלְּחֶנּוּ חָפְשִׁי מֵעִמָּךְ לֹא תְשַׁלְּחֶנּוּ רֵיקָם:
הַעֲנֵיק תַּעֲנִיק לוֹ מִצֹּאנְךָ וּמִגָּרְנְךָ וּמִיִּקְבֶךָ
אֲשֶׁר בֵּרַכְךָ ה' אֱלֹהֶיךָ תִּתֶּן לוֹ:

Ki yimakher l'kha achikha HaIvri oh HaIvria, va-avad'kha shesh shanim u-va-shana HaSh'viit t'shal'chenu chawfshi meh-imakh. V'khi t'shal'chenu chawfshi me-imakh lo t'shal'chenu reikam. HaAneik TaAnik lo mi-tzonkha u-mi-garn'kha u-mi-yikvekha, asher berakh'kha HaShem Elokekha tihten lo.

If your brother, [whether] a Hebrew man or Hebrew woman, will be sold to you [as a slave], he shall serve you for six years, and on the seventh [year] you shall send him away from you free. And when you send him away free, you may not send him away empty-handed. Rather, you must generously provide for him from your flocks and your threshing floor and from your wine-press; as HaShem your God has blessed you, you must provide for him.

Having served as slaves in Egypt for over 200 years, the Jewish people are sensitized to the extreme importance of treating others with dignity, especially employees whose efforts helped the employer succeed in his/her endeavors.

(4) *Tz'daka*
לִתֵּן צְדָקָה כְּמִסַּת יָדוֹ
Liten Tz'daka K'Misat Yado

To Give Charity According to a Person's Means
Sefer HaChinukh #479; Sefer HaMitzvot, Ahseh #195

In his magnum opus the *Mishneh Torah, Hilkhot Mat'not Aniyim* (*Laws of Gifts to the Poor* 10:7), Maimonides teaches that the highest level of *Tz'daka* is doing what it takes to make a person in need, self-sufficient by providing a job, forming a business partnership, lending money interest-free, etc. Everyone, no matter how rich or poor, must give money to *Tz'daka* - even a small amount. The ideal amount one should give is דֵּי מַחְסֹרוֹ אֲשֶׁר יֶחְסַר לוֹ/*Dei Machsoro* – **enough to make up (for that which the person [in need] is lacking)** (*Deuteronomy* 15:8).

THE BOX SCORE

Professional sports clubs are businesses with many employees. While treating employees fairly and in a dignified manner is a way to retain valuable members of your organization, unfortunately, it is not always done. An important type of sportsmanship is how team owners, front office staff, coaches, and all those who supervise others treat their employees.

Chicago White Sox and Bulls Chairman Jerry Reinsdorf is especially known for treating his employees with *Derekh Eretz v'Khavod* (**Respect and Honor**). *Halakha* (*Jewish law*) is replete with *Mitzvot* on how a person must treat an employee or others who perform services by requiring such necessities as timely pay, certain workplace benefits, and severance pay.

Chapter 12
The Power of the Pen: Acts of Sportsmanship by Journalists

The Men and Women who Write the Stories

In addition to being a professional athlete, a perennial "dream job" for boys (and today, girls as well) is to be a sports journalist. If you're a sports fan, just imagine being paid to watch games and then to write or speak about them.

Journalists can and do influence many people. Legally and ethically the journalist must only report truthful and accurate information. What should a sports journalist do when it comes to reporting information that is true but harmful to the subject's feelings or reputation?

If You Have Nothing Good to Say, then . . .

After my first book *PRAY BALL! The Spiritual Insights of a Jewish Sports Fan* was published in 1999, I worked with my publisher in trying to arrange for speaking opportunities and book signings in cities around the United States and Israel. We also solicited newspapers and other media outlets to review/publicize *PRAY BALL!*

At that time, I was told that the policy of a prominent Jewish publication was that it would only publish a book review if the writer assigned to review the book, liked it, and would recommend it. As a Jewish newspaper it was not enough to just state the truth. Adhering to the *Halakhic* (as opposed to the slang) definition of *Lashon HaRa*, the newspaper would not publish negative reviews. Even though the negative reviews would be truthful, these opinions did not have to be articulated to the publication's community of readers.

With a limited number of exceptions, this purported policy is the standard that all Jewish publications should follow; after all, according to *Halakha*, a Jew is only allowed to share negative information with others if it is the truth AND if it is absolutely necessary to disclose. If it is, then the information should only be shared with those who need to know.

Inspired by *Halakha* and the rumored, but unsubstantiated, standard of this Jewish publication, in February of 2016 (i.e., about eight months prior to the Cubs World Series Championship), I posed a question to a group of sports journalists about a matter that has bothered me since it occurred in 2003. I'm referring to the scapegoating of Cubs fan Steve Bartman discussed earlier in this book.

Here is the question that I emailed to a group of sports journalists:

"Just as newspapers and other media outlets have a policy of not including the name of a rape victim (because the potential harm caused to her outweighs the benefit to the public's 'right' to know, a newspaper's ability to sell papers, etc.), should a similar policy be adopted for fans like Steve Bartman [i.e., fans who, when identified by name, will likely experience harm or – at the very least – a disruption in their lives – even though their actions were lawful and in accordance with the rules of the particular sport]?"

Here are the (slightly edited) responses provided by three prominent sports journalists.

From Rick Telander, *Chicago Sun-Times* sports columnist, former *Sports Illustrated* senior writer, and author of *Heaven is a Playground*:
"The thing about Bartman was that it all occurred in a public place where it is tacitly assumed and agreed to that you will allow your likeness to be recorded (in photos or video) and what happens in the park will be public knowledge.

I don't think publicizing his name was completely fair, but I don't know how we limit facts that the public essentially has the right to know. Or will be found out by reasonable efforts – that is, Bartman was visually identified immediately by TV cameras, and finding out who he was, was a simple matter. If it weren't the Cubs, in such a critical, symbolic moment, almost nobody would care and Bartman would be just a tidbit and not a demarcation.

I often wonder if he could have handled the mistake better. It was, after all, something that everybody around him was doing, too – reaching for the foul ball. Nor did he get the ball. Nor did he sell it for thousands of dollars. Nor did he want any publicity. Etc. But it happened. That he has gone into seclusion almost is his choice. I don't know how I would handle the situation. Maybe I would have written a book about my travails. Maybe I would have gone on talk shows. Gone back to Wrigley only at certain times. I don't know. It's a tough nut to crack. . . .
A sexual assault victim will never be totally free again, that's for sure. The Cubs, though, can save Bartman forever. By just winning a World Series title. It's on them to set him free."

Sportscaster and talk-radio personality, Bruce Wolf, shared the following:
"Steve Bartman was *sui generis*, that is, unique. There was no way his name could or should have been kept out of the media because what he did (guilty or not) was one of the most notorious occurrences in Cubs history. There might be instances when fans' names should be kept out but I'd have to look at them on a case by case basis."

From Ed Sherman, sports media journalist and author of *Babe Ruth's Called Shot: The Myth and Mystery of Baseball's Greatest Home Run*:
"I believe that Steve Bartman was a once-in-a-lifetime situation. Make that once in a 10 million lifetimes situation. Never again will all the planets be aligned to create a scenario where an avid fan was blamed from keeping the Cubs out of the World Series.

The story was too big for Bartman's name not to be used. There was too much attention focused on him during the game telecast, and the postgame reaction was so intense. There's no way he could have remained anonymous.

However, where I believe journalists crossed the line was when they showed his parents' house, where he lived. That was reprehensible, putting him and his family at risk. All it takes is one crazy Cubs fan to find the house and do some damage.

The most amazing thing about the Bartman story is that he never has been seen again after that night. I've always said if there is one interview I'd want the most, it would be Bartman."

Update

On November 2, 2016, the Chicago Cubs won the seventh and decisive game of the World Series ending their 108-year drought. In a classy manner, as noted earlier, the following July, Cubs owner Tom Ricketts and Presidents Theo Epstein and Crane Kenney presented Steve Bartman with his very own World Series Championship ring and gave him a tour of the newly renovated Wrigley Field.

Using Rick Telander's language, the Cubs were finally able to "save Bartman forever" and "set him free."

The Men and Women who Write the Stories: A Spiritual Insight

JEWrnalism: Taking Journalism to a Higher Level

The role of the journalist is to share truthful information with their readers/viewers/listeners ("readers"). As long as it's true, that is good enough, even if the subject will experience harm.

In Jewish tradition there are stricter restrictions placed on journalists. They must not only report the truth, but also report only information that will not hurt someone else. Journalists are only permitted to convey negative facts that the readers need to know.

As can be inferred from the responses of three highly-respected, prominent sports journalists, in the professional world of American mainstream journalism, the Jewish standard is not always realistic.

Nonetheless, when it comes to reporting youth and school sports, shouldn't the student writer strive to uphold the Jewish standards for journalism?

Chapter 13
"Sportsmanship Selfies" – Extraordinary Acts of Sportsmanship towards Oneself

Sportsmanship Level III: Chapters 13-22

Extraordinary Acts of Sportsmanship for those Inside the Game: Chapters 13-17

Sportsmanship Level III: Chapters 13-22

Extraordinary Acts of Sportsmanship: Introduction

As discussed earlier in this book (see Chapter 2 *What is Sportsmanship?*), Sportsmanship Level III (SLIII) is analogous to *Rashi*'s interpretation of וְעָשִׂיתָ הַיָּשָׁר וְהַטּוֹב בְּעֵינֵי ה׳/*V'asita HaYashar v'HaTov b'enei HaShem* – **And you shall do that which is straight [fair] and good in the eyes of HaShem** (**Deuteronomy 6:18**). As a refresher, *Rashi* explains that these are acts that go **over and beyond the letter of the law** (*Lifnim MiShurat Ha-Din*). Included in SLIII are extraordinary acts of sportsmanship.

What constitutes "extraordinary"? One type of "extraordinary" is comprised of acts that one would simply not expect from others; that is, acts that would catch the observer by surprise. For example, members of a team carrying a player from the opposing team – who, after knocking the ball out of the park, broke her leg preventing her to circle the bases – around the bases to ensure that she would be awarded a home run.

Other acts in this category are ones that are historic in nature, in that they helped trigger a change in public policy or law allowing others future opportunities that were not previously available. Two examples of such acts of sportsmanship are events that led to the breaking of the color barrier in modern sports and those that helped bring about Title IX (legislation requiring equal opportunity for women in sports programs that receive federal funding).

Extraordinary Acts of Sportsmanship for those Inside the Game: Chapters 13-17

Keeping Your Cool & Controlling Your Emotions

Breaking the color barrier in professional sports was a huge challenge. When Branch Rickey, the owner of the Brooklyn Dodgers, decided that he was going to do it, he had to be extremely selective in choosing the best candidate. In addition to extraordinary baseball skills, the player had to possess a super-human capability of controlling his anger. After all, it was anticipated that wherever this African-American player would go he would be greeted with constant, cruel, bigoted taunts. The player had to be able to brush this bigotry aside and not respond.

How the Color Barrier Was Finally Broken in American Professional Sports

Being in control of one's temper is important in every walk of life, including sports. Over the years we have witnessed many athletes and coaches who have found managing their anger to be quite a challenge. Although Coach Bobby Knight led the Indiana Hoosiers to three NCAA National Championships, he lost his job after 29 years because of his temper. Yankees manager Billy Martin was hired and fired five times over the course of his eight years with the team.

Booted twice within 15 months, his second firing was after he allegedly punched a marshmallow salesman. Tennis great John McEnroe was well known for directing his temper tantrums at line judges whose calls he disputed.

Managing one's anger is a most difficult challenge to meet. Basketball coach Rick Pitino once said, "My greatest failings as a leader have come when I've lost my temper. When you can't control your emotions you can cause harm, for those kind of eruptions are harmful to the group." To mold a confident, winning team, it is important that a coach control his temper. As former New York Rangers Director of Player Personnel and former NHL coach Tom Renney stated, "If you want a team that's in control and plays with authority and is assertive and proactive and can stick to the game plan, as a coach you've got to be all of that behind the bench. . . You can't lose your emotions because that's exactly how your team will play."

As depicted in the film *42*, Brooklyn Dodgers owner Branch Rickey was very careful before he decided on which African-American player should be the person to break Major League Baseball's color barrier. Rickey realized that if this person failed, it would probably take a long time before the next black player would be brought to the MLB. Rickey had to get it right the first time. Not only did this man have to be a star player and possess great patience and courage, but he had to know how to manage his anger. It was obvious to Mr. Rickey that this player would face bigotry wherever he went.

Jackie Robinson proved to be the right choice. In addition to excelling on the field as a five-tool star player (hitting for average and power, fielding, throwing, and running), Jackie exhibited unbelievable restraint when he was the target of racial bigotry. As portrayed in *42*, instead of being warmly welcomed into "The City of Brotherly Love," Philadelphia Phillies manager Ben Chapman hurled one racial epithet after another, until Dodgers second baseman and Philadelphia native, Eddie Stanky (who later went on to manage the Chicago White Sox and two other MLB teams), confronted Chapman. Fans from ballparks across the country jeered Jackie's every move. At first, even many of his Dodgers teammates opposed #42's participation by signing a petition seeking to remove Robinson from the team.

With extraordinary strength and the support of many people, including such notables as Dodgers team captain Pee Wee Reese, MLB Commissioner Happy Chandler, and Jewish superstar Hank Greenberg, Jackie Robinson was able to restrain

---

DIDJA KNOW

that the 1954 Milan High School basketball team that won the Indiana State Championship, was the inspiration for the movie *Hoosiers* which tells the story of the 1952 championship of a fictional small town Indiana high school team, the Hickory Huskers? Led by Coach Norman Dale, portrayed by veteran actor Gene Hackman, this 1986 movie is considered by some the best basketball film of all-time. While many values may be culled from this outstanding movie, including leadership, teamwork, and taking care of one's health, a bit of trivia that many viewers may not remember is the reason why Coach Dale was dismissed as the coach of the fictional Ithaca Tigers and banned for life from coaching NCAA basketball. The reason? He hit a player (his own), something for which he felt remorseful and deeply regretted.

himself, outwardly ignoring the bigots and thus not providing integration opponents the "ammunition" to proclaim that blacks should not be admitted to MLB.

Among the many lessons that Jackie Robinson taught the world was that, at times, the best way to fight back is with silence and grace.

Keeping Your Cool & Controlling Your Emotions: Spiritual Insights

Moses: When Strength is Mistaken for Weakness

No one is perfect. Not even Moses.

Considered by many as the greatest leader in world history, Moses was not allowed into the Promised Land because, instead of speaking to a rock to draw water, as the Almighty commanded, he struck it.

Some say that Moses grew impatient and lost control of his emotions. Others dispute this interpretation, and say that Moses, in the heat of the moment, got confused and unintentionally struck the rock. After all, in a past episode, he was instructed to strike a rock to elicit the flow of water (*Exodus* 17:1-7). Whether or not he got confused, had the Almighty given Moses a pass and not punished him severely, this perhaps would have left the impression for future generations – who would read this account in the *Torah* - that the Almighty used a double-standard when punishing leaders, i.e., that leaders are permitted to disobey His word, while all others must heed it.

To further support the line of thinking that Moses had a "short fuse," some comentators feel that Moses unjustifiably – and in a fit of uncontrollable anger – killed the Egyptian taskmaster (*Exodus* 2:11-15). Others say that Moses was acting in self-defense (on behalf of an abused Israelite slave). Similarly, while some view Moses's casting down of the first set of tablets (*Exodus* 32:19) as an illustration of his terrible temper, others say that this was a sign of effective leadership. Sometimes a leader must openly display emotion to instill important lessons to his constituents.

With the theory of Moses not being able to properly manage his anger refuted, it is important now to realize that, not only was Moses able to keep his emotions in check, but actually, he can be regarded as a master of anger management.

As we know from reading the *Torah*, Moses was constantly being challenged by the Israelites. Some of their complaints and demands included: Who are you to assume leadership? Did you take us out of Egypt to die in the desert? We want meat! We want water! We demand that spies check out the land first, since we do not trust that the Almighty will let us conquer the enemies residing in the Promised Land!

Amazingly, in spite of all of these complaints and demands, Moses – somehow, some way – kept his cool.

Moses had to constantly deal with troublemakers. Two Israelites who were incessant provocateurs were *Datan* and *Aviram*. It was these two troublemakers who accused Moses of murdering the Egyptian taskmaster and then reported it to the Egyptian authorities (*N'darim* 64b). They challenged Moses when Manna was introduced (*Sh'mot Rabba* 25:10) and incited the Israelites to rebel. A major faction of the *Korach* rebellion was led by *Datan* and *Aviram* (*Numbers* 16:1). A peacemaker, Moses invited them to resolve matters. Unfortunately, they refused Moses's peace initiatives (*Midrash Tanchuma Korach* 3).

Moses had many extraordinary talents. In addition to his humility (*Numbers* 12:3), *Moshe Rabbeinu* (**Moses our Rabbi/Teacher**) should also be remembered for his incredible patience, tolerance, and last but not least, as an exemplar of anger management.

NAME THAT *MITZVAH!*

לָלֶכֶת וּלְהִדַּמּוֹת בְּדַרְכֵי הַשֵּׁם יִתְבָּרַךְ

LaLekhet U-Lhidamot B'Darkhei HaShem Yitbarakh

To Follow and Imitate the Ways of HaShem the Blessed

Sefer HaChinukh #611; Sefer HaMitzvot, Ahseh #8

A classic illustration of how the Jewish people are to imitate the Almighty is by being compassionate. An important element of compassion is being able to control our anger. God has many names. Two popular names are *HaShem* and *Elokim*. While *Elokim* represents the Almighty as a *God of law and justice* (מִדַּת הַדִּין/*Midat HaDin*), *HaShem* is the name used to express the Almighty as a *God of compassion* (מִדַּת הָרַחֲמִים/*Midat HaRachamim*). After Moses quelled the rebellious

efforts of the Israelites who were involved in the travesty of the golden calf, God punished the Israelites by afflicting them with a plague (*Exodus* 32:35). When *Moshe Rabbeinu* ascended *Har Sinai* (*Mount Sinai*) to receive the second set of tablets, the Almighty revealed to him a statement that, when recited, would invoke God's *Rachamim/* **Mercy** (*Exodus* 34:5-7). Known as the שְׁלֹשׁ עֶשְׂרֵה (יג) מִידוֹת הָרַחֲמִים/*Sh'losh Esreh* (*Yud Gimel*) *Midot HaRachamim* (*The Thirteen Attributes of Mercy*), Sefardic Jews recite this passage as a part of their everyday prayer liturgy. In Ashkenazic communities, this powerful statement is included in the *Torah* reading on all fast days (with the exception of *Yom Kippur*). On *Yom Kippur*, and other days that we recite *S'lichot* (**Penitential Prayers**), a section of this *Torah* passage is recited on multiple occasions. These awe-inspriring verses are found in *Exodus* 34:6-7:

ה' ה' קֵל רַחוּם וְחַנּוּן אֶרֶךְ אַפַּיִם וְרַב־חֶסֶד וֶאֱמֶת:
נֹצֵר חֶסֶד לָאֲלָפִים נֹשֵׂא עָוֹן וָפֶשַׁע וְחַטָּאָה
וְנַקֵּה לֹא יְנַקֶּה פֹּקֵד עֲוֹן אָבוֹת עַל־בָּנִים וְעַל־בְּנֵי בָנִים
עַל־שִׁלֵּשִׁים וְעַל־רִבֵּעִים:

HaShem HaShem Kel Rachum v'Chanun Ehrekh Apayim v'Rav Chesed veh-Emet. Notzer Chesed La-alafim Noseh Avone VaFehsha v'Cha-ta-ah, v'Nakeh Lo Y'nakeh Poh-ked Avone Avot Ahl Banim v'Ahl B'nei Vanim, Ahl Shileshim v'Ahl Ribeim.

HaShem, HaShem, God Who is compassionate and gracious, slow to anger, and abundant in loving kindness and truth. He preserves loving kindness for thousands, forgives iniquity, intentional sin, and error, and cleanses – but not completely – as He remembers the iniquity of fathers on children and grandchildren for three and four generations.

The expression "Everything in moderation, except for moderation" applies to anger. Like water, money and food, anger – if used right – can be a valuable tool. When a person channels his/her anger to correct a problem, that is positive. However, when an angry person loses control of his/her temper it is very bad. In fact, the *Talmud* (*Shabbat* 105a) equates such a person to an idolator. Maimonides (*Hilkhot Deot* 1:4) teaches about the importance of moderation:

הַדֶּרֶךְ הַיְשָׁרָה הִיא מִדָּה בֵּינוֹנִית...
וּלְפִיכָךְ צִוּוּ חֲכָמִים הָרִאשׁוֹנִים שֶׁיְּהֵא אָדָם שָׁם דֵּעוֹתָיו תָּמִיד
וּמְשַׁעֵר אוֹתָן וּמְכַוֵּן אוֹתָן בַּדֶּרֶךְ הָאֶמְצָעִית, כְּדֵי שֶׁיְּהֵא שָׁלֵם.
כֵּיצַד? לֹא יִהְיֶה בַּעַל חֵמָה נוֹחַ לִכְעֹס,
וְלֹא כְּמֵת שֶׁאֵינוֹ מַרְגִּישׁ, אֶלָּא בֵּינוֹנִי.
לֹא יִכְעַס אֶלָּא עַל דָּבָר גָּדוֹל שֶׁרָאוּי לִכְעֹס עָלָיו,
כְּדֵי שֶׁלֹּא יַעֲשֶׂה כַּיּוֹצֵא בּוֹ פַּעַם אַחֶרֶת.

HaDerekh HaY'shara he mida beinonit ... u-lfikhakh tzivu Chakhamim HaRishonim sheh-y'heh ahdahm shahm deotav tamid umshaehr otan u-mkhavein otan ba-derekh ha-emtza-it, k'dei sheh-y'heh shalem. Keitzad? Lo yiheh ba-ahl chema noach likhos, v'lo k'met sh'eino margish, ela beinoni. Lo yikhos ela ahl davar gadol sheh-raui likhos alav, k'dei sheh-lo yeh-a-seh ka-yotzeh bo pa-am acheret.

The straight [proper] path is moderation ... Therefore, our early Sages commanded that a person should always measure and focus his actions on doing that which is the middle of the road in order to be whole. How? [While] he should not be a person filled with anger, for whom it is easy to get angry, he should [also] not be like a corpse who has no feelings, rather, ... he should only express anger over a serious matter, one that is worthy to be angry about, so that the perpetrator does not commit the same act again.

DIDJA KNOW that *ChaZa"L* (*Our Sages of Blessed Memory*), based upon Moses's striking the rock (and other examples), teach that when a person is angry they are prone to make mistakes (see *Rashi* to *Numbers* 31:21)? This is why it is recommended that in such situations we should take a figurative step back, catch our breath, and sometimes even "sleep on it" before we make important decisions. Otherwise, you may later regret decisions made in the heat of anger.

THE BOX SCORE

An important element of sportsmanship is being able to control one's temper. A moody, temperamental person is no fun to be around; after all, when someone is unpredictable, one doesn't know what will provoke that person to explode.

To be a winner on the sports field, it is important that we learn to keep our cool. As players we must be careful not to lose control with our teammates, coaches, and referees. At home we must remind ourselves of the importance of not overreacting and yelling at our siblings and parents. We must take a lesson from Jackie Robinson: keys to success in every aspect of life are to be strong and to manage our anger.

There are times, however, when a leader needs to express emotion to inspire his/her constituents. Maimonides recommends that a person carefully choose when to react strongly. Moses, who had well-documented episodes of expressing his emotion, was actually a master at anger management.

To Your Health! Taking Care of Yourself

An important component of a mature thinking process is the ability to put matters into perspective and to decide what is best in the "big picture" of life. Many people are so passionate about sports that they ignore common sense and sometimes put themselves in harm's way, regardless of whether possible injuries could have long-term consequences. After all, athletes revel in the immediate gratification, fond memories, and feelings of fulfillment that they experience while playing their sports. And as even more incentive to ignore future risk, many professional athletes, during their relatively brief sports careers, are fortunate enough to earn enough money to support their families for the rest of their entire lives (if they manage their finances well).

On the other hand, some athletes are able to take a step back, analyze, and conclude that the potential negatives outweigh the positives – especially when it comes to their health and wellbeing.

Protect Yourself: Making Fully Informed Decisions

Adults assume a certain amount of personal risk when they make a decision to smoke, skydive, ride a motorcycle, become a professional window washer for high-rise buildings, or engage in any other legal activity that could be classified as potentially dangerous by the medical profession, insurance actuaries, or even society in general.

One enormously popular American activity to add to this list is competitive tackle football, especially at a collegiate or professional level. In past decades, while many people simply assumed that there was a high risk of suffering neurological (head, spine, etc.) injury, extensive supportive medical research did not yet exist. In the past decade or so, however, more and more studies have conclusively linked multiple concussions to long-term brain damage, as manifested by such maladies as dementia, amnesia, Parkinson's disease, and Parkinson's-like symptoms.

As part of his job as a staff pathologist for the Allegheny County Office of the Medical Examiner in Pittsburgh, Nigerian-born Dr. Bennet Omalu was assigned the task of performing an autopsy on Pittsburgh Steelers Hall of Fame center "Iron" Mike Webster after he passed away from a heart attack in 2002. Relentless in his work, Dr. Omalu, a brain specialist who, was not all that familiar with the game of American football at the time, studied up on the game and soon learned of the repeated blows to the brain that an NFL player incurs during the course of his lifetime. He also learned that the player position most prone to head trauma was the center, the position that Webster played.

After extensive examination of Webster's brain and other research, Dr. Omalu determined that Webster suffered from a disease that Omalu named chronic traumatic encephalopathy (CTE). CTE was a significant factor in Webster's death at the young age of 50. Leading up to his death, Webster exhibited such bizarre symptoms as erratic behavior, memory loss, depression, headaches and poor impulse control.

Dr. Omalu authored a paper, with input from other highly respected physicians, which was published in 2005 in the venerable *Neurosurgery* journal about his autopsy on Mike Webster and his discovery of CTE in the player. The article called for more study into the causes of the condition, as well as how widespread it is in professional athletes. Omalu, along with colleagues, also authored a second paper in 2006 describing his later autopsy of former Pittsburgh Steeler Terry Long, the second confirmed case of CTE. Triggered by depression resulting from CTE, sadly, Long took his own life. Still the NFL did not accept CTE as a disease caused by repeated trauma to the brain sustained by football players and in fact went to great lengths to discredit the doctors asserting the condition's existence.

Dr. Omalu later received the support of former Steelers team physician, neurologist Dr. Julian Bailes, who (because Dr. Omalu was not invited to speak) presented the doctor's findings to the first NFL league-wide concussion conference.

The work of these courageous physicians is told in the book and movie, *Concussion*, as well as in hundreds of news stories. Their efforts have forced the NFL, NCAA, and other football leagues at all levels, to begin implementing rule changes, more thorough concussion screening, and other measures to try to decrease the number of traumatic head injuries among its players. Drs. Omalu and Bailes and many others are continuing to work on definitively diagnosing CTE in living humans and, then, to develop ways to prevent it.

Because of this important research, in recent years, certain professional football players have decided to retire voluntarily at a relatively early stage of their careers. Perhaps one of the most surprising occurred in the early spring of 2015, when 24-year-old San Francisco 49ers star linebacker Chris Borland announced his retirement after his rookie season. He did it as a precautionary and not as a curative measure. And, according to an interview with the player on *ESPN*, the NFL responded by asking him to take a drug test and taking back most of his signing bonus. Borland took the financial hit to preserve his health against future "brain damage" and says he is "reluctant"to even watch football anymore, even though he loves the game. He has even agreed to participate in ongoing medical research on his brain in hopes of helping experts protect other players.

Poised to make millions of dollars in future earnings, Borland made this bold decision based upon his history of having suffered numerous concussions in the past and recent medical findings. As he told *ESPN*'s "Outside the Lines," "I just want to do what's best for my health. From what I've researched and what I've experienced, I don't think it's worth the risk."

Does this mean the end of the NFL? Absolutely not. According to *Boston Globe* reporter Christopher L. Gasper, more information allows players to make better-informed decisions. "Borland is part of the first generation of NFL players armed with enough reliable information to decide for themselves whether playing professional football is a risk worth taking." While not everyone will agree with every decision made by others, an adult of sound mind is allowed to make decisions so long as they are not contrary to the law. Sportsmanship dictates that when an athlete makes any decision – but especially one that involves great risk to his or her personal health or financial welfare – that they are able to be as fully informed as possible before making their determination.

DIDJA KNOW that another crusader in bringing the concussion problem to the forefront of the American public is former Ivy League football player and WWE professional wrestler, Chris Nowinski, Ph.D.? To help make others more aware of this crisis, in 2006, this activist wrote the book, *Head Games: Football's Professional Concussion Crisis*. Dr. Nowinski, a co-founder and president of the not-for-profit Sports Legacy Institute and codirector of the Center for the Study of Traumatic Encephalopathy at Boston University School of Medicine wrote, "My goal [in writing *Head Games*] was to raise awareness of the hidden epidemic of brain injury and its related diseases in football, and to lay out a plan for reform. The experience taught me an important lesson: books don't create change, people do." Along with Dr. Ann McKee, an esteemed clinical and research neurologist, Nowinski has dedicated his post-sports professional career to providing the necessary information on sports injuries to all those aspiring amateur and professional athletes who are considering taking their love of contact sports in general, and football in particular, to the next level.

DIDJA KNOW that the first former NHL player diagnosed with CTE (posthumously, as that was the only method of diagnosis then, as now) by the Center for the Study of Traumatic Encephalopathy at Boston University School of Medicine was former Chicago Blackhawks and New York Rangers star Reggie Fleming? Researchers will never know how many concussions Fleming had during his turbulent career (the *New York Times* wrote that the player "relished his persona as one of the most bruising players of his era"). According to the *Times*, in Fleming's day, concussion records were rarely kept, as often the head blows were often not even considered true injuries.

To Your Health! Taking Care of Yourself: A Spiritual Insight

Is There a (Jewish) Doctor in the House?

In Jewish tradition, human life is regarded as sacred. In fact, the *Talmud* (*Sanhedrin* 37a) teaches:

וְכָל הַמְקַיֵּים נֶפֶשׁ אַחַת מִיִשְׂרָאֵל
מַעֲלֶה עָלָיו הַכָּתוּב
כְּאִילוּ קַיֵּים עוֹלָם מָלֵא.

*V'khol ha-m'kayem nefesh achat MiYisrael ma-ah-leh alav HaKatuv
k'ilu kiyem olam maleh.*

***And anyone who saves another [Jew's] life, the Torah considers him as one
who has saved an entire world.***

The *Torah* (*Deuteronomy* 2:4; 4:9 & 15) also directs that we must take good care of our health. We also have a duty to heal (see *Exodus* 21:19; *Leviticus* 19:16). Physicians have a special obligation to heal because of their training.

In addition to conventional medical healing, there are many forms of spiritual intervention in Jewish tradition. There is a special prayer for the sick in the daily *Amidah*. During the public reading of the *Torah*, it is customary to recite the *Mi Shehberakh* prayer for the sick. Many people will recite chapters from King David's **Book of Psalms** (*Sefer T'hillim*) seeking Divine intervention in the healing process. One of the most inspiring *Mitzvot* is **Visiting the Sick** (בִּקוּר חוֹלִים/*Bikkur Cholim*). This *Mitzvah* requires the visitor to help care for the needs of the sick, and, subsequent to the visit, to pray for the healing of the sick person. We wish a person who is ill, רְפוּאָה שְׁלֵמָה /*R'fuah Sh'lemah –
"a complete healing"* [Hebrew version of a "speedy recovery!"].

Throughout history, there have been numerous Jewish doctors who have contributed in significant ways to the development of the field of medicine. Since 1901, about 50 Jewish doctors have been recipients of Nobel Prizes in medicine. Jewish medical luminaries include: Dr. Jonas Salk, the inventor of the polio inoculation; Dr. Albert Sabin, who developed the first oral polio vaccine; Dr. Selma Wehl, who fled Nazi Germany to become a respected physician and American Jewish leader; and Dr. Sigmund Freud, the father of psychoanalysis. Perhaps the greatest Jewish doctor of all-time, who practiced both conventional and spiritual healing, was Maimonides.

Born in 1135 in Cordoba, Spain, Rabbi Moses ben Maimon, or simply the *Rambam*, as he was known in Hebrew, was a world-renowned rabbinic scholar and physician. Forced to flee Spain because of anti-Semitism, Maimonides and his family moved to Morocco, Israel, and finally to Egypt. The *Rambam* was such an outstanding physician that he was the personal doctor of the Sultan of Egypt and his retinue.

A prodigious scholar and prolific author, Maimonides wrote many medical publications, including **Responsa** (***T'shuvot***) to questions posed to him on the *Halakhic* (i.e., Jewish legal) aspect of treating important medical conditions and situations. In addition to his medical publications, the *Rambam* wrote many other traditional Jewish publications, including the philosophical classic, ***The Guide for the Perplexed*** (*Moreh N'vukhim*), a commentary on the *Mishna*; *Sefer HaMitzvot*, a listing and discussion of the 613 *Mitzvot* (cited in the **NAME THAT *MITZVAH!*** sections of this book); and the *Mishneh Torah*, the first concise systematic treatise on Jewish law. Included in the *Mishneh Torah* (*Hilkhot Avel* Chapter 14) are guidelines on how to perform the great *Mitzvah of Bikkur Cholim* (***Visiting the Sick***).

A key principle in Jewish tradition is that protecting one's life, health, and wellbeing should be a person's top priority. In fact, the Sage Hillel advises (*Pirkei Avot* 1:14) that before a person can reach out to help others, s/he must first make sure that their own needs are cared for. (Just think about what airlines tell passengers before departure: that before you help someone else secure their oxygen mask, you must first make sure that your own is on securely.) Although quite logical, a person does not always follow this directive. Before a person performs acts of דֶּרֶךְ אֶרֶץ וְכָבוֹד/*Derekh Eretz v'Khavod* for others, they should first show this **Respect and Honor** to themselves.

A Wise Piece of Advice: A Spiritual Insight

Rabban Yochanan ben Zakkai served as the *Nasi* of the *Sanhedrin* immediately before the destruction of the Second Temple until about ten years after. Anticipating its imminent destruction, with the approval of the Roman Emperor Vespesian, *Rabban Yochanan ben Zakkai* relocated the *Sanhedrin* from Jerusalem to Yavneh. Among his many students, five were especially distinguished: *Rahbi Eliezer, Rahbi Yehoshua, Rahbi Yosse, Rahbi Shimon* and *Rahbi Elazar*.

In *Pirkei Avot* 2:13 he asks these five students:
אָמַר לָהֶם: צְאוּ וּרְאוּ
אֵיזוֹהִי דֶרֶךְ יְשָׁרָה שֶׁיִּדְבַּק בָּה הָאָדָם.
Ahmar Lahem: Tz'u ur-u eizohi derekh y'shara sheh-yidbak ba ha-adahm.
He [*Rabban Yochanan ben Zakkai*] said to them [*these five students*]: "Go out and see which is the best path for a person to cling ."

Each student gave a different answer. Here is what *Rahbi Shimon* recommended:
רַבִּי שִׁמְעוֹן אוֹמֵר: הָרוֹאֶה אֶת הַנּוֹלָד.
. . . *Rahbi Shimon omer: Ha-roeh eht ha-nolad.*

Here is a contemporary translation/interpretation of *Rahbi Shimon's* statement:
Rahbi Shimon says: "One who foresees the consequences of [*his*] actions."

THE BOX SCORE

In sports, the lure of immediate gratification, enjoyment and – at the professional level handsome financial compensation, often blinds a person from realizing the long-term effects of certain injuries on themselves. An important form of sportsmanship is looking out for one's own wellbeing by making fully informed decisions.

This is a critical lesson both in sports and in Jewish tradition.

Fair Game: The Whole Truth and Nothing But the Truth

Must a person always tell "the truth, the whole truth, and nothing but the truth"? The next story is about an athlete who volunteered the whole truth, even though he was not required to do so, which contributed toward his losing the competition.

"The Roddick Choice"

In May 2005 at the Rome Masters, top U.S. tennis player Andy Roddick was one point away from defeating Spanish opponent Fernando Verdasco and winning the match. After faulting on the first serve, the line judge called Verdasco's next serve out, giving the Spaniard a double fault. Instead of celebrating a match victory, Roddick informed the umpire that his opponent had actually aced him since the ball had nicked the line. Verdasco then rallied and won the match. Roddick's act of honesty and extraordinary sportsmanship in the heat of competition cost him the match and thousands of dollars. In his book, *The Speed of Trust*, author Steven Covey refers to this as the "Roddick Choice." Roddick had no regrets in interviews with media after the loss. "Sometimes you feel you've done something wrong and deserve to lose the match. That wasn't the case today. He just went for broke. In the second set tiebreak I didn't play a single bad shot. . . . He was playing with confidence, he just turned 180 degrees." Then the athlete generously praised the victor and talked about continuing to improve his skills playing on clay courts. Now, that's fair play.

The Whole Truth and Nothing But the Truth: Spiritual Insights

The Truth Behind the Golem

In Hebrew, the word *Emet* means "truth" or "honesty." The Almighty is referred to as: רַב־חֶסֶד וֶאֱמֶת [וְ]/*[v']Rav Chesed v'Emet* – *[and] abundant in loving kindness and truth (Emet) (Exodus 34:6)*, while His *Torah* is described as "*Emet*"– וְתוֹרָתְךָ אֱמֶת /*v'Toraht'kha Emet – And Your Torah is Truth (Psalms 119:142)*. Earlier in *Exodus* (23:7), the Almighty commands: מִדְּבַר שֶׁקֶר תִּרְחָק/ *mi-d'var sheker tirchak – Distance yourself from a false matter [or word]*.

The prophet *Zekharia* preached:

אֵלֶּה הַדְּבָרִים אֲשֶׁר תַּעֲשׂוּ
דַּבְּרוּ אֱמֶת אִישׁ אֶת־רֵעֵהוּ אֱמֶת וּמִשְׁפַּט שָׁלוֹם שִׁפְטוּ בְּשַׁעֲרֵיכֶם:
Eleh ha-dvarim asher ta-ah-su, dahb'ru emet ish et rehehu emet umishpat shalom shiftu b'sha-ah-reikhem.

"These are the matters that you shall perform: Speak the truth [every] person to his neighbor; and render judgments of truth and peace in your gates" (Zekharia 8:16).

In choosing qualified judges to assist him, Moses was advised to select:
אַנְשֵׁי אֱמֶת שֹׂנְאֵי בָצַע / *Anshei emet sohn'ei vatza*

Men of truth who abhor unjust financial gain (Exodus 18:21).

Everything that we do should be done in a truthful, honest way. Jewish tradition is replete with laws regarding how to conduct business in an honest fashion and how to ensure that a person suspected of a crime is dealt with in a fair, honest manner.

Throughout Jewish history there have been many people who are especially remembered for their honest behavior and truthful teachings. One of the most famous stories regarding *Emet* involves Rabbi Judah Loew ben Bezalel. Also known as the *MaHaRaL*, Rabbi Loew (1513–1609) served as the Chief Rabbi of Prague, Czechoslovakia. A student of **Jewish mysticism** (*Kabbala*), the *MaHaRal* was a great defender of the Jewish people. He is remembered for his ability to successfully defend the Jews of Prague against unjust government attacks. During his lifetime there was rampant anti-Semitism. Around the time of Passover, there were blood libel attacks, slanderous accusations that Jews were killing Christian children and using their blood in the manufacturing of *matza*.

Unable to successfully fend off the blood libels and other unjust anti-Semitic attacks, legend has it that the *MaHaRaL* resorted to *Kabbala*. Using clay from the shores of a nearby river, Rabbi Loew formed a human figure that was known as the *Golem* of Prague. To give him life, Rabbi Loew engraved three Hebrew letters on his forehead – א (*Aleph*), מ (*Mem*), ת (*Tav*). These letters spell – אֱמֶת (*Emet*), "truth." After all, the *Golem*, who was a giant in physical stature, was created for the sole purpose of defending the Jews of Prague. By defending them, he would reveal, protect, and promote the **truth** (*Emet*) about the unfounded anti-Semitic charges leveled against the Jews of Prague.

The *Golem* lived in Rabbi Loew's synagogue. Whenever he was needed to defend the Jews of Prague, Rabbi Loew summoned him. When the *MaHaral* felt that the anti-Semitism had subsided and the services of the *Golem* were no longer needed, he "de-activated" him by simply removing the *Aleph*, the first letter from the word *Emet* engraved on the *Golem's* forehead. Without the *Aleph, Emet* is transformed to the word מֵת /*Met* (**dead**). After all, when there is no truth, we are (spiritually) dead.

Some say that the *Golem* still resides in Rabbi Loew's synagogue in Prague. To this day, the synagogue is an historic landmark that people of all faiths and nationalities come to visit. Others say that Rabbi Loew's *Golem* has been symbolically replaced by the modern State of Israel, which defends the Jews of the world both through the efforts of its צְבָא הַהֲגָנָה לְיִשְׂרָאֵל /*Tz'va HaHagana L'Yisrael* – **the Israel Defense Forces** (צַהַ"ל /*TzaHa"L- IDF*) and by preaching the truth about Israel and **the world Jewish community** – כְּלַל יִשְׂרָאֵל (*K'lal Yisrael*).

Articulating the truth is an important way of expressing **Respect and Honor** – (דֶּרֶךְ אֶרֶץ וְכָבוֹד) /*Derekh Eretz v'Khavod*). It is also a vital component of Jewish law and life, as illustrated by the legend of Rabbi Judah Loew ben Bezalel and his *Golem*.

When is Bending the Truth/Lying Permitted?

In Jewish tradition, the obligation to "tell the truth, the whole truth, and nothing but the whole truth" outside of a legal proceeding is not absolute. Here are some of the exceptions cited in the tradition and their sources:

(1) **To save a human life**. We learn this from Abraham. Forced to temporarily leave the famine-stricken Canaan (Land of Israel) and dwell in Egypt, Abraham knew that the Pharaoh would be smitten by Sara's physical beauty and would order that Abraham be killed so that he could marry her. So Abraham directed his beloved wife to lie:

אִמְרִי־נָא אֲחֹתִי אָתְּ לְמַעַן יִיטַב־לִי בַעֲבוּרֵךְ וְחָיְתָה נַפְשִׁי בִּגְלָלֵךְ:

Ihmri na achoti aht l'ma-ahn yitahv li va-ah-vurekh v'chay'ta nafshi biglalekh.

"Please say that you are my sister in order that it will be good for me on your account and that my soul will [be allowed to] live – because of you" (*Genesis* 12:13). Isaac told a similar lie about Rebecca when they were forced to move to G'rar because of a famine (*Genesis* 26:1–11). Like his father Abraham, Isaac's life was spared. Like her mother-in-law Sara, Rebecca was not compromised in any way.

(2) **To ensure a greater good**. We learn from the episode of Jacob – at his mother Rebecca's insistence – deceiving Isaac into giving him the b'rakha (**blessing**) reserved for the b'khor (**first-born son** – *Esau*) (*Genesis* 27:1–46), that, as a last resort, one can use deception if it is the only way to ensure the greater good. In this case, not only was Isaac physically blind, but he was blind as to the great detriment that Esau's serving as his successor would cause the future of the Jewish people.

(3) **To preserve family harmony.** Literally, "peace of the home" (שְׁלוֹם בַּיִת/ *Sh'lom Bayit*), is a value that is so important that if, to preserve it a person must bend the truth, then one is permitted to do so. We learn this from the Almighty Himself, Who, when retelling to Abraham what Sara had just said about getting pregnant at age 90, He omitted mentioning a derogatory statement that she said about her 99-year-old husband: וַאדֹנִי זָקֵן/va-doni zaken – **"and my husband [master] is old"** (*Genesis* 18:12). [see *Y'vamot 65b* and *B'reshit Rabba 48:18*].

(4) **To preserve peace (between others)**. Moses's brother Aaron is described as אוֹהֵב שָׁלוֹם וְרוֹדֵף שָׁלוֹם/o-hev shalom v'rodef shalom – one who loves peace and pursues peace (*Pirkei Avot 1:12*). *Avot d'Rahbi Natan 12:3*, shares some of Aaron's unorthodox mediation techniques in bringing peace between disputants. Aaron would sit with each of the parties separately and would tell each one how badly the other felt about the rift in their relationship (i.e., Aaron would bend the truth). Moved by Aaron's "words," when the two disputants would meet, they then would embrace each other and reconcile. Although, perhaps, each of the two men now truly felt bad about the hurt they caused to the other person, in truth, this remorse was triggered by the words of (the peace-loving) Aaron.

(5) When commenting on a famous **disagreement** (*machaloket*) between the Schools of *Hillel* and *Shammai*, in his book, *Jewish Wisdom*, Rabbi Joseph Telushkin concludes that a person can bend the truth when it comes in the place of uttering **"truths that inflict hurt without achieving a greater good."** The disagreement (*K'tubot 16b–17a*) is whether a wedding guest must tell a physically unattractive bride that she is beautiful. The School of Hillel says one should bend the truth, while the School of Shammai maintains that one should not

mislead in any manner, shape, or form. The law sides with Hillel's opinion, and we are allowed to say things that will make the bride feel beautiful on her wedding day. As the famous adage states succinctly, "Beauty is in the eyes of the beholder." At a wedding, the only "beholder" whose vote counts is the groom. Since he feels that his bride is beautiful, we must only say things that will reinforce his sentiments; otherwise, stay home!

(6) **When disclosing an illness to a (very sick) patient**. According to the *Shulchan Arukh, Yoreh Deah* 338:1, a person who is very ill should recite the *vidui* (**confessional**) prayer. The text of the *vidui* includes mention of praying for one's own recovery as well as the possibility of not surviving (this particular illness). Rabbi Telushkin in *Jewish Wisdom* concludes, "According to most Rabbinic authorities, one is to make a seriously ill person aware of his or her illness, without issuing any definitive pronouncements that will deprive him or her of hope."

Chapter 14
United We Stand: Extraordinary Acts of Sportsmanship towards Teammates

Teammates

Letting a "Teammate" Win: The Lisa Kincaid Story

Lisa Kincaid. Not exactly a household name, except perhaps in the Badger State. In the great state of Wisconsin, Lisa Kincaid is a legend among track and field fans.

As a student at Palmyra-Eagle High School (1993–1996), Lisa excelled in multiple sports. Although she also lettered in volleyball and basketball, the sport in which she achieved the greatest feats was track and field. Voted the team MVP each of her four years, among the school records Lisa set include the 100-meter dash, long jump, 300-meter low hurdles and 1600-meter relay. Her high school achievements as a student-athlete earned her a track scholarship to the University of Wisconsin-Madison.

Michael Powers, Lisa's USA Junior Olympic volleyball coach, tells a warm story about Lisa's selflessness as an athlete in *Chicken Soup for the Sports Fan's Soul*.

Lisa was such an incredible athlete that she did not lose a single event in 64 consecutive high school conference meets. Ironically, the competition that she lost for the first time in her high school career was, perhaps, her greatest achievement on the track field. An extremely humble and thoughtful person, late in her junior year, Lisa's coach asked that she enter the mile race. Although this was the first time that she ever competed in this event, Lisa took an early lead, and it appeared that her win streak would be left intact. However, on the first lap, she seemed to get tired, and two athletes from another team overtook her, after which Lisa's teammate Julie did as well.

Somehow when the race concluded, not only did Lisa not finish first, but she finished in fourth place behind the two frontrunners and Julie. How could this be? Lisa, apparently, purposely finished fourth. After all, she realized that as long as one of the members of her track team finished in the top three, the team's standing in the meet would not be affected. Lisa also realized that Julie, a senior, needed to finish in no lower than third place to earn a varsity letter. Based upon past performances, going into the race, it was predicted that Julie would finish in third place behind the two runners from the other school. Once Lisa was asked to participate, she realized that, unless she finished behind Julie in fourth, Julie would never have the opportunity of receiving a varsity letter. Without harming her team, Lisa, apparently, let her winning streak come to an end, to ensure a lifetime memory of success for a high school teammate.

Teammates: A Spiritual Insight

The Wives Club: Penina Inspires Hanna's Powerful Prayer

יְהוֹשֻׁעַ בֶּן פְּרַחְיָה אוֹמֵר... וֶהֱוֵי דָן אֶת כָּל הָאָדָם לְכַף זְכוּת.

Yehoshua ben P'rachya omer . . . v'hehvei dahn et kol ha-ahdahm l'khaf z'khut.

Yehoshua the son of P'rachaya says: ". . . and judge everyone with the presumption of innocence" (Pirkei Avot 1:6).

From reading (only) the background behind the birth of the Prophet Samuel (I *Samuel* 1:1-28), one may easily conclude that jealousy and other negative feelings existed between Elakana's two wives Hanna and Penina. While Elkana favored Hanna more than Penina, after years of marriage, Hanna was unable to provide Elkana with children.

The text (1:6) states:

וְכִעֲסַתָּה צָרָתָה גַּם־כַּעַס בַּעֲבוּר הַרְעִמָה כִּי־סָגַר ה' בְּעַד רַחְמָה:

V'khiahsata tzarata gahm ka-ahs ba-avur ha-r'ihma ki sahgahr HaShem b'ahd rachma.

And her rival [Penina] angered her [Hanna] repeatedly in order to irritate her because HaShem had closed her womb.

While it appears that, driven by her jealously, Penina had (only) ill intentions as she wanted to "beat" Hanna in their "competition" for Elkana's affection, according to one source (*Bava Batra* 16a), Penina had **only good intentions** ("*l'Shem Shamayim – for the Sake of the Heavens*"). By angering Hanna, Penina wanted to inspire her rival-wife to pray with the greatest of *Kavana (fervor)*. As history bears out, driven to such a degree, Hanna prayed with such intent that her fervor while praying for a son is the standard set in Jewish tradition for measuring one's *Kavana* in prayer.

Realizing how important having a child was for Hanna, Penina – who already was the mother of multiple children – helped her rival achieve her dream of conceiving Elkana's baby.

And this baby *Sh'muel* (Samuel) was no ordinary little boy. Raised under the guidance of *Eli HaKohen* (**the Priest**), Samuel grew up to be one of the greatest prophets in Jewish history.

DIDJA KNOW
that on the first day of *Rosh HaShana* the first chapter in I *Samuel* is read as the *Haftarah*? This text parallels the *Torah* reading for that day since it touches upon the theme of *Zikhronot* (*God Who remembers*). Just as the Almighty remembered Sara by her giving birth to a son (Isaac), so too did the *Kadosh Barukh Hu* (*KB"H – the Holy One Blessed Be He*) remember Hanna. Both texts also remind us of the importance of providing a Jewish child with a proper Jewish education to ensure their moral and intellectual development.

Tolerance & Acceptance

The Powerful Message of One Arm Over Two Shoulders

Harold "Pee Wee" Reese played his entire 16-year career for the Dodgers (15 in Brooklyn and his final season in Los Angeles). He retired after the 1958 season. A 10-time All-Star shortstop and third baseman, Reese is a member of the National Baseball Hall of Fame. A career .269-hitter, Pee Wee was an excellent fielder and deft base runner. Having served as the Dodgers' captain, Reese is especially remembered for being an outstanding leader. Not only did Pee Wee help his team make seven World Series appearances, but he showed the baseball world, by example, the importance of being tolerant.

In 1947, Jackie Robinson broke Major League Baseball's color barrier, as a 28-year-old rookie playing for the Dodgers. In addition to his stellar statistics, Reese is remembered for helping Robinson gain acceptance among Dodger teammates and members of opposing teams. As mentioned in an earlier chapter, not only did players from opposing teams protest Robinson's participation in the Major Leagues, but some Dodgers players also objected. When some of Robinson's teammates circulated a petition around the Dodgers locker room wanting him to leave the team, Reese refused to sign.

During one game in either Boston or Cincinnati in the 1947 or 1948 season (historians dispute the city and year, and some question whether it even ever happened), while the Dodgers were on the field, Reese went over to Robinson and simply put his arm around him. The message that this symbolic gesture sent was that everyone needs to be more tolerant. To his teammates who refused to accept Robinson as a teammate, because he was black, Reese's message was clear: there is no room for intolerance on the Dodgers. Similarly, Reese's gesture informed the fans in the stands who were verbally abusing Robinson, as well as the entire baseball world, that prejudice and other acts of intolerance were no longer acceptable. These communications were especially meaningful coming from a respected leader like Reese who also happened to be from the South (Kentucky), which was infamous for its Jim Crow laws and other acts of intolerance.

In recognition of Reese's outstanding contribution to his team, the Dodgers retired his #1 jersey in 1984. Reese, who passed away in 1999, is remembered for being #1 in teaching the world the importance of tolerance. In 2005, this symbolic display of tolerance was honored when New York City Mayor Michael Bloomberg helped unveil a monument depicting this historical event outside of the minor league Brooklyn Cyclones' baseball stadium

Tolerance & Acceptance: Spiritual Insights

Rav Kook's Recipe for Success

Tolerance is an extremely important value in Jewish tradition. It is vital to be accepting of others, no matter what their religion, nationality, or race may be. The *Torah* teaches the importance of not discriminating against any human being, especially those who are most vulnerable. The most vulnerable include the elderly (*Leviticus* 19:32), widows and orphans (*Exodus* 22:21), and converts to Judaism (*Leviticus* 19:33). From the commandment of **Loving Your Fellow Jew** (*Ahavat Yisrael; Leviticus* 19:18; *Shabbat* 31a), we are reminded of the importance of treating all human beings the way that we ourselves would like to be treated.

There are many examples of figures in Jewish history who exemplify tolerance. One of the finest exemplars is the late Rabbi Abraham Isaac Kook ("*Rav* Kook"– 1865–1935). Born and raised in Latvia, Rabbi Kook was not afraid to practice what he believed in, even if it went against the accepted norm. At that time, many rabbinical leaders opposed **Jewish immigration to Israel** (*Aliyah*). They believed that the correct time for *Aliyah* is only after the **Messiah** (*Mashiach*) arrives. Because of this belief, many observant Jews resisted moving to Israel. Most of those who chose to settle the land were non-observant. In 1904, *Rav Kook* immigrated to Israel to become the Chief Rabbi of Jaffa. In 1921 he was named the Chief (Ashkenazic) Rabbi of Israel.

Not only was Rabbi Kook beloved and respected by observant Jews, but by a countless number of non-observant Jews as well. After all, he reached out to Jews of all back- grounds. He felt that the role played by all Jews, no matter what their level of observance, was instrumental in building a Jewish homeland. Because of his extraordinary level of tolerance, Rabbi Kook is credited with bringing many non-observant Jews closer to tradition. *Rav Kook* is remembered for his love of and tolerance for all human beings.

Sympathy & Empathy

The Bernie and Ernie Show

For three seasons (1974–1977) fans of the University of Tennessee Volunteers were treated to the outstanding, dazzling and spirited performances of Bernard King and Ernie Grunfeld. Dubbed "The Bernie and Ernie Show," King and Grunfeld had explosive chemistry on the basketball court, gaining the Vols national attention, the likes of which they had never had before.

In tribute to their magnificent performances, this dynamic duo was featured on the cover of *Sports Illustrated* and both were later chosen in the first round of the 1977 NBA draft. King was eventually elected to the Naismith Memorial Basketball Hall of Fame, after a professional career as a top scorer for teams including the New Jersey Nets, the Golden State Warriors, and his dream team, the New York Knicks. Grunfeld had a solid run as a small forward and a shooting guard and continues to have an impressive career as a leader in the NBA. Serving in executive positions for the Milwaukee Bucks (the team that initially drafted him as a player) and the New York Knicks (his last team before he retired from competition), Grunfeld currently is President of the Washington Wizards, a post that he has held since 2003.

After playing in the pros separated the two friends for a few years after leaving college, The Bernie and Ernie Show resumed once the players reunited as teammates for the Knicks in the early 1980s. The "Show" continues to this very day, as the two men remain caring friends. Their friendship was strengthened during their reunion as teammates with the New York Knicks and, in more recent times, when their jerseys were retired by their alma mater. Ernie also received a special shout-out of gratitude from Bernie at his Hall of Fame induction ceremony.

What makes this friendship particularly unique is that these two men are so different from one another and come from dissimilar backgrounds but still have such a strong connection. Grunfeld's family background helped him grow into a gregarious and outgoing adult, who believed he could do anything. King's upbringing led him to be reserved, share little of his personal struggles, and to grow more comfortable with solitude. Immigrating to America when he was a child, Grunfeld is white and Jewish and spent his teen years in the predominately upper middle class Forest Hills neighborhood of Queens, though his family lived in a tiny one-bedroom apartment. King is African American and was raised in a strict, church-going family in a Fort Greene, Brooklyn housing project when the neighborhood was tough and riddled with poverty and violence.

What initially bonded these two young men was their love of basketball and their shared New York City backgrounds: tough city teenagers finding themselves starting out their college basketball careers together in the deep South in the mid-1970s. Both had found their passion for the sport on the playgrounds in their neighborhoods. Both sought to escape the pain of being outsiders as children, and it would be here that they would learn to focus on gaining a competitive edge on the court, in order to gain acceptance from their peers and from the world.

Grunfeld and King's well-known connection on the court, I believe, was their instantly sensing in each other a "brother," no matter how different. As King so eloquently put it in a 2013 Peabody Award winning ESPN documentary about the friends, "We have a brotherly kinship and the friendship that Ernie and I have will never change."

In this author's opinion, the "glue" that bonds them is their empathy for one another. While it seems that these two men are polar opposites, upon closer examination, I believe that they share two important links: both know what pain is all about and both know how to fight for acceptance.

Born in Communist Romania, Grunfeld immigrated to the United States when he was nine years old, after his parents decided to find a new home country, because of rampant anti-Semitism. Ernie's parents were Holocaust survivors and wanted to make sure that their sons Leslie (the oldest by nine years) and Ernie were given every opportunity to flourish as Jews and also professionally as working adults. Tragically, less than two years after their arrival to the States, Leslie passed away from leukemia. Having lost his brother whom he idolized, Ernie was devastated.

In the ESPN film, Grunfeld talked about his difficulties assimilating after his 1964 arrival in New York, when he did not speak English. Nor did he play basketball. Kids made fun of him because of his inability to communicate in their native tongue. Ernie overcame his social challenges when he learned and mastered not just the English language, but the universal language of basketball. "I went on the court and I could speak the language of basketball," he said. ". . . That was my escape from everything. When I was on the court, nobody made fun of me." As his game improved, Ernie became more popular and made more friends. Ernie's parents were extremely supportive of their son as he developed into one of the best players in New York. When he came to the University of Tennessee, Ernie was considered the Big Man on Campus.

King grew up in a neighborhood known – even among residents of other poor neighborhoods around New York City – for its dangerous streets (and excellent basketball players). As the ESPN film's narrator, rapper Chuck D, pointed out, "In Brooklyn's projects, poverty and crime were rampant. And among the only alternatives to the lure of street life was basketball." One of six children, unfortunately, Bernard King, did not share a close relationship with his parents. In the documentary, King recalled that his troubled, lonely background led him to be shy, focused, and able to escape into the game – and also to problems dealing with his pain as an adult.

Although an electrifying and intense player, Bernard experienced overt prejudice while playing at the University of Tennessee, culminating in several brushes with the law. A very private person, rather than sharing his pain with others, he started relying on alcohol to ease his suffering as early as his college years. Even though he retired as a top scorer in NBA history, King was traded several times early in his career, because of his off-the-court problems with alcohol. But after a stint in rehab in the early 1980s, Bernie was a new man and, with discipline, resumed his NBA career. Soon after, he moved to the Knicks and became one of the premier players in the league. With his hometown team he was reunited with his good buddy, Ernie Grunfeld.

King's career was tragically upended, however, during a 1985 game against Kansas City, when he blew out his knee, breaking the leg and suffering severe cartilage damage, as well as a torn ligament. In those days, such an injury meant the end of an athletic career, unlike today. He required extensive surgery and retreated into isolated focus for years of dedicated rehab. During that time, he trusted only his neighbor and close friend, Grunfeld, to support him. Determined to beat the odds and return to the game, King came back two years later to the Knicks and even regained All Star status in the early 1990s with the Washington Bullets, something no other player had been able to do. Continuing knee problems forced him to retire in 1993, having scored more than 19,000 points over his career.

Ernie and Bernie both know what struggling is all about. The Jewish people have struggled throughout their history. African Americans have struggled throughout their history. Having experienced anti-Semitism, bullying, and the loss of his brother, Ernie personally knows how to successfully confront and overcome challenges. Having been raised in a home that faced poverty, recovering from a serious, life-changing injury, and fighting demons at different periods in his adult life, Bernie knows what overcoming adversity is all about.

Empathy is even more powerful than sympathy. Anyone can sympathize for another person. In order to empathize, a person must put him/herself into the other person's shoes. The easiest way to achieve mutual empathy is when two people share relatable life experiences.

Sportsmanship is all about seeing beyond the game and the ever-so-important goal of winning. Without diminishing one's efforts channeled to achieving victory, a sympathetic – or better yet, empathetic – person is best equipped to engage in acts of sportsmanship at all levels – both on and off the court.

The Bernie and Ernie Show is not just about a history of electrifying, winning basketball at the University of Tennessee. It is not even just about a friendship. But rather, it is about understanding on a deeper level: beyond people's personal histories to where they live in their hearts, and then helping them achieve their goals and applauding them when they get there.

Sympathy & Empathy: A Spiritual Insight

NAME THAT *MITZVAH!*

According to the *Torah* (*Exodus* 22:20–23), we must be especially sensitive to the needs of people who can easily be taken advantage of and bullied. Not only can we be sympathetic to those who are most vulnerable, but we can and must be empathetic. After all, we know what being "bullied" is all about; our ancestors were slaves in Egypt and were oppressed (כִּי־גֵרִים הֱיִיתֶם בְּאֶרֶץ מִצְרָיִם /Ki Gerim hehyitem b'Eretz Mitzrayim – **Because you were strangers in the Land of Egypt**).

From this passage and other sources, various *Mitzvot* are derived.

*For further details, please see **NAME THAT *MITZVAH!* in *Chapter 9* of this book.***

THE BOX SCORE

In this chapter we discussed three extraordinary acts of sportsmanship shown by one teammate to another. High school track star Lisa Kincaid, without hurting her team, apparently, allowed a teammate to finish ahead of her in a race, qualifying this teammate to earn a varsity letter. By openly supporting Jackie Robinson, Harold "Pee Wee" Reese, a player from the Jim Crow south, made it clear to all that Robinson was welcome as a member of the Dodgers and MLB. Finally, another diverse pair of (college and NBA) teammates, Bernard King and Ernie Grunfeld, were able to empathize with each other, forming a special bond, facilitating their reaching certain goals in life.

In the Jewish world we examined how Penina's behavior towards her husband's other wife Hanna, can be interpreted as a demonstration of "tough love," and may actually have helped Hanna conceive and later give birth to the prophet Samuel. We also read about Rabbi Abraham Isaac Kook, Israel's first (Ashkenazic) Chief Rabbi, and how his non-judgmental, tolerant approach toward fellow Jews of all backgrounds, brought these people closer to Judaism and helped strengthen the moral fabric of the pre-modern State of Israel.

Chapter 15
Leading by Example: Extraordinary Acts of Sportsmanship by Coaches and Captains

Celebrating Our Differences

The Best Sports Story of the Year

Retired New York high school boys' basketball coach, Jim Johnson, is a winner both on and off the court – and proved it on February 15, 2006. In, Rochester, New York's Greece Athena High School's "must-win" game against rival Spencerpost High School, Johnson decided to reward his loyal team manager, senior Jason McElwain, by allowing him to play the final minutes of the last regular season game. Although his Athena team had a double-digit lead, victory was not assured. Coach Johnson made this decision with the full support of his players and the home crowd.

J-Mac, as he is lovingly called by others, simply was not any ordinary team manager. In addition to his loyalty and dedication to the team, what had earned Jason a special place in the hearts of his coach, teammates, and schoolmates was that he was autistic. Despite this disability, his condition did not limit his dreams and aspirations.

After displaying terrifying behaviors, such as running in circles for an hour until he was sedated and banging his head against a wall during temper tantrums, Jason was diagnosed with severe autism at the age of two-and-a-half. His loving parents sought early intervention treatments, because autism can also impair a child's communication skills and ability to interact socially, delay a child's development, and have other serious effects. J-Mac himself didn't speak until age 5 and couldn't chew his food until nearly a year later.

But at a young age, J-Mac became interested in sports, especially basketball. Unfortunately, his physical skills were not strong enough to earn a spot on his school teams. Yet, realizing how passionate he was for basketball, Coach Jim Johnson gave Jason the opportunity to serve as the manager of the varsity squad. Before the fated game, Johnson gave Jason the chance to suit-up and sit on the bench with the varsity players. There was no promise that he would be given any playing time, though he told him he would try since it was the last game.

With four minutes and nineteen seconds remaining in the fourth quarter, Coach Johnson made a decision that not only would change J-Mac's life, but the lives of many others as well. It was Jason's time to contribute on the court to his beloved team's success. After missing his first two shots, Jason developed a hot hand hitting one shot after the other. In the final minutes of the game, Jason scored an amazing 20 points, making six of 10 three-pointers. He finished as the game's leading scorer. When the final buzzer sounded, the fans stormed the court mobbing the unlikely hero.

The next day, Jason's heroic story was shared on the local news. Soon after that, it went viral, making J-Mac a national celebrity; he met such people as President George W. Bush, Oprah Winfrey (who interviewed him on her show), and Magic Johnson. J-Mac's story was so moving that ESPN presented him with an esteemed ESPY Award for the Best Moment in Sports in 2006, beating out such feats as Kobe Bryant's 81-point game.

Not only did Coach Johnson's decision to give Jason the opportunity to play create a most memorable, "feel-good" moment in time for Jason, but it also gave him a platform to become a spokesman on behalf of autism. In addition to his serving as a coach and supermarket employee, Jason – whose #52 jersey was officially retired by his alma mater in 2013 – is an ambassador for autism awareness, research, and cure, speaking around the United States raising money and awareness for this most important cause. He has even written a book titled, *The Game of my Life*, with assistance of co-author Daniel Paisner.

Coach Johnson's decision to give a dedicated student some playing time has also been credited with inspiring numerous other school coaches to be more inclusive in their programs, encouraging them to engage more students with autism and other developmental disabilities to actively participate in prep sports.

It's good to be a winner, both on and off the court. Just ask J-Mac and his hero, Coach Jim Johnson.

Anne Burke and the Founding of the Special Olympics

When I first learned in 2000, that Chicago Alderman Ed Burke and his wife Anne were trying to adopt a black toddler who had been in their care as a foster child, I was not surprised. After all, it was well known to me that the Burkes were a "power couple" who promoted inclusivity. They were champion advocates on behalf of the most vulnerable members of society.

In addition to their extraordinary deeds of adoption, Anne was a primary founder of the Special Olympics. Although the Special Olympics could not have been expanded into the international program that it is without the work of the late Eunice Kennedy Shriver and the funding led by the Joseph P. Kennedy, Jr. Foundation, it was Anne Burke who created and implemented the template for this outstanding organization.

Back in 1965, Anne Burke was 21 years old and a physical education instructor for the Chicago Park District. She volunteered to teach sports classes for intellectually disabled youth at a Chicago Park District program funded by the Kennedy Foundation. In Anne Burke's own words, "I had never even seen a retarded person. Parents wouldn't bring them to the parks because kids would make fun of them. I got the [able] kids in the park to be my junior counselors, so they were not making fun of [the disabled kids]. After a year, I had about 100 kids, and people were saying, 'This is good.'" (In those days, such disabled individuals were known as "mentally retarded".)

This game-changing experience got Anne Burke thinking big. Why not have an Olympic type event in Chicago "to bring more disabled to the program and so that Chicagoans could see that these children had abilities"?

Meanwhile on the East Coast, similar ideas were running through the mind of Eunice Kennedy Shriver. Inspired by her mentally challenged sister, Rosemary, with whom she shared a close relationship, Eunice Shriver was motivated to do as much as she could to promote programs to enhance the lives of the mentally disabled.

The two women met in Washington, D.C. Anne Burke then submitted a proposal for funding to the Kennedy Foundation, which led to a $25,000 grant to hold what became the pilot program for Special Olympics. Known as the Chicago Special Olympics, Anne Burke produced a fabulously successful meet on July 20, 1968. Originally intended only to attract participants from Illinois and states nearby, this first event ended up with representatives from 26 states and Canada.

What emerged from the passion and extraordinarily organized leadership of Anne Burke culminating in the amazing Chicago Special Olympics of 1968 led to the creation by the Kennedy Foundation of Special Olympics, Inc. An international organization with a presence in each of the 50 United States, Special Olympics continues to impact upon the lives of a countless number of mentally challenged as well as able people.

We all know how the Kennedy family turned out, but what became of the 21-year-old physical education instructor with ambitions to change the world? While raising her family, Anne attended and graduated law school. Her life's mission was, in large part, devoted to improving the lives of the disabled and at-risk children. Burke's law career culminated into serving as an Illinois Supreme Court Justice. It is clear from her career and life choices that she continues to believe in the power of service and including everyone in our nation's public life.

Shaya's Story

One of the most moving emails that I have ever received was an account entitled *Shaya's Story*. I received this from multiple sources in about the year 2000. This true story is described fully in Rabbi Pesach Krohn's book *Echoes of the Maggid* and bears the title *Perfection at the Plate*.

In this brief story, Rabbi Krohn describes in detail a speech given by the father of a learning disabled child at a fundraising dinner for the school which his son, Shaya, attended. After lauding the virtues of the school and its dedicated staff, the father asks the rhetorical question, "Where is Hashem's perfection?" He immediately responds, "I believe that when Hashem brings a child like this into the world, the perfection that He seeks is in the way people react to this child." Shaya's dad then retells the story that led to his most thoughtful, philosophical response.

The father tells how one time when he and Shaya walked past a park at a *Yeshiva* that Shaya attended on Sundays, they saw boys that Shaya knew playing baseball. Shaya told him that he would like to join the game. The father then relayed Shaya's request to the boys, and a member of the team that was losing, invited Shaya to be a part of his team. The team ended up rallying, and with two outs in the bottom of the ninth inning and the bases loaded with "Shaya's team" down by only two runs, Shaya was due to bat. Not only did his teammates insist that he hit, but one of his teammates assisted him. Even with this support, Shaya only hit a weak grounder to the pitcher. Instead of simply tossing the ball to first base and ending the game, the opposing pitcher lobbed the ball to right field. When the right fielder threw the ball (also purposely) over the third baseman's head, everyone yelled, "Run to second, run to second!" With the support of players from both teams, Shaya hit a "walk-off grand slam." After he stepped on home plate, all 18 players from both teams hoisted Shaya on their shoulders and gave him a hero's tribute.

The father then concluded his speech by sharing: "That day, those 18 boys reached their level of perfection. . . ."

THE BOX SCORE

Although inclusivity may appear to be a modern invention, its principles have been clearly articulated in the *Torah*. While being reminded of the 200-plus years of slavery in Egypt, the Jewish people are commanded that they must reach out to include all people, especially society's most vulnerable who, oftentimes, are shunned by members of the mainstream.

The stories of Jason McElwain and his compassionate coach along with the creation of the Special Olympics are inspirational reminders of the importance of reaching out to those less fortunate and ensuring that they are provided with opportunities comparable to those in the mainstream. *Shaya's Story* teaches that making decisions to include those with disabilities in mainstream activities should not require the involvement of an adult. At a young age, youth need to be taught the importance of inclusivity.

Inclusivity is a special type of sportsmanship and *Derekh Eretz v'Khavod.*

NAME THAT *MITZVAH!*

Be Inclusive of All People – Especially the Most Vulnerable

According to the *Torah*, we must reach out to and be inclusive of all people, especially those who can be exploited easily. The *Torah* (*Exodus* 22:20-23) lists three groups in particular: the widow (אַלְמָנָה/*Ahlmana*), orphan (יָתוֹם/*Yatom*), and convert to Judaism (גֵּר/*Ger*). The reason why we should be especially vigilant is that we know what being mistreated is all about; after all, we (i.e., our ancestors) were slaves in Egypt and were oppressed (כִּי־גֵרִים הֱיִיתֶם בְּאֶרֶץ מִצְרָיִם/*ki gerim hehyitem b'Eretz Mitzrayim* – **Because you [the Jewish People] were strangers in the Land of Egypt**). From this passage and other sources, various *Mitzvot* (previously listed in this book) are derived.

Only the *Torah* and its (Divine) Author are Perfect

שֶׁלֹּא לְהוֹסִיף עַל הַמִּצְוֹת וּפֵרוּשָׁן

Shehlo L'hosif Ahl HaMitzvot U-Pherushan

Not to Add to the Mitzvot and Their Interpretations

Sefer HaChinukh #454; *Sefer HaMitzvot, LT* #313

שֶׁלֹּא לִגְרֹעַ מִכָּל הַמִּצְוֹת וּפֵרוּשָׁן

Shehlo LiGroah MiKol HaMitzvot U-Pherushan

Not to Deduct from the Mitzvot and Their Interpretations

Sefer HaChinukh #455; *Sefer Ha Mitzvot, LT* #314

These two *Mitzvot* are learned from the *Biblical* verse:

אֵת כָּל הַדָּבָר אֲשֶׁר אָנֹכִי מְצַוֶּה אֶתְכֶם
אֹתוֹ תִשְׁמְרוּ לַעֲשׂוֹת
לֹא־תֹסֵף עָלָיו וְלֹא תִגְרַע מִמֶּנּוּ׃

Et kol ha-davar asher Anokhi m'tzaveh etkhem, ohtoh tishm'ru la-asot, lo tohsef ahlahv v'lo ti-grah mi-mehnu.

Everything that I command you, you shall observe and perform; do not add to nor diminish from it (*Deuteronomy* 13:1).

We are also reminded by these two *Mitzvot* that no human being, plant, or animal are without flaw; only the Almighty and His *Torah* are perfect. As the Psalmist King David wrote:

תּוֹרַת ה' תְּמִימָה מְשִׁיבַת נָפֶשׁ

Toraht HaShem T'mima m'shivat nahfesh

The Torah of HaShem is perfect, restoring one's soul (*Psalms* 19:8).

"May Their Memories be for a Blessing:" Paying It Back Posthumously

After a person passes away s/he is best remembered for the way that they led their life. At times a person is also remembered posthumously for how they distributed the assets of their estate.

Coach Dean Smith & His Lettermen

One of the most winning college basketball coaches of all time was University of North Carolina's (UNC) Dean Smith. A reserve guard on the legendary 1952 Phog Allen-coached Kansas Jayhawk NCAA title team, Smith distinguished himself as a bright and progressive coach and leader who truly cared about the wellbeing of his players.

In addition to winning two NCAA championships (1982 and 1993) as coach of the UNC Tar Heels, Smith is remembered for introducing the "foul-line huddle" where, before shooting a free throw, a player would relay to his four teammates a play call from their coach. Smith also is credited with popularizing the four-corner offense. This was a stalling technique oftentimes used by Smith's Tar Heels teams to preserve a narrow lead during the final minutes of a game. Essentially it was a hybrid of "keep-away" and "chicken," in which the UNC players would hold-off from trying to score by passing the ball amongst teammates, daring the opposition to steal the ball or foul one of the Tar Heels. The four-corner offense was so successful that it forced the NCAA to introduce the shot clock, something that was already employed in the NBA.

In the on-the-court category of sportsmanship, "Thank the Passer" was a trademark of Dean Smith-led teams (as well as Coach John Wooden's teams). This ritual established the culture of generosity and team play that was the essence of both men's coaching styles: Any player who scored a basket was required to briefly acknowledge his teammate who assisted with the pass. Even the smallest gesture demonstrated that a player remembered he was part of a team.

Off-the-court, Smith was a trailblazer among his southern white coaching colleagues. While others recruited only white players, Smith began recruiting African-American players in the 1960s. A graduate of KU with a degree in mathematics, Smith also placed a high priority on academics. In fact, about 95% of the men who played for him at UNC graduated, including Michael Jordan and Vince Carter, both of whom returned to UNC to complete their bachelor's degrees during their respective NBA careers.

In addition to being an innovator during his lifetime, perhaps the most creative innovation of Smith was not revealed to the public and its actual beneficiaries until after he passed away. About a month after his death on February 7, 2015, all of the players who earned a varsity letter while playing for Coach Smith during his 36-year tenure at UNC received a $200 check with a cover letter from a lawyer based in Charlotte, North Carolina. Attorney Tim Breedlove, the Trustee of the Dean E. Smith Revocable Trust, sent a letter to each of the 184 Tar Heel basketball lettermen whom Smith mentored from 1961–1997.

The personalized letters read in part:

". . . Each player was important and special to Coach Smith and when he prepared his estate plan, Coach wanted to reach out to each of his letterman [sic]. Accordingly, Coach directed that following his passing, each letterman be sent a two hundred dollar ($200.00) check with the message 'enjoy a dinner out, compliments of Coach Dean Smith.' Enclosed is a check in the amount of two hundred dollars ($200.00) with notation 'dinner out.'"

Although it is my opinion that Dean Smith's players would have always remembered their beloved coach for his acts of kindness even without this extraordinary "dinner-out-on-me" gift, by giving them the aforementioned posthumous present, Smith reminded us all of the importance of exhibiting sportsmanship-type behavior at all times, both on and off the court.

Paying It Back Posthumously: Spiritual Insights

The Magnanimous Beneficence of Anne Scheiber

A good secretary is a person who is not only adept at customary office skills, but is shrewd and protective of his/her boss.

In December 1995, a lawyer persistently tried to schedule a meeting with Yeshiva University President Rabbi Dr. Norman Lamm, but the rabbi's secretary was equally persistent in trying to shield him from such a meeting. After all, she was concerned that the lawyer was trying to distract Rabbi Lamm from his work. The secretary finally relented and scheduled the meeting.

At the meeting, the attorney presented Rabbi Lamm with a handwritten note from his deceased client, Ms. Anne Scheiber, in which she discussed her life, highlighting the discrimination that she endured in the workforce during the first half of the 20th century. A law school graduate and seasoned bookkeeper, Scheiber claimed that her government employer, discriminated against her because she was both Jewish and a woman.

From the time of her retirement in 1944 until her death in 1995, the reclusive Ms. Scheiber became an astute investor in blue-chip stocks, taking her initial life savings of $5,000 and parlaying it into a portfolio of stocks valued at more than $20 million. Anne Scheiber felt that the best use of her fortune would be to assist Jewish women in their pursuit of equal treatment in the workforce. Even though Ms. Scheiber did not know anybody from Yeshiva University (YU), she felt that this institution of higher learning was best equipped to help her reach her goals – albeit, posthumously.

Yeshiva University used this magnanimous gift to establish the Anne Scheiber Scholarship Fund. According to the YU website, this fund was established "for financially and academically deserving Jewish women studying at Stern College for Women . . . and Albert Einstein College of Medicine . . . 'who have indicated their desire to assist in the development of humanity, and alleviate pain and suffering.'" Because of Anne Scheiber's generosity, many Jewish women have graduated from medical school and other professional disciplines.

NAME THAT *MITZVAH!*

In Jewish tradition, it is important for parents to pass along to their descendants the Jewish values by which they led their lives, as well as their real and personal property. After the Israelites captured *Eretz Yisrael* (the Land of Israel), the land was then divided among all of the tribes (with the exception of *Levi*, as their job was to administer the Holy Temple). It was important that each tribe retain its own identity, as much as possible, both in terms of the land that its members owned and the customs they practiced. Accordingly, per the *laws of inheritance* (נַחֲלוֹת/*Nachalot*), the first heirs were the sons of the deceased. An Israelite woman assumed the identity of the tribe of her husband and shared in his inheritance. Oftentimes, Israelite women would "switch" tribes when they married a man from a different tribe. The intricate laws of *Nachalot* (*inheritance*) are described in *Sefer HaMitzvot, Ahseh #248* (the final *Mitzvah Ahseh* in Maimonides's collection of 248 – corresponding to the 248 limbs/organs in the human body). In *Sefer HaChinukh #400* [מִצְוַת דִּינֵי נְחָלוֹת/ *Mitzvat Dinei N'chalot - The Mitzvah of the Laws of Inheritance*], the author elaborates upon Maimonides's description. The *Torah* source for this *Mitzvah* is *Numbers* 27:8-11 which states:

וְאֶל־בְּנֵי יִשְׂרָאֵל תְּדַבֵּר לֵאמֹר
אִישׁ כִּי־יָמוּת וּבֵן אֵין לוֹ
וְהַעֲבַרְתֶּם אֶת־נַחֲלָתוֹ לְבִתּוֹ:
וְאִם־אֵין לוֹ בַּת וּנְתַתֶּם אֶת־נַחֲלָתוֹ לְאֶחָיו:
וְאִם־אֵין לוֹ אַחִים וּנְתַתֶּם אֶת־נַחֲלָתוֹ לַאֲחֵי אָבִיו:
וְאִם־אֵין אַחִים לְאָבִיו וּנְתַתֶּם אֶת־נַחֲלָתוֹ
לִשְׁאֵרוֹ הַקָּרֹב אֵלָיו מִמִּשְׁפַּחְתּוֹ וְיָרַשׁ אֹתָהּ
וְהָיְתָה לִבְנֵי יִשְׂרָאֵל לְחֻקַּת מִשְׁפָּט
כַּאֲשֶׁר צִוָּה ה' אֶת־מֹשֶׁה:

V'el B'nei Yisrael t'daber lehmor, ish ki yamut u-ven ein lo, v'ha-avartem et nachalato l'vito. V'im ein lo bat u-ntatem et nachalato l'echav. V'im ein lo achim u-ntatem et nachalato la-achei aviv. V'im ein achim l'aviv u-ntatem et nachalto, li-shero hakarov elav mi-mishpachto v'yarash otah, v'ha-y'ta liVnei Yisrael l'chukat mishpat, ka-asher tziva HaShem et Moshe.

And to the Children of Israel speak these words saying: "When a man dies and does not have a son, his inheritance should be transferred to his daughter. If he [also] does not have a daughter, then you shall give his inheritance to his brothers. If he has no brothers, then you shall give his inheritance to the brothers of his father. And if his father does not have any brothers, then you shall give his inheritance to his relative who is closest to him of his family, and he shall inherit it. And this shall be for the Children of Israel a statute of judgment as HaShem commanded Moses."

The intricacies of these most important, but complex, *Halakhot* (*laws*) are delineated further in the *Shulchan Arukh, Choshen Mishpat* 276–289.

THE BOX SCORE

We are reminded by the accounts of Coach Smith and philanthropist Anne Scheiber of the importance of proper estate planning. In Jewish tradition, the proper distribution of assets after a person's death is very important as it helps ensure that one's material assets are used in a way that properly reflect the values by which the deceased led their life.

In many ways, Coach Dean Smith and Ann Scheiber were polar opposites. Smith led a very public life, while Scheiber chose an exremely reclusive one. One thing they shared in common was a desire to teach valuable lessons after their deaths through their estate planning. Coach Smith chose to express his gratitude (a form of sportsmanship) by giving each of his 184 lettermen the token gift of a dinner out to remind them they were always members of his team. Scheiber, in turn, made a magnanimous gift (an off-the-charts expression of *Derekh Eretz v'Khavod*/**Respect and Honor**) to enable many women to study medicine and other disciplines and, hopefully, to have opportunities she did not have because of discrimination.

Chapter 16
Opponents, But NOT Enemies: Extraordinary Acts of Sportsmanship towards Opponents

How Do We Treat the Opposition?

The Concession Golf Club: Jack Nicklaus and Tony Jacklin

Ever wonder about the origin of certain names?

When it comes to football fields, baseball stadiums, and other arenas, nowadays, it is usually rather easy to figure out. Just follow the money. After all, stadium-naming rights are an important revenue stream for many professional and college teams.

There is a certain golf course, however, whose name and the meaning behind it is far more valuable than the amount of money a corporate sponsor would ever pay.

Two legendary retired golf pros, American Jack Nicklaus and Britain's Tony Jacklin, led the design of the Concession Golf Club, in Bradenton, Florida. First opened in 2006, this course earned its name from a world famous act of sportsmanship by Nicklaus towards Jacklin in the 1969 Ryder Cup competition.

Founded in 1927, the Ryder Cup match is played every other year between a U.S. and a European team of golf pros. In 1969, the competition was between the teams fielded by the United States and England. In an exciting, tight match, after 17 holes the score was tied. Unlike other tournaments where sudden death would be played in the event of a tie after the 18th hole, in this tournament a tie is permitted. On the 18th hole, an up-and-coming 29-year-old star from the US, Jack Nicklaus, was able to finish off the hole with a putt from five feet away. To tie the American team, a rising British star, 25-year-old Tony Jacklin, would need to make a two-foot putt. With millions of people from around the world watching, Nicklaus did an amazing thing. Instead of putting Jacklin on the spot and subject him to possible embarrassment in front of his home crowd in England if he were to miss the putt, he decided to concede the putt. So, before Jacklin could make the shot, Nicklaus picked up and removed Jacklin's ball marker. Nicklaus was quoted in *Golf Digest* as saying, "I don't think you would have missed it, but I wasn't going to give you the chance, either."

DIDJA KNOW that according to American humorist/author Mark Twain, "It's good sportsmanship not to pick up lost golf balls while they are still rolling"? What do you think Twain meant by that?

That year, there was no single winner of the Ryder Cup match – the tie essentially meant that the United States and Great Britain shared the honor but since America had won in 1967, they kept the trophy that year. Not only was this the beginning of a long friendship between two magnificent golf pros from different parts of the world, but it was the inspiration for Nicklaus and Jacklin deciding to name a golf course they designed together – over 30 years later – The Concession Golf Club.

How Do We Treat the Opposition? Spiritual Insights

NAME THAT *MITZVAH!*

שֶׁלֹּא לְהַלְבִּין פְּנֵי אָדָם מִיִּשְׂרָאֵל

Shehlo L'halbin P'nei Ahdahm MiYisrael

Not to Cause the Face of a Fellow Jew to Turn White (from Shame)
Sefer HaChinukh #240; Sefer HaMitzvot, LT #303

Our Sages teach that when a person publicly embarrasses a fellow Jew, it is analogous to killing him, since he has caused the blood to drain from his face. Although this is a *Torah* commandment for Jewish people to observe, it can and should be universalized, that is, applied to people of all faiths and backgrounds. (For further details see *Chapter 6*, section titled *Public Shaming: A Spiritual Insight*.)

DIDJA KNOW

that the Hebrew word for a *tie* (*in sports*) is תֵּיקוּ (*Teiku*), and that it is anacronym for תִּשְׁבִּי יְתָרֵץ/קֻשְׁיוֹת וּבְעָיוֹת *Tishbe Y'taretz Kushyot uV-ayot* (*the Tishbite* [*Elijah*] *will resolve all* [*unresolved*] *questions and problems*)? Based upon a deep philosophical principle (i.e., that when *Mashiach* [the **Messiah**] comes, all unresolved *Halakhic* [**Jewish legal**] matters will be settled), this word is an example of how modern Hebrew oftentimes evolves from *Biblical* or *Talmudic* terms.

How Do We Treat the Opposition (Even) When He Is the Enemy?

Defying the Evil Spirit of the Nazis: Luz Long Advises Jesse Owens

Although athletic achievement is the hallmark of the Olympic Games, often, historical messages of the political kind are also delivered in this venue. In 1936, Germany hosted the Summer Olympics in Berlin and Hitler wanted to use these games, in part, to show the world that his desired Aryan race was superior to all others, especially blacks and Jews.

Jewish sprinters Marty Glickman and Sam Stoller were held back by their coaches at the last minute from competing in the 400-meter relay as members of the U.S. team. The coaches claimed they needed faster runners, because the German team was faster than expected – despite the Americans being a solid favorite. Yet, Marty Glickman claimed throughout his life that the decision was an anti-Semitic act at worst, or kowtowing to the Germans at best – and his allegations were supported, though not in written documents, by the other runners who were not removed (including Jesse Owens and Ralph Metcalf who took their places in the relay) and even the president of the Olympic committee at the time. According to the *New York Times*, Stoller called the occasion, "the most humiliating episode in my life."

African Americans Jesse Owens and Ralph Metcalfe participated in multiple events, including the relay. Owens strenuously protested when Glickman and Stoller were pulled. At the time, the track superstar had already won three of four gold medals (his historic fourth was that relay). Those wins sent, a powerful message to Hitler and his Nazi followers that members of the so-called Aryan race were **not** superior to the rest of the world. And Owens's defense of his teammates against the decision of their coaches shows what an honorable man he was, as well.

One of Owens's events was the long jump. To qualify for the semifinals in the long jump competition, an athlete had to clear 7.15 meters (23.46 feet). This distance is one that Owens had cleared during high school and should have posed no great challenge for him. However, understandably, he became nervous, causing him to foul in his first two attempts by taking off from beyond the starting line. He knew that he had only one more opportunity to qualify for the semifinals.

After Owens's second failed attempt, a tall 23-year-old German, Carl Ludwig "Luz" Long, the greatest long jumper in Europe at that time, came over to Jesse and recommended that he mark the take-off line several inches in front of the actual line. Long felt that this would prevent his American rival from fouling and thus being disqualified. Heeding his opponent's advice, Owens advanced to the semifinals and then on to the finals where he won the gold medal. Luz Long finished right behind Owens, earning a silver medal.

After Owens's victory, in front of Hitler and 100,000 spectators, Long went over to congratulate Jesse and lifted his hand symbolically crowning him as the champ. After the Olympics, according to Owens, he and Long stayed in contact with each other, While Owens died of lung cancer in 1980 at the age of 66, Long had barely reached the age of 30, as he was killed in 1943 while fighting for Germany and the Nazis during World War II.

Jesse Owens remarked about his camaraderie with his opponent, "It took a lot of courage for him to befriend me in front of Hitler. You can melt down all the medals and cups I have, and they wouldn't be a plating on the 24-karat friendship that I felt for Luz Long in that moment."

How Do We Treat the Opposition (Even) When He is the Enemy? Spiritual Insights

Jonathan and David

Talk about an awkward friendship. Jonathan, the son of King Saul and his heir apparent, was best friends with David. An accomplished musician (lyrist) and poet (*Book of Psalms*), David was Saul's top soldier and the popular choice among the Israelites to succeed him. Because of David's immense popularity, Saul was insanely jealous of and did not trust David – to the point of wanting to kill him. Jonathan, however, realized that David was better suited than he to succeed Saul, and viewed himself as David's top aide/supporter:

וְאַתָּה תִּמְלֹךְ עַל יִשְׂרָאֵל וְאָנֹכִי אֶהְיֶה לְךָ לְמִשְׁנֶה/V'atah timlokh ahl Yisrael v'anokhi eh-yeh l'kha l'mishneh – **"And you [David] will rule over Israel and I [Jonathan] will be second to you"** (Samuel I: 23:17).

In spite of Jonathan's close friendship with David, Saul still perceived David as a threat to his sovereignty. Saul made his intentions of killing David clear to Jonathan. Caught in the midst of this conflict, Jonathan decided to do the right thing and protect his pal. Instead of encouraging his dear friend to attend a feast hosted by King Saul to celebrate the upcoming **new month** (Rosh Chodesh), Jonathan advised David to hide from the wrath and jealousy of his father. He also devised a secret signal for David that directed him as to what he should do when Jonathan came with an assistant to the field where David would be hiding and shot three arrows:

וְהִנֵּה אֶשְׁלַח אֶת־הַנַּעַר לֵךְ מְצָא אֶת הַחִצִּים
אִם־אָמֹר אֹמַר לַנַּעַר
הִנֵּה הַחִצִּים מִמְּךָ וָהֵנָּה קָחֶנּוּ וָבֹאָה
כִּי שָׁלוֹם לְךָ וְאֵין דָּבָר חַי־ה':
וְאִם־כֹּה אֹמַר לָעֶלֶם
הִנֵּה הַחִצִּים מִמְּךָ וָהָלְאָה
לֵךְ כִּי שִׁלַחֲךָ ה':

V'hineh eshlach et ha-na-ahr lekh m'tza et ha-chitzim, ihm ahmor omar la-na-ahr, hineh ha-chitzim mim'kha va-hehna kachenu va-vo-ah, ki shalom l'kha v'ein davar chai HaShem. V'ihm ko omar la-elem, hineh ha-chitzim mim'kha va-hala, lekh ki shilachakha HaShem.

"And behold I will send the lad [saying to him] 'Go and find the arrows.' If I say to the lad: 'The arrows are on this side of you, [then this is a signal for you to] take them and return, because there is peace for you, and there is no concern, as HaShem lives.' However if I tell the young man thus: 'The arrows are beyond you,' [then this is a signal for you to] go, for Hashem has sent you away" (Samuel I 20:21-22).

When Jonathan came to the field, he warned David that his life was still in danger and that he must flee, and they bid each other farewell:

וַיֹּאמֶר יְהוֹנָתָן לְדָוִד
לֵךְ לְשָׁלוֹם אֲשֶׁר נִשְׁבַּעְנוּ שְׁנֵינוּ אֲנַחְנוּ
בְּשֵׁם ה' לֵאמֹר
ה' יִהְיֶה בֵּינִי וּבֵינֶךָ
וּבֵין זַרְעִי וּבֵין זַרְעֲךָ עַד עוֹלָם:

Va-yomer Y'honatan l'David, lekh l'shalom asher nishbanu sh'neinu anachnu, b'shem HaShem lehmor, HaShem yi-yeh beini u-veinekha, u-vein zari u-vein zarakha ahd olam.

And Jonathan said to David: "Go in peace as the two of us have sworn in the name of HaShem, saying HaShem will [be a witness] between me and you, and between my descendants and your descendants – forever" (*Samuel* I 20:42).

David survived Saul's paranoia and rose to become the King of Israel. Tragically, along with his father and two younger brothers, Jonathan died in a fierce battle against the Philistines (*Samuel* I 31:1-6).

NAME THAT *MITZVAH!*

שֶׁלֹּא לַעֲמֹד עַל דַּם רֵעִים

Shehlo LaAmod Ahl Dahm Rei-im

Not to Stand By Idly While Someone's Blood is Shed
Sefer HaChinukh #237;
Sefer HaMitzvot, LT #297

Realizing that David was not really an enemy of King Saul, when Jonathan warned David he fulfilled the *Mitzvah* of not to stand by idly. After all, his recommendation to his dear friend helped save David's life. Were Jonathan to support his father's sick (presumably, undiagnosed mental illness) desire to murder David, by not warning his friend, he would, very possibly, have violated this ever-so-important *Mitzvah*.

Spontaneous Acts of Kindness

The Most Inspirational Home Run Ever

What is the most inspirational home run in the history of baseball? Was it Babe Ruth's "called shot" in the 1932 World Series against the Chicago Cubs? Was it Bobby Thomson's "shot heard round the world" that beat the Dodgers and catapulted the New York Giants into the 1951 World Series? One could make a case that Carlton Fisk's homer that he "waved fair" in Game 6 of the 1975 World Series is the most inspirational of all time. For millennials, perhaps the most memorable, inspirational round-tripper was the one hit by St. Louis Cardinals 2011 World Series MVP David Freese to send the Series to Game 7.

If this were a multiple-choice test, my answer would be "None of the above." Although a strong argument can be made for each of these great home run moments, I believe the most inspirational one in the history of baseball was hit by Sara Tucholsky.

Who in the world is Sara Tucholsky?

Sara is a former outfielder for the Western Oregon University women's softball team. In April 2008 in the second game of a doubleheader against Central Washington University in a must-win game for playoff contention, Sara – a five-foot-two-inch senior outfielder with a career batting average of .153 who had never hit a homer in high school or college – cleared the centerfield fence and appeared to have just hit a three-run homer.

In her excitement, Sara missed stepping on first base and, when she turned back, she hurt her knee so badly that all she could do was crawl back and tag first base. There was no way that she could round the remaining three bases and complete her home run trot. Sara's teammates knew that if they would assist her in rounding the bases, Sara would be called out. According to the umpire (whose ruling was later found to be incorrect), had Western Oregon substituted a pinch runner, the play would have been ruled a two-run single with the pinch runner taking first base only.

Then something virtually unheard of in the world of competitive sports – at any level – happened. According to the *New York Times*, Central Washington's strong first baseman Mallory Holtman asked the umpires, "Excuse me, would it be OK if we carried her [Sara] around and she touched each bag?" The umpires then huddled and decided that this was permissible. Mallory then enlisted the help of her teammate, shortstop Liz Wallace, and with hands crossed and locked together, the two teammates of the opposing team carried the injured Tucholsky around the base path stopping at each bag to give Sara the opportunity to tag the base. After rounding third base, Sara Tucholsky, with her newfound "legs," completed her home run trot when she stepped on home plate. Sara's homer, enabled by the compassionate gestures of Holtman and Wallace, later proved to be the winning run as Western Oregon knocked Central Washington out of playoff contention and eventually won their conference title.

Had Mallory and Liz not done what they did, in great likelihood, the outcome of the game would have been different, perhaps allowing Central Washington to make the playoffs. In hindsight, which is always 20/20, did Holtman regret her decision? Not at all, as the *New York Times* reported: "She [Sara] hit it over the fence. She deserved it. Anybody would have done it. I just beat them to it." Did Mallory act contrary to what she was taught? Just the opposite; according to Mallory, her coach, Gary Frederick, taught his players that "winning is not everything."

This story received national attention from both the sports and general media, as such acts of sportsmanship in any sport at any level are rare. Western Oregon Coach Pam Knox quickly realized the significance of this event, when she spoke with USA Today: "When it happened I knew it was the best moment in my coaching career. I started calling my friends and family and they cried when I told them the story. So I knew this was something bigger than just me being emotional."

To me it's a "no-brainer" that Sara Tucholsky's only career homer is the most inspirational home run in the history of baseball. As inspirational as Ruth's "called shot," Thomson's "shot heard round the world," Fisk's waved round-tripper, and Freese's walk-off are, they all pale in comparison to what Mallory Holtman and Liz Wallace did to enable Sara to bask in a life highlight. It also allowed sports participants and fans the world over to learn what sportsmanship is all about.

When it comes to a celebrity sports star who best exemplifies spontaneous acts of sportsmanship, my vote goes to Central Washington University's first baseman, Mallory Holtman.

Spontaneous Acts of Kindness: A Spiritual Insight

In Search of (Matriarch) Sara's Successor

A good leader in any realm learns how to choose a top-notch staff and then makes sure that s/he delegates tasks to trusted members of their staff.

For his "chief of staff," Abraham was fortunate to choose a smart and loyal man named Eliezer. After the death of Abraham's beloved wife Sara, the main task that remained for our first patriarch was to ensure that Isaac married a woman whom he not only loved and respected but who was capable of succeeding Sara as the second matriarch of *B'nei Yisrael* (*the Children of Israel*). Abraham delegated Eliezer with the most important assignment of finding a woman who was worthy of and who desired to marry Isaac, subject, of course, to the consent of both future husband and wife.

In establishing the criteria for the next matriarch, Eliezer wanted to make sure that this special woman possessed, in particular, the virtue of **kindness** (חֶסֶד/ *Chesed*). Eliezer articulated these standards in his conversation with the Almighty:

וְהָיָה הַנַּעֲרָ אֲשֶׁר אֹמַר אֵלֶיהָ הַטִּי־נָא כַדֵּךְ וְאֶשְׁתֶּה
וְאָמְרָה שְׁתֵה וְגַם־גְּמַלֶּיךָ אַשְׁקֶה
אֹתָהּ הֹכַחְתָּ לְעַבְדְּךָ לְיִצְחָק
וּבָהּ אֵדַע כִּי־עָשִׂיתָ חֶסֶד עִם־אֲדֹנִי:

V'haya ha-na-ahra asher omar eleha hati na khadekh v'eshteh, v'am'ra sh'teh v'gahm g'malekha ashkeh, ota hokhachta l'avd'kha l'Yitzchak, u-va edah ki asita chesed ihm adoni.

"And it shall be that the young woman to whom I shall say 'please tip your jug [i.e., pour water] so that I may drink,' and she [then] says [on her own initiative] 'you drink and I will also provide water to your camels,' You [HaShem] have proven that she is [the right woman] for Your servant Isaac and through her I will know that You have performed acts of loving kindness with my master" (Genesis 24:14).

Soon after clearly articulating the parameters necessary for a potential matriarchal candidate to be deemed suitable to be Isaac's wife, a young woman, Rebecca, appeared and immediately expressed her kindness to Eliezer, perhaps even over-and-beyond his criteria. The passage in the *Torah* along with commentary teaches us that Rebecca acted spontaneously and expressed her great *Chesed* (*Loving Kindness*) to Eliezer in different ways:

- Instead of handing a jug to the travel-weary Eliezer for him to lift and drink from, Rebecca tipped the jug so that Eliezer only needed to exert minimal effort.

- When watering the camels, Rebecca did not distinguish between them. Rather, she treated them equally and gave them water simultaneously by pouring water into a trough so that all of the camels could partake at the same time.

- It is estimated that Rebecca needed the equivalent of 140 gallons of water in order to quench the thirst of the camels. She retrieved and carried all of the water on her own without any assistance.

- The words וַתְּמַהֵר/וַתָּרָץ – *va-t'maher/va-tarotz* (**and she hurried/and she ran**) (*Genesis* 24:18 & 20), teach us that Rebecca performed these acts of *Chesed* with great zeal. She did it because she wanted to, not because she had to. Rebecca did not have to be told to perform Acts of Loving Kindness; rather, her acts were spontaneous. She met Eliezer's criteria for the next matriarch of Israel – she had *Chesed* (*Loving Kindness*) in her DNA.

When Rebecca returned with Eliezer, she and Isaac realized right away that they had each met their *b'shert* (i.e., **soul mate**). *Midrashic* literature (*Genesis Rabba* 16) teaches that during Sara's lifetime, a light was always lit in Sara's tent, a blessing was found in her dough, and the Divine Presence would be hovering over her tent. After Sara died, all three of these phenomena stopped. However, the first time Rebecca entered the tent, as Isaac's bride-to-be, all three of these miracles reoccurred.

NAME THAT *MITZVAH!*

Being a Good Host – הַכְנָסַת אוֹרְחִים (*Hakhnasat Orchim*)

By greeting Eliezer, a stranger in her eyes, in the manner that she did, Rebecca, just like her future father-in-law and mother-in-law would have done, performed this most important *Mitzvah*. Although it is universally understood that *Hakhnasat Orchim* is a *Mitzvah*, it is not one that is specifically listed in either *Sefer HaChinukh* or *Sefer HaMitzvot*. It is a **Rabbinic Commandment** (*Mitzvah D'Rabbanan*). The Sages agree that, by properly inviting and caring for guests, one performs an important act of *Chesed* (*Loving Kindness*). They differ as to exactly under which *Torah*-ordained Commandment such acts of *Chesed* belong. (For further details, please see the section titled *The Fans: What is Acceptable Behavior? Spiritual Insghts* in *Chapter 9* of this book.)

Losing on Purpose

The Art of "Tanking"

"Throwing a game" or "Tanking" are terms oftentimes associated in the popular imagination with players who secretly conspire with professional gamblers to purposely commit acts that change the outcome of a game or series. If such acts are completed "successfully," the corrupt players are rewarded handsomely for their efforts. I think that most, if not all, sports historians will agree that the most notorious incident ever was the shameful case of the 1919 World Series between the Chicago White Sox and Cincinnati Reds.

Referred to by many as the "Black Sox," the team actually earned this nickname not because of the betting scandal, but rather because their owner was known to be so stingy that he charged the players 25 cents to clean their uniforms. So instead of wearing spotless white uniforms, the slighted players chose to wear dirty, black baseball apparel.

Although the White Sox were heavily favored to win the Series, they lost it. After this upset, it was alleged that eight Sox players accepted payments from professional gamblers to purposely lose the World Series. In spite of the fact that these eight players were acquitted by a Cook County Court (believed to be corrupt), MLB's first commissioner, former judge John Kenesaw Mountain Landis, banned these eight players for life from organized baseball. Hence, the origin of the expression and book/movie title *Eight Men Out*.

There have also been other point-shaving and game-fixing scandals in other sports at different levels of competition.

A more recent form of "tanking" is when a team does not try its hardest or play its best players because, in the minds of its coaches, executives (and sometimes even players), more can be gained from losing than winning. For many years, the order of the teams selecting in the NBA and other professional sports' drafts was determined strictly by final standings; the worse the record, the higher the pick. The teams with the worst record from each of the two divisions would then simply flip a coin to determine which team would have the overall #1 draft pick. In 1985, a lottery system was introduced to the NBA draft that expanded the number of teams who had a chance to win the right to pick #1. Over the years, this process has been modified several times to make it a fairer system.

A major benefit of a lottery system versus simply a coin flip between the league's two worst teams is that it presents less incentive, and thus, less of a conflict of interest for a team to "accidently, on-purpose" lose repeatedly (also referred to as "tanking"). By allowing the 14th worst team to participate in a lottery for the #1 draft pick, the theory is that teams are less tempted to try anything other than their hardest to win.

Although playing for home court advantage is usually seen as an incentive for most teams even after they have clinched a playoff spot, sometimes a playoff-bound team feels that it has a greater likelihood for success to qualify for the next playoff round if

it lost and played the team with the better record in the opening round.
Although this may seem rational, out of respect for the integrity of the sport, such behavior is totally unacceptable.

In a bizarre case in February 2015, two Tennessee women's high school basketball teams played each other and, through their blatantly incredible sloppy level of play, they made it abundantly clear to the referees and opposing players and fans that they were trying to do everything they could to lose. After all, the losing team would face the easier team to beat in the next round of the playoffs.

Some of the more blatant acts making it obvious to the referees that both teams were trying to "tank" include:

- One team intentionally missing 12 of its 16 free-throw attempts;
- A team's refusal to advance the ball past the half-court line in the requisite 10 seconds, in order to cause a turnover;
- Intentional three-second violations;

The one that "takes the cake" happened when a player tried shooting the ball into the wrong basket, but was stopped because of a 10-second violation. At the conclusion of the game, the referees filed a complaint with high school officials, which led to a series of punishments. These penalities included banning both teams from the high school state playoffs that year, as well as fining and placing both schools on probation.

By trying to purposely lose, the biggest losers ended up being both playoff-bound teams.

The Unpopular Popovich Decision

One of the most successful basketball coaches of all time, San Antonio Spurs' coach Gregg Popovich, has led his team to five NBA Championships. Thrice-named Coach of the Year, Popovich is especially admired for his keen ability to manage players. A strategy of his which has drawn great criticism recently is his decision to rest aging star players at the end of a long stretch of games. On November 29, 2012, "Coach Pop" sent four star players (Tony Parker, Tim Duncan, Manu Ginobili, and Danny Green) back home to San Antonio to rest and kept them out of a nationally televised game against the defending NBA champion Miami Heat at a game in Miami. None of these four stars had any known injuries. With the exception of Danny Green, all of the players were well into their thirties (old by NBA standards). Coach Popovich's rationale is that, to win championships, a coach must ensure that his players are strong enough at the end of the regular season to be effective contributors during the playoffs. Unfortunately, sometimes when teams reach the playoffs, their key players are suffering from fatigue or injuries and are unable to perform at a championship level. Before the game, Coach Pop told reporters, "We've done this before in hopes of making a wiser decision, rather than a popular decision. It's pretty logical."

Unfortunately, former Commissioner David Stern did not agree with Coach Popovich's strategy, and fined the Spurs $250,000. In the words of the Commissioner, "I apologize to all NBA fans. This was an unacceptable decision by the San Antonio Spurs . . ."

Coach Popovich's strategy can be viewed as both an act of good sportsmanship as well as badsportsmanship. It depends on from whose perspective you are analyzing the situation.

After all, Coach Pop's decision basically came down to him protecting his (older) players' health and the potential to win in the playoffs vs. the NBA's desire for TV viewers and fans who have paid big bucks to see star players, despite their fatigue. Money versus autonomy – a basic human political conundrum.

Is Coach Popovich's occasional one-game tanking good or bad sportsmanship? You make the call!

Losing on Purpose: Spiritual Insights

Giving Lot, Lots of Land

The Patriot Abraham refused to shirk any responsibility – whether real or perceived. After his brother Haran died, Abraham (at that time known as Abram) assumed responsibility for Haran's son Lot. Nephew Lot proved to be a challenge and was not grateful for the good that his Uncle Abraham (and Aunt Sara) provided for him. Through their beneficence, Lot accumulated land and livestock. When his shepherds had a dispute with the shepherds of Abraham, it was Abraham who conceded and gave Lot his choice of land. In a narcissistic fashion, Lot chose the better land and left the inferior for his uncle (*Genesis* 13:1-12). Although Abraham deserved to keep the choice land, he chose "to lose on purpose," probably in order to preserve a relationship with Lot and honor his brother Haran's memory.

Sibling Rivalry

A special relationship is the one between siblings. Many times, brothers and sisters can be best friends. At times, siblings can be embroiled in conflict with one another. In the world of psychology, the inherent competitive relationship between siblings is known as sibling rivalry. At its roots, siblings compete for the attention, love, and affection of their parents.

Sometimes sibling rivalry can manifest itself on the sports field or court. While, on too many occasions, siblings who participate in the same sport have an acrimonious relationship with one another, at times they are able to restrict the competitive nature of their relationship to only the times when they play against each another. Off the field or court, those athletes maintain a close, warm rapport with one another. Although this is the way a sibling relationship should be, unfortunately, many times this is not the case.

The following story is an "extraordinary" display of sibling rivalry between two of the greatest players in the history of women's tennis.

Competitors on the Court, Best Friends Off

In the world of sports, one of the most heartening sibling stories is the close and unique relationship between two of tennis's greatest stars, Venus and Serena Williams. During their illustrious careers, which began in the mid-1990s when they were teenagers, at times they were ranked as tennis's top two women players. Although they have not always maintained the top two spots in tennis rankings, they have remained #1 when it comes to sisters who have remained close friends, in spite of competing against one another. In fact, during a chapter of their professional lives, the two sisters shared a home. Later they bought homes on the same street, allowing themselves the option of spending maximum time with each other.

When Venus and Serena played against each another in the Lipton Championship in April 1999, it marked the first sister vs. sister final in professional tennis in 115 years. Since that historic competition, the sisters have been opponents in the final round of such venerable tournaments as the U.S. Open, Wimbledon, and the Australian Open. At their first finals meeting, Venus, the older sister by 15 months, beat Serena. As time passed, though, Serena would, more often than not, emerge as the victor.

Even though they are competitors with one another, because of their close relationship, the taste of victory is dulled somewhat when one sister beats the other. After defeating Serena in the 2001 U.S. Open, Venus stated, "I always want Serena to win. It's strange. I'm the bigger sister. I'm the one who takes care of her. I make sure she has everything even if I don't. I love her. It's hard."

In a most philosophical manner, Serena tempered the awkward feeling of competing against her sister. After winning the U.S. Open in 2002, Serena stated, "I prefer to play Venus because that means that we have reached our maximum potential and that we'll both go home winners. For me, I'm happy to play her in the finals."

On January 28, 2017, Venus and Serena met for the 28th time in their professional careers. This time they both qualified for the final round of the Australian Open. Serena was the winner, and with this victory, she became the all-time leader in women's tennis for the most Grand Slam title.

After this historic victory, here is what the sisters had to say:

Venus: "Congratulations, Serena, on number 23 [Grand Slam titles]. I have been right there with you. Some of them I have lost right there against you. It's been an awesome thing, your win has always been my win, you know that."

Serena: "There's no way I would be at 23 without her [Venus]; there's no way I would be at 1 without her. . . She's my inspiration. She's the only reason I'm standing here today, and the only reason that the Williams sisters exist."

Venus and Serena Williams serve as outstanding role models in illustrating how sisters can be both competitors and best friends. Their sibling rivalry is an extraordinary act of sportsmanship.

Sibling Rivalry: A Spiritual Insight

The Sister Act: Rachel Shares the Signals with Leah

Right before the *Chupah* wedding ceremony, it is traditional for the groom to visit his bride and place the veil over her face. This mini-ceremony is known as *Badeken* (**checking**). A reason for this ritual is that the groom wants to make sure that the woman dressed in the bridal gown is really the lady who he intends to marry, and that his future father-in-law did not switch daughters on him. After all, Jacob of the *Torah* was misled by his father-in-law Laban when he ended up marrying Leah instead of his true love, Rachel, the younger sister.

When we read the *Torah* text (*Genesis* 29:15-26) it is fair to conclude that this "mix-up" was caused exclusively on account of the deceit of Laban. However, when examining the discussion in the *Talmud* (*M'gilla* 13b & *Bava Batra* 123a) about this episode, we realize that the intended good sportsmanship of Rachel also contributed towards this outcome.

According to the *Talmud*, Rachel and Jacob anticipated that Laban may try substituting his older daughter Leah for her younger sister Rachel, since it was common for daughters to marry in their birth order. In an attempt to try to overcome this possible trick by Laban, Jacob and Rachel agreed that Rachel would give Jacob special secret signals to reassure him that it was indeed Rachel whom he was marrying. However, at the last moment, Rachel felt bad for Leah and, not wanting to cause her any shame, she shared these secret signs with her older sister. So when the night of the wedding arrived, Jacob looked to "his" bride for the "high sign" and, unbeknownst to him, it was Leah who delivered the correct signs.

In the case of these *Biblical* sisters, their sibling rivalry was even more complicated than the type that usually exists between sisters. Here, both women were competing for the love of the same man.

From Rachel's act, we learn that the relationship between siblings can be so close that, at times, they may even be willing to act in a selfless manner that may impair their future relationship. [In order to prevent such acts from occurring in the future, the *Torah* (*Leviticus* 18:18) – which was given about 400 years later – prohibits a man from marrying sisters. In approximately 1000 CE, the French Rabbinic Authority *Rabbenu Gershom*, prohibited polygamy.]

Practicing Acts of Sportsmanship

Team Spirit Institute Volunteers PRACTICING
Acts of Sportsmanship on the Chicago Bulls' court
at the United Center. Photos courtesy of
Team Spirit Institute/David Blachman, Photographer.

Top: Chicago
Blackhawks
Great Stan Mikita.
Photo courtesy
of the Chicago
Blackhawks.

Bottom:
A Striking Photo
PBA Legend
Carmen Salvino
jumping while
bowling a strike.
Photo courtesy of
Carmen Salvino.

To learn more
about both athletes'
special brands of
sportsmanship and
the innovations they
introduced to the
sports of hockey and
bowling, please read
Chapters 2 & 3.

			DALLAS BRONCOS											
IO	BP	MP	PLAYER	1	2	3	4	5	6	7	8	9	IO	R
			CARMEN SALVINO	20	39	57								
			RED ELKINS											
			JACK AYDELOTTE											
			DON BICKFORD											
			J.B. SOLOMON											

TOTAL SCORE

Crosstown Hall of Famers

To learn about how "Mr. Cub" (Ernie Banks, left) exemplifies hope, and "The Big Hurt" (Frank Thomas, right) illustrates might, please read *Chapters 3 & 25*.

Both photos courtesy of National Baseball Hall of Fame and Museum, Cooperstown, New York.

Top Left: **Brian Piccolo Touchdown!**
Top Right: Brian and wife Joy with daughters
(left to right) Traci, Kristi and Lori.
Photos courtesy of the Piccolo Family.

Bottom: Left-Right: Chicago Bears Owner & Coach
George "Papa Bear" Hallas, Assistant Coach
Phil Handler with Joy and Brian Piccolo on the day
Brian signed contract to play with the Bears.
Photos courtesy of the Piccolo Family.

"A coach is a teacher."

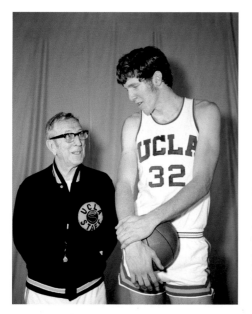

Coach (teacher) John Wooden with star player (student) Bill Walton. Photo courtesy of University of California, Los Angeles (UCLA).

To learn more about Coach John Wooden and Hall of Famer Bill Walton's teacher-student relationship, please read *Chapter 5*.

The Starting Five (left to right): Rabbi James, Max, Rita and Sophie Gordon & Bill Walton at Chicago's O'Hare International Airport in 2006. Photo courtesy of the Gordon Family/ Marilyn Gordon, Photographer.

Special Teamers

Top: F. Scott Fitzgerald (1896–1940) (Everett Historical/ Shutterstock.com). Bottom: Minnesota Viking Brent Novoselsky holding son Alec in 1994. Photo courtesy of the Novoselsky Family/ Andrea Novoselsky, Photographer.

To learn more about the connection between F. Scott Fitzgerald and Brent Novoselsky, besides both attending Ivy League schools (Fitzgerald – Princeton University and Novoselsky – University of Pennsylvania), please read *Chapter 5*.

The Scapegoating of Alfred Dreyfus and the Revival of Zionism (Chapter 9)

Top Left: Captain Alfred Dreyfus.
Photo Courtesy of the Library of Congress,
LC-DIG-ggbain-17080.
Top Right: Theodore Herzl on old Israeli
10 Shekel Banknote. (vkilikov/Shutterstock.com)

Bottom: The Degradation of Alfred Dreyfus
(Right) And A Caricature From The Anti-Semitic
Paris Newspaper, "La Libre Parole" (Left).
(Sa'ar Ya'acov/National Photo Collection,
State of Israel)

Top Left: Sports Journalist, Ed Sherman.
Top Right: *Chicago Sun-Times*
Sports Columnist, Rick Telander,
surrounded by Rabbis Gordon in 2011.
Photo courtesy of Team Spirit Institute/
Mark Weksler, Photographer.

Bottom: Sports Journalist,
Bruce Wolf, next to Aaron (left) &
Mark Weksler in 2007. Photo courtesy
of Team Spirit Institute.

Not Afraid to Be a Trailblazer

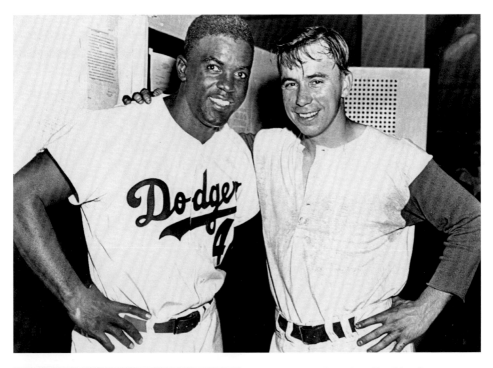

Top: **One Arm Over Two Shoulders?**
While Pee Wee Reese actually did put
his arm around Jackie Robinson in the clubhouse,
did he also do so on the field? Photo courtesy
of National Baseball Hall of Fame and Museum,
Cooperstown, New York.

To learn more about this debate among
historians, please see *Chapter 14*. You may also
want to check-out *Chapter 13* that discusses more
of Jackie Robinson's extraordinary contributions
to sports and U.S. history.

Bottom: Dr. Julian Bailes at World Premiere
Gala Screening of Sony Pictures *Concussion*
at AFI Fest 2015 in Hollywood, CA/see *Chapter 13*.
(Eric Charbonneau/Invision for Sony Pictures/
AP Images)

Top: Newlyweds Ed and Anne Burke at
the inaugural 1968 Chicago Special Olympics
held at Soldier Field.

Right: Justice Burke in a recent photo.
Both photos courtesy of Justice Anne M. Burke.

Defying the Evil Spirit of the Nazis: Luz Long Advises Jesse Owens (Chapter 16)

Top: Jesse Owens and Luz Long at the
Berlin Olympics, 1936.
Bottom: Jesse Owens and fellow Olympians
staying warm between events, 1936.

Both photos courtesy of the
Jesse Owens Family and The Ohio State
University Archives.

Ezra Schwartz — z"l: Sportsman, Fan and Jewish Patriot (Chapter 19)

Top: Ezra pitching for the Maimonides School M-Cats in June 2015.

Top Right: In October 2015 Ezra got together with friends to watch a Patriots' game in Israel.

Bottom: Gillette Stadium, Patriots vs. Titans, December 2015 (Robert Kraft hugging Elon Schwartz); Avi Schwartz is in the orange coat. (Elon and Avi are Ezra's brothers.) Photos courtesy of Dr. Ari and Ruth Schwartz (Ezra's Parents).

Top Left: Maimonides (1135–1204) on 1 Shekel 1986 Banknote from Israel. (Georgios Kollidas/Shutterstock.com)

Maimonides was the first to write a systematically indexed code of Jewish law ([still used today] known as the *Mishneh Torah/Yad HaChazaka* – see *Chapter 13*).

Top Right: Rabbi Abraham Isaac Kook (1865–1935) served as the first Chief Ashkenazic Rabbi of pre-State Israel/see *Chapter 14*.

Photo courtesy of the Library of Congress, LC-DIG-npcc-25595.

Bottom: Louis Brandeis (1856–1941). (Everett Historical/Shutterstock.com) Brandeis was the first Jewish U.S. Supreme Court Justice/see *Chapter 24*.

Jewish Firsts and Sportsmanship/*Derekh Eretz v'Khavod* (continued)

Top Right: Sandy Koufax – the first Jewish MLB pitcher to pitch four no-hitters and to be inducted into the Baseball Hall of Fame/see *Chapters 27 & 28.* Photo courtesy of National Baseball Hall of Fame and Museum, Cooperstown, New York.

Bottom Right: Rebecca Yoshor – Yeshiva University's first female athlete to be named an Academic All-America. Photo courtesy of Yeshiva University.

Bottom Left: Anne Frank – the first person (who perished in the Holocaust) whose diary was published in over 60 countries (and in 70 languages)/ see *Chapter 3.* (Tony Baggett/ Shutterstock.com)

Yankee Stars (On & Off the Field) and (Pin)Stripes

Top Left: Artist Robert Thorn's depiction of Babe Ruth's Called Shot. Image courtesy of National Baseball Hall of Fame and Museum, Cooperstown, New York.

Top Right: Lou Gehrig delivering his Luckiest Man speech on Lou Gehrig Appreciation Day, July 4, 1939 at Yankee Stadium. Photo courtesy of National Baseball Hall of Fame and Museum, Cooperstown, New York.

Bottom: Battery Mates Yogi Berra (left) and Whitey Ford. Photo courtesy of National Baseball Hall of Fame and Museum, Cooperstown, New York.

To learn about Lou Gehrig, Babe Ruth and Yogi Berra's special expressions of Sportsmanship (on & off the field), please see *Chapters 18* and *23*.

Performaing Acts of Sportsmanship

Team Spirit Institute Volunteers PERFORMING Acts of Sportsmanship / *Derekh Eretz v'Khavod* / **Respect and Honor** on (and off) Chicago Bulls' court at the United Center.
Top Left and Bottom photos: Courtesy of Team Spirit Institute/ David Blachman, Photographer.

Top Right photo: Courtesy of Team Spirit Institute/Marilyn Gordon, Photographer.

To learn more about Sibling Sportsmanship, please read *Chapter 16*.

Chapter 17
Forgive and Forget: Extraordinary Acts of Sportsmanship involving Game Officials

Forgiveness

According to mediaeval British poet Alexander Pope, "To err is human, to forgive divine." It's easy to make a mistake, but it takes a super-human effort to forgive someone who has harmed you with his or her mistake.

The "Most Perfect" Perfect Game

It is easy to be gracious when something good happens. However, to be kind when you are wronged is a display of sportsmanship of the highest order.

As of this writing, only 23 perfect games have been pitched in the more than 140-year history of Major League Baseball. On June 12, 1880, Lee Richmond of the Worcester Ruby Legs recorded MLB's first perfect game when he beat the Cleveland Blues 1-0. The 23rd perfect game was pitched by Felix Hernandez of the Seattle Mariners against the Tampa Bay Rays on August 15, 2012. Hernandez's "perfecto" should actually have been MLB's 24th, but for an error committed by MLB veteran umpire Jim Joyce.

With two outs in the ninth inning of the June 2, 2010 game between the Detroit Tigers and Cleveland Indians, Jason Donald of the Indians hit a grounder to Tigers first baseman Miguel Cabrera who fielded the ball and then threw to pitcher Armando Galarraga for what appeared to be the 27th and final out of the game. Surprisingly, Joyce called Donald safe, ruining Galarraga's perfect game. (An instant replay clearly showed that the base runner was out. Since 2014, plays such as this would be reviewed [and over-turned] by virtue of MLB instant replay regulations.)

Had Galarraga lashed out at the umpire in a fit of anger, it would have been understandable; after all, the blown call caused the pitcher to miss out on being a member of a club even more exclusive than President of the United States. But how did the wounded Tiger react? Instead of arguing with the first base umpire, Galarraga accepted the call and then promptly retired the next batter. When responding to reporters after the game, Galarraga remarked, "I got a perfect game. Maybe it's not in the book, but I'm going to show my son the CD." When Joyce, who by his own tearful admission, "cost that kid a perfect game," apologized to the player in person after the game, Galarraga comforted the veteran umpire by giving him a hug and telling him, "Nobody's perfect."

One of the most prestigious awards in sports is the *Sports Illustrated* Sportsman of the Year. Although Armando Galarraga was not chosen, he was nominated for this award by at least one *SI* writer, Joe Posnanski, who wrote, in November of that year, "But because of the way

DIDJA KNOW that in MLB history there have been fewer unassisted triple plays (15) than perfect games (23)?

DIDJA KNOW that in the 2013 World Series Jim Joyce (correctly) called obstruction on Will Middlebrooks, the Red Sox shortstop, for tripping the Cardinals' Allen Craig who was attempting to score after a wild throw from BoSox catcher Jarrod Saltalamacchia? Rarely called, Joyce was not afraid of making a controversial call that ended Game 3 of the World Series.

he handled it, Armando Galarraga DID throw a perfect game. In many ways, it was the most perfect game in baseball history."

Forgiveness: A Spiritual Insight

The Mark of a *Tzadik* (Righteous Person)

In Jewish tradition, ***forgiveness*** is known as מְחִילָה/*M'chila*. It is an integral component of the **repentance** (*T'shuva*) process. *Maimonides* teaches that when one person has wronged another s/he must not only compensate the aggrieved party for his/her damages, but also apologize and ask for forgiveness. As long as the wrongdoer is sincere in his/her request and provides appropriate compensation, the person who was wronged must grant *M'chila* (*Mishneh Torah, Hilkhot T'shuva* 2:9). If a person refuses to forgive, then s/he is considered as one who bears a grudge, an act prohibited by the *Torah* (*Leviticus* 19:18). Since the only person who can grant *M'chila* is the person who was actually wronged, it is impossible to be forgiven for such crimes as murder.

For all sins, those interpersonal in nature along with those between a Jew and God, ultimately we must ask forgiveness from the Almighty. This is a major theme in daily life with a special focus assigned during the High Holy Day season.

Throughout Jewish history there have been many examples of people who have been terribly wronged and who have granted *M'chila*. One of the best examples of someone who forgave others for their egregious sins against them was Joseph in the *Torah*. Although Joseph's youthful arrogance and enormous talents provoked jealousy among his brothers, nonetheless, his brothers sinned horribly by selling Joseph as a slave and misleading their father Jacob by telling him that Joseph had been slain.

The *Torah* (*Genesis* 50:15–21) relates that, after Jacob passed away, Joseph's brothers apologized and begged that he forgive them. Although their request was largely motivated by their concern that Joseph would retaliate against them, nevertheless, Joseph forgave them and promised to look out for their welfare:

וְאַתֶּם חֲשַׁבְתֶּם עָלַי רָעָה אֱלֹקִים חֲשָׁבָהּ לְטֹבָה
לְמַעַן עֲשֹׂה כַּיּוֹם הַזֶּה לְהַחֲיֹת עַם־רָב:
וְעַתָּה אַל־תִּירָאוּ אָנֹכִי אֲכַלְכֵּל אֶתְכֶם וְאֶת־טַפְּכֶם
וַיְנַחֵם אוֹתָם וַיְדַבֵּר עַל־לִבָּם:

V'atem chashavtem alai ra-ah Elokim chashava l'tova, l'ma-ahn ahso ka-yom ha-zeh l'hachayot am rav. V'ata ahl tira-u anokhi akhalkel etkhem v'et top'khem, vaynachem otahm vaydaber ahl libam.

"While you intended evil for me, Elokim [the God of Justice] intended good, in order for me to perform what is today, to keep alive a vast nation. And now do not be afraid; I will sustain you and your young children." And he [Joseph] comforted them and he spoke to their heart (*Genesis* 50:20-21).

For this act, along with other noble deeds, Jewish tradition refers to Joseph as *Joseph the Righteous* (*Yoseph HaTzadik*).

There is an old saying that if God didn't intend for us to make mistakes, He wouldn't have put erasers at the end of pencils. To err is human. To correct our mistakes and apologize is also human. To accept an apology and forgive is the proper Jewish way.

We all have disagreements with others in all facets of lives: at home, at school, and on the sports fields. As we learn from the unfortunate incidents between Joseph and his brothers, sometimes disagreements can escalate to a dangerous level. We learn from Joseph's readiness to forgive his brothers that apologies and forgiveness are integral ingredients in leading a healthy and productive life.

THE BOX SCORE

It takes courage to apologize. It is extremely difficult **not** to bear a grudge. It is even more challenging to forgive someone when they have really hurt you. Forgiving someone who has wounded you is an extraordinary act of sportsmanship/ דֶּרֶךְ אֶרֶץ וְכָבוֹד – *Derekh Eretz v'Khavod* (**Respect and Honor**). In the world of sports we learn this from Armando Galarraga forgiving umpire Jim Joyce. In Jewish history this important lesson is taught by Joseph granting *M'chila* (**forgiveness**) to his brothers.

Chapter 18

Remember Those Who Pay To Watch You Play: Extraordinary Acts of Sportsmanship by Players towards Fans

Gratitude

Achieving success is a team effort. It is important for a successful person to express his/her gratitude to those who helped him/her along their path forward.

Lou Gehrig: The Luckiest (and Most Grateful) Man

Lou Gehrig was known as the "Iron Horse." Until Cal Ripken, Jr., broke his consecutive-games-played record in 1995, Lou Gehrig was the first person who came to mind when hearing the words "durable" and "reliable." Gehrig died just shy of the age of 37 possibly from Amyotrophic Lateral Sclerosis (ALS), or possibly from brain trauma (see my earlier chapter on CTE). (Ironically the disease that – in common usage – bears his name, "Lou Gehrig's disease," may not have been the condition that led to his death, after all - according to the latest research.) A Hall of Famer who won the Triple Crown in 1934 and holds the American League record with 185 RBIs in a single season, Gehrig is also remembered for teaming up with Babe Ruth as baseball's all-time most powerful duo.

In addition, Lou Gehrig is well remembered for his gratitude. After playing 13 consecutive seasons without missing a single game, Gehrig started slowing down in 1938 and began the 1939 season not feeling well. After performing far below his standards, before the ninth game of the season, Gehrig removed himself from the Yankees' starting lineup, ending his streak at 2,130 games. Subsequently, he went to the Mayo Clinic where he was diagnosed with ALS.

On July 4, 1939, the New York Yankees and more than 60,000 fans showed their appreciation to the Iron Horse by honoring him at Yankee Stadium on Lou Gehrig Appreciation Day. Gehrig expressed his gratitude with his famous "Luckiest Man" farewell speech.

In this seemingly unscripted message, Lou Gehrig said, in part: "Fans, for the past two weeks you have been reading about the bad break I got. Yet today I consider myself the luckiest man on the face of this earth. I have been in ballparks for 17 years and have never received anything but kindness and encouragement from you fans. . . When you have a father and a mother who work all their lives so you can have an education and build your body – it's a blessing. When you have a wife who has been a tower of strength and shown more courage than you dreamed existed – that's the finest I know. So I close in saying that I may have been given a bad break, but I've got an awful lot to live for."

In this moving and magnificent speech, Lou Gehrig, a man who was suffering from a debilitating disease that was rapidly moving through his body, expressed gratitude to all those who contributed to the quality of his life.

Known also as "Baseball's Gettysburg Address," the "Luckiest Man" speech is the exemplar of all speeches expressing gratitude. Over the years, athletes have articulated their gratitude in many speeches, especially when receiving an award.

The Hakarat HaTov Hall of Fame

In Jewish tradition, **gratitude** is known as *Hakarat HaTov* (literally, ***recognizing the good***). We should recognize the positive in every situation. Instead of viewing the proverbial cup of life as being half empty, we should consider it half-full. Rather than *kvetch* (**complain**) about what we do not have, we should express our gratitude towards our fellow human beings and to the Almighty for all that we do have.

One traditional way that a Jew expresses his/her gratitude to God is by reciting **blessings** (b'rakha/b'rakhot). When the fictional Rabbi of Anatevka in *Fiddler on the Roof* was asked if there was a blessing for the Czar, he responded: "A blessing for the Czar? Of course! May God bless and keep the Czar . . . far away from us!"

Although Jewish tradition does not have a blessing for everything, there are blessings that mark many important activities. Before and after we eat, we recite appropriate blessings. When a Jew wakes up, s/he expresses their gratitude by reciting the *Modeh Ahni* (***I Thank You Gratefully***) prayer. There is even a blessing after a person relieves themselves! Another common way that a person shows his/her gratitude is by saying *"Barukh HaShem"* (**Blessed is God**).

In the *Bible* and *Talmud* there are many individuals who are cited for expressing their *Hakarat Hatov* (**Gratitude**):

- After Sara's death, Abraham entrusted Eliezer, his "chief of staff," to find a wife for Isaac. When he discovered Rebecca, who met all the criteria to be the successor to Sara, Eliezer, a non-Hebrew, praised God and said: *Barukh HaShem* – ***"Blessed is HaShem!"***:

וַיֹּאמֶר בָּרוּךְ ה' אֱלֹקֵי אֲדֹנִי אַבְרָהָם
אֲשֶׁר לֹא־עָזַב חַסְדּוֹ וַאֲמִתּוֹ מֵעִם אֲדֹנִי
אָנֹכִי בַּדֶּרֶךְ נָחַנִי ה' בֵּית אֲחֵי אֲדֹנִי:

VaYomer Barukh HaShem Ehlokei adoni Avraham, asher lo azav chasdo va-amito m'ihm adoni, anokhi ba-derekh nachani HaShem beit achei adoni.

And he [Eliezer] exclaimed: "Blessed is HaShem the God of my master Abraham Who has not removed His loving kindness and truth from my master; I have been on the road and HaShem has guided me to the house of my master's brothers" (Genesis 24:27).

- Rabbi Shlomo Riskin in his *Haggadah* (*The Passover Haggadah*) points out that at the end of his life, when Jacob blessed his grandsons *Menashe* and *Ephraim* (Joseph's sons), he stated (*Genesis* 48:16):

הַמַּלְאָךְ הַגֹּאֵל אֹתִי מִכָּל רָע
יְבָרֵךְ אֶת־הַנְּעָרִים וְיִקָּרֵא בָהֶם שְׁמִי וְשֵׁם אֲבֹתַי אַבְרָהָם וְיִצְחָק
וְיִדְגּוּ לָרֹב בְּקֶרֶב הָאָרֶץ:

HaMalakh ha-goel oti mi-kol rah, y'varekh et ha-n'arim v'yikareh va-hem sh'mi v'shem avotai Avraham v'Yitzchak, v'yidgu la-rov b'kerev haAretz.

"The Angel Who has redeemed me from all evil, may He bless the youth and instill in them my name, and the names of my fathers Abraham and Isaac. And may they multiply in abundance like fish, in the midst of the land."

Having suffered such tragedies as fleeing from the wrath and jealousy of his brother Esau, the separation from his parents, the abuse inflicted upon him by his father-in-law/uncle Laban, the rape of his daughter Dina, and the separation from his son Joseph, of all the Patriarchs, Jacob had the most to complain about. But, yet, instead of expressing bitterness, he articulated words of *Hakarat HaTov.*

- Jethro, whose daughter *Tzipora* married Moses, was also a person who expressed his gratitude. Like Eliezer, Jethro was not born a Hebrew, but yet showed gratitude to the God of Israel for all the good that He bestowed upon Israel (*Exodus* 18:9-10).

- Throughout the **Book of Psalms** (סֵפֶר תְּהִלִּים / *Sefer T'hillim*), its author, King David praises the *Kadosh Barukh Hu* (**Holy One Blessed Be He**). The word *T'hillim* means **praises**.

- **Joshua and Caleb** returned from their spy mission in Israel and, among all of the 12 spies, issued the only positive report about the Israelites' chances of conquering the **Land of Israel**/*Eretz Yisrael* (*Numbers* 13). They had a positive attitude and were grateful to the Almighty for being allotted the opportunity to conquer the Land. Caleb and Joshua were rewarded by being the only two members of their generation to be allowed to enter *Eretz Yisrael.*

- Not recognizing *Rahbi Akiva*'s wife Rachel, when she and a multitude of others went to see *Rahbi Akiva* when he returned from a prolonged time away devoted to *Torah* study, *Rahbi Akiva*'s students literally stood in Rachel's way. *Rahbi Akiva,* not only identified this woman as his wife, but he credited Rachel for inspiring him to learn (*N'darim 50a*):

שֶׁלִּי וְשֶׁלָּכֶם שֶׁלָּה הוּא.‏-*Shehli v'shehlakhem shehla hu.*

"What is mine (i.e., what I [Akiva] have accomplished in Torah learning) and what is yours (i.e., what you [my students] have accomplished in Torah learning) is her's (i.e., is all on account of my wife Rachel and her sacrifices)."

DIDJA KNOW that the popular Passover *Seder* song *Dayenu* has an extremely deep meaning?

Although the meaning of the verses may not be known by all *Seder* participants, the one word refrain is easy to learn and the tune is both catchy and fun; hence, it is enthusiastically recited.

Like all passages in the *Pesach Haggadah*, the *Dayenu* has a profound meaning. While the word *Dayenu* means *It would have been enough!* each of the 15 verses describe, in chronological order, a Divine miracle bestowed upon Israel, beginning with the Exodus from Egypt and concluding with the building of the Holy Temple (**Beit HaMikdash**). After each of these miraculous events we respond with one word: דַּיֵּנוּ/*Dayenu* – *It would have been enough!*

The number 15 and *Hakarat HaTov* have a strong connection in that there are 15 chapters in the book of the *Psalms* (a book dedicated to praising the Almighty) that begin with the words – *Shir HaMaalot* (*A Song of Ascents*) and there were 15 steps in the *Beit HaMikdash* on which the Levites stood while singing praises to God.

One of the 15 statements which, at first blush, does not seem to make sense is:

אִלּוּ קֵרְבָנוּ
לִפְנֵי הַר־סִינַי
וְלֹא נָתַן לָנוּ
אֶת הַתּוֹרָה-
דַּיֵּנוּ!‏

Ihlu kervahnu lifnei Har Sinai v'lo natan lanu et HaTorah – Dayenu!

Had He brought us close to Mount Sinai and not given us the Torah – Dayenu!

After all, how could have just being at Mount Sinai and **not**

receiving the *Torah* been enough?

Various explanations have been posited. Rabbi Shlomo Riskin suggests in his *Haggadah* that the preparation to receive the *Torah* was in itself a valuable experience that could stand on its own. During this intense three-day period, the Israelites purified their bodies and cleared their minds of unchaste thoughts. Plus by simply standing together in unity at Mount Sinai in anticipation of the *Torah,* they were still able to experience the **Divine Presence** (*Sh'khina*). Rabbi Riskin notes further that sometimes the preparation can take longer than the actual experience (e.g., cooking takes longer than eating; among some Chassidic Jews, preparing to pray is a longer process than the actual *davening/**praying**).

Not only is this true with cooking and prayer preparations, but it is especially relevant in the world of sports. The time that most athletes train and prepare is much greater than the actual time that they compete. Just think of some of the Olympic events like swimming and gymnastics.

DIDJA KNOW that the *Tanna Ben Zoma* (*Ethics of Our Fathers* 4:1) defines a wealthy person as someone who is grateful for all that s/he has? In his words:

בֶּן זוֹמָא אוֹמֵר: ...
אֵיזֶהוּ עָשִׁיר?
הַשָּׂמֵחַ בְּחֶלְקוֹ.‏

Ben Zoma Omer: ... Eizehu ashir? HaSameach b'chelko.

Ben Zoma says: ... *"Who is wealthy? One who is happy in [i.e., accepts] his lot [in life]."*

THE BOX SCORE

It is always important to express our gratitude in life. In the world of sports it is expressed by "high fives," fist bumps, hats thrown onto the hockey rink after a player scores a hat trick, standing ovations, trophies, performance bonuses, and speeches. We should be inspired by Yankees great Lou Gehrig to be even more appreciative of what we have in life and to always express our gratitude to those who have aided and encouraged us.

We should have a positive attitude and be grateful to others and ultimately to the Almighty for everything that we have in life. In Jewish tradition, *Hakarat HaTov* (**gratitude**) is expressed by handshakes, embraces, saying *Kol HaKavod* (**all of the honor**) or *Yishar Koach* (**may your strength be increased**) to a person who has performed a mitzvah and by praising God through prayers and blessings. We should be inspired by Eliezer, Jacob, Jethro, Joshua, Caleb, King David, and *Rahbi Akiva* to be even more appreciative of what we have in life and to always express our gratitude.

Bringing the Game Back to its Roots

An important expression of sportsmanship (i.e., Honor and Respect) is openly showing how grateful a person is to the patrons.

A Real "Buddy" to the Fans

Don't you just hate it when you go to a store and the clerk treats you like he's doing you a HUGE favor by taking care of you? Personally, I resent such behavior.

Unfortunately, sometimes employees forget that they have jobs because of the customers who choose to patronize the business that employs them. It's nice to be appreciated.

To recognize the commitment of fans, many teams will host a fan appreciation day, usually at the end of the season, giving a "shout-out" to the loyal fans who support the team. Sometimes a player who retires or is traded will place an ad in the local newspapers thanking the fans for their support.

Perhaps the most remarkable expression of appreciation by players to fans that I have heard about is a "ritual" performed by a journeyman MLB player. In 2015, the *Wall Street Journal* and other media sources published a moving story about a relief pitcher named Earl Carlyle.

Known as "Buddy," Carlyle behaves like the meaning of his name. Before many road games, during batting practice, Buddy selects a buddy, that is, a youngster in the stands who is wearing a baseball glove or mitt, and does what many players do: he tosses him/her a ball. However, instead of going back to his own practice, Carlyle does something rather unique. He asks the child to throw the ball back to him. What this exchange does is it starts a game of catch, between a Major League ballplayer and a young fan.

Playing catch is one of the most basic scrimmages in all of sports. Made famous in the epic film *Field of Dreams*, "having a catch" is a simple way of creating and then strengthening a connection between two people. Many times it's an intergenerational relationship between parent and child or grandparent and grandchild. In this case it's between a Major League Baseball player and an adoring young fan.

Carlyle, who has bounced around from city to city since his MLB debut in 1999, making multiple stops along the way in the minor leagues, has played for manifold teams including the Braves, Dodgers, Yankees and Mets. He has also played overseas in Japan and South Korea. Being a father and never the beneficiary of a huge MLB contract, Carlyle has a certain appreciation of the game of baseball and for its fans – especially the youth -- not found among your average player.

Why does he do what he does? In Buddy Carlyle's own words, "It's something that's easy for me to do. I figure it's something they'll always remember."

No wonder they call him "Buddy."

Bringing the Game Back to its Roots: A Spiritual Insight

Having a Jewish Catch

As an American father, an activity that has provided a strong bond between my children (a son and two daughters) and me is playing catch. Known also as "having a catch," this all-American activity was popularized by Kevin Costner in his role as Ray Kinsella in the movie *Field of Dreams*.

Beginning at ages four and five, my two oldest children, Max and Rita, spent many hours with me over the next decade or so in front of our suburban Chicago home intensely engaged in baseball fielding drills. While they enjoyed – and were quite proficient at – fielding ground balls, and then beating the imaginary runner with their pinpoint throws to first base, their favorite exercise was catching pop-ups. I would test the strength of my arm by tossing a used tennis ball as high as I could over the mature trees that decorated our front lawn. Max and Rita (and later Sophie, who is four years Rita's junior) would take turns tracking the flight of the ball, sometimes through the branches of trees, planting their feet in the proper manner and then waiting for the ball to land in their gloves. Their faces would light-up with huge smiles as they squeezed the ball with both their gloved and bare hands.

My father-child memories of having a catch are not unique, as they are shared by many other American parents. Fathers and sons have expanded to fathers and daughters, which in turn has spawned mother-daughter and even mother-son duos. Playing catch is a rite of passage through which many parents and children pass before our children disappear in front of our very own eyes and become adults. Once parents themselves, the cycle of this great American tradition repeats itself.

As a Jewish father, the activity that has forged the most durable union with my (now young adult) children is having the honor of studying *Torah* (and other Judaic studies) with them, highlighted by preparing each of them for their *Bar Mitzvah* service and *B'not Mitzvah* ceremonies. The *Mitzvah* of *Talmud Torah* (teaching *Torah* to your children) is one of the most important responsibilities that parents have. Although parents often delegate this duty to professional teachers and tutors, some parents have the special opportunity to actually be their child's primary Jewish educator – at least when it comes to preparing them for their *Bar/Bat Mitzvah*.

With this background in mind, one, perhaps, can better understand why the Patriarch Jacob (*Yaakov Avinu*) gave what appeared to be preferential treatment to his son Joseph. A common criticism of Jacob is that he **unreasonably** favored his son Joseph. As it is stated in the *Torah* (*Genesis* 37:3):

וְיִשְׂרָאֵל אָהַב אֶת יוֹסֵף מִכָּל בָּנָיו כִּי בֶן זְקֻנִים הוּא לוֹ וְעָשָׂה לוֹ כְּתֹנֶת פַּסִּים:

V'Yisrael ahav et Yosef mi-kol banav ki ven z'kunim hu lo v'asah lo k'tonet pasim.

And Israel [Jacob] loved Joseph more than any of his sons, because he was a son born to him when he was old; and he [Israel] made him a tunic of fancy wool.

Did Joseph earn the right to be treated more favorably than the rest of his brothers? We can find an answer to this question by carefully examining the term *ben z'kunim*. According to *Rashi* and *Ibn Ezra*, **the most direct meaning** (*p'shat*) of the term *ben z'kunim* (literally, **the son of old age**) is that Joseph was born to an elderly father. According to *Ibn Ezra*, Jacob was 91 years old when Joseph was born. Looking only at the *p'shat* of the term *ben z'kunim* we then might erroneously conclude that Jacob acted unreasonably in showing apparent favoritism to Joseph. After all, should a child be given preferential treatment by a parent simply because he was born when the parent was old?

When, however, we examine the term *ben z'kunim* more closely, we can find an interpretation that views Jacob in a more favorable light. Jacob rewarded his son Joseph for behavior which we want to see from all Jewish children, as he spent time with his father engaged in the ideal father-son activity; that is, studying *Torah* together. (In my "sports mind," this is the Jewish version of "having a catch.")

According to the *Targum Onkelos* and the *Ba-ahl HaTurim*, the term *ben z'kunim* refers to **one who possesses Torah knowledge**. After all, Joseph was the son of Jacob the Patriarch who was especially known for his *Torah* study and knowledge. In the words of the *Targum*, Joseph was a *Bar-Chakim* (**a wise son**). In commenting on the *Targum Onkelos*, *Rashi* explains that Jacob taught Joseph all that he had learned at the Academies of *Shem* and *Ever*. The *Ba-ahl HaTurim* points out further that the word *z'kunim* is a *notrikun* (**acronym**) for the six **orders** (*s'darim*) of the *Mishna*. Similarly, the Sages teach that, in addition to **elder**, the word *zaken* can also be interpreted as a contraction for זֶה שֶׁקָּנָה חָכְמָה/*zeh shehkana chawkhma* (**he who has acquired wisdom**).

Based upon the last explanation of the term *ben z'kunim* we learn that the reason why Jacob treated Joseph so favorably was because he was rewarding his son for his dedication to the study of *Torah*. Further support for this most positive interpretation can be learned from the *Torah's* usage of the name *Yisrael* (**Israel**), which is used only when the third Patriarch is engaged in a spiritual endeavor, as opposed to *Yaakov* (**Jacob**), the name used when he performed mundane tasks.

Jacob was doing what all Jewish parents should do; that is, to encourage our children to lead a life devoted to the study of *Torah* and to the performance of the *Mitzvot*. This should be the top item on the agenda of all Jewish parents.

By studying *Torah* together, this famous *Biblical* father and son duo participated in an activity that, thank God, is still extremely popular and critical for fathers and sons/parents and children to engage in. In many ways it is the Jewish expression of the all-American pastime of "having a catch"– parent and child.

DIDJA KNOW
that, after moving to Egypt (*Genesis* 46), according to *Midrashic* literature (*Tanchuma* 6), Jacob established a similar relationship with his grandson *Ephraim* as he had with Joseph? They regularly learned together. This is the reason why Jacob chose to bless *Ephraim* first instead of his older brother *Menashe*.

THE BOX SCORE

Known in Hebrew as הַכָּרַת הַטּוֹב/Hakarat HaTov (or in some communities – *HaKoros HaTov*), expressing one's **gratitude** is extremely important. It is a significant manifestation of sportsmanship.

We learn from Buddy Carlyle, a family man who never achieved star status in the MLB, that a classy (and spot-on) way for a professional baseball player to thank his "customers" is by engaging young fans in a game of catch. In addition to strengthening the bond between player and fan, "having a catch" is also a classic American way of reinforcing the parent-child bond.

In Jewish tradition, the most important way that a parent can strengthen a bond with a child is by studying with him/her *Torah* (and other Jewish texts). When doing so, not only is a father fulfilling the *Mitzvah* of *Talmud Torah*, but also strengthening his relationship with his son. The *Biblical* Jacob was especially close with his son Joseph (and grandson *Ephraim*) because they learned together. By transmitting the teachings of the *Torah*, through both word and deed, a parent helps instill in his/her child the importance of displaying *Derekh Eretz v'Khavod* in everything they do in life. While Joseph and *Ephraim* were grateful to their father/grandfather for studying with them, Jacob was also grateful. After all, through them he was able to fulfill his duties as our third Patriarch of ensuring future generations of the Jewish people committed to the study and teachings of the *Torah*.

Chapter 19
The 110% Club: Extraordinary Acts of Sportsmanship by Team Executives

Going Above and Beyond

The "Wasted" Draft Pick

"Always give 110 percent." Of course this is a mathematical impossibility but the expression is used to convey the idea that one can give more than his or her maximum effort. This sound piece of advice has been offered by parents, teachers, and coaches. Striving for 110 percent can also be applied to our schoolwork, friendships, religious practices, and the sports that we play.

In the world of sports, there are many examples of players who have gone above and beyond in their efforts to succeed. These players include Pete Rose, who always ran to first base and slid head first to maximize his efforts, and Cal Ripken, Jr., who always tried his hardest while playing in a record 2,632 consecutive baseball games. Giving 110 percent is not reserved strictly for players, but is also an important ideal for coaches, managers, and sports executives.

A coach who is remembered for giving and demanding maximum effort from his players was the legendary Arnold "Red" Auerbach (1917–2006). Selected in 1980 as the greatest coach in the history of the NBA, Auerbach led his Boston Celtics team to nine NBA titles, including eight in a row (1959–1966) – still unequaled by any other coach. After retiring from coaching in 1966, Auerbach became a successful Celtics' executive. In 1980 he was voted the NBA Executive of the Year.

Although all of these astounding accomplishments required giving 110 percent, perhaps Auerbach's greatest expression of going above and beyond the call of duty was for an act that he performed in 1982. That year he used the Celtics' final pick in the NBA Draft to select Landon Turner, one of Indiana's greatest players under legendary Indiana University Hoosier Coach Bobby Knight. The previous season, Turner led his Hoosiers team to the NCAA Championship. Known for his work ethic and team play, Turner was a perfect fit for the Celtics brand of winning basketball. What was admirable and unusual about Auerbach's decision was that Turner was paralyzed since the summer of 1981, a result of a car accident, without any medical hope to ever play basketball again.

Realizing that it would take a miracle for Turner to ever play for the Celtics, Auerbach wanted to help the Hoosiers' star realize the dream of being selected in the NBA draft. Although Auerbach "wasted" his pick in the conventional manner, his 110 percent deed as a general manager brought great respect and joy to Landon Turner as well as honor to the storied Celtics' franchise.

It was an extraordinary act of sportsmanship.

Going Above and Beyond: A Spiritual Insight

Treating Your Employees with Respect and Dignity

One of the more celebrated examples of an employer who has gone above and beyond in his treatment of employees is Aaron Mordecai Feuerstein. Well known for many years in New England for his commitment to corporate social responsibility and his leadership in the Jewish community, Feuerstein became internationally known in December 1995.

While celebrating with family and friends his 70th birthday, Aaron Feuerstein was informed that Malden Mills, the company founded by his grandfather, was on fire. The fire ultimately destroyed three of the company's nine buildings and halted the work of some 3,000 laborers. Four days later, Feuerstein, CEO of Malden, announced that his plans were to rebuild Malden as quickly as possible and to continue, without any disruption, to compensate his employees.

This decision was a shock to the business world because when confronted with similar situations, many CEOs would have decided to either keep the millions of dollars of insurance payments for themselves or to rebuild in another country where taxes, labor, and other production costs were far less costly. Not so for Aaron Feuerstein. An observant Jew, Mr. Feuerstein is no ordinary CEO. Inspired by the teachings of Jewish tradition and the legacy of his father and grandfather who previously owned and ran Malden Mills, Feuerstein continued to treat his employees not as fungible expenses, but rather as priceless assets. He was committed to his valued employees and their families as well as the New England economy.

Malden Mills was rebuilt and, since the devastating fire, has experienced both successes and failures. In March 2002, while still in the midst of a corporate bankruptcy, Feuerstein reaffirmed his 1995 decision to rebuild when he stated in a television interview, "Yes, it was the right thing to do."

In the non-sports business world, Aaron Feuerstein's decision in 1995 to rebuild Malden Mills was clearly an act that exceeded the expectations dictated by the norms of society.

"Going above and beyond" is an important ideal to pursue in all endeavors that a person undertakes. Not only will it often "get you places" in the world, but, more importantly, it is the right thing to do.

In Hebrew we refer to this category of behavior as either לִפְנִים מְשׁוּרַת הַדִּין/ Lifnim MiShurat HaDin (***more than the law requires***) or יוֹשֶׁר/Yosher (***equity***). In the world of sports, we can view these as extraordinary acts of sportsmanship. They are truly amazing expressions of דֶּרֶךְ אֶרֶץ וְכָבוֹד/ Derekh Eretz v'Khavod (***Respect and Honor***).

יוֹשֶׁר/*Yosher* or לִפְנִים מְשׁוּרַת הַדִּין/*Lifnim MiShurat HaDin* directs individuals as well as ***Jewish courts of law*** (בֵּית דִּין/בָּתֵי דִּין - *Beit Din/Batei Din*) to go above and beyond the letter of the law when making a decision. In Judaism, the number 18 is considered to be a lucky number since it corresponds to the word חַי/*Chai* (**alive**). Accordingly, giving 118% is a contemporary expression of the ancient principle of Yosher. In contemporary legal terms, this venerable Jewish principle can be translated as *equity*.

Lifnim MiShurat HaDin directs judges to incorporate into their legal renderings such equitable ideals as promoting peace and *compromise* (פְּשָׁרָה/*p'shara*). *Rahbi Yochanan* states that the reason why the Second Temple was destroyed was because Jewish courts did not incorporate *Lifnim MiShurat HaDin* into their judgments (*Bava M'tzia 30b*). According to this principle, before a home can be put on the market for sale, the adjacent/abutting neighbors must first be given the right of first refusal (*Matzranut*). The *Talmud* (*Bava M'tzia 83a*) teaches that *Yosher* also directs employers to treat their employees with an extra measure of fairness.

The *Torah* source for equity (*Yosher/Lifnim MiShurat HaDin*) is Deuteronomy 6:18:

וְעָשִׂיתָ הַיָּשָׁר וְהַטּוֹב (בְּעֵינֵי ה׳)
V'ahsita HaYashar v'HaTov (b'Einei HaShem)

And you shall do that which is straight [fair] and good [in the eyes of HaShem].

The Medieval luminary *Rashi* teaches that, from these words, we learn the importance of **compromise** (פְּשָׁרָה/*P'shara*) and going over and beyond the letter of the law לִפְנִים מְשׁוּרַת הַדִּין - *Lifnim MiShurat HaDin* when resolving conflicts. We learn that it is not enough to only fulfill the *Mitzvot*, (i.e., that which we are commanded to do) but rather, we must go over and beyond accepted standards while performing them.

Although neither Maimonides (*Sefer HaMitzvot*) nor Rabbi Aharon HaLevy (*Sefer HaChinukh*) include this concept as one of the 613 *Torah Mitzvot*, logically, it can be included as an expression of:

מִצְוַת אַהֲבַת יִשְׂרָאֵל
Mitzvat Ahavat Yisrael
***The Mitzvah of Loving Your Fellow Jew; Sefer HaChinukh #243; Sefer HaMitzvot, Ahseh #206;* or**

לָלֶכֶת וּלְהִדָּמוֹת בְּדַרְכֵי הַשֵּׁם יִתְבָּרַךְ
LaLekhet U-Lhidamot B'Darkhei HaShem Yitbarakh

To Follow and Imitate the Ways of HaShem the Blessed Sefer HaChinukh #611; Sefer HaMitzvot, Ahseh #8

Honoring the Memory of a Young Sportsman

In Memory of Ezra Schwartz: *Kol HaKavod* Robert Kraft

One of the "perks" of being famous or wealthy is that you have the opportunity to take a public stance on important, but controversial issues, and bring much-needed attention to it.

Unfortunately, on too many occasions, celebrities take the easy way out, choosing not to get involved. Robert Kraft, the owner of the NFL's New England Patriots, is not such a person.

Raised in a traditional Jewish home, Mr. Kraft and his beloved wife Myra – of blessed memory – support many philanthropic causes in both the Jewish and general communities. Known to have a warm relationship with his employees, including coaches and players, during the season following Myra's passing, his Patriots players wore a patch on their uniforms with the initials "MHK" (Myra Hiatt Kraft) emblazoned on them.

A number of years ago, an American Football in Israel (AFI) player recognized Robert Kraft in an Israeli hotel lobby and told him that the AFI needed a stadium to house its flag football league games. Kraft stepped up immediately and provided the necessary funds to build Jerusalem's Kraft Stadium.

From my own personal experiences, I know that the opportunity to play a game you adore in the land you love not only brings you a sense of comfort away from home, but also fosters your love of Israel. During the 2010-2011 academic year, along with my wife Marilyn, I had the opportunity to watch our son Max – who was studying in Israel – and his teammates play flag football, under the lights, at *Itztadiyon* (**Stadium**) Kraft. For Max and the many other young (and some not so young) flag football players, sports and Israel became more meaningful because of this experience.

I had not been back to Israel since visiting my son. In 2015, horrified by the latest intifada, Marilyn and I deemed it essential that at least one of us go to Israel as soon as possible to provide our youngest child Sophie, an 18-year-old seminary gap student, with *chizuk* (**strength/support**). On November 16, I embarked on a five-day trip (by myself representing Marilyn and our older children Max and Rita) with the singular purpose of spending time with Sophie, and encouraging her to keep on studying in Jerusalem's Old City, while constantly being cautious and fully aware of her surroundings.

For the first three days of my visit, Sophie and I thrived. While she gained strength, so did I. Through the magic of smartphones, we, in turn, passed this strength along to Marilyn, Max, and Rita. Sophie proudly introduced me to her rabbis, teachers, and friends. I attended school programs. During our breaks, while Sophie studied, I either worked at my "office" in the Old City apartment where I stayed or went to *daven* (**pray**) at the *Kotel* (**Western Wall**), which was a mere "roll out of bed" for me.

On Thursday, November 19, things changed drastically. While shopping in Jerusalem's *Meah Sh'arim* neighborhood, I received two *JPost* alerts. First I learned of a stabbing in Tel Aviv resulting in the deaths of two Jewish men who were *davening* (**praying**) *Mincha* (**the afternoon service**) during their lunch break. Next I read about a terrorist shooting that just took place on the highway near the Gush Etzion Junction. The early reports spoke of the deaths of an 18-year-old and 50-year-old man. While I felt sad, the crime did not have a face. It was not personal.

Several hours later, it became personal when Sophie came by my apartment to pick me up for dinner. She shared that the two men who were murdered by a Palestinian terrorist were Ezra Schwartz, an 18-year-old graduate of the Maimonides School in Brookline who was studying in Israel, and a *yeshiva* instructor, Rabbi Yaakov Don. Ezra was on his way, with Yeshiva classmates, to a **Chesed (Loving Kindness)** mission, to beautify *Oz v'GAoN*, a nature preserve dedicated in memory of three Israeli youth who were kidnapped and brutally murdered by Palestinian terrorists in 2014. In a separate vehicle, Rabbi Don was travelling to meet his sons - students at another yeshiva nearby.

While neither Sophie nor I personally knew either terror victim, as fellow gap students, Sophie and Ezra shared Ida Crown Jewish Academy and Maimonides friends.

We ate dinner together at her seminary, *Midreshet HaRova*, amidst a pall of silence.

After dinner, I joined Sophie at a school-wide meeting led by one of the school's administrators.While Sophie and I gained some strength and perspective from this meeting, along with thousands of members of the American-Israel *yeshiva* community, we were grieving from this devastating, horrific disregard for human life.

I did not regain my vigor until Monday, November 23, a day after I returned from Israel. I finally felt some sense of consolation after watching the introduction to the National Anthem on the Monday Night Football game aired on ESPN between the New England Patriots and Buffalo Bills.

It was reported earlier in the day that, after learning that Ezra Schwartz was a huge Patriots fan, Robert Kraft decided to honor the memory of Ezra with a moment of silence before the game played in Massachusetts. To have it aired by ESPN, it is my understanding that Mr. Kraft had to have the verbiage approved by the network.

During this moment of silence, millions of viewers worldwide got the opportunity to see what the face of terror victims look like. A photo was displayed of Ezra, a handsome, sports-loving man-child, wearing a football jersey with anti-glare charcoal painted under his eyes, surrounded by the warm, loving embrace of friends. Along with this photo was the caption, "In Memory of Ezra Schwartz." Ezra, Hebrew for "help," represented all terror victims who were remembered during that brief moment in time. The moment of silence helped to remind us that acts of terror abruptly end the lives of innocent Jews and non-Jews in Israel and worldwide, and that families can never fully recover from such cowardly evil acts.

Not only did this moment of silence, made possible by the courage of Robert Kraft, bring some comfort and consolation to my family and millions of others (most importantly, I hope, to Ezra's family and friends), it also alerted the millions of naïve people around the world that the terror that Jews continue to endure in Israel and worldwide is just as horrific as, if not worse than, all acts of terror.

In Hebrew when someone steps up, takes a stand, and does the right thing, we say *Kol HaKavod* – **all of the honor**. In that spirit, Robert Kraft, *Kol HaKavod* for doing what many others would never have the integrity, strength, and courage to do. New England Patriots owner Robert Kraft used his high profile status to honor the memory of a super Patriots fan, Ezra Schwartz, while also honoring his Jewish homeland, Israel. This is a huge expression of *K'vod HaMet* (**Honoring the Deceased**).

May the memory of Ezra Schwartz and all of Israel's *K'doshim* (**holy martyrs**) throughout our history be for a blessing.

Update

On February 5, 2017, in perhaps the greatest comeback in the history of sports, the New England Patriots defeated the Atlanta Falcons 34-28 in overtime in Super Bowl LI. Among those in attendance at Houston's NRG Stadium were Ezra Schwartz's parents and siblings. They were VIP guests of Robert Kraft.

Ezra's mother, Mrs. Ruth Schwartz, shared with me that Robert and Daniel Kraft visited the Schwartz family during Shiva, and that Robert Kraft himself called to invite them to Super Bowl LI. During this telephone call, Robert Kraft and Dr. Ari Schwartz, Ezra's father, "had a very emotional conversation about Myra and Ezra."

Honoring the Memory of a Young Sportsman: A Spiritual Insight

NAME THAT *MITZVAH!*

כְּבוֹד הַמֵּת/*K'vod HaMet*
(*Honoring the Deceased*)
Originating from *Deuteronomy* 21:23, there are both positive and negative *Torah* Commandments that a Jewish person must provide a speedy burial for a fellow Jew, ideally within 24 hours of his/her death:

שֶׁלֹּא לְהָלִין הַתָּלוּי
Shehlo L'halin HaTalui
Not to Allow a Corpse to Hang (Overnight)
Sefer HaChinukh #536;
Sefer HaMitzvot, LT #66; &

לְקָבְרוֹ בּוֹ בַיוֹם וְכֵן כָּל הַמֵּתִים
L'kov'ro Bo VaYom V'Khen Kol HaMetim
To Bury a Person on the Same Day that S/he Died (via Capital Punishment or in any other Manner); *Sefer HaChinukh* #537; *Sefer HaMitzvot, Ahseh* #231

Under the general rubric of כְּבוֹד הַמֵּת / *K'vod HaMet* (*Honoring the Deceased*), we have many other related Rabbinic-ordained *Mitzvot* and traditions including burying all Jews in shrouds (תַּכְרִיכִים/*takhrikhim*); participating in the actual burial (i.e., by placing earth into the grave); prohibiting autopsies on a Jewish corpse (unless there is an exceptional reason); escorting the deceased to the grave; not eating or drinking in a cemetery; and not reinterring the remains of others, unless it is for an extraordinary purpose including burial in Israel or amongst other relatives.

In many Jewish communities, in order to ensure that *K'vod HaMet* is fully practiced, an organization known as a *Chevra Kaddisha* [literally, *holy society*] is formed comprised of men and women. These organizations wash and prepare the body for burial in a traditional, respectful, compassionate process known as a

טָהֳרָה/*Tahara* (*Ritual Purification*), and provide support where needed.

Another term used to describe these traditions is חֶסֶד שֶׁל אֱמֶת/*Chesed Shel Emet* (literally, *Loving Kindness* of Truth; also translated as [*an Act of*] *True Loving Kindness*), since the beneficiary of such acts is unable to reward the one who performs these acts of kindness.

Maimonides (*Mishneh Torah, Shoftim, Hilkhot Ahvel* 14:1) states that ensuring the proper burial of a Jew is another illustration of *Mitzvat Ahavat Yisrael*/*Loving Your Neighbor* (*Sefer HaChinukh* #243 & *Sefer HaMitzvot, Ahseh* #206).

Just as with the great *Mitzvah of Bikkur Cholim* (discussed in Chapter 23), according to *Chazal* (*our Sages of Blessed Memory*), proper burial per Jewish tradition (and implied other acts of *K'vod HaMet*) is also a manifestation of *Mitzvat Ahavat Yisrael* (*The Mitzvah of Loving Your Fellow Jew*) – *Sefer HaChinukh* #243; *Sefer HaMitzvot, Ahseh* #206; as well as

לָלֶכֶת וּלְהִדַּמּוֹת בְּדַרְכֵי הַשֵּׁם יִתְבָּרַךְ
LaLekhet U-Lhidamot
B'Darkhei HaShem Yitbarakh (*To Follow and Imitate the Ways of HaShem the Blessed*) – *Sefer HaChinukh* #611; *Sefer HaMitzvot, Ahseh* #8.

As stated by *Rahbi Chama the son of Rahbi Chanina* (*Sotah* 14a), one of the ways that we fulfill this Divine Command is by burying the dead, just as the Almighty buried Moses.

Also, according to the commentary of *Nachmanides* (cited in the introduction of this book), *K'vod HaMet* can also be seen as an example of *HaYashar v'HaTov*, doing that which is straight [fair] and good in the eyes of *HaShem*. (*Deuteronomy* 6:18).

THE BOX SCORE

In Jewish tradition it is simply **not** enough
to do only that which is required. One must go above
and beyond.

Three Jewish men (coincidentally all from the Boston-area)
who went over and above what was dictated by
societal norms, were business executive Aaron Feuerstein
who chose the wellbeing of displaced employees over
corporate convenience; the legendary Red Auerbach who
used a Celtics' draft pick to select a college player who
was paralyzed; and New England Patriots' owner Robert
Kraft who helped bring comfort to a grieving family and
community by honoring the memory of a loyal Patriots fan
on a nationally televised game.

In the world of sports, such acts are manifestations of
sportsmanship of the highest order.

The principle of *Lifnim MiShurat HaDin* (***going over
and beyond the letter of the law***) directs us to do all that
we can to ensure the fair treatment of employees,
customers and others. It is an extraordinary expression of
Derekh Eretz v'Khavod (***Respect and Honor***).

Chapter 20

All Women (and Men) are Created Equal: Extraordinary Acts of Sportsmanship by Legislators and Activists

Equality for Women in Sports

For years, women were relegated to second class when it came to providing funding for sports programs in academic institutions and salaries for professional athletes. Because of the efforts of many women and men, the "playing field" has slowly been leveling – though it remains imperfect – with the passing of Title IX.

The Impact of Title IX

March 10, 2014 was an historic day in the history of women in sports, with a particular emphasis on Jewish women.

On that day, *Sports Illustrated* (*SI*) published in its *Faces in the Crowd* section the following:

Rebecca Yoshor | Houston | Basketball

Yoshor, a 6-foot senior forward at Division III Yeshiva University, had 20 rebounds in the Maccabees' season finale, . . . , an 83-80 win over NYU-Poly, to finish her season as the NCAA leader in rebounds per game—among men and women—with 16.0. Last year Yoshor was the school's first female athlete to be named an Academic All-America.

My daughter Rita, a hardnosed point guard and one of "Yosh's" teammates, gave me, a longtime subscriber to *SI*, a heads-up as to what I should expect to find when my magazine arrived in the mail. Not only did I take pride in the accomplishments of one of my children's friends, but I marveled on how far we have come in promoting women's sports at all levels.

The evolution toward equal funding for women's sports largely began with the passing of the landmark Title IX of the Education Amendments Act of 1972. Known simply as "Title IX," this legislation prohibits discrimination by virtue of one's sex in all federally funded educational programs, among other things. It is best known for its application to sports, but has also been applied to other issues, including sexual harassment. Since being signed into law in 1972 by President Richard M. Nixon, federal court opinions and further legislative amendments have helped better clarify the meaning of the law and expand it.

Many people were instrumental in helping bring to fruition Title IX's passage and implementation. They include the late Congresswoman Edith Louise Starrett Green and tennis legend Billie Jean King.

A ten-term representative from Oregon, Edith Green is best remembered for her work on behalf of education and for her early opposition to the Vietnam War. The daughter of schoolteachers and a former teacher herself, Green championed other educational initiatives including the Higher Education Facilities Act (1963) and the Higher Education Act (1965). Known as "Mrs. Education" or "the mother of higher education," Green also worked on behalf of women's rights. Most notably, she was a powerful advocate on behalf of the Equal Pay Act which was signed into law in 1963.

The founder of the Women's Sports Foundation, in addition to a stellar career as a professional tennis player, Billie Jean King fought relentlessly for equality in women's sports. An outspoken advocate for equal pay for women tennis players, King was the first woman to win over $100,000 in prize money in one year (1971). Threatening to boycott the U.S. Open in 1973 if women were not paid the same as men, the tournament conceded to her demands, becoming the first Grand Slam to award equal prize money to both sexes. (It was 11 years later before a second Grand Slam tournament agreed to equal pay – the Australian Open.) In 1974, King established the co-ed World Team Tennis circuit with her then-husband Larry King. Another major triumph for equality in professional tennis was Billie Jean King's convincing victory in straight sets over Bobby Riggs in 1973 in what was dubbed "The Battle of the Sexes." King's career totals include winning 39 major singles, mixed-doubles, and doubles championships. One of her greatest recognitions was being named the first-ever *Sports Illustrated Sportswoman of the Year* in 1972.

In addition to the financial benefits and recognition gained by playing in organized sports for academic or professional institutions and the protections from sexual harassment and bullying, one of the greatest ways that the passage/implementation of Title IX has helped is by improving women's health. According to the *New York Times*, research published in the *Evaluation Review* journal showed that "the increase in girls' athletic participation caused by Title IX was associated with a 7 percent lower risk of obesity 20 to 25 years later, when women were in their late 30s and early 40s." The paper went on to point out that research demonstrates that even a small loss of weight can reduce the risk for diabetes and other health issues. Other benefits for women include higher levels of self-esteem, lower usage of drugs and tobacco, and unwanted pregnancy.

Female athletes throughout the United States owe their opportunity to compete on equal footing with their male counterparts to many people, including tennis legend Billie Jean King and the late Congresswoman Edith Green.

Equality for Women in Sports: A Spiritual Insight

The Daughters of *Tz'laphchad*

The inspiration for many Jewish women of all contemporary streams of Jewish life to step up and respectfully challenge matters that do not appear to be fair lies in the story of the daughters of (*B'not*) *Tz'laphchad* (*Numbers* 27:1-11). (Please see Chapter 15 in this book.)

After the death of their father, these five sisters, who had no brothers, approached Moses requesting that the ancestral land that *Torah* law would require be passed on only to sons, instead be passed on to them. Moses, the final, human arbiter among the Israelites on Jewish legal matters, did not know what to do, so he petitioned the Supreme Court's Chief Justice (i.e., the Almighty). The Holy One Blessed Be He pronounced the following rendering which initiated a new chapter in Jewish law regarding inheritance:

כֵּן בְּנוֹת צְלָפְחָד דֹּבְרֹת
נָתֹן תִּתֵּן לָהֶם אֲחֻזַּת נַחֲלָה בְּתוֹךְ אֲחֵי אֲבִיהֶם
וְהַעֲבַרְתָּ אֶת־נַחֲלַת אֲבִיהֶן לָהֶן:

Kehn B'not Tz'laphchad dov'rot, naton tihten lahem achuzat nachala b'tokh achei avihem, v'haavarta et nachalat avihen lahen.

The daughters of Tz'laphchad speak correctly. You shall surely give them a hereditary holding among the brothers of their father, and you shall cause the inheritance of their father to be transferred to them (Numbers 27:7).

Rashi and other commentators point out that the motivation behind *Machla, Noa, Chagla, Milka* and *Tirtza* (i.e., the five daughters') request for equality in ancestral land distribution was their love of *Eretz Yisrael* (**the Land of Israel**) and their desire to keep the land that belonged to their father in their family's possession (*Rashi* on *Numbers* 27:1). Since the land was divided among the tribes, and *Tz'laphchad* was a descendant of *Menashe*, to retain their portion, the five daughters had to marry men from the Tribe of *Menashe*.

Because what they proposed was consistent with the intent of the law of inheritance, *B'not Tz'laphchad* were successful in setting a precedent on how a person's possessions (real and personal property) normally pass to the next generation. Since *Machla* and all four of her sisters were sincere in their love of family and passion for Israel, they were each granted equal shares of land in Israel.

In many ways, this new addition to the laws of inheritance is "the Title IX of the Daughters of *Tz'laphchad*."

THE BOX SCORE

Legislators perform acts of sportsmanship by creating laws that help bring equality to those entitled to it. In the *Torah* we read about *B'not* (**the daughters of**) *Tz'laphchad* (*Numbers* 27:1-11) who successfully petitioned Moses to create an exception to the laws of inheritance to ensure that women, who had no brothers, received a fair share of ancestral land upon the death of the familial landowner. This is an expression of extraordinary *Derekh Eretz v'Khavod* (**Respect and Honor**) to the deceased parents, daughters, and the Land of Israel.

Chapter 21
"The Whole Is Greater Than the Sum of its Parts:" Extraordinary Acts of Sportsmanship by Unions and Lawyers

Union Leaders and Lawyers

Just because society says it is okay to do something does not always mean that it is okay. According to Jewish, American, and many other countries' labor laws, workers and employees are entitled to certain rights. At times, current laws do not reflect the goals of society or provide honor and respect to all, and thus need to be amended or expanded or even instituted. Through courageous efforts of brave people, the appropriate changes can be, and often are, realized.

The Contributions of Marvin Miller

In 1966, Marvin Miller was hired by the Major League Baseball Players Association (MLBPA) to be its executive director. Leaving a prominent position as a labor economist for the powerful United Steelworkers of America, Miller took a professional risk when assuming this leadership role for the underfunded and understaffed players' union. After all, before his arrival, the MLBPA was considered to be a weakling among professional organizations; in fact, it was described by Dahlia Lithwick in the book *Jewish Jocks* as "a fairly toothless fraternal group."

For anyone skilled enough to play in the MLB, it should be, and it is for many, a great honor to be a member of this elite fraternity. After all, this is a dream shared by a countless number of ambitious little boys around the world. Before Miller's tenure, little economic power came with this "great honor." Players were essentially at the mercy of the owners.

With the wisdom gained from being raised by parents who were active in their support for organized labor (his father was a clothing salesman and his mother a union public school teacher), along with his wealth of prior work experiences, Miller quickly realized that injustices were being done to the players. From an economic perspective, they were being exploited by the owners. For example, the "reserve clause," a paragraph included in every MLB player's contract, bound the player to that team until management decided otherwise. This left players essentially as – in former U.S. Senator Sam Ervin's words, "well-paid slave(s)"– unable to choose their teams. Additionally, all grievances a player had with his team were arbitrated by the commissioner, who had an inherent conflict of interest since the owners hired him.

Having assessed these injustices, Miller quickly realized that the players association could be transformed from a "toothless fraternity" into a powerful union, a collective bargaining unit that could obtain for its members what the law entitled the players to receive. As with all labor leaders, the major obstacle that Miller faced was changing the mentality of the players and inspiring them to buy in to his philosophy. In a relatively short time, Miller gained the respect and confidence of the players. Over the course of the nearly 17 years with the organization, his efforts led to significant changes that benefited the players and the game (and team owners) as well.

Here are some of the major accomplishments achieved by the Miller-led MLBPA:

(1) A player's right to have a grievance heard by an independent arbitrator, whose decision would be binding;

(2) A practical end of the reserve clause, achieved through the courage of Curt Flood (please see next passage) and wise legal decisions of arbitrator Peter Seitz and a federal court which upheld Seitz's decision;

(3) With the fall of the reserve clause and an agreement as to when a player would be considered a free agent, salaries rose. When Miller began his tenure the average salary was $19,000 and when he retired in 1982 it was $241,000;

(4) Players gained the right to be represented by an agent;

(5) An increased pension plan funded in part by television revenue;

(6) Safer working conditions, including padded outfield fences, better locker rooms, and more player-friendly scheduling of games;

(7) With greater earnings and improved benefits, most MLB players no longer needed an offseason job. As full-time employees, they were better able to train, thus raising the level of the player and game.

Marvin Miller's bold innovations in baseball spilled over into the other major professional sports in the United States, leading to similar improvements in benefits and salaries for players in the National Football League, National Basketball Association, and National Hockey League. While game ticket prices for MLB, NFL, NBA, and NHL games have risen dramatically, making it very difficult for many fans to attend, the players and owners have reaped great benefits – and one might say excesses. For example, the total revenues for MLB owners in 1965 were about $50 million. In 2016, their revenues were approaching $10 billion.

While directly improving the lives of MLB players (and indirectly, players from other major sports leagues) would qualify as an act of sportsmanship in my definition, it was met with hard feelings from many members of MLB management. (And admittedly, the outsize salaries paid to players these days are jaw-dropping.) In spite of receiving recommendations from former MLB commissioners Bud Selig and Fay Vincent and other respected leaders in the baseball world, Marvin Miller has repeatedly been rejected from inclusion in Baseball's Hall of Fame. Nonetheless, his efforts in legally leveling the playing field between players and owners have been recognized by the United States Supreme Court. In 2012, a little more than six months before he passed away, Miller became the first non-justice to have his portrait hanging in the halls of the United States Supreme Court.

Civil Disobedience

Arthur Goldberg's One and Only Case Before the U.S. Supreme Court

Civil disobedience is defined by the *Oxford American Dictionary* as the "refusal to comply with certain laws considered unjust, as a peaceful form of political protest."

In addition to flouting laws that are unjust, another approach is to challenge such laws in a court of law.

In 1970, two individuals of diverse backgrounds teamed up to challenge such a law. Although they did not prevail in this specific case, their efforts helped pave the way for professional athletes to receive better pay and more benefits, especially for those represented by labor unions.

This story is about an African-American baseball player named Curt Flood and a Jewish labor attorney with an impressive resume named Arthur Goldberg.

In 1997, Curt Flood passed away at 59. Many avid baseball fans do not remember him. After all, he is not a member of the National Baseball Hall of Fame and he spent most of his career overshadowed by Hall of Famers Lou Brock and Bob Gibson. As a player, Curt Flood was a solid .293 career hitter. Known as an outstanding fielder, Flood won seven Gold Glove awards for his play in the St. Louis Cardinals outfield. A National League All-Star for three seasons, he helped lead the Cardinals to two World Series Championships.

On January 16, 1970, Curt Flood sued Major League Baseball challenging its reserve clause. Flood alleged that the reserve clause, which obligated a player to play for the same team unless the team decided to trade him, violated the United States Constitution's 13th Amendment's prohibition against involuntary servitude and slavery. Although at the time, he was earning what was then considered to be a high salary, $90,000 a year, he felt that it was wrong for a player to be so severely limited in choosing where he wanted to play and for how much. Instead of agreeing to be traded to and playing for the Philadelphia Phillies, Flood chose to sit out the 1970 baseball season and to pursue his claim for justice.

The court held in favor of Major League Baseball. The league argued that the reserve clause should not be equated with involuntary servitude as a player had a choice to seek employment in other occupations. The baseball establishment further argued that abolishing the reserve clause would lead to free agency and would eventually ruin baseball. In their decisions, the courts held that because of tradition, the MLB should be exempted from the antitrust laws. In the federal district court opinion, Judge Irving Ben Cooper stated, "Baseball has been the national pastime for over one hundred years and enjoys a unique place in our American heritage . . . The game is on a higher ground; it behooves us to keep it there . . ." In a 5–3 decision by the U.S. Supreme Court, Justice Harry Blackmun stated for the majority: "The longstanding exemption of professional baseball from the antitrust laws . . . is an established aberration . . ."

Even though Flood did not prevail in his lawsuit, it eventually led to other players fighting MLB management; an arbitrator struck down the reserve clause in 1976, and free agency was born. Unfortunately, at the time, Flood was shunned by many members of the mainstream world of Major League Baseball. "I lost money, coaching jobs, a shot at the Hall of Fame. But when you weigh that against all the things that are really and truly important, things that are deep inside you, then I think I've succeeded."

Arthur Goldberg was born in Chicago to a poor immigrant family in Chicago. Greatly inspired by Jewish tradition, after graduating from Chicago's Northwestern University School of Law, he dedicated his law practice to advancing the rights of America's labor force. He served as JFK's secretary of labor before being appointed to the U.S. Supreme Court in 1962. Three years later, Goldberg shocked the world when he accepted President Lyndon Johnson's offer to abdicate his lifetime seat on the Supreme Court and become the U.S. Ambassador to the United Nations. In this capacity, Goldberg greatly assisted Israel in its fight for survival before, during, and after the 1967 Six Day War. As a lawyer, Goldberg appeared only once before the Supreme Court: in Curt Flood's case.

not deliver pointed, persuasive arguments. He lost his place. He did not answer justices' questions directly. He clumsily listed Flood's season-by-season batting averages. He went past his allotted time. He repeated himself."

While we do not know whether a better prepared Arthur Goldberg would have been able to sway two more of the justices in his favor, it is fair to learn from this the important role that preparation and focus play in a person's performance. Sometimes it's better to turn down an assignment rather than accept it and not be able to give it your all.

Civil Disobedience: A Spiritual Insight

Shifra & Puah: Women Who Ensured the Future of the Jewish People through an Act of Civil Disobedience

When enslaving the Israelites did not slow down the Jewish male birth rate enough to assuage Pharaoh, he ordered the midwives who delivered the Hebrew babies, *Shifra* and *Puah*, to kill any Israelite boys that were born. Because *Shifra* and *Puah* had too much *Kavod, Derekh Eretz,* and *Yirah* (**reverence**) for God and the Jewish nation, they risked their lives and refused to follow Pharaoh's command.

When the two midwives were summoned by Pharaoh to explain their insubordination, they simply stated:

כִּי לֹא כַנָּשִׁים הַמִּצְרִיֹּת הָעִבְרִיֹּת
כִּי־חָיוֹת הֵנָּה
בְּטֶרֶם תָּבוֹא אֲלֵהֶן הַמְיַלֶּדֶת וְיָלָדוּ:

Ki lo kha-nashim haMitzriyot haIvriyot, ki chayot hena, b'terem tavo alahen ha-m'yaledet v'yaladu.

Because the Hebrew women are not like the Egyptian women. Rather, they are like wild animals; before the midwife arrives, they have already given birth (*Exodus* 1:19).

While some commentators (see *Rashi, Exodus* 1:19) state that *Shifra* and *Puah* were actually Moses's mother *Yocheved* and sister Miriam, others (see *Abarbanel*) state that they were Egyptian women who had no vested interest in saving the Israelites. These brave midwives risked their lives in order not to follow an immoral edict or law. In his article *On Not Obeying Immoral Orders*, former Chief Rabbi of England Lord Rabbi Jonathan Sacks refers to *Shifra* and *Puah*'s refusal to obey Pharaoh as "the first recorded instance in history of civil disobedience."

Not only did the Almighty reward *Shifra* and *Puah* and spare their lives and protect them, but their acts of Divine sportsmanship were rewarded by having dynasties descend from them.

To learn more about the noble acts of *Shifra* and *Puah*, see the *Torah* text (*Exodus* 1:15–21) and such Rabbinic sources as *Sh'mot Rabba* 1:13 and *Sotah* 11b.

THE BOX SCORE

As stated in the introduction to this section (Sportsmanship Level III), "one category of extraordinary acts of sportsmanship are ones that are historic in nature, in that they helped trigger a change in public policy or law allowing others future opportunities that were not previously available to them." Such accomplishments are almost always achieved by people who are willing to take risks in possibly compromising their own physical survival, financial security, or standing/acceptance in society.

Treating employees and workers (even those who are paid handsomely) with proper respect and honor (דֶּרֶךְ אֶרֶץ וְכָבוֹד/*Derekh Eretz v'Khavod*) is a form of sportsmanship. Sometimes these achievements can only be accomplished by challenging the status quo, as Curt Flood and Arthur Goldberg did.

The midwives *Shifra* and *Puah* have a special place in Jewish history as women who, at the risk of their own lives, were not afraid to disobey the command of Pharoah, allowing the Israelites to survive.

Chapter 22
Muckrakers and Prophets: Extraordinary Acts of Sportsmanship by Journalists

Don't Shoot the Messenger

With captive audiences of readers, journalists have the wonderful opportunity to positively influence society. One way they can do so is by pointing out the generally unrecognized ills of the world and incite public outrage, making the appropriate people take responsibility, and propose solutions. Since the early 1900s, the journalists who have chosen this route have been known as muckrakers.

Rick Telander: A Contemporary Sports Muckraker

The term "muckrakers" refers specifically to pre-World War I journalists in the United States who had the courage to expose corruption in government, business and other noted areas. The earliest muckrakers were pioneering investigative journalists. They include Upton Sinclair, who uncovered major problems in the meat industry in his breakthrough novel, *The Jungle* and Edwin Markham, who called out child labor abuses in his book, *Children in Bondage*. Although the muckraker era of journalism technically ended more than 100 years ago, I agree with others and still consider contemporary journalists muckrakers, especially investigative reporters who expose social issues that other journalists choose to overlook.

In sports journalism there are a number of present day muckraking journalists who come to mind. Among them is award-winning, Chicago-based writer Rick Telander. Currently a featured columnist for the *Chicago Sun-Times*, Telander has also written for decades for the venerable *Sports Illustrated* and *ESPN, The Magazine*. A graduate of the prestigious Medill School of Journalism at Northwestern University, Rick Telander attended Northwestern on a football scholarship. An Academic All-Big Ten selection, he was drafted by the Kansas City Chiefs and later cut during training camp.

In addition to his creative, informative, and insightful prose, Telander is known for writing about problems in the world of sports that needed to be fixed. Although he has written on many different sports, the journalist honed his expertise in college football as *Sports Illustrated's* beat writer. During this time, he exposed many of the scandals at major Division I schools as well as addressed the issue of how the NCAA makes millions of dollars off its football players who do not share in its monetary bonanza. In his 1989 book, *The Hundred-Yard Lie: The Corruption of College Football and What We Can Do to Stop It*, Telander deals with these and other issues. He continues to investigate the powers that be and, in recent years, has written stories on college coach salaries and violence surrounding Chicago schools.

Rick Telander has also been in the frontlines of bringing to the public's attention the dangers of football, specifically in causing concussions. In an enlightening series of articles in the *Sun-Times*, Telander wrote about a number of his former Northwestern Wildcat teammates – some of whom also played in the NFL, all who suffer from lingering football injuries. The sensitively phrased question (which I am paraphrasing) that he posed to each of his friends was whether the thrill and benefits derived from playing football outweigh the physical problems that they incurred and continue to experience?

Journalists, like Rick Telander, are blessed with the skills needed to clearly investigate and articulate the world's problems – and have the opportunity to influence public policy as a result. This is the highest level of sportsmanship when journalists use their talents to enlighten us on important issues, thus stoking the fires of change.

Don't Shoot the Messenger: Spiritual Insights

אַתָּה הָאִישׁ! / Ata Halsh– "You Da Man!"

"You da man!" This popular phrase is commonly exclaimed in many different forums with a particular regularity in the world of sports. It has different meanings depending upon whom you ask. To some, these three "words" are reserved for the team star or leader. According to others, this statement is a form of recognition, recognizing a job well done.

We learn from the first instance that this statement was documented that "You da man!" is actually an expression of responsibility; it was proclaimed by a person whose role it was to remind others of their shortcomings and inspire them to lead more upstanding, ethical lives.

One of the greatest *Biblical* figures was King David. David, the son of Jesse, was a most talented and courageous man. He is especially remembered for his musical genius, special friendship with Jonathan (son of Saul) and his leadership qualities. However, like any human being, David was imperfect.

His greatest sin was that he violated the tenth of the Decalogue (**Ten Commandments**), the prohibition of coveting (*Exodus* 20:14; *Deuteronomy* 5:18). King David committed this egregious misdeed when he admired Batsheba, who was married to a man named *Uriah*. David was so attracted to Batsheba that he wanted to marry her. This caused David to abuse his powers as King of Israel and order that Uriah, who was an officer in Israel's army, be sent to the front lines of battle. Because of David's cruel order, *Uriah* was killed and David then married "the widow" Batsheba.

During the days of the *Bible*, there were Hebrew prophets. In addition to communicating directly with the Almighty and serving as leaders, the prophets also functioned as the moral conscience of the Israelites. Whenever necessary, they would reprimand the Children of Israel, and then remind them to behave appropriately and take responsibility for their behavior. The prophet Nathan lived at the time of David and was not intimidated by the fact that David was the King of Israel. Not afraid to confront David and make him take responsibility for his actions, the prophet accomplished this by telling David a story about a rich man who stole a lamb from a poor man. David became so enraged by this story that he interrupted Nathan and proclaimed:

DIDJA KNOW that President Theodore "Teddy" Roosevelt, who Is well known for saying: "Speak softly and carry a big stick; you will go far," is credited with coining the noun "muckraker"?

חַי ה' כִּי בֶן מָוֶת הָאִישׁ הָעֹשֶׂה זֹאת

Chai HaShem ki ven ma-vet HaIsh ha-oseh zot

"As HaShem lives the man who did this deserves to die!"
(*II Samuel* 12:5)

David's response gave Nathan the opening to make David accept responsibility for his reckless behavior. The Hebrew prophet confronted the Hebrew king and said to him, **אַתָּה הָאִישׁ!**/Atah HaIsh (*Samuel* II 12:7). When translated into modern day English this phrase means, *"You da man!"*

The responsibility of serving as the moral compass of the modern-day Jewish community is often assumed by its rabbinic leaders. The role of the rabbi is to teach, both through traditional texts and by personal example. Although untenured rabbis cannot be as bold as the Prophet Nathan, for fear of losing their job, they can and should still point out issues in society that are in conflict with Jewish tradition and then propose solutions to their constituents.

One of the rabbis who is best known for inspiring others to lead a more ethical, moral life is Rabbi Yisrael Salanter (1810–1883). Inspired by the teachings of Rabbi Zundel, the Lithuanian-born Rabbi Salanter dedicated his life to Jewish scholarship and teaching. In addition to *Torah*, Prophets, Scriptures, *Talmud*, and Codes, Rabbi Salanter stressed the importance of including *Mussar* in the curricula of *Y'shivot*. Roughly translated as **moral, ethical teachings**, *Mussar* stresses the need to self-examine our moral behavior and always look for ways to improve. It focuses on taking the lessons from the traditional texts and applying it to one's own personal behavior.

Rav Salanter is credited with establishing the *Mussar* movement. From his influence, *Mussar* slowly became incorporated into the curricula of mainstream *Y'shivot*. Not only did the *Y'shivot* begin to require courses in *Mussar*, using such texts as Rabbi Moshe Chaim Luzzatto's (1707–1746) *M'silat Y'sharim* (**Path of the Just**), but many *Y'shivot* added a new position to their faculty known as the *Mashgiach Ruchani* (**Spiritual Supervisor**).

One of the many famous quotes attributed to Rabbi Salanter is, "A rabbi they don't want to drive out of town is no rabbi, and a rabbi who lets himself be driven out of town is no man."

Through his *Mussar* teachings and by personal example, Rabbi Yisrael Salanter reminded every Jew of the importance of taking responsibility for their own actions and to always aspire to improve their *Midot* (**character attributes**). *Rav Salanter*, a muckraker himself, teaches that we must all be our own muckraker.

NAME THAT *MITZVAH!*

As stated earlier, The definition of לְשׁוֹן הָרַע /
Lashon HaRa is *truthful, but negative speech.*
The general rule is that, even though it is true, we
are prohibited from uttering it. However, when it
is absolutely necessary to do so, we are allowed,
but only to those people who need to know. The
clear exceptions to the general prohibition include
when one was a witness to a crime. In such cases,
the proper authorities must be notified so that
the alleged offender does not keep harming
others. The more difficult exceptions are in the
cases of *Shidduchim* (*matches intended for
marriage*) and job references. In his book, *Jewish
Literacy,* Rabbi Joseph Telushkin analyzes a
famous case in American political history and
whether the press was correct in sharing personal
medical information about a certain candidate
for national office.

Chapter 23
Sportsmanship Level IV: Acts of Sportsmanship Off the Field

Giving Back

Valuable life lessons can and should be learned from the sports we play and watch. A person displays Level IV of Sportsmanship when s/he internalizes Levels I, II and III, and then manifests honor and respect in all facets of their life

"Show me the Money!"

"Show me the money!" This line, which was made famous in the movie *Jerry Maguire*, stereotypes the perceived primary function of today's sports agents: to negotiate the most lucrative contracts for their athlete clients. Too often, sports stars spend their money on personal comforts like deluxe homes, luxury cars, and vices, while ignoring the needs of their community. Many squander millions in life earnings and subsequently declare bankruptcy.

However, California-based sports agent Leigh Steinberg, who served as a consultant for the box-office hit film *Jerry Maguire* and inspired the creation of the title role, is also known for getting athletes involved in philanthropy. In addition to representing the financial interests of his clients, Steinberg insists that his clients "show him the money" and consider establishing foundations and other programs that will benefit society.

Some of Steinberg's former clients worked hard to give something back. Retired Tampa Bay Buccaneer Warrick Dunn helps single-parent families purchase homes. Former quarterback Warren Moon's *Crescent Moon Foundation* awards college grants. San Francisco 49ers' legend Steve Young's *Forever Young Foundation*, aids children struggling with physical, emotional or financial difficulties. And retired defensive tackle Russell Maryland – nicknamed "The Conscience" by college teammates because he persistently nudged them to do their homework and play their hardest – has worked to help at-risk young people in Texas and his home town of Chicago. Many of these charitable efforts are focused on the same communities in which the benefactor/athlete grew up or in cities where they played.

In addition to negotiating billions of dollars in contracts, Leigh Steinberg has facilitated the distribution of a multitude of charitable monies benefiting local communities.

In Steinberg's own words, "To this day . . . if I walked home and told my dad I'd negotiated a $10 million contract he'd just say, 'Gee, that's great.' But if I told him I had set up a community program that helped kids, he'd throw his arms around me and really get excited. Because of that, I had to make a difference somehow."

Since the release of the movie *Jerry Maguire*, Steinberg has suffered ups and downs dealing with such problems as alcoholism, divorce, agent decertification and bankruptcy. With much work, he has come back from his fall from grace and is, once again, working as a sports agent.

With professional sports generating greater profits, valuations of most teams in the billions, and increasingly off-the-chart player and coach salaries, charitable giving and community development have become more and more common in the sports community – for altruistic reasons, but also financial and tax considerations are influential. Many, if not all, professional sports teams (at the highest level of the sport) have established charitable foundations that provide funding for important programs in their local communities. More and more players have set charitable priorities and provided for these causes through their foundations and volunteer efforts.

Giving Back: A Spiritual Insight

The *Gabbai Tz'daka*

Historically the Jewish community has been an exemplar of taking care of its own members and not being dependent upon the good graces of government. Jewish law mandates that all Jews perform *G'milut Chasadim* (***Acts of Loving Kindness***) both through their physical actions (e.g., *Bikkur Cholim* – ***Visiting the Sick***, and *Nichum Avelim* – ***Comforting the Bereaved***, etc.) and also by providing financial assistance to individuals and organizations in need. The latter is commonly referred to as צְדָקָה (*Tz'daka*). The great scholar Maimonides/ *Rambam* (1135–1204) in his magnum opus on Jewish law, the *Mishneh Torah* (sometimes referred to as the *Yad HaChazaka* – ***Strong Arm***), emphasizes the importance of doing all that one can to assist the impoverished, while bringing the least amount of shame to the beneficiary.

The *Rambam* also points out that the highest (of eight) level of *Tz'daka* is achieved not by giving an outright gift, but rather by providing the person in need with a mechanism to become self-sufficient. This may include a job offer or an interest-free loan to establish a business. Historically, because of the generosity of many individuals, along with the great value placed on education and earning a livelihood, and only accepting welfare from others as a last resort, there are relatively few Jews today who need assistance. While there may be relatively few, nonetheless, there are still many Jewish people in need of some type of financial assistance.

While it has become fairly common for the community to show gratitude, as it should, to the many generous individuals who step up and contribute their own money to assist others, oftentimes, we neglect to recognize those who inspire others to give – the fundraisers.

The model for the contemporary Jewish communal (professional and volunteer) fundraiser is the community *Gabbai* (literally, ***Collector***) of years past. While the term *Gabbai* today is commonly given to the man who assigns *Aliyot* and other synagogue honors, the primary function of the *Gabbai* during the *Talmudic* and post-*Talmudic* eras was that of a fundraiser.

Every community would appoint a *Gabbai* whose role was to collect *Tz'daka* (both obligatory and voluntary amounts) from the members of that particular community. Each week (usually on Friday) after he collected these monies, he then distributed funds to poor members of the community as well as for other charitable public purposes. **The public fund that the Gabbai managed** was known as the *Kupa*. Jews back then could fulfill their obligation to give *Tz'daka* by giving directly to a worthy person or organization or could do so by giving to the *Kupa* (through the *Gabbai*).

Understandably, for a community to entrust their charitable contributions to a public fund, the fund manager had to be unquestionably trustworthy, possessing impeccable credentials. The role model for serving as a *Gabbai* was *Rahbi Chanina ben T'radyon* (*Bava Batra* 10b; *Avoda Zara* 17b). Based upon these *Talmudic* passages, according to Maimonides (*Mishneh Torah, Hilkhot Mat'not Aniyim* 10:8), the three most important qualifications that a *Gabbai* must possess are that he must be **trustworthy** (*Neh-ehmahn*), **wise** (*Chakham*), and **know how to manage money properly** (*v'yodeah l'hanhig k'shura*).

Also known as *Chanania ben T'radyon*, this great *Tanna* lived in the Galilean city of *Sikhin*. Although he lived a most honorable life, unfortunately, he also endured great personal tragedies. The father of *B'ruria* (who was married to *Rahbi Meir* and who had a tragic death), *Rahbi Chanina ben T'radyon* is also well-known for encouraging Jews to share *divrei Torah* (**words of Torah**) when in each other's company. As he stated in *Pirkei Avot/Ethics of Our Fathers* 3:3:

רַבִּי חֲנַנְיָא בֶּן תְּרַדְיוֹן אוֹמֵר:
שְׁנַיִם שֶׁיּוֹשְׁבִין וְאֵין בֵּינֵיהֶן דִּבְרֵי תוֹרָה, הֲרֵי זֶה מוֹשַׁב לֵצִים . . .
אֲבָל שְׁנַיִם שֶׁיּוֹשְׁבִין וְיֵשׁ בֵּינֵיהֶם דִּבְרֵי תוֹרָה, שְׁכִינָה שְׁרוּיָה בֵינֵיהֶם . . .

Rahbi Chanania ben T'radyon omer: Sh'naim sheh-yosh'vin v'ein beineihen divrei Torah, harei zeh moshav letzim . . . Aval sh'naim sheh-yosh'vin v'yesh beineihem divrei Torah, Sh'khina sh'ruya veineihem . . .

Rahbi Chanania ben T'radyon says: "Two [Jews] who sit together and do not exchange words of Torah, is [considered] a session of the scornful . . . However, two [Jews] who sit together and exchange words of Torah, the Sh'khina [Divine Presence] rests amongst them . . ."

Like *Rahbi Akiva* and many other *Tannaim* who lived during the time of the Hadrianic Decrees which outlawed the teaching of *Torah* (approx. 130 CE), *Chanina ben T'radyon* refused to stop teaching and eventually was caught and tortured to death (*Avoda Zara* 17b–18a). This powerful account is recounted as a part of the special *Musaf* Martyrology liturgy on *Yom Kippur*.

THE BOX SCORE

As in the days of the *Talmud*, it is important today
that we appoint (both on the professional and volunteer
levels) individuals who possess similar qualities as
Rahbi *Chanina ben T'radyon* who inspire members of
the Jewish community to give as much as they are able,
who then manage these charitable funds honestly
and prudently, and make sure that they are distributed
to worthy beneficiaries.

A sports figure expresses Level IV of Sportsmanship
by incorporating the positive life lessons learned on the
field/court and then expressing them outside of the
sports venue. One such expression is charity, which is
being performed more and more by professional
athletes who have established charitable foundations and
other instruments to share their bounty with those
less fortunate. It is important to give a "shout-out" to
Leigh Steinberg and other sports agents who encourage
their clients to become even more charitable.

Providing Opportunity to be Self-Sufficient

Paying It Forward: Yogi Berra's Magnificent Act of Kindness

When the non-sports fan hears the name "Yogi Berra," often s/he will associate it with one of his many malapropisms or, as they are better known, "Yogi-isms." "It ain't over till it's over." "Baseball is 90 percent mental. The other half is physical." These are but a few of his profound and often funny quotes.

While remembering his Yogi-isms like everyone else, the diehard sports fan will also remember Berra as perhaps the greatest catcher of all time. In addition to his three MVP awards and 15 All-Star Games, Yogi, a true team player and leader, helped lead his beloved Yankees to 14 World Series appearances, 10 of which ended with World Championships.

A quiet, humble man, Yogi Berra performed numerous acts of kindness that were not known outside of his immediate circle of family and friends. One story came to light around the time of his 90th birthday in 2015, a few months before his death.

Choosing to drop out of school in 8th grade to help his immigrant parents against their wishes, Berra lost jobs at a coal yard and working on a Pepsi truck because he kept ducking out to play baseball. A native of St. Louis, when he was 15, Yogi was offered a contract from his hometown Cardinals but he rejected it because he was only offered a minimal $250 signing bonus, $250 less than his friend Joe Garagiola. With the guidance, encouragement, and recommendation of his local American Legion team leader, Leo Browne, Berra was signed to a minor league contract by the New York Yankees with a more respectable $500 signing bonus

Apparently, Yogi Berra was profoundly influenced by Mr. Browne's taking an interest in him. About 50 years later a local entrepreneurial teenager, Carlos Lejnieks, raised by an immigrant single mother, approached Berra and asked him to participate in a baseball memorabilia show that he was organizing. Impressed by this teen, Berra agreed and negotiated a discounted fee for his participation.

Unfortunately Carlos, who excelled academically, later dropped out of high school briefly to help his mother support the family. When young Mr. Lejnieks returned to school, he was told that it would be quite a challenge for him to be admitted to a top college. The high school student then reconnected with Berra who agreed to write a letter of recommendation to Brown University. After being accepted,

DIDJA KNOW that the Yogi Berra Museum and Learning Center, in addition to being a unique repository of memorabilia related to the life and times of this great American treasure, also sponsors educational programs that focus on the values that Berra personified both on and off the field, like sportsmanship, social justice, and respect? Located in Berra's adopted hometown of Montclair, New Jersey, this institution plays an important role in ensuring the amazing legacy of this Yankee great. (For further information, see http://yogiberramuseum.org)

Brown University's admissions dean told Carlos that Berra's letter was a key reason why he was admitted.

Lejniek excelled at Brown. After a short but successful career on Wall Street, Carlos followed his heart to public service. He is now President and CEO of Big Brothers Big Sisters of Essex, Hudson, and Union Counties in New Jersey, an organization that pairs youth in underserved communities with mentors.

From Leo Browne to Yogi Berra to Carlos Lejnieks to New Jersey's "little" brothers and sisters, one could conclude that: "paying it forward is all about paying it forward." Since Yogi Berra was never documented as saying this, let us just call this an "honorable Yogi-ism."

Providing Opportunity to be Self-Sufficient: A Spiritual Insight

Maimonides's Highest Level of Charity

NAME THAT *MITZVAH!*

Tz'daka

לָתֵן צְדָקָה כְּמִסַּת יָדוֹ

Liten Tz'daka K'Misat Yado

To Give Charity According to a Person's Means
Sefer HaChinukh #479;
Sefer HaMitzvot, Ahseh #195

In his compendium on Jewish law, the *Mishneh Torah, Hilkhot Mat'not Aniyim* (*Laws of Gifts to the Poor* 10:7*), Maimonides teaches that the highest level (of eight levels) of *Tz'daka* is doing what it takes to make a person in need, self-sufficient by providing a job, forming a business partnership, lending money interest-free, etc. While the next seven levels all deal with giving a person in need a charitable gift, they are ranked in terms of how much potential shame may be involved. The highest of these seven levels is providing money in confidence where neither the donor nor the benificary know the other person's identity.

Visiting the Sick

The Babe

In an interview in 2013, Babe Ruth's granddaughter, Linda Ruth Tosetti, shared the following about her famous grandfather:

"When it came to children, there was nothing he would not do. He would go to the hospitals and ask to see the sickest children. When he entered the room all the kids went crazy. Children who could not sit up, did. The ones who could not walk, ran to him. They forgot they couldn't. It must have been incredible to see! "

The most inspirational story of the Bambino visiting a sick child is one that has become legendary. In 1926, Johnny Sylvester, then an 11-year-old die-hard Yankee fan, was severely injured after falling off of a horse. While convalescing in his family's Essex Fells, New Jersey estate, during the World Series between the St. Louis Cardinals and New York Yankees, according to one account, Johnny told his father that the only thing that could lift his spirits was a baseball from the World Series. A few days later, Johnny received a package via airmail from

St. Louis, containing autographed balls from both teams. The one from the Yankees had the autographs of Babe Ruth and a few of his teammates. On the ball, the Sultan of Swat also scribbled: "I'll knock a homer for you on Wednesday." Sure enough, not only did the Babe deliver on his bold promise, but he went above and beyond, as on October 6, during Game Four, Ruth hit – not one – but three home runs.

Unfortunately for Johnny, the Yanks lost the Series in seven games. However, on October 11, the day after the Cards' clinching victory, Babe Ruth went to visit young Mr. Sylvester in Essex Fells. The following day, the *New York Daily News* ran the front page headline, "'DR.' BABE RUTH AT BEDSIDE," accompanied by a photo of the Bambino shaking hands with a beaming Johnny Sylvester.

Johnny recovered from his injury, graduated from Princeton University, and later became a prominent businessman. He also rose to the rank of lieutenant in the U.S. Navy and served his country during World War II.

This inspirational story is memorialized in the book, *Babe & the Kid*, by Charlie Poekel, as well as in the documentary film, *I'll Knock a Homer for You: The Timeless Story of Johnny Sylvester and Babe Ruth.*

Visiting the Sick: A Spiritual Insight

Reb Aryeh: A Rebbe with a Cause

וְאָמַר רַבִּי חָמָא בְּרַבִּי חֲנִינָא:
מַאי דִּכְתִיב אַחֲרֵי ה' אֱלֹקֵיכֶם תֵּלֵכוּ?
וְכִי אֶפְשָׁר לוֹ לְאָדָם לְהַלֵּךְ אַחַר שְׁכִינָה?...
אֶלָּא לְהַלֵּךְ אַחַר מִדּוֹתָיו שֶׁל הַקָּדוֹשׁ בָּרוּךְ הוּא.

V'amar Rahbi Chama B'Rahbi Chanina:
Mahy dikh'tiv – Acharei HaShem Elokeikhem telekhu?
V'khi efshar lo l'ahdam l'halekh achar Sh'khina? . . .
Elah l'halekh achar midotav shel HaKadosh Barukh Hu.

[And] Rahbi Chama the son of Rahbi Chanina said: "What is the meaning of the verse: Acharei HaShem Elokeikhem telekhu – Follow HaShem your God (Deuteronomy 13:5)? Is it possible for a person to [physically] follow the Divine Presence? . . . But rather, [this verse teaches] that we should follow [i.e., imitate] the attributes of the Holy One Blessed Be He.

Just as He clothes the naked . . ., you should clothe the naked. The Holy One Blessed Be He visited the sick . . ., you too should visit the sick. The Holy One Blessed Be He comforted mourners . . ., you too should comfort the bereaved. The Holy One Blessed Be He buried the dead . . ., you too should bury the dead" (Sotah 14a).

The great *Mitzvah* of *Bikkur Cholim* (**Visiting the Sick**) all began when the Almighty, through his angel Raphael, visited 99-year-old Abraham who was recuperating from his *B'rit Mila* (*Bris*) which he had three days earlier. Since that time, about 4,000 years ago, many people have fulfilled *Mitzvat Bikkur Cholim*, lifting the spirits of a countless number of healthcare patients.

A champion of visiting the sick was Rabbi Aryeh Levin (1885–1969). Known as the *Tzaddik* (**Righteous Man**) of Jerusalem as well as simply *"Reb Aryeh,"* Rabbi Levin emigrated from Europe to *Eretz Yisrael* (the **Land of Israel** or, as some refer to pre-state Israel, Palestine) in 1905. There he served as a member of the administration of *Etz Chaim Talmud Torahs*. In addition to his role in Jewish education, Rabbi Levin made it a regular practice to visit the sick and other people who were isolated, even reaching out to lepers who others feared to visit.

In 1931, Chief Rabbi Abraham Isaac Kook offered *Reb Aryeh* a position that he had already unofficially assumed, the prison chaplain to Jewish prisoners. During this time, the British, who ruled over Palestine, presented numerous challenges to the Jews already living in Israel as well as those trying to immigrate. To meet these challenges, the Jews organized the Jewish Resistance Movement, a group of underground resistance fighters, forming such organizations as the *Haganah* and *Palmach*. When these brave men and women were caught, many were subjected to harsh prison sentences and sometimes even sentenced to death for their "political crimes."

Known as being non-judgmental to Jews of all backgrounds, *Reb Aryeh* brought hope and light to hundreds of prisoners. He regularly visited one of the prisons on *Shabbat* morning where he ran a morning *Minyan* (**service**) for the inmates. Many stories about *Reb Aryeh's* compassion towards the sick and others that he visited are recorded in such books as Simcha Raz's *A Tzaddik in Our Time: The Life of Rabbi Aryeh Levin*. A story written by David Rossoff in his article, *Aryeh Levin, Father of Jewish Prisoners*, blends together *Reb Aryeh's* great compassion for the Jewish prisoners, his passion to perform *Bikkur Cholim*, and the abundant love and commitment that he had for his family.

The story told by Rossoff describes how *Reb Aryeh* once was reading the *Torah* during the *Shabbat Shacharit* (morning) service at the prison when one of the guards interrupted and asked the rabbi that he come with him immediately as there were people waiting for him. Not wanting to compromise the integrity of the service, *Reb Aryeh* asked the guard to wait until he was done reading from the *Torah*. The guard was persistent, and after waiting a few minutes, he insisted again that Rabbi Levin stop and come with him. Sensing the urgency of the request, *Reb Aryeh* asked that one of the inmates continue the *Torah* reading, and the esteemed Rabbi left with the prison guard.

As he approached the prison entrance, *Reb Aryeh* saw that his son-in-law was there and right away realized that there was a serious problem. Together they walked back to his daughter's home, where Rabbi Levin soon learned that his daughter was stricken with an illness that caused paralysis. Although the doctor felt that over time she would regain partial use of her affected limbs, he said that it would be years before she would fully recover.

Having learned about the tragedy in *Rav Levin's* family, the following *Shabbos*, the inmates wanted to know how the daughter was doing. *Reb Aryeh* responded, "As well as can be expected." During the *Torah* service, after the first *Aliya* (honor), *Reb Aryeh* recited the *Mi Shehberakh* prayer for the welfare of the prisoner who had just finished reciting the blessings over the *Torah*. Instead of pledging money for *Tz'dak*a, which is customarily done, the first honoree pledged one day of his life for the recovery of *Reb Aryeh's* daughter. The next five men who had *Aliyot* each increased their "pledges." After the seventh *Aliya*, the *Oleh LaTorah* (man who was honored), a prisoner named Dov Tamari – who later became a professor at the world renown Technion Israel Institute of Technology – made the ultimate pledge, "What is our life in prison worth compared to the our rabbi's anguish? I pledge all the remaining days of my life to the complete recovery of our rabbi's daughter." Moved by the compassion expressed by these men for his daughter and their devotion to their beloved rabbi, *Reb Aryeh* was overcome by emotion.

At the conclusion of *Shabbat*, *Reb Aryeh* learned that his daughter had made significant progress in her recovery. A few days later she returned to normal. As we know, the bravery of these "prisoners" was integral in establishing the modern State of Israel. In addition to this huge achievement, we see that the power of their prayers and love also helped bring about a medical miracle.

NAME THAT *MITZVAH!*

Bikkur Cholim (Visiting the Sick)
Although not directly enumerated in *Sefer HaChinukh* or Maimonides's *Sefer HaMitzvot* – and technically a *Mitzvah D'Rabbanan* (**Rabbinic-ordained Commandment**) – according to *Chazal* (**our Sages of Blessed Memory**), the great *Mitzvah of Bikkur Cholim* (**Visiting the Sick**) is an expression of various **Torah-ordained Commandments** (*Mitzvot D'Oraita*), including.

מִצְוַת אַהֲבַת יִשְׂרָאֵל
Mitzvat Ahavat Yisrael
The Mitzvah of Loving Your Fellow Jew
Sefer HaChinukh #243;
Sefer HaMitzvot, Ahseh #206

According to Maimonides (*Mishneh Torah, Hil'khot Ahvel* 14:1): "It is a Rabbinic ordained *Mitzvat Ahseh*/**Positive Commandment** to visit the sick, comfort mourners, bury the deceased, provide a wedding for the bride, and to escort (i.e., host) guests . . . These are considered *G'milut Chasadim* (**Acts of Loving Kindness**) that one performs through action (as opposed to by donating money), and have no minimum or maximum amount. . . . Although all of these *Mitzvot* are Rabbinically-ordained, they are all examples of (the *Torah*-ordained *Mitzvah*) *V'Ahavta l'reiakha kamokha* – **And you shall love your neighbor** as yourself, all those acts that you would want others to perform to you, you should perform to your brother."

לָלֶכֶת וּלְהִדָּמוֹת בְּדַרְכֵי הַשֵּׁם יִתְבָּרַךְ

LaLekhet U-Lhidamot B'Darkhei HaShem Yitbarakh

To Follow and Imitate the Ways of HaShem the Blessed

Sefer HaChinukh #611; Sefer HaMitzvot, Ahseh #8

As stated by *Rahbi Chama the son of Rahbi Chanina* (*Sotah* 14a), one of the ways that we fulfill this Divine Commandment is by visiting the sick, just as the Almighty did to Abraham when he was recuperating from his *B'rit Milah/Bris* (at age 99).

It has been noted by Rabbi Yitzchok Silber in his book *The Code of Jewish Conduct* that when a visit is so vital that it is an important factor in helping save a sick person's life, the visitor is also performing other *Mitzvot* including שֶׁלֹּא לַעֲמֹד עַל דַּם רֵעִים / *Shehlo LaAmod Ahl Dahm Reiihm – Not to Stand By Idly While Someone's Blood is Shed;* [*Sefer HaChinukh #237; Sefer HaMitzvot, LT #297*] and לְהָשִׁיב אֲבֵדָה לְיִשְׂרָאֵל / *L'Hashiv Aveda L'Yisrael – To Return a Lost Object to a Fellow Jew;* [*Sefer HaChinukh #538; Sefer HaMitzvot, Ahseh #204*].

The following episode illustrates how *Bikkur Cholim* can be viewed as an example of **Shehlo LaAmod Ahl Dahm Reiihm**. The *Talmud* (*N'darim 39b-40a*) relates the story of how one time a student of *Rahbi Akiva* was ill and none of the other students or sages went to visit him, with the exception of *Rahbi Akiva*. While visiting, *Rahbi Akiva* cleaned the floor of his sick student's room. At the end of *Rahbi Akiva's* visit the student exclaimed, "*Rah-bi heh-ch'yatani* – **Rabbi you have given me life.**" Based upon this episode, *Rahbi Akiva* stated: "*Kol mi sh'eino m'vaker cholim k'ilu shofekh dahmim* – **Anyone who does not visit the sick, it is as if he is committing murder** [literally, spilling blood; i.e., killing the sick person]."

V'ah-sitah HaYashar V'haTov b'einei HaShem – **And you shall do that which is fair [straight] and good in the eyes of HaShem** (*Deuteronomy 6:18*). Although not listed as one of the 613 *Mitzvot* in the *Sefer HaChinukh* or *Sefer HaMitzvot*, the *Mitzvah* of *Bikkur Cholim* has been cited in the *Morasha Syllabus* titled בִּקּוּר חוֹלִים / *Bikkur Cholim* as fitting naturally into the interpretation of Nachmanides

regarding this statement. As stated earlier in this book, the *Ramban* writes that, since the *Torah* cannot list every "fair and good" act, the *Torah* provides this "catch-all" phrase for which many acts not specifically listed comfortably fit.

Key components of *Mitzvat Bikkur Cholim* (the *Mitzvah* of Visiting the Sick) include:

- The *Mitzvah* is incumbent upon all Jews (rich or poor; learned or ignorant; etc.).
- The visitor must perform an act that brings comfort to the patient. It is all about the person who is sick, not the visitor. This deed varies according to the needs/wishes of the patient. These acts may include bringing the *Choleh* (*sick person*) meals, reading to him, listening to her, paying his bills, washing their floor as *Rahbi Akiva* did, etc.
- Subsequent to the visit, the visitor should say a prayer for the sick person (either in or outside of the patient's presence). A [simple, short] recommended prayer is:

הַמָּקוֹם יְרַחֵם עָלֶיךָ בְּתוֹךְ חוֹלֵי יִשְׂרָאֵל

HaMakom Y'rachem ahlekha b'tokh cholei Yisrael – **May the Omnipresent have compassion on you amongst the sick people of Israel.** (*Shulchan Arukh, Yoreh Deah, Hilkhot Bikkur Cholim* [**the Laws of Visiting the Sick**] *335:6*).

- If performed properly, the visit will remove 1/60 of the remaining illness of the sick person (*N'darim 39b*).
- One fulfills this *Mitzvah* by visiting both Jews and non-Jews (*Shulchan Arukh, Yoreh Deah, Hi'lkhot Bikkur Cholim* [**the Laws of Visiting the Sick**] *335:9*).
- The visitor should show compassion (and empathy if possible). It is related in the *Morasha Syllabus* that once when *Reb Aryeh* accompanied his wife to the doctor when she had a medical issue with her foot, he told the physician, *Doctor, ha-regel shel ishti koevet lahnu* – **"Doctor, my wife's foot hurts us."**
- בִּקּוּר / *Bikkur* and בֹּקֶר / *Boker*: Scholar, author, and psychologist Rabbi Reuven Bulka, Ph.D., in his book *Judaism on Illness and Suffering*, notes that the fact that the words for "morning" (בֹּקֶר / *boker*) and "visit" (בִּקּוּר / *bikkur*) are very similar teaches a very valuable lesson. In Rabbi Bulka's words: "When we visit the sick, we are, in effect, charged with the responsibility of showing them the 'morning,' or bright side, of life."

Honor Your Parents

Honoring Wanda Durant and Other Sports Moms and Dads

Although the source of the *Mitzvah* of *Kibbud Av VaEm* (**Honoring One's Father and Mother**) is the *Torah* (*Exodus* 20:12; *Deuteronomy* 5:16), it is an imperative that is quite logical in nature and similar directives have been adopted by other religions and cultures. There are many examples of people of all different backgrounds and faiths who observe this great commandment.

For scores of athletes, when they sign their first professional contract, they achieve financial security for the first time in their lives. Many express their great love and respect for their parents, as former NBA star Shaquille O'Neil did, by purchasing for them homes and other material objects that they were unable to afford. Other professional athletes establish scholarships in honor of their parents. Along with his mother, former NBA star Grant Hill established a scholarship at Duke University Divinity School in honor of his father, former Yale University and NFL star Calvin Hill. Retired NFL lineman Chris Zorich honored his late mother Zora through the works of a charitable foundation that he founded that included the "Care to Share" family food distribution program.

One of the most inspirational stories of an athlete who honors his mother on a regular basis, through his upstanding character as displayed both on and off the court, is Golden State Warriors' forward Kevin Durant.

Referred to in a sporting goods store commercial as "the nicest guy in the NBA," the former Oklahoma City Thunder player's respect for, and abundant appreciation of, his mother came to the attention of the world at the end of the speech he delivered on May 6, 2014 – five days before Mother's Day – when accepting the Maurice Podoloff Trophy as the 2013-2014 NBA Most Valuable Player. Although "KD" thanked all of his Thunder teammates, his brothers, his father, his grandmother, his coach, Thunder personnel, and others, this speech is best remembered for the gratitude that he expressed to the last person on his long list, his mother, Wanda.

Along with his older brother Tony, Kevin Durant was raised primarily by his mother after his father Wayne left the family when Kevin was 1. Inspired in large part by her own mother, Barbara Davis, Wanda raised her two sons to set goals and to work their hardest to achieve them. These goals included being independent, educated, possessors of upstanding character, and contributors to society. In addition to purchasing for his mom a dream home and other material possessions, Kevin went way beyond, using his MVP award as a platform to laud his mother. In so doing, KD gave his mom Wanda the best Mother's Day gift a child could ever give.

DIDJA KNOW

that, although I would argue that the true origin of Mother's Day is indeed the *Torah* (after all, a child should make every day Mother's [and Father's] Day, by showing honor and reverence to his/her parents), President Woodrow Wilson formalized the national holiday in 1914, by signing a law establishing the second Sunday of the month of May as Mother's Day?

DIDJA KNOW

that Kevin Durant wears the #35 on his jersey to honor the memory of his beloved childhood coach and mentor, Charles "Big Chucky" Craig, who was killed at age 35?

Here are some of the words from that speech:

"Everybody told us we weren't supposed to be here. We went from apartment to apartment by ourselves. . . . When something good happens to you, I don't know about you guys, but I tend to look back to what brought me here. . . . You [referring to his mother] made us believe. You kept us off the street. You put clothes on our backs, food on the table. When you didn't eat, you made sure we ate. You went to sleep hungry. You sacrificed for us. You're the real MVP."

The speech went viral and was the inspiration for a Lifetime movie, *The Real MVP: The Wanda Durant Story*, which was first aired on television the night before Mother's Day 2016.

As a professional athlete, businessman, philanthropist and community leader, and family man, Kevin Durant expresses a global application of honoring one's parents.

Honor Your Parents: Spiritual Insights

The Universal Deeds of Honoring and Revering Our Parents

Question: "How many Jewish mothers does it take to change a light bulb?" Answer: "None; so, I'll sit in the dark!"

Mothers in general and Jewish mothers in particular have been the butt of jokes for a long time.

In the language of comedian Rodney Dangerfield (birth name, Jacob Cohen), mothers get "no respect."

Not only do mothers and fathers deserve respect and honor but, according to Jewish tradition, children are obligated to respect their parents. The fifth of the Ten Commandments states: כַּבֵּד אֶת אָבִיךָ וְאֶת אִמֶּךָ /Kabed et avikha v'et imekha – *Honor your father and mother* (*Exodus* 20:12). Children are also commanded to revere their parents (*Leviticus* 19:3): אִישׁ אִמּוֹ וְאָבִיו תִּירָאוּ/Ish ihmo v'aviv tira-u – [*Every*] *man: his mother and his father he shall revere*.

Honor (*Kavod*) refers to honoring one's parents both through spoken words and actions. These activities include not addressing them by their first name, notifying one's parents that they should not worry, allowing parents to sleep, and assisting them in any manner that they need.

Reverence (*Yirah*) guides a child to act towards a parent in the same manner that he or she would act before a ruler who has the power to punish. A child is prohibited from interrupting his/her parents, sitting in their regular chair (think: Archie Bunker and his loveable son-in-law, "Meathead"), and contradicting them in a disrespectful manner.

According to Jewish tradition, a child must observe the *Mitzvah* (Commandment) of **Honoring his/her Parents** (*Kibbud Av VaEm*) throughout the child's life. After a parent has passed away, this *Mitzvah* is observed by saying the Mourner's Kaddish prayer, giving *Tz'daka* (**charity**) in their memory, and by living an exemplary lifestyle. The reward for observing this *Mitzvah* is long life. Similarly, a child must also observe the *Mitzvah* of Revering Parents throughout their life.

Although honoring one's parents is based in the *Torah*, as noted earlier, it is a practice that is quite logical in nature and has been adopted by other religions and cultures. There are many examples of people of all different backgrounds and faiths who observe this great Commandment. As recorded in the *Talmud* (*Kiddushin* 31a; *Avoda Zara* 23b-24a), an exemplar of this *Mitzvah* was a righteous gentile named *Dama the son of N'tina*. The *Talmud* relates the story of how *Dama* was offered an exorbitant sum of money to sell to certain Sages precious stones to be used for the *Ehphod* garment worn by the *Kohen Gadol* (**High Priest**). To get the key for the safe where these stones were stored, *Dama* would have to wake up his father. Out of respect for his father, he refused to wake up his dad from his nap and was rewarded by having a *Para Aduma* (**Red Heifer** – see *Numbers* 19:1-22) born to his herd.

Jewish tradition and history is replete with examples of individuals who have been role models for the great *Mitzvah* of *Kibbud Av VaEm*. Joseph of the *Torah* had a special bond with his father Jacob and heeded his words even when it put Joseph at risk (see *Rashi's* commentary on *Genesis* 37:13). Although Esau was a wicked man, his one redeeming quality is that he showed great honor to his father, Isaac. In the *Talmud* (*Kiddushin* 31b) we read about *Avimi*, a Sage with five adult sons all who were rabbis, who showed great honor and respect to his aging father *Rahbi Abahu*. We also read about *Rahbi Tarfon* who took extra special care of his mother (*J. Talmud Peah* 1:1).

A modern day example of *Kibbud Av VaEm* is the esteemed Rabbi Shlomo Zalman Auerbach – *ZTz"L* (1910–1995) of blessed memory. Considered one of the greatest **arbiters of Jewish law** (פּוֹסֵק–פּוֹסְקִים/*Posek-Poskim*) of his generation, in addition to his scholarship, Rabbi Auerbach is also remembered for his commitment to the Land of Israel (born in Israel, he never travelled outside of it) and his impeccable observance of both those **Commandments between a Jew and God** (*Mitzvot Bein Adam LaMakom*) and **those between fellow human beings** (*Mitzvot Bein Adam LaChaveiro*). He treated people from all walks of life with dignity and made himself accessible to their inquiries. Throughout his life, *Rabbi Auerbach* manifested a special measure of honor and respect towards his parents.

When *Rav Auerbach* was a youth, he realized that his mother had a hearing impairment that required a hearing aid. Knowing that his father was unable to afford one, the young *Shlomo Zalman* saved prize money won for his scholarship to buy the hearing aid. When *Rav Auerbach* discovered that his mother would not wear the hearing aid on the Sabbath because she felt that it would violate the laws of the Sabbath, he dedicated many hours to meticulously researching and then writing an

Halakhic opinion which explains how, why, and under what conditions a hearing-impaired person could wear a hearing aid without violating the Sabbath. Not only did Rabbi Auerbach enhance the *Shabbos* experience of his mother, but that of countless additional hearing-impaired Jews as well!

NAME THAT *MITZVAH!*

מִצְוַת כִּבּוּד אָב וָאֵם
Mitzvat Kibbud Av VaEm
The Mitzvah of Honoring Parents
Sefer HaChinukh #33;
Sefer HaMitzvot, Ahseh #210

A child is obligated to honor his/her parents throughout the child's entire lifetime. This *Mitzvah* applies equally to a young child being raised in their parent's home, as well as to an adult child caring for his/her elderly parents. We must honor our parents in all ways: through our interactions with them, by serving them, in how we speak to/with them, and in how we act towards others and conduct our lives (as this is a reflection of how parents raised their children). The *Shulchan Arukh* (*Yoreh Deah, Hilkhot* 240:5) cites as examples, that if the parent is unable to take care of him/herself, the adult child must step up and make sure that the parent is fed and cared for in all ways in a dignified manner. After a parent passes away, a child fulfills this great *Mitzvah* by mourning for 12 months, observing *Yahrtzeit*, and acting in ways that bring honor to their memory.
A son is obligated to recite *Kaddish* for the 11 months (approximate) after the burial of each parent. The source of this *Mitzvah* is the fifth of the Ten Commandments, stated both in *Exodus* 20:12 and *Deuteronomy* 5:16. Although it is common to refer to the tablet that contains the last five Commandments as the tablet that deals with *Mitzvot Bein Ahdahm LaChavero* (***Interpersonal Commandments***), the *Mitzvah* of *Kibbud Av VaEm* does not appear on it. Rather, as

the fifth Commandment, it appears on the first tablet, the one that is generally regarded as the tablet that is dedicated to *Mitzvot Bein Ahdahm LaMakom* (***between Man and the Omnipresent***). This apparent discrepancy has been explained that the honor and reverence that a child is obligated to display to his/her parents is similar to the honor and reverence that a Jew is obligated to show God. After all, parents are agents of the Divine, charged with the awesome duty of ensuring that their children are taught the *Torah*, both in word and deed (see *Kiddushin* 30b). Honoring our parents makes a lot of sense; after all, not only do they give us life, but as the agents of the Almighty, by raising children in a proper Jewish environment and manner, they help ensure for their offspring a secure place in **The World to Come** (*Olam HaBah*).

מִצְוַת יִרְאַת אָב וָאֵם
Mitzvat Yirat Av VaEm
The Mitzvah of Revering Parents
Sefer HaChinukh #212;
Sefer HaMitzvot, Ahseh #211

Based upon *Leviticus* 19:3, the *Sefer HaChinukh* teaches that, in addition to honoring his/her parents, a child should also revere them. As noted earlier, a child should have reverence for one's parents in a similar manner that a person would fear a person in power who can punish those who are disrespectful towards him. The *Shulchan Arukh* (*Hilkhot Yoreh Deah* 240) cites as examples that a child should not sit in a parent's chair, contradict their words, or address them by their first names.

THE BOX SCORE

Although it is derived from the *Torah*, honoring parents is a universal principle practiced by people from all walks of life (including Kevin Durant and other sports figures). This *Mitzvah* teaches us that we should honor our parents at all stages of our lives, at every opportunity.

So, the next time someone asks you, "How many Jewish mothers does it take to change a light bulb?" Your answer should be: "None. After all, her children will do it!"

Respect Your Elders

Shaq Buries a Friend

Throughout the rich history of the NBA's Lakers franchise, the team has had the benefit of having many outstanding "big men" play for them. In Minneapolis, their original home city, 6'10" center George Mikan led the team to four NBA championships during the course of a six-year span (1949–1954) and was voted best player of the first half of the 20th century by the Associated Press in 1950. In Los Angeles, the Lakers were led by such outstanding centers as Wilt Chamberlain, Kareem Abdul-Jabbar, and Shaquille "Shaq" O'Neal.

Shaq led the LA Lakers to three consecutive NBA titles (2000–2002). While a Laker, O'Neal forged a friendship with former superstar Mikan. The modern-day Laker "big man" understood the inordinate contributions that his elder made, not only to the Lakers franchise, but to all NBA players who played after Mikan retired. While George Mikan was paid meagerly and did not receive a generous pension, O'Neal became a multi-millionaire from his NBA career. He realized that without the sacrifices made by Mikan and other past NBA stars of the early years, the great fame and wealth that O'Neal and most modern day NBA stars continue to enjoy would have never happened.

On June 1, 2005, George Mikan passed away at age 80 from complications of diabetes and kidney disease. At the time of his death, Mikan and his family were struggling with financial hardship. Realizing this, the protégé Shaq offered to pay for the entire cost of the funeral for his mentor. Crediting Mikan as a player who helped lay the framework for the success of his NBA career, Shaq stated simply, "Without No. 99 [Mikan's jersey number] there's no me. . . . I know what he was and I know what he did."

Respect Your Elders: A Spiritual Insight

The Sad Demise of the Circle Maker

Choni HaM'ahgel (**Choni the Circle Maker**) was one of the many righteous sages who lived during the first century BCE. *Choni* earned this nickname since he once prayed to the Almighty for rain to fall and boldly stated that he would not move from the area that encircled him, until ample rain fell. Not only were *Choni*'s prayers answered, but it rained so hard that he had to pray to the Almighty that He stop the rains (*Taanit* 23a).

Even righteous *Torah* scholars are not perfect and can learn from their mistakes. One time *Choni* saw an old man planting a carob tree. Knowing that it takes 70 years before a tree bears fruit, *Choni* asked the old man why he bothered to plant a tree that would not bear fruit during his lifetime. The old man replied that he "bothered" to do so since he appreciated that he was only able to enjoy the fruit from carob trees because members of earlier generations planted those trees:

כִּי הֵיכִי דְּשָׁתְלֵי לִי אֲבָהָתַי, שָׁתְלֵי נַמִּי לִבְרָאי.

Ki heikhi di-shatlei li ahvahatai, shatlei nahmi li-vrahi.

"Just as my ancestors planted for me, I also plant for my children (**ibid**)."

Choni then fell into a deep sleep from which he did not awaken for 70 years. When he awoke, not only had he outlived the members of his generation, but the next generation as well. Realizing that he had outlived all of his friends and colleagues, he became distressed and passed away.

THE BOX SCORE

Unlike the "old man" in the above cited *Talmudic* passage, unfortunately, it took 70 years of hibernation – wasted years – for *Choni* to learn from his mistakes and realize that we must appreciate and show our gratitude for the contributions of members of past generations and be ready to pay it forward to future generations.

Not erring in this manner, Shaq appreciated the sacrifices that George Mikan and members of his NBA generation made for the modern day players and acted like a "big man" by engaging in an act of off-the-court sportsmanship by paying tribute to the memory of Mikan.

Patriotism

Pat Tillman: Leaving the NFL for a "Greater Calling"

Greatly impacted by the tragedies of September 11, 2001, Pat Tillman took a leave of absence from a lucrative career as an NFL player and, along with his brother Kevin, enlisted in a U.S. Army Rangers regiment. For their bravery, the Tillman brothers received the Arthur Ashe Courage Award in 2003. After serving in Iraq, Pat was then deployed to Afghanistan, where he was killed by "friendly fire" in 2004. The Army later awarded Tillman with a Silver Star and Purple Heart. Both the Arizona Cardinals, the only team for whom Tillman played during his four-year NFL career, and his alma mater, Arizona State University, retired the player's jersey numbers soon after he died.

In addition to foregoing millions of dollars in future earnings as an NFL player, Pat Tillman volunteered for a war for which there was no draft. A *summa cum laude* college graduate (in only 3.5 years), Tillman felt a great sense of loyalty, not just to his country, but also to his team. After all, he rejected a more lucrative offer from the Super Bowl XXXIV champion St. Louis Rams to play for his home team, the Arizona Cardinals.

In the words of his Cardinals coach Dave McGinnis, "Pat knew his purpose in life. He proudly walked away from a career in football to a greater calling." Pat Tillman paid the ultimate price for a brand of sportsmanship we call patriotism.

Patriotism: A Spiritual Insight

Israel Advocacy

The first Israeli-born player in the NBA, Omri Casspi truly appreciates the role of Israel as the Jewish homeland. He is also grateful for the religious freedoms allowed him by both his birth country of Israel and the country where he works, the United States. Additionally, Casspi has embraced his status as a role model for Jews around the U.S. and the world and as an outspoken goodwill ambassador for Israel.

Descended from Polish Jews on his mother's side, who were forced to flee World War II Europe because of anti-Semitism, as well as Moroccan Jews (father's family), Casspi truly comprehends that Jews need a safe, secure modern State of Israel.

He is reminded of this message on a regular basis, having been raised in the city of Yavneh, located only 25 miles from the Gaza Strip. In a 2014 telephone interview with Ailene Voisin, a reporter for *The Sacramento Bee*, Casspi stated regarding the Israel-Gaza conflict: "Everyone is scared and on edge. My dog (Butch) follows me everywhere, even into the bathroom. I tried to sleep last night, but then the sirens go off, and you can hear when the Iron Dome missiles connect with an incoming rocket. The whole house trembles. My sister and my parents, we just run to the nearest bomb shelter. Believe me, this is just terrible."

Having served in the Israel Defense Forces, Casspi also understands he high price that Jews must pay for a homeland.

A member of the Israeli National Team, Casspi and his teammates often are met by hostile crowds. When traveling in Europe and other countries, the team is accompanied by top security personnel and is advised to hide their team apparel that identifies which country they represent.

Omri Casspi knows first-hand and from family history what anti-Semitism/Zionism is all about. Yet, instead of running from or denying his heritage, Omri chooses to be an advocate on behalf of his homeland, Israel. In addition to inspiring Jewish NBA fans around the United States and Canada, Casspi is an unofficial spokesman/emissary for Israel.

Prompted by many well-intended questions from teammates, Omri was inspired to organize his first trip to include a group of former and current teammates, all non-Jews, to travel with him (and that time, with former NBA player and countryman Gal Mekel) to Israel for one week during the summer of 2015. While in Israel, this entourage of players got to experience, firsthand, how unique and essential Israel is for the survival of the Jewish people. In addition to seeing

DIDJA KNOW that, in addition to having a Hall of Fame baseball career, one in which he hit 521 home runs and batted .344, Ted Williams was also a great patriot and war hero? The "Splendid Splinter" missed playing in nearly five baseball seasons while he served in the U.S. military during World War II and the Korean War. As a Marine fighter in Korea, Williams showed great courage, flying about 39 combat missions, and taking enemy fire on three occasions. Can you imagine what Williams's career stats would have been had he not missed such a significant amount of playing time?

what first-time tourists see, they also had the experience of volunteering at two basketball camps where Jewish, Palestinian, and Druze youngsters all played together. In an interview about the 2015 visit, Casspi said, "I'm in the unique position to show my best friends it's the only country in all of the Middle East that you can . . . practice Islam, you can practice Christianity, you can be Jewish."

As an advocate for Israel, Omri Casspi expresses an important type of *Derekh Eretz v'Khavod* (**Respect and Honor**) by using his celebrity status as a platform to help his homeland fight the anti-Semitic untruths spewed by so many around the world. He is a true patriot of his homeland, Israel.

Love Peace and Pursue Peace

Suzyn Waldman is a trailblazer.

The longest-tenured woman broadcaster in the history of Major League Baseball, Ms. Waldman has served as the color commentator for New York Yankees radio broadcasts on WFAN since 2005. In addition to her color commentary, Waldman conducts the (pre- and post-game) interviews along with certain other game day broadcasts. Prior to this appointment, she had been covering the Yankees beat for WFAN, New York City's premier all-sports radio station since 1987.

After a formidable career as an actress, in 1987 she switched gears and entered the male-dominated field of sports journalism.

What is her unique, special brand of sportscasting? Ms. Waldman, when interviewed by Milwaukee journalist, Duane Dudek, said that during a game, she attempts to: "bring out the humanity of a situation. To find one or two things that fans can't get by reading the paper or watching TV."

Well-respected by longtime Yankees owner – the late George Steinbrenner ("the Boss"), in 1999 Waldman was given the seemingly insurmountable challenge to bring peace between Steinbrenner and Yankee legend Yogi Berra by the station's executive producer, Mark Chernoff. Chernoff proposed that Waldmann hold this peace summit on a live broadcast of Waldman's evening radio show.

Upset regarding the manner in which he was fired as the Yankees manager after only 16 games in 1985 (instead of personally delivering the news, the Boss sent a representative), the Hall of Fame catcher vowed never to return to the Yankees so long as George Steinbrenner owned the team. Despite numerous pleas from friends and family members, the proud and stubborn Berra refused to relent.

That is until Waldman got involved . . . .

After Ms. Waldman communicated with both parties, the two men agreed to make amends as part of her live broadcast on January 5, 1999 at the recently-opened Yogi Berra Museum & Learning Center in Montclair, New Jersey, a municipality in which Berra resided for many years.

At this meeting Steinbrenner apologized to Berra, and Berra accepted the apology. Yogi even relented and allowed the Yankees to honor him on July 18th of that year at "Yogi Berra Day" at Yankee Stadium.

To open the "Yogi Berra Day" celebration, Don Larsen – the only player to ever pitch a perfect game in the World Series (in 1956) – threw out the ceremonial first pitch to the catcher who also played that historic series – his Yankee teammate, Yogi Berra. To add further glory to that special day – made possible by the reconciliation facilitated by Suzyn Waldman – Yankee pitcher David Cone threw the 16th perfect game in MLB history.

Love Peace and Pursue Peace: A Spiritual Insight

הִלֵּל אוֹמֵר:
הֱוֵי מִתַּלְמִידָיו שֶׁל אַהֲרֹן;
אוֹהֵב שָׁלוֹם, וְרוֹדֵף שָׁלוֹם,
אוֹהֵב אֶת הַבְּרִיּוֹת וּמְקָרְבָן לַתּוֹרָה.

Hillel omer: H'vei mi-talmidav shel Aharon; ohev Shalom, v'rodef Shalom, ohev et ha-b'riyot u-mkar'van LaTorah.

[The Sage] Hillel says: "Be of the students of Aaron; loving peace and pursuing peace, loving people and bringing them closer to the Torah" (**Ethics of Our Fathers** 1:12).

Aaron is remembered for various distinctions. He was Moses's older brother who served as his spokesman. The first *Kohen Gadol* (**High Priest**), Aaron was charged with the awesome responsibility of overseeing the daily religious affairs of the *Mishkan* (**Tabernacle**).

A people's person, Aaron not only loved peace, but actively pursued it. In *Avot D'Rahbi Natan*, Aaron's legendary tactics in facilitating peace between two individuals are described. He would actively pursue each of the two disputants, sit down with them individually, and then tell each one how distraught the other person feels about their unresolved dispute. Upon learning of the other person's contrition, the next time the two individuals met they embraced, thus burying the hatchet.

Aaron, along with his sons, was the first person to bestow the Priestly Blessing (*Numbers* 6:22–27), when he gave this three-fold blessing to the Children of Israel. In this fifteen-word passage the first blessing (for one's material welfare) is comprised of three words. The second blessing (for spiritual needs) is five words. Finally the most challenging blessing is the third one, comprised of seven words. This blessing is for **peace** (שָׁלוֹם/*Shalom*).

There's No Place Like Home

An important display of sportsmanship by many professional athletes is assisting their home and/or team communities through acts of volunteerism and charity. On rare occasions athletes have the opportunity to express their gratitude to those "who raised him/her," by actually playing for their hometown teams.

Long Live the King! The (Self-Imposed) Exile and Return of LeBron James

If the average basketball fan were asked to articulate the first four words that come to mind when hearing the name "LeBron James," in great likelihood, they would choose such words as: "great," "dominating," "amazing," and "awesome."

When I freely associate after hearing the same name, the words "pressure," "hype," "expectations," and "relief" emerge. (If one has trouble remembering these words, try the following acronym: PHER [pronounced "fair"].) Known for his tough, but fair, play and unique, one-of-a-kind style, this "word" describes LeBron James's long journey from high school stardom to bringing the first NBA championship to his hometown team, the Cleveland Cavaliers.

Pressure and Hype.

In 2003, the Cleveland Cavaliers won the NBA draft's lottery and were rewarded with the #1 pick. As expected, the lowly Cavs selected 18-year old LeBron James's, a "can't miss" athletic phenom from northeast Ohio, who had just graduated from nearby Akron's St. Vincent-St. Mary High School.

Talk about pressure. For years, James had been hyped in the media as the future face of the NBA, the heir apparent to Michael Jordan, who had just retired.

Expectations.

Since their inception in 1970, the Cavs had never played in an NBA Finals, let alone, won the NBA championship. In fact, the last professional team from Cleveland to win a title was the "old" Browns who won the NFL championship in 1964 (two-plus years before Super Bowl I). The city of Cleveland was starved for a champion and their expectations of LeBron James were that he would lead the Cavaliers to a championship – very soon.

While James played like a seasoned veteran during his first season, earning him the NBA's Rookie of the Year award, and the Cavs more than doubled their victory total from the previous season, the team still did not qualify for the playoffs. "King James" continued to perform at this extraordinary level, playing in the NBA All-Star game in each of his next six Cavalier seasons. In the 2006–2007 season, in spite of a second-place finish in the East Conference, James led the Cavs to the NBA Finals where they were swept by the San Antonio Spurs. In the 2008-2009 and 2009-2010 seasons, in spite of winning more than 60 regular season games in each of these campaigns, the Cavaliers failed to reach the NBA Finals.

In 2010, LeBron James became an unrestricted free agent. He was now free to choose any team to play for. He decided to join fellow All-Stars Dwyane Wade and Chris Bosh (also top five picks in the 2003 NBA Draft) and play for the Miami Heat. James gave this reason for his choice in his public announcement in July of that year: "I think the major factor and the major reason in my decision was the best opportunity for me to win and to win now and to win into the future also."

As a member of the Heat for the next four seasons, James's team reached the NBA Finals each season, winning back-to-back championships in 2012 and 2013. After the 2013-2014 season, once again, LeBron James became an unrestricted free agent.

As was the case four years earlier, there were many teams competing, trying to recruit James to their team. Some made major personnel changes to adjust their salary cap space, while other teams asked their stars to actively reach out to James.

Unlike the outcome in 2010, this time, King James chose to return home to play for the Cavaliers. In his own words, as told to Lee Jenkins, a senior writer for *Sports Illustrated*: ". . . I want to give them hope when I can. I want to inspire them when I can. My relationship with Northeast Ohio is bigger than basketball. I didn't realize that four years ago. I do now. . . . When I left Cleveland, I was on a mission. I was seeking championships, and we won two. . . . Our city hasn't had that feeling in a long, long, long time. My goal is still to win as many titles as possible, no question. But what's most important for me is bringing one trophy back to Northeast Ohio."

Relief.

The 2016 NBA Finals featured a rematch from the previous year: the NBA champion Golden State Warriors vs. the runner-up Cleveland Cavaliers. Led by LeBron James, the Cavs came back from a 3–1 deficit, swept the final three games, and claimed their first NBA Title in team history. In addition to the overwhelming joy felt by James, his Cavalier teammates, and Cleveland sports fans, there was also a tremendous sense of relief. In the words of *Sports Illustrated* Senior Writer, Lee Jenkins, "[Kevin] Love could feel an actual weight lifting from his teammate's [LeBron James] 250-pound frame."

Not only did the King return to his kingdom from his self-imposed exile, but he restored to his home the great feeling of being champions once again. He did this all by playing fairly (PHERly); that is, by withstanding extreme pressure, exceeding overwhelming hype, and surpassing expectations. At the end, the King and the members of his kingdom breathed a collective sigh of relief.

And they all lived happily ever after . . .

There's No Place Like Home: Spiritual Insight

The Sage *Hillel*'s Delicate Balancing Formula

Looking for a meaningful quote? I recommend checking-out the *Talmudic* Tractate of *Pirkei Avot* (literally, **Chapters of the Fathers**; many times translated as **Ethics of Our Fathers**).

DIDJA KNOW that certain researchers give some credit for the beginning of a turnaround in Cleveland – from a dying Rust Belt city where the population was plummeting to one that appears to be sprouting growth and embracing renewal – to LeBron James's return to play for the Cleveland Cavaliers? According to Richey Piiparinen, a researcher and director for The Center for Population Dynamics at Cleveland State University, "Something is happening. The river burned in '69 . . . Everybody left . . . We were the first region that died. And then recently, we've seen trends pointing to this return migration, this boomerang effect. LeBron is the face of it because his boomerang was so iconic."

DIDJA KNOW that the LeBron James Family Foundation sponsors all third grade at-risk students enrolled in Akron public schools through 12th grade? Any of these students who graduate high school with at least a 3.0 average are guaranteed four-year scholarships to the University of Akron. For further information go to: http://lebronjames familyfoundation.org.

DIDJA KNOW that when LeBron James was 13 years of age he participated in Sunday night open gym at the Shaw JCC in Akron? Keith Dambrot, who is Jewish, supervised this weekly activity. Today the head basketball coach at the University of Akron, Dambrot coached LeBron to two state high school basketball championships as the coach at Akron's St. Vincent-St. Mary High School.

In a 2012 interview with the *Cleveland Jewish News* Dambrot shared: "Basically, I opened up the Jewish center and let any kid pretty much come and work out every Sunday evening. LeBron was a sponge. He was with a group of boys who had been coming for a year or so. He's the type of guy that learned quickly, just wanted to be taught."

Replete with wise advice from many of the leading scholars of the time, this tome offers life lessons from the "Who's Who" of *Tannaitic* Sages (approximately 20-200 CE).

One of these sages is *Hillel*. Known for his sensible and practical teachings, *Hillel* teaches:

אִם אֵין אֲנִי לִי, מִי לִי?
וּכְשֶׁאֲנִי לְעַצְמִי, מָה אֲנִי?
וְאִם לֹא עַכְשָׁיו, אֵימָתָי?

Ihm ein ahni li, mi li? U-Khshehahni l'ahtzmi, ma ahni? V'ihm lo akhshahv, eimatai?

If I am not for myself, then who will be? And when I am (only) for myself, what am I? And if not now, then when?

THE BOX SCORE

While we are taught the importance of looking out for the welfare of others, in order to be able to effectively accomplish this goal, according to the teaching of the Sage *Hillel*, we first must ensure our own wellbeing.

Although LeBron James wanted to win championships for his home state Cleveland Cavaliers, after seven seasons, when he saw that he was not successful in accomplishing this goal James chose to join a team where he felt he would win the coveted NBA title. The King took care of his own needs by winning two Championship Rings in four years, and then decided to express his gratitude to fellow Northeast Ohioans by returning to the Cavaliers. Sure enough, in his second season back, King James achieved his ultimate professional dream.

Operating out of a sense of urgency, in 2014, James realized that the time was now for him to help the Cavaliers and Cleveland sports fans win a championship for this franchise and city that so desperately wanted to be a winner after more than five decades.

Tz'daka

לָתֵן צְדָקָה כְּמִסַּת יָדוֹ
Liten Tz'daka K'Misat Yado

To Give Charity According to One's Means
Sefer HaChinukh #479;
Sefer HaMitzvot, Ahseh #195

Based upon the teachings of Maimonides (*Mishneh Torah, Hilkhot Mat'not Aniyim/Laws of Gifts to the Poor* 7:13) and other Sages, the order of priority of giving to the poor is: (1) the poor from a person's own family; (2) the poor of a person's town; (3) the poor of Israel; and (4) the poor of the Diaspora.

The Unbreakable Bond Between Siblings

As technology becomes more and more sophisticated, communication has become easier and more accessible. Towards the end of the 20th century, personal computers, cell phones, and the Internet exploded into the public sphere and quickly became an indispensable fixture in almost every household of means in countries around the world. Email and then texting and instant messaging became a common mode of communication.

The 21st century has witnessed the proliferation of such social media as Twitter, Instagram, and Facebook. Today, if a person with enough money to buy a cell phone or a tablet or a computer and internet access wants to reach out to someone – whether they are as close as next door or across the world - they have many choices.

Back in the "old days," a long-distance call from Europe to the United States was quite costly. Today, such calls can be free. If people want to see each other while chatting they can use such programs as Skype and FaceTime.

While technology has provided us with so many options in communication, there are still certain relationships that can only be nurtured in person, face-to-face.

When Smartphones Aren't Smart Enough

One of the greatest female athletes is Women's National Basketball Association (WNBA) superstar Elena Delle Donne. Passionate about her sport, as an 18-year-old, she brought a whole new meaning to being "homesick."

For many, college is a hard adjustment. After all, classes are less frequent and more challenging. There is less structure. For those who live on campus, it takes time to get adjusted to living away from home. Dorm rooms do not provide the same luxuries as home. No matter how hard the college cafeteria staff may try, no one's food can match Mom's (or Dad's).

Recruited by numerous universities, Delle Donne chose to play for the perennial powerhouse University of Connecticut Huskies. Coached by legendary Geno Auriemma, UConn continues to be a top team in the nation. In the fall of 2008, after spending only two days on campus, Delle Donne decided to leave the university, expressing to the public that she felt "burned out" from basketball. It appeared, though, that it wasn't just basketball burnout that caused her to leave, but also her close relationship with her family:

Delle Donne was homesick. Most of all she missed her older sister, Lizzie.

Lizzie is not your average "big sister." Born blind and deaf with autism and cerebral palsy, the only way others communicate with Lizzie is through her sense of smell and touch. Elena, brother Gene, and parents Ernest and Joan mainly communicate with Lizzie with hand-overhand sign language. Because of her disabilities, the only way that Elena and others can communicate with Lizzie is in-person.

Extremely close with Lizzie, Elena transferred to nearby University of Delaware so that she could resume regularly spending time with her big sister. At the University of Delaware, Elena excelled in basketball, leading the Blue Hens to national prominence. Selected #2 overall in the 2013 WNBA draft by the Chicago Sky, Delle Donne has earned the league's Rookie of the Year (2013) and MVP (2015) awards. With the exception of 2016–2017, Delle Donne rejected offers to play basketball overseas during the WNBA off-season, choosing instead to be closer to Lizzie and family in Delaware.

Unfortunately for the Sky and the city of Chicago, Delle Donne's desire to spend more time with Lizzie propelled her to request a trade to the Washington Mystics on February 2, 2017, so she could be within commuting distance to Delaware.

In a moving piece on the Internet entitled "Lizzie," Elena Delle Donne writes about her relationship with Lizzie: "Therein lies one of the biggest lessons Lizzie has taught me: communication is so much more than words. That lesson has transcended all of my relationships. It's changed how I communicate with those that I'm closest to. Language is important but actions – doing, touching – is above all. Giving someone a huge hug is sometimes way more effective than saying anything."

No matter how smart phones may be, they can never replace face-to-face experiences with others.

Elena Della Donne teaches, by example, a unique type of sportsmanship – the importance of going above and beyond in helping care for family and others.

The Unbreakable Bond between Siblings (and other Family Members): Spiritual Insights

When it Comes to Brothers, a Half is Equal to a Whole

Before forgiving his brothers, when he was the viceroy of Egypt, it seems that any act that Joseph performed towards his brothers was negative. Or at least that's the way it was interpreted. Joseph proudly described his dreams in great detail in a manner that conveyed to his brothers (and parents) that he was superior to them. According to the *Midrash* (*Tanchuma* 7), based upon *Genesis* 37:2, he shared with his father stories about alleged evil acts performed by his brothers. And the list goes on.

But this was not always the case.

According to this same *Midrashic* source, Joseph looked out for his half-brothers born to Jacob's wives, Bilha and Zilpa. While Leah's sons may have bullied them by treating them like slaves, Joseph treated them with **true brotherly love** (אַחֲוָה / *Achava*). Unfortunately, when he relayed this news to Jacob, it just made Leah's sons hate him even more.

Being the children of Leah (and Rachel's) maidservants, these half-brothers were viewed as "second class" by Leah's sons, and therefore were more vulnerable to mistreatment by Leah's elitist sons.

Joseph showed that when it comes to brothers, a half is equal to a whole.

An Unbreakable Familial Bond

When Joseph ordered that his brother Benjamin be kept as a slave, because the goblet was found in his sack, Judah pleaded that Joseph reconsider and take him (Judah) instead. From a simple reading of the text (*Genesis* 44:18–34) Judah's argument that led to Joseph finally revealing his true identity was that a permanent separation of Benjamin from his father would cause Jacob's death. The most powerful phrase that Judah articulated to describe the close father-son bond shared by Jacob and Benjamin was:

וְנַפְשׁוֹ קְשׁוּרָה בְנַפְשׁוֹ

V'nafsho k'shura v'nafsho

"... and his [Jacob's] soul is bound up with his [Benjamin's] soul."

THE BOX SCORE

We learn from basketball superstar Elena Delle Donne and the *Biblical* Joseph how strong the bonds can (and should) be between family members and the importance of looking out for those who are vulnerable – especially if they are siblings or other family members.

While Elena Delle Donne expresses a special type of off-the-court sportsmanship, we are reminded by Joseph that דֶּרֶךְ אֶרֶץ וְכָבוֹד / *Derekh Eretz v'Khavod* (**Respect And Honor**) extends to the way we treat all family members.

The Swimming All-Star

Retired shortstop Nomar Garciaparra's MLB resume includes: six-time All-Star; American League Batting Champion (1999/.357 and 2000/.372); and a career batting average of .313. He had a most successful baseball career, playing for the Red Sox, Cubs, Dodgers, and A's. He is still involved with the game as a baseball analyst for Sportsnet LA. In addition to his being a husband (to soccer legend Mia Hamm) and father of three children, Nomar's personal résumé also includes rescuing two women from possibly drowning in the Boston Harbor.

In October 2005, while working on a condominium that he owned, Nomar and his uncle Victor Garciaparra heard a scream and a splash. Nomar ran out the door towards the harbor to investigate. In addition to the first woman, a second woman also fell, hit her head on the pier, and landed in the water. Nomar dove into the water, swam towards the two women, and was able to reach them. Reports that day noted that, in order to bring the women safely to shore, Victor then also jumped from the condo's balcony (approximately a height of 20 feet) to assist in the rescue.

Because both Nomar and his uncle were apparently comfortable (and possibly also trained) in water rescue, they were able to bring these women to safety. Although Nomar Garciaparra led the American League in the number of double plays turned as a shortstop in 1997 (113) – along with his DP partner Uncle Victor – this was the most important double play of Nomar's life.

Doing What's Right: Spiritual Insights

Elijah: The Unintimidated Resuscitator

Based upon the words לֹא תַעֲמֹד עַל־דַּם רֵעֶךָ /Lo Tah-ah-mod ahl Dahm Reiehkha– **Do not stand idly by when your fellow's blood is shed** (*Leviticus* 19:16), a Jew is commanded (*Sefer HaChinukh* #237) to do all that s/he can (without putting their own life in peril) to save the life of another human being. From this same verse we are also commanded not to withhold testimony in court when that information can save someone's life or prevent a financial loss.

Homiletically, this *Mitzvah* also directs a person to be strong
and to do the right thing, even if the leaders of a given
community/society and the majority of its members are
corrupt. This latter interpretation of the above *Mitzvah* best
describes one of the key roles of the ancient Prophets. A major
task of theirs was to "call out" others even though it may
have endangered their own wellbeing.

One of the most revered prophets in Jewish history was
Elijah. Two of his greatest confrontations were with Israel's
King Ahab and his Phoenician wife, Jezebel.

In one instance when Queen Jezebel introduced the
Israelites to the pagan idol *Baal*, Elijah challenged 450 priests
of *Baal*, hired by the evil queen, to a competition to see who
the real god of Israel was. The Almighty responded with a
large fire, causing the Israelites gathered to exclaim, "*HaShem
Hu HaElokim, HaShem Hu HaElokim*" – "***HaShem (the God
of Compassion) is the God (of Justice), HaShem is the God!***" (*I Kings* 18:39).
At the direction of Elijah, the Israelites then killed the 450 priests of *Baal*.
To save his own life, Elijah was forced to flee and hide for 40 days until Jezebel's
anger dissipated.

Later, Elijah, unintimidated by King Ahab and Queen Jezebel, reprimanded
King Ahab for unjustly ordering the execution of Navot (with the assistance
of Jezebel) because Ahab coveted his vineyards: הֲרָצַחְתָּ וְגַם יָרָשְׁתָ /*HaRatzachta
v'gahm yarashta* – "***Have you murdered and also inherited?***" (*I Kings* 21:19).

Elijah also had the opportunity to fulfill *Mitzvah* #237 in its literal sense
when he resuscitated the son of the owner of the property where he was living
(*I Kings* 17:17–24). Elijah's protégé, the Prophet Elisha, also saved a boy in a similar
manner (*II Kings* 4:8–37).

Chapter 24
The Enforcers

**Sportsmanship Enforcers,
Facilitators and Promoters:
Chapters 24-30**

Enforcing Sportsmanship

In an ideal world, there would be no need for third parties to enforce sportsmanship, as the participants (players and coaches) would follow all the rules and act in a sportsmanlike manner. If a player committed a foul, s/he would immediately take responsibility for their infraction, and then subject her/himself to the appropriate punishment.

In organized sports, with some exceptions like golf, we do not rely on self-enforcement; rather, we engage referees, umpires, and other trained professionals to judge the conduct of the players. Whenever someone violates a rule, the offender is cited and the appropriate punishment is meted out. When a coach or player acts in an unsportsmanlike manner – beyond violating a basic rule of play – often, the referee/umpire can stop play and penalize the offender and team.

Referee Jerry Markbreit Invents a New Unsportsmanlike Conduct Penalty

One of the greatest NFL referees of all time expanded the definition of unsportsmanlike conduct in a 1986 game between the Chicago Bears and their archrival, the Green Bay Packers.

In the second quarter of a game during the season following the Bears first (and to date, only) Super Bowl victory, Packers cornerback Mark Lee intercepted a pass thrown by Chicago's "Punky QB" Jim McMahon. Two full seconds after the end of the play, Packers defensive nose tackle Charles "Too Mean" Martin picked-up McMahon as he was walking to the sidelines and dumped him headfirst onto the turf. Veteran NFL official Markbreit caught a full view of this assault, immediately flagged Martin, and, without hesitation, ejected him from the game. Ejections are issued so rarely in the NFL that this was Markbreit's first in his then nine-year career as a league referee. When announcing his decision over the public address system, Markbreit introduced a new term to the NFL, "stuffing." Soon thereafter, the NFL incorporated this term as additional grounds to eject a player from a game.

In making this landmark decision, Markbreit reflected years later, "A lineman dreams of intercepting a pass and running for the winning touchdown. An official's dream is to have something happen in a football game where you not only react correctly, but you also contain the animosity, control the game, and save the day. And brother, that's exactly what I did."

After 43 consecutive seasons of officiating football (the last 22 in the NFL, officiating 161 games, according to the ref), in 1999, Jerry Markbreit began a new phase of his distinguished career, contributing as an off-the-field sports judge. First he served as an instant replay official and later as head trainer of NFL referees. Always putting player safety first, he was later locked out, along with other experienced former officials (the total experience of these officials amounted to over 250 years), after refusing to train unqualified replacement officials during a league labor dispute in 2012.

In every sport, the officials, like Jerry Markbreit, are entrusted to keep order, protect players, and to ensure that unsportsmanlike behavior is appropriately penalized, hopefully deterring others from doing so in the future.

"Level I" of enforcing sportsmanship is to make sure that technical rules are followed. In all sports, this includes ensuring that the permitted number of players are on the field/court. In football, for example, the officials must make sure that players are not offside or delaying the game. In basketball, some examples of breaches the referees must look for include players traveling with the ball, illegally guarding opposing players, or forcefully touching opposing players when guarding them. In hockey, the officials closely monitor players so they do not trip opponents or use their sticks in improper ways.

"Level II" of sportsmanship enforcement is to make sure that the players and coaches act in a sportsmanlike (i.e., respectful) manner to one another and to the referees and other officials. Ideally, this includes ensuring that there is no inappropriate language or fights on the field or court – in practices or during play. In basketball, for example, technical fouls are called to punish Level II infractions, allowing the non-penalized team the opportunity to shoot a free throw and then to retain possession. In football, a team can be penalized for an offense by moving the ball back 15 yards. When extreme unsportsmanlike conduct is exhibited by players and/or coaches in team sports (which happens more often in baseball and basketball), the referees may even mete out the most severe penalty – ejection from the game. Usually, the league will investigate further, and sometimes may suspend the offender for a number of games and/or also levy a fine upon him/her and/or their team.

Game officials are extremely important contributors to sports as they ensure that the order of the game and dignity of the sport are maintained. Their role is to make sure that both the written and unwritten rules of sportsmanship are followed at all times.

Charles Martin passed away in 2005 at the age of 45. Although Jim McMahon played in the NFL through the 1996 season for seven teams over 15 seasons, according to Markbreit, he was never the same after that vicious hit. As the ref told *ESPN*, "Every time I saw [McMahon] after that, in Philadelphia or Green Bay, he'd come out and get ready for the first snap and when he saw me, he'd stop and say, 'Hey Jerry, how are you? Good to see you.' But for all intents and purposes, that play ended his career. He was never the same after that."

Isolation: The Penalty Box

In the world of ice hockey, when a player is penalized, not only is his team forced to play with one less skater during the duration of the penalty, but the offending player must sit by himself, isolated from all others until he has served his time or the opponent scores a goal. Known as the penalty box, this is where a penalized skater is secluded.

Some say that the innovation of hockey's penalty box was inspired by the sport of rugby, where a penalized player is sent to sit alone in an area known as the "sin bin."

Although not backed (nor refuted) by any researcher, I believe that the underpinnings of the penalty box reflects one the principles of basic behavioral psychology, as espoused by B.F. Skinner: reinforcement changes behavior. That is, when we want a person (and all those watching) to learn from their own behavior, we can provide that person with positive reinforcement for good behavior and negative reinforcement for any bad acts. By sending a player to and isolating him in the penalty box (negative reinforcement) for an indiscretion, he, along with all the other players at the game, is reminded that what he did was wrong and unacceptable. Granted, it is only a few minutes, but it still makes the point. Ejection would be the ultimate negative reinforcement for unsportsmanlike behavior.

In law, effective punishment serves many purposes, including rehabilitation and deterrence. By isolating a player, not only does the penalty box give the offender the opportunity to ponder (ideally) and (hopefully) resolve to correct his misconduct by exhibiting exemplary behavior in the future, but it also sends a clear message to all the other players to learn from the mistakes of the offender and to be deterred from committing similar acts.

So, when done right, in sports or law, negative reinforcement, through penalties, can have a positive impact. Earlier (see *Chapter 2*), we read, for example, how the public punishment of sitting in the penalty box, as observed by his young daughter, helped inspire hockey legend Stan Mikita to become one of the most sportsmanlike players in the history of the NHL. In that case, penalties helped a player grow and become a better role model for his children and for his fans.

Enforcing Sportsmanship: Spiritual Insights

Here Come Da (Jewish) Judges . . .

After the ***flood*** (*Mabul*), all descendants (in perpetuity) of Noah were commanded to observe ***seven Torah Commandments*** (*Sheva Mitzvot B'nei Noach*). One of the ***Seven Noahide Laws***, is to establish a just legal system. The directive *Tzedek Tzedek Tirdof* – ***Justice Justice you shall pursue*** (*Deuteronomy* 16:20), provides the overarching philosophy on how to manage all judicial systems, with the exemplar being the one identified in the *Torah* and described in greater detail in the *Halakhic* codes. Some of the elements of a just judicial system include: (1) the requirement to appoint highly qualified judges (*Deuteronomy* 16:18-19); (2) the obligation for judges to apply equal, fair standards to all litigants (*Deuteronomy* 16:19); and (3) the stern warning against the dangers of bribes (ibid).

According to Maimonides in his magnum opus (*Mishneh Torah, Hilkhot Sanhedrin* 2:7), to be considered qualified to sit as a judge, a candidate must possess the following seven *midot* (***character traits***): (1) *Chawkhma/***Wisdom;**

(2) *Yira/**Reverence** (for the Almighty); (3) *Anivut/**Humility;*** (4) *Sinat Mamon* (literally, ***"hatred of money"*** – i.e., ***utter disdain for bribes***); (5) *Ahavat HaEmet/ **Love of the Truth**); (6) *Ahavat HaB'riyot/**Love of** [**Fellow**] **Human Beings**; and (7) **Ba-ahl Shem Tov/*One who Possesses a Good Name***.

Throughout Jewish history, ***Jewish/Rabbinic courts*** (*Beit Din; Batei Din*, plural) have been meticulously organized and operated. During the days of the *Talmud*, there were courts of three, 23, and 71 *Dayanim* **(judges)**. Each court heard different types of cases. The court of 71 *Dayanim* was known as the *Sanhedrin HaGadol* (**Great Sanhedrin**) and its chambers were located next to the Temple in Jerusalem. Today, in many Jewish communities, there are *Batei Din* which render decisions regarding business, religious, and domestic matters.

During the course of Jewish history, many individuals have been cited for their contribution to the promotion of justice. The Prophetess Deborah functioned as a judge, "holding court" under a palm tree (*Judges* 4:5). And, of course, who could forget King Solomon and his ability to adjudicate difficult matters such as a baby's maternity (*I Kings* 3:16-28)?

Perhaps the greatest judge in Jewish history was none other than Moses. Following the (unsolicited) advice given to him by his sincerely, concerned, father-in-law Jethro, Moses established the first multi-tiered court system (*Exodus* 18:13-26) which serves as a model for all similar court systems, including the U.S. federal and state courts to this very day.

With this background in mind it is no surprise that in modern times, there have been many outstanding Jewish attorneys, academics, and judges who have made substantial contributions to the pursuit of justice. In Israel, two of the foremost legal scholars who have helped Israel incorporate Jewish law into its modern-day legal system (*Mishpat Ivri*) are the late Supreme Court Justice Menahem Elon and Bar Ilan University Law Professor Nahum Rakover.

In the United States, we remember such luminaries as Louis Brandeis and Benjamin Cardozo, the first two Jews appointed to the U.S. Supreme Court.

In 1916, during World War I and with growing anti-Semitism in the United States, President Woodrow Wilson made a bold move and nominated who he considered the best-qualified candidate, Louis Dembitz Brandeis, to fill a vacancy on the U.S. Supreme Court. After 125 days, Brandeis was confirmed, in spite of vast opposition against Brandeis's confirmation by prominent individuals who claimed that his views were too radical (but some were most likely against Brandeis's nomination primarily because he was a Jew). He served with distinction on the U.S. Supreme Court for more than 22 years. Known as a proponent of individual liberty and a staunch opponent of unchecked governmental power and corporate interests, Brandeis promoted free speech, while also being sensitive to an individual's right to privacy.

In 1932, President Herbert Hoover, a Republican, once again nominated another Jew, Benjamin Cardozo. At the time, Cardozo was a New York state appellate judge, having been a member of the court for 18 years. An expert in commercial law, Cardozo was the author of the opinion in *MacPherson vs. Buick Motor Co.*, a trailblazing case in the area of consumer rights in matters of product liability. As a U.S. Supreme Court Justice, along with Justice Brandeis, Justice Cardozo was known for his support of New Deal programs. Cardozo is also credited for helping refine criminal law.

Both secular Jews, Justices Brandeis and Cardozo were supporters of the establishment of a Jewish state and were active in other Jewish organizations and causes. While Waltham, Massachusetts's Brandeis University is named in the Justice's honor, the legacy of Justice Benjamin Cardozo was honored through the 1976 establishment of Yeshiva University's Benjamin N. Cardozo School of Law, in New York City.

While sitting together on the Supreme Court, both Justices Cardozo and Brandeis shared another unfortunate distinction. In addition to enduring acts of anti-Semitism from outsiders, they were both the targets of acts of blatant anti-Semitism directed towards them by one of their own, fellow Supreme Court Justice James Clark McReynolds. It was three years before McReynolds would even speak to Brandeis once he was confirmed as a fellow justice – because he was Jewish. He also directed his staff not to communicate with Justices Brandeis and Cardozo. According to writer Ian Millhiser, there is no official photograph of the justices for 1924 because "a seniority-based seating chart required McReynolds to sit next to Brandeis, and McReynolds simply refused to be photographed next to his Jewish colleague."

After Cardozo's premature death in 1938, on January 5, 1939 President Franklin D. Roosevelt nominated Harvard Law Professor and American Civil Liberties Union co-founder Felix Frankfurter to succeed Cardozo. Because of the succession of Jewish Supreme Court Justices, the notion of a "Jewish seat" on the Court came to be known. (On February 13, 1939, Justice Brandeis retired from the US Supreme Court.) Upon Frankfurter's retirement in 1962, after a distinguished 23-year Supreme Court career, President Kennedy nominated famed Jewish labor attorney and former U.S. Secretary of Labor Arthur Goldberg to fill the so-called "Jewish seat."

At the urging of President Lyndon B. Johnson, Goldberg resigned his life tenure on the Court after sitting only three years, to serve as the U.S. ambassador to the United Nations (a decision he later regretted). A staunch opponent of U.S. involvement in the Vietnam War, then-Ambassador Goldberg was a key ally of Israel during the 1967 Six Day War and played a significant role in drafting UN Resolution 242, which calls for "a just and lasting peace in the Middle East." (For more about Arthur Goldberg see *Chapter 21*.)

President Johnson then nominated his friend, Abe Fortas, to fill the "Jewish seat" vacated by Goldberg. As a lawyer for Clarence Earl Gideon, Fortas's argument before the Supreme Court led to the historic ruling that states are required to provide legal help to the poor. He served about four years on the Supreme Court. Fortas was one of the justices who ruled in the *Miranda vs. Arizona* case that criminal suspects must be informed of their rights to an attorney and to remain silent before police questioning.

The "Jewish seat" then remained empty for almost a quarter of a century, until President Bill Clinton nominated first Ruth Bader Ginsberg in 1993, and then Stephen Breyer the following year. Today, Justices Ginsburg and Breyer are joined on the bench by a third Jewish justice, former U.S. Solicitor General and Harvard Law School Dean Elena Kagan.

Shot'rim (Enforcement Officers)

שֹׁפְטִים וְשֹׁטְרִים תִּתֶּן־לְךָ בְּכָל־שְׁעָרֶיךָ

Shof'tim v'shot'rim ti-ten l'kha b'khol sh'arekha

Judges and enforcement officers
you shall appoint in all of your gates [cities]
(Deuteronomy 16:18).

While it may be easy to understand the role of the **judges** (*Shof'tim*), it is not as easy to discern the exact role of the **officers** (*Shot'rim*).

Based upon *Midrash Tanchuma 2*, *Rashi* explains that the main job of the *Shot'rim* was to enforce the judgments of the *Shof'tim* (**judges**). They were even permitted to use corporal punishment if necessary. In modern Hebrew, a *Shoter* is a **police officer**. In many ways the *Shot'rim* referenced in the *Torah* played a similar role as police officers do today; that is, to make sure that the members of society follow the law.

The term *Shoter* is also mentioned in other parts of the *Bible*. One reference occurs when describing the Egyptian slavery. In the *Torah* we read (*Exodus* 5:6-18) that the *Shot'rim* were the Israelite foremen who supervised the work of the slaves and served as a buffer between the slaves and the **Egyptian taskmaster**s (*nog'sim*). *Rashi* (*Exodus* 5:14) explains that when the Israelite slaves were unable to manufacture their daily quota of bricks, the *Shot'rim* had compassion and did not pressure or punish them for non-compliance. Rather, they assumed responsibility and were the subject of severe lashings from the hands of the Egyptian taskmasters. The Almighty rewarded these righteous *Shot'rim* by making them members of the original *Sanhedrin* (the judicial assembly of 71 [including Moses] Israelite men in the desert).

The *M'tzora*

In Jewish history and tradition, isolation has been used as a form of punishment to influence a wrongdoer to correct their actions while also deterring others from committing similar acts. Perhaps the most common use of isolation was as a punishment for a *M'tzora*.

The *Torah*, along with the *Talmud* and Codes, teaches the laws of the *M'tzora*. Often incorrectly translated as a "leper," a *M'tzora* was a person who was afflicted with an apparent dermatological (i.e., skin) disease known as צָרַעַת (*Tzaraat*) that had symptoms similar to those exhibited by a medical leper. Unlike the medical leper, the cause of the *M'tzora*'s affliction with *Tzaraat* was the commission of any one of seven spiritual sins (*Arakhin* 16a), most notably, speaking negatively about someone else. In this light, the *Talmud* (*Arakhin* 15b) teaches that מְצֹרָע (*M'tzorah*) is actually an acronym/contraction for מוֹצִיא שֵׁם רַע/*Motzih Shem Rah* (**One who defames** [*literally, one who releases an evil name*]). According to *Halakha* (**Jewish law**), unless the matter must be disclosed, a person is prohibited from speaking negative words about someone else – even if they are truthful.

In addition to the aforementioned physical symptoms, the *M'tzora* was temporarily evicted from the community and forced to sit in isolation, after which s/he went through a series of stages of purification before s/he were permitted to re-enter mainstream society (*Leviticus* 14:1-20). The reason that a *M'tzora* was forced to dwell in isolation was to punish the offender in a like manner as the harm that s/he caused the afflicted party. Known as מִדָּה כְּנֶגֶד מִדָּה/*mida k'neged mida* (**a measure for a measure**), just as his/her speech isolated the afflicted party by causing others to stay away from the subject of the negative talk, so too s/he is now isolated from their community (*Arakhin* 16b).

Perhaps the most famous case of a person who was afflicted with *Tzaraat* because she spoke *Lashon HaRa* was Miriam, one of the holiest women in Jewish history. In the *Torah* (*Numbers* 12:1), we read:

וַתְּדַבֵּר מִרְיָם וְאַהֲרֹן בְּמֹשֶׁה עַל אֹדוֹת הָאִשָּׁה הַכֻּשִׁית אֲשֶׁר לָקָח
כִּי אִשָּׁה כֻשִׁית לָקָח:

Va-t'daber Miryam v'Aharon b'Moshe ahl odot ha-isha HaKusheet asher lakach, ki isha Khusheet lakach.

And Miriam and Aaron spoke against Moses regarding the Kushite woman that he took [as a wife], because he took a Kushite woman [as a wife].

Based upon various commentaries, we can explain this passage in the following manner. Miriam learned from Moses's wife, *Tziporah*, that Moses had not been intimate with her for some time. Not realizing that the Almighty had instructed

Moses to act in that manner at this time – because of his extreme level of holiness – Miriam misperceived that Moses and *Tziporah* were experiencing trouble in their marriage. As a concerned big sister, she implored assistance from Aaron who, based upon Miriam's account, also became concerned. So out of their love for their younger brother, they approached Moses. Perhaps they reached this erroneous conclusion because of a subtle sense of jealousy? After all, Miriam and Aaron were also prophets and when it came to matters of טָהֳרַת הַמִשְׁפָּחָה/ *Taharat HaMishpacha* (*family purity*), they were treated in the same manner as any Hebrew. What they failed to realize was that Moses was at a level of holiness unlike any prophet in history.

Because Miriam did not think through this very private matter, and instead reached an erroneous conclusion, causing embarrassment to her brother, she was punished by becoming a *M'tzoraat*. Miriam was removed from the Camp of Israel and placed in isolation. Moses then uttered the shortest prayer recorded in the *Bible* imploring of the Almighty to heal his beloved sister:

קֵל נָא רְפָא נָא לָהּ
Kel na r'fa na la

God please, please heal her [Miriam] [now] (Numbers 12:13).

The Almighty answered Moses's prayer and removed all physical symptoms from Miriam, who remained isolated for an additional seven days after which she rejoined the Camp of Israel.

Because Miriam's actions, no matter how well-intended they may have been, caused Moses some emotional isolation from his wife, *Tziporah*, Miriam was punished in kind, ***measure for measure*** (מִדָּה כְּנֶגֶד מִדָּה/*mida k'neged mida*).

THE BOX SCORE

In the world of organized sports, the first line of people whose duty it is to enforce the rules (sportsmanship) are the referees, judges, umpires, and other officials. From NFL referee extraordinaire Jerry Markbreit, we learn that, in addition to having a thorough knowledge of all the rules, an official must, at times, be able to think "out of the box" to ensure the integrity of that particular game and sport.

In Jewish tradition, the concept of **Reward and Punishment** (שָׂכָר וָעֹנֶשׁ/*Sakhar VaOnesh*) is integral. One of the punishments in the days of the *Torah* was isolating a wrongdoer from mainstream society. To properly adjudicate and, when necessary, punish a wrongdoer, ensuring that there is a society filled with דֶּרֶךְ אֶרֶץ וְכָבוֹד / *Derekh Eretz v'Khavod* (**Respect and Honor**), every community must establish courts with highly-skilled and honest judges. These judges must treat all litigants fairly, and the litigants, in turn, must abide by the judges' decisions. In *Biblical* times, there were also *Shot'rim* who, like the sports referees, enforced the decisions (judgments) of the judges.

Because we do not live in a perfect world where everyone follows the applicable laws and rules, and when they deviate from them they police themselves, every society must have in place a proper judicial/punishment/enforcement system.

Chapter 25
Controlling Your Emotions

Obstacles and Challenges

The Big Bad Four: Greed, Jealousy, Anger and Competition

Four of the main causes of unsportsmanlike behavior are greed, jealousy, envy, anger, and the "mishandling" of competition. While it is a positive attribute to try our hardest to be the best we can in all of our endeavors, it is an extreme display of human weakness if we are willing to do so at any cost.

Baseball's Dark Ages

A dark period in modern Major League Baseball history was the "Steroid Era," from approximately the late 1980s through the mid-to-late 2000s (a few fear a return of doping, now that players are hitting more home runs, though others have claimed the increase is due to very specialized swing adjustments). During this time frame, it is believed that numerous players used steroids and other performance enhancement drugs (PEDs) in violation of MLB rules and, at times, in violation of the law as well. (For simplicity sake, I am going to use the terms "steroids" and "PEDs" interchangeably, referring to those substances which were banned by MLB.)

What was the root cause of this steroids scandal? In addition to MLB not having effective rules against the usage of steroids and weak mechanisms of enforcement, what drove many players to cheat was their motivation to perform better than their competitors. After all, there are limited roster spots on an MLB team. To make a team, one must have a higher batting average, a superior fielding average, a stronger WAR (Wins Against Replacement) and lower ERA (Earned Run Average) than the next guy. The financial earning differential between a player with a 10-year career in AAA minor league baseball vs. the MLB is in the tens of millions of dollars. For many players, the potential long-term health dangers associated with taking these drugs were worth the gamble to acquire financial security for their family. Additionally, PED users were rarely caught, and when they were, their punishments were not lifetime bans. Simply put, for many, this kind of cheating was worth the risk.

For the established MLB star, who was already earning multimillions annually over a multi-year contract, the motivation to take PEDs was simply greed. They were not satisfied with the achievements that they had already legitimately earned. They merely wanted to amass even better stats and even more money. And at times, this greed was fueled in part by jealousy and envy.

Although he has vehemently denied "knowingly" taking steroids, one of the greatest stars suspected of using these banned substances was former San Francisco Giants (and Pittsburgh Pirates) slugger, Barry Bonds. According to *San Francisco Chronicle* reporters Mark Fainaru-Wada and Lance Williams in their exposé on doping, *Game of Shadows*, the first time the Giants' superstar used steroids was not until after the 1998 season when his trainer Greg Anderson, gave him the drug Winstrol (stanozolol), a favorite among bodybuilders.

Among its effects, this PED helped Bonds get rid of the pain and fatigue that he experienced after workouts, allowing him to intensify his energy levels. By then, Bonds already had won three National League MVP Awards (1990, 1992, and 1993) and was destined to become a first-ballot Hall of Famer.

During the 1998 season, however, things changed. The talk of baseball was the home run competition between Sammy Sosa and Mark McGwire, who were chasing Roger Maris's single season home run record. (McGwire later admitted to using PEDs and Sosa was strongly suspected of it, despite his denials. In spite of amassing Hall Of Fame career statistics, both sluggers have been denied entrance to the Hall of Fame.)

Fainaru-Wada and Williams pointed out, "As McGwire's pursuit of the home run record became the constant topic of the nation's media, and as McGwire was celebrated as the best slugger of the modern era and perhaps the greatest slugger who had ever lived, Bonds became more jealous than people who knew him well had ever seen."

For example the authors described that, when the Cardinals visited other cities, certain teams began to rope off the area around the batting cage in order to control access to McGwire during batting practice. In July of 1999, when Bonds saw the ropes for the first time on his hometown field when the Cards came to town, he angrily started knocking down the ropes and saying to the security guards: "Not in my house!"

Obstacles and Challenges: A Spiritual Insight

The *Chofetz Chaim's* Grocery Store

While the Chasidic Rabbi Zusya of Hanipoli (see *Chapter Three*) may have set the benchmark for "ideal" competition (i.e., against one's potential), when it comes to the more common form of "head-on" or "direct" competition (i.e., participant vs. participant or team vs. team), we look to the esteemed sage Rabbi Israel Meir HaKohen Kagan (1838–1933) as our role model.

Better known by the name of his most famous publication, (*Sefer*) *Chofetz Chaim*, Rabbi Kagan is an exemplar of how to conduct oneself in business in a free market economy. While there is extensive antitrust legislation in American law pro-hibiting monopolies, in Jewish law, there are even more regulations/restrictions to ensure fair competition. Based upon the prohibition of **boundary encroachment/** *Hahsagat G'vul* (*Deuteronomy* 19:14), Jewish law permits competition among local residents so long as the market can bear it, and no existing business is forced to close. (For further details see the next **DIDJA KNOW?**)

Early on in his career as a *Torah* scholar in Poland, with the support of his wife, the *Chofetz Chaim* decided that he was not going to depend on serving as a pulpit rabbi to support his family. Instead, he decided to devote himself to scholarship, teaching, and publishing. To supplement these pursuits, along with his wife, Rabbi Kagan opened up a small grocery store. While his wife managed the store, the *Chofetz Chaim* assisted by meticulously auditing the bookkeeping to make sure that all business was conducted in the most honest and scrupulous manner.

Because of his extreme honesty, which paved the way for the most competitive prices, plus the great respect that the *Chofetz Chaim* earned from others, the Kagan family business was the most popular grocery store in town. To ensure that his competitors could still survive, the *Chofetz Chaim*'s policy was to close his store each day as soon as it made enough money to pay for his family's daily needs. That way, the local shoppers were "forced" to support the competing grocers as well.

In Jewish tradition, we are supposed to conduct ourselves with great דֶּרֶךְ אֶרֶץ וְכָבוֹד (*Respect and Honor*) in all that we do– both on and off the field, at home and in our businesses, as exemplified by *Torah* scholar/businessman Rabbi Israel Meir HaKohen Kagan (a/k/a the *Chofetz Chaim*) and his *Rebbetzin* (*title bestowed upon a Rabbi's wife*).

Good vs. Bad Sportsmanship

Might, Proper Perspective and Honesty

What separates the players who consistently exhibit good sportsmanship from those who do not?

Various characteristics; in addition to honesty/integrity, these traits include the possession of might, proper perspective, and courage.

For the definitions of "might" and "proper perspective" in Jewish tradition, we look to the wisdom of the Sages *Ben Zoma* and *Akavya ben M'halalel* as stated in **Ethics of Our Fathers**/*Pirkei Avot* (4:1 and 3:1). As exemplars of "might," we look to a series of heroes in Jewish history [*Midrash Tanchuma (Balak* 1)], beginning with Moses, who – in this author's opinion - suppressed their evil inclinations to achieve feats that benefited humankind.

DIDJA KNOW that in recognizing the important value of a person's property, Rabbi HaLevy and Maimonides cite a unique *Mitzvah* that prohibits a Jew from encroaching upon someone else's property boundaries? This *Mitzvah* has also been interpreted in certain instances as placing limitations on competition when it could adversely affect the ability of a person to make a living. Based upon the opinion of *Rav Huna*, the son of *Rav Yehoshua* (*Bava Batra* 21b), there is a general *Halakha* (law) that residents of one town can stop ("cease and desist") an out-of-town merchant from doing business in the new town, provided that the "visiting" merchant does not pay taxes in the new town (*Shulchan Arukh, Choshen Mishpat, Hilkhot N'zikei Sh'khenim/ Laws of the Damages of Neighbors* 156:7). To promote various activities and societal goals, a number of exceptions are carved out of this general principle, including:

(1) Out-of-town perfume merchants who did not pay local taxes, were still allowed to go door-to-door (but not open a stationary store), since helping single women become more attractive (with the purpose of finding suitable husbands) is a most desirable endeavor in Jewish tradition (ibid 156:6); and

(2) Out-of-town *Torah* scholars trying to make a living, thus enabling them to devote more time to their scholarship and teaching, were allowed to sell their wares without any geographic limitations (ibid).

The Big Hurt's So Good

In the *Talmud* (*Ethics of Our Fathers* 4:1), the Sage *Ben Zoma* asks a series of four rhetorical questions. One of these is:

אֵיזֶהוּ גִבּוֹר? הַכּוֹבֵשׁ אֶת יִצְרוֹ,
שֶׁנֶּאֱמַר (מִשְׁלֵי ט"ז: לב):
טוֹב אֶרֶךְ אַפַּיִם מִגִּבּוֹר, וּמוֹשֵׁל בְּרוּחוֹ מִלֹּכֵד עִיר.

Eizehu Gibor? HaKovesh et yitzro, shehnehehmahr (Mishlei 16:32): Tov erekh apayim mi-Gibor, u-moshel b'rucho mi-lokhed ihr.

Who is mighty? One who conquers/subdues his (evil) inclination, as it is stated (Proverbs 16:32): "A person who is slow to anger is better than a mighty person (Gibor), and one who conquers his (evil) inclination is better than a person who conquers a city."

Greed, jealousy, envy, excessive desire for success that leads to cheating, and anger are common manifestations of a person's evil inclination. The mighty person is one who is able to subdue these passions.

During the steroids era, there were many players who either did not even consider using PEDs or who refused to succumb to their baser inclinations to take the drugs. One such player was Chicago White Sox legend Frank "The Big Hurt" Thomas. Long an outspoken advocate for mandatory drug testing by MLB, Thomas was the only active player who agreed to be interviewed by former U.S. Senator George Mitchell for his investigation into drug use in baseball, known as the "Mitchell Report," which was published in 2007.

Over the course of his 18-year (16 with the ChiSox) MLB career, Thomas hit 521 home runs and had a career batting average of .301. Like the great Red Sox star Ted Williams, Thomas was known for being an extremely patient, selective hitter, waiting for not just any strikes to cross the plate, but ones that he had a particularly good chance of converting into base hits. Understandably, The Big Hurt led the American League in bases on balls (walks) on multiple occasions. Thomas had his share of critics who, during his career, felt that he wasn't worthy of being elected to Baseball's Hall of Fame, since he was primarily a designated hitter (DH). But the Big Hurt's extraordinary accomplishments as a hitter and his mighty character paved the way for him to be the first MLB player who played a majority of his games as a DH to be voted into the Cooperstown shrine. In fact, Thomas was elected on the very first year (2014) that he was eligible.

Some people are driven to suppress any natural inclinations toward unsportsmanlike behavior and cheating by the fear of getting caught. Others are able to subdue their "evil" urges simply on principle; that is, if something is against the rules, they will not do it, no matter the reward, and their sense of honesty wins.

251

DIDJA KNOW that White Sox broadcaster Ken "Hawk" Harrelson is credited with giving Frank Thomas the nickname "The Big Hurt"? Here is the story behind the origin of this famous nickname. Hawk described how it happened in a Chicago television special, "Welcome to Cooperstown, Frank Thomas:"

"I just blurted it out one day. I kept saying, 'he hurt it, he hurt it, he hurt it.' He'd kill one into left center, 'he hurt it.' One day he hits a home run ... I'm watching him go around first base ... and I said, 'The Big Hurt' and it just blurted out and that's how that came about. It turned out to be a pretty good nickname for him."

Still others may also be very pragmatic and that tendency will help them put things into their proper perspective. In the case of athletes deciding whether or not to take PEDs, the proper perspective would be to take a figurative step back and realize how the potential physical harm would, in great likelihood, deprive them of living longer and enjoying good health.

It is my opinion that, while Frank Thomas was and continues to be motivated to take care of his health, what especially drove him not to use steroids or other PEDs and to repeatedly speak out against such practices is that he is a principled and honest person. In fact, after he hit his 500th career home run, The Big Hurt declared, "It means a lot to me because I did it the right way."

Good vs. Bad Sportsmanship: A Spiritual Insight

Using Your Talents in Beneficial Ways

In Jewish history, one of the most celebrated contrasts between two highly-talented people – one who used his skills to improve the world and the other to commit evil acts – was that between Moses and *Bilam*. Cited by the *Torah* as the most humble person on the face of the earth (*Numbers* 12:3), Moses was able to suppress any desire to satisfy personal (ego) needs for success and was focused on channeling his great talents for the betterment of the Jewish people and the world. On the other hand, while *Bilam* had the need to flaunt his talents, his goal was to fulfill the meaning of his name (בְּל–עָם *bil* or *bahl ahm*; which is to **destroy the nation** [i.e., the Nation of Israel]).

In announcing the death of Moses, the *Torah* (*Deuteronomy* 34:10) states:

וְלֹא קָם נָבִיא עוֹד בְּיִשְׂרָאֵל כְּמֹשֶׁה
V'lo kahm navih ode b'Yisrael k'Moshe

And [another] prophet in Israel has not arisen like Moses.

Regarding this, the *Midrash* (*Sifre*) responds to the inherent question, of why was it necessary to qualify this statement:

אֲבָל בְּאֻמּוֹת קָם. וְאֵיזֶה? זֶה בִּלְעָם בֶּן בְּעוֹר.

Ahval b'umot kahm. V'eizeh? Zeh Bilam ben B'or.

However, in the non-Jewish nations [a prophet like Moses] has arisen. And which one? This is Bilam the son of B'or.

Although this *Midrash* is an exaggeration, as Moses clearly had the most intimate relationship with the Almighty, more than any other prophet, nonetheless it is an entrée to view how *Bila*m squandered his talents. *Midrash Tanchuma (Balak* 1) expands on this by sharing that, for every great leader in Jewish history, we can find a gentile counterpart who used his skills to try and destroy Israel. While King Solomon built the *Beit HaMikdash* (Holy Temple), Nebuchadnezzar, the Babylonian king, destroyed it. Similarly, while King David used his wealth to help the Israelites, Haman used his riches to try to annihilate the Jews of Persia.

The message of these *Midrashim* is that every human being is endowed with talents and the potential to use them for the betterment of the world. What differentiates those who use it for the positive from those who squander their talents is **might** (גְּבוּרָה/*G'vurah*) – according to *Ben Zoma's* definition; that is, whether or not a person is able to subdue his/her *Yetzer HaRa* (**Evil Inclination**).

THE BOX SCORE

Jewish tradition teaches that every human being is born with two inclinations: one good and the other bad, and is endowed with **free choice** (בְּחִירָה חָפְשִׁית / *B'chira Chawfsheet*). It is everyone's challenge to control their *Yetzer HaRa* (**Evil Inclination**) and instead follow the path of their *Yetzer HaTov* (**Good Inclination**). In the world of sports, Hall of Famer Frank "The Big Hurt" Thomas chose **not** to take PEDs despite the fact that others did. In Jewish tradition we see that Moses used his talents for good, while *Bilam* followed the path of his *Yetzer HaRa* and squandered his talents on trying to destroy Israel.

Chapter 26
Remembering What's Important in Life

Keeping the Game in Perspective

An often-used expression is "to put things into their proper perspective." This means to learn how to properly prioritize and to be sure not to overreact to life's everyday occurrences.

In competitive sports, for the vast majority of participants, the outcome of the game will not have a major impact upon their lives beyond the immediate aftermath of that particular contest.

For professionals or high-level amateurs, one's performance could impact upon whether or not they qualify for an event or a career in a particular sport. Unless a fan is betting money (legally, of course) on a sporting event, while a victory by one's favorite team may bring an immediate sense of gratification, ultimately, it will not make much of a difference in one's life.

Another important element that fuels sportsmanship is perspective. Sometimes participants put such a high value on the outcome of their individual and team's performance that they are motivated to act in unsportsmanlike ways. A player may commit a flagrant foul or break a rule of the game. Similarly, fans often can be nasty to players or umpires who they feel erred or to fans of the opposing team.

Unfortunately, many times, it takes an occurrence outside of the sports world for fans, players, and all other participants to take a figurative step back to gain a proper perspective of the sport. Usually, these events are of a personal nature, such as an illness to or death of a loved one. On rare occasion, it is an event in history.

Steve Kerr: Family First

Steve Kerr has excelled in almost all of the challenges that he has undertaken. After a stellar basketball career at the University of Arizona, Kerr went on to the NBA where he had a 15-year career eclipsed by retiring with the highest three-point shot percentage in NBA history. This record still stands today.

A career that was highlighted by being a vital member of five NBA Championship teams (three with the Bulls and two with the Spurs), Kerr was especially regarded for his leadership skills. Steve Kerr delayed becoming a coach because of its requisite time demands that would compromise his role as a husband and father. Instead, he chose the route of administration and broadcasting, serving as the general manager of the Phoenix Suns and as a TNT broadcaster. In 2014, when his children were older, Steve Kerr accepted an offer to become the head coach of the Golden State Warriors. Without any NBA or college head coaching experience, Kerr led his team as a rookie coach to a Warriors team record 67 regular season victories and an NBA Championship. The following season his Warriors won an NBA all-time best 73 regular season games, while losing to LeBron James and the Cleveland Cavaliers in the seventh and final game of the Finals. Then in 2017, the Kerr-coached Warriors defeated the Cavaliers in a rematch to regain their championship crown.

Although it appears that Steve Kerr has lived a glamorous life, he has not.

At age 18, Kerr suffered a tragic personal loss. His father, Malcolm Kerr who was president of the American University in Beirut, was assassinated by terrorists. The senior Kerr's mission in life was to help facilitate peace in the Middle East. Instead, he himself was a victim of terror. Rather than allowing the loss of his beloved father ruin his own life, Steve Kerr used his father's memory and, possibly also his violent death, as a means to motivate him to succeed in life and to also realize the importance of maintaining a proper perspective.

According to close friend, former college teammate, and Warrior assistant coach, Bruce Fraser, "I think the death of his father helped Steve as a basketball player because he realized it was just basketball . . . The weight of a miss, the weight of a loss, the weight of a big moment . . . they just didn't mean anything to him anymore."

Even before the unexpected death of his father, Steve Kerr had a better appreciation of life than many of his peers since, as a child of international academics, he, along with his three siblings, had the opportunity to live in different parts of the world. At times the Kerrs witnessed firsthand the impoverished lifestyles of others. As Kerr said in an interview with the *Mercury News*, "I developed a lot of compassion living in Egypt, seeing the poverty. The discussions around the dinner table about world politics and understanding how fortunate we were – all that helped me gain perspective on life."

No matter how important it was/is for Steve Kerr to win as a player, executive, and coach, ultimately, basketball – to him – is simply only a game. By integrating his professional career with spending time with a loving and supportive family and interests outside of basketball, Kerr is able to provide balance to his life which assists him in maintaining a proper perspective. The coach summarized the central theme behind his coaching and his life in the *Wall Street Journal*: "I think perspective is important. I try to mention it as a coach occasionally – just remember that it's still [only] a basketball game."

A Tragedy in Perspective

One of the most seminal events in the twenty-first century, was the series of terrorist attacks launched on the United States on September 11, 2001. The deadly strikes, for a time, shaped people's perspective on every aspect of life from politics to personal relationships, to, yes, even sports.

For example, the quite minor consequence of a weeklong postponement of baseball games also provided an opportunity for all those involved (players, coaches, umpires, fans, etc.) to find a much deeper meaning in that season's World Series. In the 2001 World Series, the upstart Arizona Diamondbacks played the legendary New York Yankees. In all other years, it is fair to say that most non-New Yorkers would cheer against the Yankees since they had already won a record 26 World Series Championships. 2001, however, was different. Having survived the worst terrorist attack in U.S. history that destroyed New York's famed Twin Towers, killing more than 2000 people, baseball fans saw a Yankees series victory as a way to help bring comfort to a city writhing in pain, grief, and sorrow. According to comedian, actor and huge Yankees fan Billy Crystal, "For the first time I think in the history of baseball, people around the country were pulling for the Yankees to win."

Although the Yankees lost the Series that year by losing Games 1, 2, 6, and 7 in Arizona, they still helped bring the Big Apple closer to healing by winning all three games played in historic original Yankee Stadium.

Perhaps one of the most exhilarating moments in MLB history was when then-President George W. Bush, while wearing a bulletproof vest, threw out the ceremonial first pitch of Game Three – the first played in New York City – to a Secret Service agent dressed in a Yankee uniform. Supervising were other agents dressed as MLB umpires. According to ABC News, the president said, "The gravity of the moment never really hit me until the first step coming out of that dugout. I remember the noise and it was deafening. I remember looking around the stadium, this giant crowd. Standing on the mound at Yankee Stadium was by far the most nervous moment of my presidency." It probably didn't help that famous Yankee shortstop, Derek Jeter, told Bush right before the pitch, "Don't bounce it. They'll boo ya."

While in Manhattan, players from both teams volunteered to visit with and help bring comfort, relief, and hope to the beleaguered residents of New York City, especially those who lost loved ones in the Twin Towers attacks, as well as surviving first responders. In Game 7, baseball's greatest closer of all-time, Mariano Rivera, blew a save opportunity leading to the Yankees' loss of the Fall Classic. When reflecting back on the Series on the tenth anniversary of 9-11, MLB's all-time leader in saves put his mistake in its proper perspective: "I think it was the best World Series we ever played in. Because of the way we had to fight. And just because . . . of the way we played."

How could a person complain about a blown save and a lost World Series when these hard fought games of America's Pastime helped bring comfort to millions of New Yorkers and Americans who were grieving the loss of and injuries to thousands of innocent fellow Americans?

It shouldn't take tragedy to force people to "put these things into their proper perspective," whether it is in politics, business, or sports. Unfortunately, too often, it takes heartbreak to remind us that sports and life are not always about winning, but rather, on how we play the game.

Sportsmanship, too, is ultimately all about on how we play the game and internalizing the mantra, "Remember, it's only a game!"

Keeping the Game in Perspective: A Spiritual Insight

Proper Perspective: "I'd rather be called a fool"

The *Tanna Akavya ben M'halalel* was regarded as a *Talmid Chakham* (**brilliant Torah scholar**) and a man of great integrity. In the *Talmud* (*Edyot* 5:6), he is recorded as taking an opposing view to the majority in four particular issues in Jewish law. When it came to the time to be considered for the position of *Av Bet Din* (the second most powerful position of the *Sanhedrin*/Jewish court), *Akavya ben M'halalel* was told that the only matter that would prevent him from being offered this most important and prestigious position was that he publicly opposed the Sages in these four particular matters. To help ensure his smooth functioning in this role, this great *Tanna* was asked to retract his *Halakhic* renderings in these matters. *Akavya ben M'halalel* refused, stating on principle:

אָמַר לָהֶן: מוּטָב לִי לְהִקָּרֵא שׁוֹטֶה כָּל יָמַי,
וְלֹא לַעֲשׂוֹת שָׁעָה אַחַת רָשָׁע לִפְנֵי הַמָּקוֹם,
שֶׁלֹּא יִהְיוּ אוֹמְרִים: בִּשְׁבִיל שְׂרָרָה חָזַר בּוֹ.

Amar la-hen: Mutav li l'hikareh shoteh kol yamai, v'lo le-asot sha-ah achat rasha lifnei HaMakom, shehlo yihyu om'rim: bishvil s'rara chazar bo.

He said to them: "I would rather be called a fool my entire life, than become [even] for a single moment an evil man before the Omnipresent, so that they [people] would not say: he changed his mind [strictly] for authority [i.e., political gain]."

Surprisingly, the *Halakhic* renderings of *Akavya ben M'halalel* are only recorded in one additional text (*N'gaim* 1:4). This *Tanna* is also quoted for his great insights regarding having the proper perspective in one's life.
As we know, when things are going well for a person, it is relatively easy to become arrogant. In *Pirkei Avot* (3:1), *Akavya* prescribes the perfect formula on how to prevent oneself from becoming arrogant:

עֲקַבְיָא בֶּן מַהֲלַלְאֵל אוֹמֵר:
הִסְתַּכֵּל בִּשְׁלֹשָׁה דְבָרִים, וְאֵין אַתָּה בָא לִידֵי עֲבֵרָה:
דַּע, מֵאַיִן בָּאתָ, וּלְאָן אַתָּה הוֹלֵךְ,
וְלִפְנֵי מִי אַתָּה עָתִיד לִתֵּן דִּין וְחֶשְׁבּוֹן.
מֵאַיִן בָּאתָ? מִטִּפָּה סְרוּחָה.
וּלְאָן אַתָּה הוֹלֵךְ? לִמְקוֹם עָפָר רִמָּה וְתוֹלֵעָה.
וְלִפְנֵי מִי אַתָּה עָתִיד לִתֵּן דִּין וְחֶשְׁבּוֹן?
לִפְנֵי מֶלֶךְ מַלְכֵי הַמְּלָכִים הַקָּדוֹשׁ בָּרוּךְ הוּא.

Akavya ven M'halalel omer: Histakel bi-shlosha d'varim, v'ein ata va lidei aveira: Dah, meh-ayin bata, u-l'ahn ata holekh, v'lifnei mi ata atid liten din v'cheshbon. Meh-ayin bata? Mi-tipa s'rucha. U-l'ahn ata holekh? Li-mkom afar rima v'toleha. V'lifnei mi ata atid liten din v'cheshbon? Lifnei Melekh Malkhei HaM'lakhim HaKadosh Barukh Hu.

Akavya the son of M'halalel says: "Reflect upon three things and you will not come into the hands of sin: Know [remind yourself] from where you came, and to where you will [ultimately] go, and before Whom you will present the judgment and account of your life.
From where did you come?
From a putrid drop.
And to where are you [ultimately] going?
To a place of dust, maggots and worms.
And before Whom will you present the judgment and account of your life?
Before the Supreme King of Kings, the Holy One Blessed Be He."

As illustrated by his rejecting the offer of the position of *Av Bet Din*, since he would have to go back on what he truly believed, *Akavya ben M'halalel* showed that he fully appreciated his (and all human beings') humble beginnings and ends. He truly viewed life in its proper perspective.

THE BOX SCORE

We learn from NBA great Steve Kerr and from the venerable *Tannaitic* sage *Akavya ben M'halalel* that to be successful in life, we must have a proper perspective on where we came from and to where we are ultimately headed. By doing so, we are able to exhibit true sportsmanship; that is, treat all others with the proper דֶּרֶךְ אֶרֶץ וְכָבוֹד / *Derekh Eretz v'Khavod* (**Respect and Honor**) that they deserve!

Chapter 27
And the winner is...

Awards Night

For many people, playing in a sportsmanship-like manner is rewarding in and of itself, but it is always nice to be formally recognized for such exemplary behavior. In addition to reinforcing a person's positive behavior, publicly rewarding such acts also can inspire others to do the same. This is especially true in youth sports.

Sportsmanship Awards in Professional and Amateur Sports

Formally recognizing players and coaches for a blend of top-notch competitive play mixed in with a high-level of sportsmanship has been around for many years. The trend in professional sports is to issue an award to players for their sportsmanship both on the field/court/ice as well as in the community. Many times, separate awards are presented, while at times, only one (combined) award is given. In youth and school leagues where there is (and should be) a greater emphasis placed on the process (i.e., how the game is played) rather than the outcome (i.e., winning at any cost), it is common for sportsmanship and other "process" awards to be presented to multiple participants.

What follows is a brief survey of the sportsmanship awards presented by various professional sports leagues, along with the NCAA and high schools. I then propose three additional sportsmanship awards. I have taken the liberty to intersperse this survey with stories about the awards, awardees, or people after whom particular awards are named, with the hope that it will encourage the reader who is involved in youth sports to enhance the existing sports awards program at his/her school or youth sports league.

National Hockey League

The Lady Byng Memorial Trophy

Perhaps Frank Boucher is the best example of any coach in any sport who taught sportsmanship solely by virtue of the way he played the game. A member of the Hockey Hall of Fame, Boucher played for and later coached the New York Rangers starting more than 90 years ago. He passed away in 1977. As we all know, hockey can, at times, be a very violent sport, one in which fighting and poor sportsmanship is quite common. It is somewhat ironic that, to my knowledge, the NHL was the first professional major sports league to give an award to the player who exhibits the best sportsmanlike behavior. Known as the Lady Byng Memorial Trophy, this award is presented each year to the player who "exhibited the best type of sportsmanship and gentlemanly conduct combined with a high standard of playing ability." Over the years, many different players have won this award. Only one player has ever won it more than five times. That person is Frank Boucher, who won it seven times! After the seventh time, the NHL gave him the original trophy and decided to make a new one since he was such a good sport.

King Clancy Trophy

According to the National Hockey League's website, "The King Clancy Memorial Trophy is an annual award given to the player who best exemplifies leadership qualities on and off the ice and has made a noteworthy humanitarian contribution in his community."

This award, which has never been presented to any player more than one time, is named in memory of Hall of Famer Francis M. "King" Clancy, a former NHL player, coach, and executive. Past recipients have included NHL greats Bryan Trottier and Ray Bourque. The first awardee (in 1988) was Lanny McDonald of the Calgary Flames.

National Basketball Association

The Joe Dumars Trophy

As the president of player personnel for the Detroit Pistons, a position that he held for 14 years (2000-2014), Joe Dumars directed the day-to-day affairs of this top NBA team. Since leaving this position, Mr. Dumars has served as an advisor to his beloved Pistons. He does all of his work in a quiet manner, not visible to most basketball fans. He tries his hardest to be fair and act in a classy, sportsmanlike manner.

In his capacity as team president, in 2004, Dumars helped lead the Pistons to an NBA Championship. The next season, the Pistons fell one game short of duplicating this feat. As a player, Joe was known for his hard work, keen shooting, tough defense, and sportsmanship. Along with Isiah Thomas, Dennis Rodman and Bill Laimbeer, Dumars helped lead his Pistons team to back-to-back NBA Championships (1988–1989 and 1989–1990). His display of sportsmanship on the court during the 1995–1996 season earned him the honor of being the first recipient of the NBA's Sportsmanship Award.

His continued display of sportsmanship made him worthy of having this award later named in his honor. In announcing this to the public, NBA Deputy Commissioner Russ Granik stated: "Joe Dumars represents the best of the NBA. Throughout his 14-year career, Joe carried himself with dignity and integrity and showed that one can be both a great athlete and a great sportsman. It is with enormous pride that we will from now on be giving the 'Joe Dumars Trophy' to our annual Sportsmanship winner." This prestigious award is presented to the player who best "exemplifies the ideals of sportsmanship on the court – ethical behavior, fair play and integrity."

The J. Walter Kennedy Citizenship Award

Named in memory of the NBA's second Commissioner, J. Walter Kennedy, who served the league with great distinction (1963–1975), this award is presented each year by the Professional Basketball Writers Association (PBWA) "to the player, coach, or athletic trainer who shows outstanding service and dedication to the community."

Past recipients have included Dave Bing and Kevin Johnson, who both became city mayors (Detroit and Sacramento respectively), Doc Rivers, who ascended to become one of the NBA's top coaches, and Joe Dumars (see preceding passage).

The 2013–2014 recipient was former Chicago Bulls standout Luol Deng who never forgot his past. Born in the Sudan to a distinguished Dinka tribe family, Luol – along with his family – fled to Egypt because of political unrest when he was a young child. When Luol's father – a former member of the Sudanese Parliament – was granted political asylum, the Deng family moved to England. Recognized for his charitable work on behalf of various organizations, the star hoopster founded the Luol Deng Foundation, which uses basketball to inspire hope in young men and women in Africa, the United Kingdom and the U.S. Upon receiving the distinguished award, Deng stated, in part: "It's an honor to be recognized for any award, but this one is special because it represents who I am as a person and where I came from."

Women's National Basketball Association

Kim Perrot Sportsmanship Award

The Kim Perrot Sportsmanship Award is given annually "to a player who exemplifies the ideals of sportsmanship on the court, including ethical behavior, fair play, and integrity."

A talented point guard who helped lead her Houston Comets team twice (1998 and 1999) to the WNBA Championship, Kim Perrot died of cancer on August 20, 1999, at the age of 32. After playing professional basketball in Israel and a number of European countries, Perrot made the inaugural Comets team, as a developmental player, at an open try-out. She soon became a starter and was known as a floor leader, top defensive player, and role model for sportsmanship. Before the start of the 1999 season, Kim was diagnosed with an aggressive form of lung cancer. While battling her illness, Kim envisioned the creation of a youth center especially designed for teenagers who were battling life-threatening illnesses. This center would be a place for these teens and their families to relax, study, have fun, and take a break from medical treatments. Through Kim's efforts, as well as the generosity of the Comets and their fans, today Kim's Place is a reality. Housed in Houston's world renowned M.D. Anderson Cancer Center, Kim's Place provides the opportunity for teens and their families to experience respite during trying times.

WNBA Cares Community Assist Award

Each month of the WNBA season (i.e., May, June, July, and August), this award is presented to "a WNBA player for their outstanding efforts in the community, and for ongoing philanthropic work. . . ."

Major League Baseball

The Roberto Clemente Award

Roberto Clemente played his entire 18-year career for the Pittsburgh Pirates. Clemente excelled in all of baseball's major skills (i.e., hitting, fielding, throwing, and base running). The 1966 recipient of the National League Most Valuable Player (MVP) Award, Clemente won the Gold Glove award as the best fielder at his position 12 times and had 200 or more hits during four of eighteen seasons. When his career came tragically to an end in 1972, he had amassed exactly 3,000 base hits. The player also led his team to the World Series Championship in 1960. Clemente was the first Hispanic to earn many baseball achievements, including the first to be named league and World Series MVP and the first to win a World Series as a starting player.

Not only was Clemente a star on the field, but off the field as well. In addition to a well-known devotion to his family, Clemente also demonstrated great caring for others, especially people who needed help. His humanitarian leanings led him to Nicaragua in 1972, after an earthquake rocked the country, killing and injuring tens of thousands. Clemente wanted to make sure that food, clothing, and medical supplies would be brought to the earthquake victims as quickly as possible, and on New Year's Eve of that year, he boarded an old, overstuffed plane so that he could personally deliver supplies directly to devastated families. Sadly, his plane crashed, killing him and everyone else on board.

Clemente's teammate on the Pirates, catcher and outfielder Manny Sanguillén, would have been on the plane but he lost his car keys and didn't make it to the airport. Sanguillén was so ravaged with grief over losing his longtime friend that he missed the memorial service, so that he could swim the ocean near the crash site, looking – in vain – for Clemente's body, which was never found.

After just a few months, Roberto Clemente was inducted into Baseball's Hall of Fame – again, the first Hispanic to attain this honor. Up to that point, a player was not eligible before five years had passed after his baseball career had ended. But due to the circumstances of his death, they waived that rule for Clemente. (The rule was later changed to enable consideration after six months for candidates who die while still actively playing on a major league team.)

Because of his sportsmanship on the field and extraordinary community service, MLB renamed the recently established "Commissioner's Award" after Clemente in 1973. The coveted Roberto Clemente Award is presented annually to one player who "demonstrates the values Hall of Famer Roberto Clemente displayed in his commitment to community and understanding the value of helping others."

National Football League

The Art Rooney Award

Although the penalty for unsportsmanlike conduct has been around for many years, the NFL did not formally award one of its players with a sportsmanship award until 2015, when the league introduced the Art Rooney Award. Candidates are selected by their fellow teammates for demonstrating ". . . on the field the qualities of great sportsmanship, including fair play, respect for opponents, and integrity in competition." Former players choose the winners, which are announced each year at an awards ceremony held the night before the Super Bowl.

Art Rooney Sr. founded the Pittsburgh Steelers in the early 1930s and is one of the NFL's pioneers. According to current Steelers President Art Rooney II, "My grandfather cared about integrity in the game of football, and the recipient of this award should be proud his peers look at him in such a respectful manner."

Walter Payton: Man of the Year Award

After his death in 1999, at age 45, the NFL added the name of running back Walter Payton to its annual "Man of the Year" award. The Walter Payton Man of the Year Award "recognizes a player's off-the-field community service as well as his playing excellence." Payton, who played his entire 13-season Hall of Fame career with the Chicago Bears, was beloved by players and fans for his amazing play and involvement in the community. Payton earned the nickname "Sweetness" in college because he was a sweet guy and for his smooth running on the football field. Walter's legacy of compassion and charitable work continues through the work of the Walter and Connie Payton Foundation, founded by the star player and his wife to aid low income kids and was later expanded to help struggling elderly seniors obtain assisted living housing. And to perpetuate Walter's passion for providing a college education to those who cannot afford it, the Payton Family Foundation was established, which provides college scholarships.

Major League Soccer

Xbox Individual Fair Play Award

Presented annually, the Xbox Individual Fair Play Award is given to a player whose sportsmanship qualifications are determined by "objective criteria such as fouls committed, cards received, games and minutes played, as well as subjective evaluation of sportsmanlike behavior." A past winner of this prestigious award is MLS legend Brian McBride who won it in 2003 as a member of the Columbus Crew.

Xbox Team Fair Play Award

The Xbox Team Fair Play Award is given each year to a team whose sportsmanship qualifications are determined by "objective criteria such as fewest fouls committed and cards received and on the subjective evaluation of sportsmanlike behavior." Since its inception in 1997, the Columbus Crew has received this award the most, a total of five times.

National Collegiate Athletic Association

NCAA Student-Athlete (and Team) Sportsmanship Award(s)

This award is presented to a male and female student-athlete from each of the six NCAA divisions "who have distinguished themselves through demonstrated acts of sportsmanship and ethical behavior." The criteria for selection include the candidate's: positively affecting their community's sports culture; selflessness; display of acts of integrity; and sportsmanship. (For this award, an act of sportsmanship is defined as "behavior exhibited during competition by student-athletes based on values, respect and integrity.")

Additionally, each year one team is recognized for its exemplary acts of sportsmanship and presented by the NCAA with a team sportsmanship award.

NCAA Bob Frederick Sportsmanship Award

Named in memory of Dr. Bob Frederick, a former Kansas and Illinois State athletic director, first awarded in 2009, this award is presented annually to one NCAA coach, staff member or administrator "who possesses a demonstrated history of sportsmanship. The individual will have displayed the utmost respect for NCAA intercollegiate athletics and all who participate by leading by example and promoting positive fan involvement in and out of the competition setting."

High School Sports Awards

Many of the 50 U.S. states have formal programs to promote sportsmanship among its student-athletes, coaches, administrators, parents, and/or fans. Just as in professional and collegiate sports leagues, it is common for awards to be granted to worthy high school student-athletes and other participants.

Illinois has developed a solid program promoting and reinforcing sportsmanship. In the Illinois High School Association's (IHSA) "Do What's Right!" program, annual sportsmanship awards are presented to individual high schools, sports conferences, and student-athletes. Additionally, "Sport A Winning Attitude" certificates are given to "a coach, player, team, official, or spectator [who] has demonstrated exemplary sportsmanship at an IHSA interscholastic contest."

Authors Choice: And the Winner Is...

If I had my own award to give out it would be the Team Spirit Institute's Lifetime Achievement Sportsmanship Award, and it would go to UCLA basketball coach John Wooden (highlighted in *Chapter 5* of this book).

Why Coach Wooden? There are many reasons, but here are a few.

Although no human being in the history of the world has been considered perfect and, accordingly, is subject to criticism for some deficiencies, among sports figures, John Wooden is as close to an ideal role model that there is. When defining sportsmanship as ***Respect and Honor*** (דֶּרֶךְ אֶרֶץ וְכָבוֹד/*Derekh Eretz v'Khavod*), Coach Wooden has practiced and preached the importance of treating others with respect and honor throughout his life and in all of his various relationships. In addition to "talkin' the talk," he has also "walked the walk."

As a college basketball player, Wooden was a three-time All American, leading Purdue to the Helms Foundation's unofficial national championship in 1932. He was also named national player of the year. Before the establishment of the NBA, Wooden played professionally. Nicknamed the "India Rubber Man" for the many times that he dived on the floor (and bounced back), Wooden combined exceptional skill and extraordinary acts of hustle and sportsmanship to benefit his team.

Wooden considered coaching to be an extraordinary opportunity to impact upon the lives of his student players. In addition to basketball skills, Wooden also set out to teach them life skills. According to the esteemed coach, more important than winning on the court was being a success off of it. Integrity was the foundation of his existence and the core of his curriculum.

Known for his aphorisms, affectionately referred to as "Woodenisms," the coach stressed to his players the importance of leading an upstanding, moral life. "Your true happiness comes from giving, not getting. It's a basic precept of all great religions: The Golden Rule."

Coach Wooden taught the importance of competing against a person's own potential. He often quoted his father, exclaiming, "Make each day your masterpiece." He would add, "Merely try to do your best, every day. . . True success can come only from the satisfaction one gets from knowing you did the best you are capable of doing." If everyone tried their hardest, thus achieving greatness, it follows then that the team comprised of such individuals would also be successful.

Often, when speaking to youth, Coach Wooden would hand out his business card, which contained his sportsmanship pledge (see *Chapter 30*). Although he was raised in rural Indiana, notorious for its segregation and blatant prejudices towards blacks, Coach Wooden was a strong proponent against racism. Referred to as "color blind," when asked by a reporter what type of racial problems existed on the UCLA Bruins basketball team, black UCLA star hoopster Curtis Rowe responded, "You don't know our coach, do you? He doesn't see color, he sees ballplayers."

When the first African-American hoopsters had trouble securing housing at UCLA, Wooden arranged with two Jewish fraternity houses for these players to be admitted into their lodging.

Although competitive, Coach Wooden was known for acting in a respectful, sportsmanlike manner to his opponents even in defeat. Pete Newell coached the University of California Berkeley team from 1954-55 through 1959. During this five-year span, his Golden Bears and Wooden's UCLA Bruins were pretty evenly matched. Newell commented about Wooden, "He never expressed frustration, personal difficulties, or anger in those years that I was beating him, just the opposite."

A true example of sportsmanship, Wooden also behaved in an upstanding, ethical, loving manner to his family. Deeply devoted to his wife Nell, the love of his life, he and his wife dedicated their lives to raising their four children as well as being an active part of the lives of their numerous grandchildren and great-grandchildren. After Nell passed away in 1985, Coach Wooden, who had retired from coaching 10 years earlier, lived an additional 25 (meaningful) years, continuing to lead his family and educate multitudes of others through his writings, lectures, and motivational speeches.

An epitome of sportsmanship also is a citizen who displays great patriotism. A Naval veteran, Wooden was a staunch patriot. The coach, though more conservative politically, might find himself discussing the hot topics of the day with some of his more liberally-minded players – and could also respectfully disagree while maintaining their admiration.

Possessing views that advocate love, respect, peace, and contribution to one's community – whether the source is religion or family teachings or from experience – is an important component of someone who displays sportsmanship. A devout Christian, in his magnum opus, known as "The Pyramid of Success," Coach Wooden includes at the apex of this structure, next to "Patience," the virtue of "Faith."

Many times, the only reward that someone who displays consistent acts of sportsmanship receives is the intrinsic reward of seeing your progeny and protégés mature into upstanding citizens and community leaders. Coach Wooden had this great satisfaction with his children, grandchildren, and great-grandchildren, as well as with countless numbers of his Bruins players.

Sometimes an exemplary sportsman is also rewarded with consistently winning the games in which he competes. In this way also, the Wizard of Westwood is unique in that he won the most NCAA Championships of any coach in men's sports college history. Although Wooden is especially remembered for his amazing 10 NCAA Championships during a 12-year span (including seven consecutive) as the Coach of the UCLA Bruins, few realize that he did not win his first championship until his 15th season as UCLA's coach. He possessed great patience, perseverance, and class while pursuing his dream of being a championship coach.

For all of the above-cited reasons and more, it is with great pride that I present (posthumously) the Team Spirit Institute's Lifetime Achievement Sportsmanship Award to the greatest coach of all-time: Coach John R. Wooden.

Author's Choice: A Spiritual Insight

And the winner is...

Although many men and women in Jewish history are worthy of receiving the prestigious Team Sprit Institute's Lifetime Achievement Award, the person who is most fitting is **Abraham our Patriarch** (*Avraham Avinu*), with a supporting award going to his beloved wife, **Sara our Matriarch** (*Sara Imenu*).

Using the definition for sportsmanship of דֶּרֶךְ אֶרֶץ וְכָבוֹד / *Dereckh Eretz v'Khavod*, throughout his lifetime, and in all of his relationships, Abraham displayed the ultimate of **Respect and Honor** to others.

For starters, nobody expressed their great love of and belief in the Almighty more than Abraham (*Ethics of Our Fathers* 5:4):

עֲשָׂרָה נִסְיוֹנוֹת נִתְנַסָּה אַבְרָהָם אָבִינוּ וְעָמַד בְּכֻלָּם,
לְהוֹדִיעַ כַּמָּה חִבָּתוֹ שֶׁל אַבְרָהָם אָבִינוּ.

Asara nisyonot nitnasa Avraham Avinu v'amad b'khulam, l'hodia kama chibato shel Avraham Avinu.

Abraham our Patriarch was tested for 10 trials, and he withstood them all; this teaches how great Abraham our Patriarch's love [of HaShem] was.

Among these 10 trials were the command of *"Lekh L'kha"* (*Genesis* 12:1) to leave his homeland and family; having a *b'rit mila/bris* (**circumcision**) at age 99 (*Genesis* 17:24); and being asked to sacrifice his son, Isaac (*Genesis* 22:1-2).

Abraham showed great respect for his family. Deeply distressed by the demand placed upon him by his wife Sara to banish Hagar and her son from his household (*Genesis* 21:9-13), the Almighty assured Abraham that Sara was justified in making her demand; after all, *Yishmael* was engaged in acts of murder, immoral relationships, and idol worship (see *Rashi* to *Genesis* 21:9), and was a terrible influence upon Isaac, Abraham's successor Patriarch.

Although Abraham's late brother, Haran, was not fully supportive of him in promoting his belief in monotheism (see *Rashi* to *Genesis* 11:28), Abraham still showed great respect by assuming the responsibilities of serving as the guardian to Haran's son, Lot.

Even though Lot proved to be selfish and narcissistic, Abraham sought to make peace between his own and his nephew's shepherds who were quarrelling by allowing Lot the opportunity to choose first which land he desired. Naturally, Lot chose the land that was more fertile for grazing (*Genesis* 13:5–12). Later, when Lot and his family's lives were threatened, Abraham risked his and his followers' lives by staging a war against the Four Kings who had kidnapped his troubled nephew (*Genesis* 14:1–24).

We learn from *Genesis* 18:1-22 and accompanying *Rashi* commentary that *Avraham* and *Sara* are the (human) founders of another form of *Derekh Eretz v'Khavod*; that is the *Mitzvah* of *Hachnasat Ohrchim*/**Welcoming in Guests** (see **NAME THAT MITZVAH!** in *Chapters 9* and *10*). While recuperating from his *Bris*, Avraham refused to sit still and, instead, actively sought out wayfarers. Upon seeing three human figures who were strangers, Abraham welcomed them into his tent, gave them water to wash themselves, food, and drink. It turned out that these three "men" were angels of God, who came to visit the recuperating *Avraham*, tell *Sara* and Abraham about Sara's pregnancy, and also share with them news of the upcoming destruction of **Sodom and Gomorra** (סְדֹם וַעֲמֹרָה /*S'dom VaAmorah*).

As discussed in Chapter 9, *Ushpizin* is a mystical tradition to welcome exalted (*Biblical*) guests into our *Sukkot* (huts) on each of the seven nights of the festival of *Sukkot*. Fittingly, on the first night of the holiday, we welcome Abraham, whose Kabbalistic emanation is *Chesed* (**Loving Kindness**), as expressed in many ways including through the *Mitzvah* of **Welcoming in Guests** (*Hakhnasat Orchim*) which he and Sara initiated.

Not only did Abraham have respect for "stranger-angels" who appeared to be human beings, but he also had tremendous respect for humankind, even if (too) many of its members were evil. This is especially evident by his pleading with the Almighty to spare the lives of the citizens of *S'dom* and *Amorah* (*Genesis* 18:20–32).

An important principle in Jewish tradition is *K'vod HaMet* (**Respect for the Deceased**). Abraham remains the model for proper burial and mourning practices in Jewish tradition for the respectful, compassionate, and loving manner in which he ensured the proper burial of and mourning for his beloved wife, Sara (**Genesis** 23:1–20).

Finally, *Avraham* showed great *Derekh Eretz v'Khavod* for the continuity of the Jewish people that he (along with Sara) founded. This is most realized by his commissioning his trusted aid (sort of an ancient version of today's chief of staff) Eliezer to go and find a woman that Isaac would love (and vice-a-versa) and one who was fitting to be Sara's successor (*Genesis* 24:2–9). The *Midrash* teaches us that Rebecca proved to be the perfect wife for Isaac and second Matriarch for the Jewish people (see *Rashi* to *Genesis* 24:67).

Abraham was rewarded by the Almighty for his many acts of *Derekh Eretz v'Khavod* (a Jewish formula for sportsmanship), by being blessed with both material wealth, and most importantly, by being the founder of a great nation known today as the Jewish people. God fulfilled his promises to Abraham by making him the progenitor of a people rich in both quality and quantity:

כִּי בָרֵךְ אֲבָרֶכְךָ וְהַרְבָּה אַרְבֶּה אֶת זַרְעֲךָ
כְּכוֹכְבֵי הַשָּׁמַיִם וְכַחוֹל אֲשֶׁר עַל שְׂפַת הַיָּם

Ki varekh avarekh'kha v'harba arbeh et zarakha, k'khokh'vei ha-shamayim v'khachol asher ahl s'fat ha-yam

For I will surely bless you and make your progeny abundant like the stars in the heavens and like the sand on the sea shore (Genesis 22:17) . . .

For all of the above cited reasons, plus more, it is with great pride that I present (posthumously) the inaugural Team Spirit Institute's Lifetime Achievement *Derekh Eretz v'Khavod* Award to the founding Patriarch of the Jewish people: אַבְרָהָם אָבִינוּ / *Avraham Avinu* (**Abraham Our Patriarch**) with a Best Supporting Matriarch Award going to his beloved wife, Sara (שָׂרָה אִמֵּנוּ) /*Sara Imenu*/ **Sara Our Matriarch**.

THE BOX SCORE

The Winners:

Coach John R. Wooden:
Team Spirit Institute's Lifetime Achievement
Sportsmanship Award

Abraham Our Patriarch (*Avraham Avinu*):
Team Spirit Institute's Lifetime Achievement
Derekh Eretz v'Khavod Award

Sara Our Matriarch (*Sara Imenu*):
TSI's Best Supporting Matriarch Award

Authors Choice #2: And the winner is...
If you were asked to select one person from sports history and one from Jewish history who is remembered "forever" for one single act of sportsmanship/ *Derekh Eretz v'Khavod*, what individual and which act would you pick? Why?

Regarding "*Rahbi*" *Elazar ben Durd'ya* who successfully performed *T'shuva* (**Repentance**), it was stated:

יֵשׁ קוֹנֶה עוֹלָמוֹ בְּשָׁעָה אַחַת.
Yesh koneh olamo b'sha-ah achat

There are those who acquire their [secure place in] the World [to Come] in one moment (*Avoda Zara* 17a).

Inspired by this statement, I call these honors the Team Spirit Institute's (TSI) *Yesh Koneh Olamo B'Sha-ah Achat* Awards.

271

Here are my choices, and why:

From the world of sports, I select Sandy Koufax. Although he is considered by many the greatest left-handed pitcher of all-time, what most American Jews remember best about Koufax was his decision not to pitch in the opening game of the 1965 World Series because it fell on *Yom Kippur*. Koufax made this decision out of his deep respect for his religion and all those Jewish fans who admired him. Koufax was a secular Jew, who it is believed did not even attend synagogue services that *Yom Kippur* day, but, instead, "laid low" in his St. Paul, Minnesota hotel room. In an era when American Jews were still reeling from the loss of more than six million brothers and sisters murdered in the Holocaust and were praying for the survival of the nascent modern State of Israel, Sandy Koufax's action gave Jews of that generation, and of future generations, a very needed shot in the arm proving the importance of openly and proudly identifying as a Jew.

In the "Jewish World (exclusively)," my pick for the TSI *Yesh Koneh Olamo B'sha-ah Achat Derekh Eretz v'Khavod* Award is *Menashe*.

The oldest son of Joseph, born in Egypt, *Menashe* was the first *b'khor* (**firstborn son**) in the (recorded) history of the world, who, when passed over for a blessing or other perceived entitlement, did not retaliate against his younger brother. Beginning with Cain and Abel, and continuing with the sons of our Patriarchs (Ishmael and Isaac; Esau and Jacob; Leah's sons and Joseph), we have seen that once "slighted," the *b'khor* acted out against his younger brother. An accomplished, competent political aide (top assistant to Joseph), *Menashe* realized that his younger brother, *Ephraim* – a (pre-Sinai) *Torah* scholar - was better suited to receive the blessing of the first born. *Menashe*'s act of *Derekh Eretz v'Khavod* was that he did not act out against *Ephraim*.

THE BOX SCORE

In addition to acquiring their places in the annals of Sportsmanship/*Derekh Eretz v'Khavod* history with one single act, American sports immortal Sandy Koufax and *Torah* hero *Menashe* both possessed extraordinary restraint in taking the high road and doing that which is right. Both of their award-winning acts were passive in nature and we reward them for their inactions.

Chapter 28
In the Name of Heaven

Kiddush HaShem

Public displays of an athlete's respect for his/her's religion play out in different ways among other athletes and fans. Some display it so openly that it can be a "turn-off" to other players and fans, while other athletes express it in a more discreet manner that can, at times, be inspirational. When a Jewish athlete expresses his/her respect for Judaism in a low-key manner, it can be considered an act of *Kiddush HaShe*m (***Sanctification of God's Holy Name***), as s/he is representing the Jewish people in a way that portrays a positive image of all Jews to both non-Jews and Jews.

While the 1960s was a decade only 20 years removed from the Holocaust and Jews were stereotyped by many as passive, weak people, the first story inspired great pride among all Jews as it was a low-key "in-your-face" portrayal to the gentile world that Jews can indeed be strong, handsome, and athletic.

By the turn of the millennium, Jews were so well-accepted in American society that it became common for many different male professionals (i.e., doctors, lawyers, accountants, professors) to wear a *Kippa* (***yarmulke; skullcap***) at the work place. During the 1960s, such a phenomenon was extremely rare. While triggering a great sense of pride among Jews (especially Orthodox), the second story showed the world how an observant Jew can perform at the highest levels of all professions, including sports.

The *Kiddush HaShem* Heard Around the World

A story is told that when Los Angeles Dodgers manager Walt Alston came to the mound to take ace Don Drysdale out of the game after he allowed six runs in the first three innings, Drysdale said to his skipper, "I bet now you're wishing I was Jewish."

This remark was made during the first game of the 1965 World Series between the visiting Dodgers and the home team, the Minnesota Twins. Drysdale, the Dodgers #2 pitcher, started in the Series opener in place of the team's #1 starter, Sandy Koufax. (See *Chapter 27*.) Although he was a secular Jew who never even celebrated becoming a *Bar Mitzvah*, Koufax knew that Jews, especially youth, looked up to him as a role model and, out of respect for his religion, he chose not to pitch that day. Although Jews (including some rabbis) around the Twin Cities claimed that he was in their synagogues for services, author Jane Leavy, who wrote a biography about the Dodger phenom, insists that Koufax never left his hotel room. Koufax, famously reluctant to give interviews, has never revealed what he did that day.

Sportsmanship is all about *Derekh Eretz v'Khavod/***Respect and Honor***. Known for being a person who enjoyed his privacy and who minimized his time in the spotlight, Sandy Koufax chose not to play on *Yom Kippur* because he was a dignified, polite, and respectful man. In fact, in his tome, *American Jews and America's Game: Voices of a Growing Legacy in Baseball*, the author Larry Ruttman describes how gracious Koufax was even when he declined Ruttman's invitation for an interview.

Although Sandy was not the first, or last, Jewish ballplayer to sit out a game on *Yom Kippur*, his case is probably the best known due to the fact that it was the first game of the World Series, and because it occurred at a rather critical time for Jewish acceptance in mainstream American Jewish society.

Sandy Koufax's well-publicized decision brought great pride and inspiration to Jews of all ages and backgrounds, both fans and non-followers of sports. Koufax's bold act of sportsmanship (i.e., respect towards his religion and people), also brought the intrinsic reward of *Kiddush HaShem*, great honor to the Jewish people among the other nations of the world.

The *Kiddush HaShem* Kid

"Tamir Goodman Signs Multi-year Deal to Play for Maccabi Tel-Aviv"

Newspapers around the world ran headlines like this in July of 2002 after basketball phenom, Tamir Goodman, announced that he would play professional hoops in Israel.

In the winter of 1999, the world outside of Maryland first learned of a teenager named Tamir Goodman. *Sports Illustrated* and other major media sources began to tell us about this then high school superstar who had plans to play basketball at the University of Maryland.

What was especially unique about this recruit is that he was a product of a yeshiva high school. Like so many other Jewish parochial school students, Tamir woke up early each morning to *daven* (**pray**) with his schoolmates and did not classes until late each evening. And like so many other Jewish day school students, he loved basketball. What distinguished Goodman from other yeshiva students was his extraordinary basketball talent.

Not only is Tamir known as "JJ," short for the "Jewish Jordan," but he truly played in a "Jordanesque" manner. He is so talented that when the University of Maryland, a perennially top basketball program, extended a scholarship to the young Mr. Goodman, they understood that Tamir intended to remain a fully observant Jew. They realized that Tamir would only eat Kosher food, wear his *kippa* when he played basketball, and that, in observance of *Shabbat* (**Sabbath**), he would not play on Friday nights and Saturdays.

Although Goodman's plans changed, in that he attended and played basketball for Towson University, another NCAA Division I school, instead of the University of Maryland, his commitment to Judaism remained the same. After his college career, Tamir decided to turn pro and play in his homeland, Israel. Tamir, whose mother is Israeli, also served in the ***Israel Defense Forces*** (*IDF*)/ צָהַ"ל (*TzaHa"L*).

DIDJA KNOW that Sandy Koufax does not have the most career wins by a Jewish MLB pitcher? That distinction belongs to another southpaw, Kenny Holtzman. Koufax posted 165 victories to Holtzman's 174.

DIDJA KNOW that in their only match-up (on September 25, 1966), Holtzman beat Koufax 2–1 in Wrigley Field? A Cub rookie, the 20-year-old, defeated the 30-year-old Koufax who retired after the World Series that year because of painful arthritis.

In sports, it is common for athletes to have nicknames. In addition to the "Jewish Jordan" and "JJ," a moniker that I feel was also appropriate for the amazing hoopster when he was a high school upperclassman was the "*Kiddush HaShem Kid*." After all, even as a teenager, Tamir taught both Jews and non-Jews around the world by example that a person does not have to compromise their religious beliefs and observances to be successful in any profession or walk of life.

The *Torah* teaches that every action we take in life falls into one of two general categories. It is either a *Kiddush HaShem* (**Sanctification of God's Holy Name**) or a *Chillul HaShem* (**Desecration of God's Holy Name**). When we perform a *Mitzvah* or other type of act endorsed by the *Torah*, we are doing something which is a *Kiddush HaShem*. When one does something contrary to the law or spirit of the *Torah*, one is engaging in a *Chillul HaShem*.

Although no longer a "kid," today Tamir goes around the world inspiring Jews of all ages through his coaching, presentations, and motivational speeches on how important it is to always act in a *Kiddush HaShem* manner. Tamir speaks passionately about **Sportsmanship** / דֶּרֶךְ אֶרֶץ וְכָבוֹד as well as the other values that we learn from playing basketball. One of the life stories that he shares is a lesson that his late father taught him about the importance of exhibiting sportsmanship at all times, even after victory. As a youngster, one time after Tamir scored the winning bucket, he was so exuberant that he celebrated in front of all those in attendance, including members of the opposing team. After the game, young Tamir's father reminded him that, even after victory, a Jew must exhibit proper **Sportsmanship** / דֶּרֶךְ אֶרֶץ וְכָבוֹד (*Derekh Eretz v'Khavod*) by being humble and not doing anything that might shame another person – including one's opponent.

Chapter 29
May I Quote You on That?

May I Quote You on That?

The word יח /Chai (**live; alive**) is a "lucky" word in Hebrew, as Judaism sanctifies life. A popular pendent worn by men and women is one bearing this word. The Gimatria (**numerical value**) of the Hebrew letters of this word is 18. Often, people give monetary gifts in denominations of 18. The Torah (Leviticus 18:5) commands the Jewish people to *live by them* [*the Mitzvot*]/ וָחַי בָּהֶם.

While there are numerous quotes about sportsmanship, here are my favorite 18:

"True sportsmanship is . . . Always taking the high road . . ."
Lorii Myers, *3 Off the Tee: No Excuses: The Fit Mind–Fit Body Strategy Book, Volume 3*

"I think sportsmanship is knowing that it is a game, that we are only as good as our opponents, and whether you win or lose, to always give 100 percent."
Sue Wicks, 2000 Winner of WNBA's Kim Perrot Sportsmanship Award

"One man practicing sportsmanship is far better than a hundred teaching it."
Knute Rockne

"In my day we patted the guy who beat us on the back, wished him well, and that was it."
Louis Zamperini, *Devil at My Heels: A Heroic Olympian's Astounding Story of Survival as a Japanese POW in World War II*

"I never thought about losing, but now that it's happened, the only thing is to do it right."
Muhammad Ali

"The only way to prove that you're a good sport is to lose."
Ernie Banks

"A lion never roars after a kill."
Attributed by many to Coach Dean Smith (Coach Smith, however, attributed It to Randy Wiel who served as an assistant coach under him at University of North Carolina)

"Sportsmanship is making sure you have respect for the guy you're playing across from."
Hall of Fame Quarterback Warren Moon

"Be fair. Play hard."
Dan Venezia, Retired Professional Baseball Player;
Author, *Coach Dan on Sportsmanship*

"Golf is a game of respect and sportsmanship; we have to respect its traditions and its rules."
Jack Nicklaus

"Sometimes I think sportsmanship is a little bit forgotten in place of the individual attention."
Cal Ripken, Jr.

"For when the One Great Scorer comes to mark against your name, He writes – not that you won or lost – but how you played the Game."
Grantland Rice, American Sportswriter in poem
Alumnus Football

"If you win through bad sportsmanship that's no real victory."
Babe Didrikson Zaharias

"Sportsmanship next to the Church is the greatest teacher of morals."
President Herbert Hoover

"[Y]ou are never really playing an opponent.
You are playing yourself, your own highest standards, and when you reach your limits, that is real joy."
Arthur Ashe

"Play to win, observe the rules, and act like a gentleman."
Attributed to: Clair Bee, American college basketball coach

"It's good sportsmanship not to pick up lost golf balls while they are still rolling."
Attributed to: Mark Twain

"I'll be a good sport when I win or I lose. No whining, complaining or making excuses. I'll always keep trying one hundred percent. To give my best effort in every event. This sportsmanship pledge will bring out my best. Coach Wooden has taught me to be a success."
Coach John R. Wooden's Sportsmanship Pledge

May I Quote You on That? Spiritual Insights

Here are my top 18 quotes from the *Torah* and other traditional texts that embody spiritual sportsmanship:

הָבוּ לַה' כְּבוֹד שְׁמוֹ
Havu LaShem k'vod Sh'mo
Give HaShem the honor due to His name.
Psalms 29:2

תְּנוּ כָּבוֹד לַתּוֹרָה.
T'nu Kavod LaTorah.
Give honor to the Torah.
Siddur/Prayer Book

דֶּרֶךְ אֶרֶץ קָדְמָה לַתּוֹרָה.
Derekh Eretz Kadma LaTorah.
Respect precedes [even] the study of Torah.
A Rabbinic statement [apparently] derived from
Tanna D'vei Eliyahu Rabba Parasha Aleph and VaYikra Rabba 9:3

דַּעֲלָךְ סְנֵי, לְחַבְרָךְ לֹא תַּעֲבֵיד.
זוֹ הִיא כָּל הַתּוֹרָה כּוּלָהּ
וְאִידָךְ פֵּירוּשָׁה הוּא; זִיל גְּמוֹר!
D'alakh s'nei, l'chavrakh loh ta-aveid. Zo he kol HaTorah kula
v'idakh perusha hu; zil g'mor!
That which is hateful to you do not do onto your
neighbor. This is the entire Torah and the rest is commentary;
go [and] study!
Hillel in Shabbat 31a

וְעָשִׂיתָ הַיָּשָׁר וְהַטּוֹב בְּעֵינֵי ה'
V'ahsita HaYashar v'HaTov b'einei HaShem
And you shall do that which is straight [fair] and good
in the eyes of HaShem.
Deuteronomy 6:18

וְנִשְׁמַרְתֶּם מְאֹד לְנַפְשֹׁתֵיכֶם
V'nishmartem m'od l'nafshoteikhem
And you shall diligently guard your souls.
Deuteronomy 4:15

בֶּן זוֹמָא אוֹמֵר . . .
אֵיזֶהוּ מְכֻבָּד? הַמְכַבֵּד אֶת הַבְּרִיּוֹת.

Ben Zoma omer: . . . Eizehu m'khubad? Ha-m'khabed et ha-b'riyot.

Ben Zoma says: . . . "Who is worthy of honor? One who honors
[i.e., treats with respect] others."

Ethics of Our Fathers 4:1

כַּבֵּד אֶת אָבִיךָ וְאֶת אִמֶּךָ

Kabed et avickha v'et imekha

Honor your father and your mother.

Exodus 20:12; Deuteronomy 5:16

מִפְּנֵי שֵׂיבָה תָּקוּם וְהָדַרְתָּ פְּנֵי זָקֵן

Mi-p'nei seiva takum v'hadarta p'nei zaken

In the presence of a gray haired person you shall rise; and you shall
honor the presence of an elder [or sage].

Leviticus 19:32

וּמוֹרָא רַבְּךָ כְּמוֹרָא שָׁמַיִם.

U-Mora rabakh k'mora Shamayim.

And the reverence that one [i.e., a student must show]
his Rabbi [teacher] is similar to that which he must show Heaven
[i.e., the Almighty].

Ethics of Our Fathers 4:15

נְצֹר לְשׁוֹנְךָ מֵרָע וּשְׂפָתֶיךָ מִדַּבֵּר מִרְמָה:

N'tzor l'shon'kha meh-ra u-sfahtekha mi-daber mirma.

Guard your tongue from evil and your lips from speaking deceitfully.

Psalms 34:14

הַמַּלְבִּין פְּנֵי חֲבֵרוֹ בָּרַבִּים כְּאִלּוּ שׁוֹפֵךְ דָּמִים.

HaMalbin p'nei chavero ba-rabim k'ilu shofekh damim.

Someone who causes the face of another to turn white
[i.e., shames him] in public, it is as if he has spilled blood
[i.e., committed murder].

Rabbinic statement based (apparently) on Ethics of Our Fathers 3:15

לֹא תַסִּיג גְּבוּל רֵעֲךָ

Lo Tasig g'vul reh-akha

Do not move the boundary of your fellow.

Deuteronomy 19:14

לֹא תִרְאֶה אֶת שׁוֹר אָחִיךָ אוֹ אֶת שֵׂיוֹ נִדָּחִים
וְהִתְעַלַּמְתָּ מֵהֶם
הָשֵׁב תְּשִׁיבֵם לְאָחִיךָ:

Lo tireh et shor achikha oh et seiyo nidachim, v'hitalamta meh-hem,
hashev t'shivem l'achikha.

**You shall not see your brother's ox or sheep wandering
and hide yourself from them; [rather,] you shall surely return
them to your brother.**

Deuteronomy 22:1

וְלִפְנֵי עִוֵּר לֹא תִתֵּן מִכְשֹׁל

V'lifnei ihver lo tihten mikhshol

And before a blind person you shall not place a stumbling block.

Leviticus 19:14

בְּיוֹמוֹ תִתֵּן שְׂכָרוֹ

B'yomo tihten s'kharo

**On that [same] day [that he worked] you shall pay
[i.e., the worker] his wages.**

Deuteronomy 24:15

שְׁמוֹנֶה מַעֲלוֹת יֵשׁ בַּצְּדָקָה
זוֹ לְמַעְלָה מִזּוֹ.

Sh'moneh ma-alote yesh ba-tz'daka zo l'mala mi-zo.

There are eight levels of charity each one higher than the next.

Maimonides, Mishneh Torah, Laws of Gifts to the Poor 10:7

וַיָּבֹא אַבְרָהָם לִסְפֹּד לְשָׂרָה וְלִבְכֹּתָהּ

Va-yavo Avraham lispod l'Sara v'li-vkota

And Abraham came to eulogize Sara and to weep for her.

Genesis 23:2

Chapter 30
Conclusion:
The Last Word

Winning isn't everything; it's how you treat others that counts most.

While winning is important at any level of competition, it is clearly not everything – especially at a youth (schools and leagues) level. Simply put: we cannot win at any cost. While teaching the importance of winning, we must also emphasize that we cannot sacrifice the significance of treating all others connected with our competition with proper **Respect** (*Derekh Eretz* / דֶּרֶךְ אֶרֶץ) and **Honor** (*Kavod*/ כָּבוֹד). This is the true definition of **Sportsmanship** / דֶּרֶךְ אֶרֶץ וְכָבוֹד (*Derekh Eretz v'Khavod*).

In this regard, players must treat members (players and coaches) of the opposing team in a dignified manner. Teammates must act in a proper way towards one another. The fans in the stands also must display proper sportsmanship towards the players, managers, umpires, and to each other. Players must act respectfully towards their coaches and the referees. Similarly, coaches and referees should not abuse their positions of authority and mistreat any players, coaches, or fans in any way. Likewise, a code of Sportsmanship/*Derekh Eretz v'Khavod* must exist for members of the media, especially when covering youth sports. Even the public address announcer plays an important role in modeling and promoting sportsmanship.

For many student-athletes, the most influential educators that they encounter in their academic careers are their coaches. Accordingly, coaches – as reinforced by parents – must take full advantage of this opportunity to positively influence their student-athletes. We must fully utilize the sporting experience, both as participants and fans, to teach the importance of **Sportsmanship** / דֶּרֶךְ אֶרֶץ וְכָבוֹד and other valuable life lessons (e.g., leadership, teamwork, health and focus) to our most precious resource – our children.

In the book of *Isaiah* (49:6), the Israelites are commanded by the Almighty to behave in an upstanding manner, not only for the benefit of the Jewish people, but as an example for all of the nations of the world: וּנְתַתִּיךָ לְאוֹר גּוֹיִם / *u-ntatikha l'ohr goyim* – **And I will make you a light for the nations**.

In this book, I have presented four levels of sportsmanship through the stories of many men and women who exemplify different aspects of sportsmanship. From the world of athletics, I chose players, coaches, administrators, and others from all different sports, competing at all different levels. From Jewish history, I have selected men and women from the *Torah*, Prophets, *Talmud*, and modern Jewish history who are exemplars of the many categories of דֶּרֶךְ אֶרֶץ וְכָבוֹד / *Derekh Eretz v'Khavod* (**Respect and Honor**).

It is my sincere hope – as a parent, educator and sports enthusiast – that the **PRAY BALL! Spiritual Values Series**, beginning with its first book **PRAY BALL 2!!** *Spiritual Insights into Sportsmanship* – its stories, lessons, and the examples set by the celebrity sports stars and Jewish historical figures highlighted – inspire us to further advance our holy mission and to continue to serve as a light for the nations – both on and off the field.

Acknowledgements and Sources

Acknowledgements

Hakarat HaTov. Gratitude. Recognizing the good. Giving credit where credit is due.

In the world of sports this is expressed by high fives, fist bumps, hats thrown onto the hockey rink, standing ovations, trophies, and performance bonuses. In Jewish tradition, it is manifested by handshakes, honoree dinners, greetings of יִישַׁר כֹּחַ *Yishar Koach* and כָּל הַכָּבוֹד / *Kol HaKavod*, and by simply saying, "thank you."

For all practical purposes ***PRAY BALL 2!!*** *Spiritual Insights into Sportsmanship* took 18 years to complete. Since the publication of my first book in 1999, the focus of my "spare" time during these nearly two decades has been directed to writing, piloting, rewriting and editing the materials that comprise the core of this new volume.

PRAY BALL 2!! *Spiritual Insights into Sportsmanship* has come to fruition through the support and assistance of many people. In the spirit of *Hakarat HaTov*, it is important particularly to recognize and thank some of these individuals. In advance I apologize to all those whose names I, inadvertently, omitted.

- My parents, Rabbi Nathan – *z"l* (of blessed memory) and Esther Gordon, for bringing me into this world and for instilling in me the importance of combining and applying Jewish and secular education (*Torah U-Mada*) to help make our world a better place. Sadly my father, brilliant and spot-on with his insights, passed away shortly before the publication of this book.
- My wife Marilyn for her love, support, honest critiques of my work as well as for giving-up Saturday nights and many other social opportunities to enable me to write this book and moonlight as an author/writer.
- Our children (now all young adults) Max, Rita (Carmi), and Sophie, all accomplished in their own rights – professionals, students, athletes and fans – for teaching me how to be a sports parent who exhibits proper Sportsmanship (*Derekh Eretz v'Khavod*), and providing me with valuable suggestions and stories for writing and marketing my ideas.
- My "Aunt" Rae and "Uncle" Lenny Hochman – both of blessed memory – for inspiring me to become a sports enthusiast (fan and player) by taking me to my first sporting event – a Chicago White Sox game.
- A very special thank you to my dear friends and fellow Team Spirit Institute officers Alan Molotsky (Vice President) and Mark Weksler (Treasurer). Not only have they expressed their friendship with countless hours of donated professional services (legal and accounting) and counsel, but they are men whose professional and family relationships truly define their upstanding character.
- Tom and Leslie Silverstein for their confidence in my abilities to create an educational resource to enrich the lives of Jewish youth. I am most grateful to the Silversteins and to all other supporters for their beneficence.

- My editors Jennifer Samors Eberling (English) and Ken Cooper (content) for their critical analysis (most of which I accepted).

- My sports fact-checker Lori Azim who applied the same deliberate, thorough, meticulous system with my manuscript as she does with the writings of her *New York Times* best-selling author-clients, and in so doing set a new (much higher) bar for my writing.

- My proofreaders, Marilyn Goldman, Aaron Goldman, Robert Chimberoff, Noam Domsky, Yehoshua Merzel, and Sruli Prero for their meticulous review of the manuscript before it went to press.

- Rabbi Noah Baron, an alumnus of the Yeshiva University *Torah Mitzion Kollel* of Chicago, for ensuring the accuracy of my *Biblical, Talmudic, Midrashic, Halakhic,* and other traditional Jewish citations and interpretration of these sources.

- Rabbi Yona Reiss *SHLIT"A* (Chicago Rabbinical Council's *Av Bet Din* and a *Rosh Yeshiva* at Yeshiva University) for always being available for *Eitzot* (advice).

- Rabbi Dr. Jerold Isenberg, Hebrew Theological College Professor & Chancellor Emeritus, for Hebrew, Judaic and technical insights and recommendations.

- Team Spirit Institute summer interns Audrey Fretzin, Ari Karesh and Rebecca Shiner, who assisted in the research, fact-checking and documentation of this book's numerous sources. A special shout-out to my daughter Sophie, who recruited these high school friends for this most important work.

- Beth Brzozowski for ensuring that the massive number of sources consulted in writing this book were accessible and well organized.

- My educational consultants Rabbi Dr. Burton Cohen, Dr. Martin Oliff and Rabbi Moshe Simkovich, who spent coutless hours reviewing the second draft of my manuscript and then provided keen, valuable insights on how to make the book accessible and reader-friendly to Jews of all backgrounds and educational venues from all streams of North American Jewry.

- Accomplished author, publisher, book industry entreupeneur Dr. Neal Samors for guiding me in establishing the Team Spirit Press, a division of Team Spirit Institute.

- *New York Times* bestselling author Jonathan Eig and academic scholar and author Rabbi Zev Eleff, Ph.D., for validating **PRAY BALL 2!!** *Spiritual Insights into Sportsmanship* as both a sports book and Jewish educational resource.

- Scholar, psychologist, prolific author Rabbi Reuven Bulka, Ph.D., for generously answering any and all inquiries.

- To all those in the sports world, academics and field of Jewish education who reviewed and wrote endorsements of this book. This list includes: Marci Dickman, Dr. Erwin Epstein, Rabbi Vernon Kurtz, Rabbi Menachem Linzer, Rabbi Elazar Muskin, Brent Novoselsky, Mark Potash, Rabbi Howard Jacoby Ruben, Dr. Jonathan Sarna, Ed Sherman, Morton Steinberg, Bruce Wolf and Rebecca Yoshor.

- Avrom Fox for guiding me through the process of distributing/selling books.
- Chicago Bulls Chairman Jerry Reinsdorf and President/COO Michael Reinsdorf for generously allowing special entrance to the United Center in order to take photographs for this book.
- Attorneys Larry Levine and Adam Klein of the law firm of Katten, Muchin, Rosenman, LLP for facilitating the United Center photo shoot opportunity.
- Colleen Quinn and Ross Lipschultz for coordinating the details of and graciously hosting the photo shoot.
- All of the photo "models" and their parents: Chava, Ken, Yaakov and Hadassah Avner; Avi Dobkin; Ezra and Sara Perlow; Robbie, Audrey, Sophie, Eli and Esther Fretzin; Phil and Avi Samuels; and "referee" Mark Weksler. Kudos to my children for serving as models, helping me recruit additional models, and designing the TSI uniforms.
- David Blachman for his outstanding photography. Eighteen years after snapping (with real film) the front cover and author's photos that decorate my first book, David returned to shoot (this time, digitally) the photos for my new book. Although technology has changed since 1999, David Blachman's high quality has not wavered.
- Sam Silvio, *PRAY BALL 2!!'s* masterful graphic designer for his patience, creativity and professionalism.
- Artist and graphic designer par excellence, Shikma Benmelech, for skillfully integrating the Hebrew text with the English.
- Adam Rhine and Raphaël Freeman, for helping to trouble shoot and correct challenges that arose in the graphic design of the book.
- My dear friends Phyllis and Otto Waldmann for their sage advice, counsel, guidance, and support.
- To all those who assisted me in searching for, locating, sharing and authorizing my use of photos in this book and on the Team Spirit Institute website. These individuals include: Dr. Julian Bailes; Illinois Supreme Court Justice Anne M. Burke; Kristi Piccolo Dolby (and other members of the Piccolo family) and Megan Kono of Rush University Medical Center; Gene Honda; John Horne, Coordinator of Rights & Reproductions at the National Baseball Hall of Fame Library; Attorney/Author Neville L. Johnson; David Khabinsky of Yeshiva University; Chicago Cubs Executive Vice President Michael Lufrano and Archivist Kristina Maldre Jarosik; Brent Novoselsky; Marlene Owens Rankin, Stuart Rankin (daughter and grandson of Jesse Owens) and Archivists Tamar Chute and Michelle Drobik of OSU Libraries University Archives; Raymond Ridder, Golden State Warriors, Vice President, Public Relations; Adam Rogowin, Vice President, Communications and Will Chukerman of the Chicago Blackhawks; Carmen Salvino; Ed Sherman;

Rick Telander; Alex Timiraos of UCLA; Joseph Williamson of Major League Baseball Properties, Inc.; Bruce Wolf; and Rebecca Yoshor.

- A very special thank you to Dr. Ari and Ruth Schwartz (the parents of Ezra Schwartz – z"l) for opening up their hearts and sharing with me a glimpse of their beautiful family. I hope the words and photos shared in this book further perpetuate the wonderful legacy of Ezra and bring added comfort to all members of the Schwartz family and community. I am grateful to my cousin Emily Levine Rapalino for introducing us.

- Paul Cibulka and all other representatives of the Friesens Corporation involved in this project for printing such an attractive-looking, reader-friendly book.

- My favorite sports teams: the Chicago White Sox, Chicago Bulls, University of Michigan Wolverines and Northwestern University Wildcats for providing me with both entertainment and, even more importantly "spiritual" material.

- Finally, to the Almighty for giving me the gift of life each day, something that I do not take for granted.

Sources

Sports/General

Books

Aaseng, Nathan. *True Champions: Great Athletes and Their Off-the-Field Heroics.* New York: Walker & Co., 1993.

Araton, Harvey. *Driving Mr. Yogi: Yogi Berra, Ron Guidry, and Baseball's Greatest Gift.* New York: Houghton Mifflin Harcourt, 2012.

Ashe, Arthur and Frank Deford. *Arthur Ashe: Portrait in Motion.* New York: Houghton Mifflin, 1975.

Bausum, Ann. *Muckrakers: How Ida Tarbell, Upton Sinclair, and Lincoln Steffens Helped Expose Scandal, Inspire Reform, and Invent Investigative Journalism.* Washington, DC: National Geographic Children's Books, 2007.

Bee, Clair and Ken Norton. *The Science of Coaching.* New York: Roland Press, 1959.

Bjarkman, Peter C. *Baseball Legends: Ernie Banks.* New York/Philadelphia: Chelsea House Publishers, 1994.

Brown, Bruce Eamon. *1001 Motivational Messages and Quotes: Teaching Character Through Sport.* Monterey, CA: Coaches Choice, 2003.

Cahan, Richard, Michael Williams, Neal Samors. *Real Chicago Sports: Photographs from the Files of the Chicago Sun-Times.* Chicago: Chicago's Neighborhoods, Inc., 2005.

Canfield, Jack, Mark Victor Hansen, Mark & Chrissy Donnelly, Jim Tunney. *Chicken Soup for the Sports Fan's Soul.* Deerfield Beach, FL: Health Communications, 2000.

Dickson, Paul. *The Dickson Baseball Dictionary* 3rd edition. New York: W.W. Norton & Company, 2009.

Eig, Jonathan. *Ali: A Life.* New York: Houghton Mifflin Harcourt, 2017.

Eig, Jonathan. *Luckiest Man: The Life and Death of Lou Gehrig.* New York: Simon & Schuster, 2005.

Eig, Jonathan. *Opening Day: The Story of Jackie Robinson's First Season.* New York: Simon & Schuster, 2007.

Eisenberg, John. *The Streak.* New York: Houghton Mifflin Harcourt, 2017.

Fainaru-Wada, Mark and Lance Williams. *Game of Shadows: Barry Bonds, BALCO, and the Steroids Scandal That Rocked Professional Sports.* New York: Gotham, 2006.

Feldman, Bruce. *Cane Mutiny: How the Miami Hurricanes Overturned the Football Establishment.* New York: New American Library, 2004.

Foer, Franklin and Marc Tracy, editors. *Jewish Jocks: An Unorthodox Hall of Fame.* New York/Boston: Twelve Books, 2012.

Ginott, Haim G. *Between Parent and Teenager.* Toronto: MacMillan Company, 1969.

Gladwell, Malcolm. *David and Goliath: Underdogs, Misfits, and the Art of Battling Giants.* New York: Little, Brown and Company, 2013.

Golenbock, Peter. *Wrigleyville: A Magical History of the Chicago Cubs.* New York: St. Martin's Press, 1999.

Gordon, James M. *Pray Ball! The Spiritual Insights of a Jewish Sports Fan.* Jerusalem: Gefen Publishing House, 1999.

Harris, Greg. *Jews in Baseball: A Painting by Ron Lewis.* JewishBaseballPlayer.com.

Herzog, Brad. *Inspiring Stories of Sportsmanship.* Minneapolis: Free Spirit Publishing, 2014.

Johnson, Neville L. *The John Wooden Pyramid of Success: The Biography, Oral History, Philosophy and Ultimate Guide to Life, Leadership, Friendship and Love of the Greatest Coach in the History of Sports.* Rev. second ed. Los Angeles: Cool Titles, 2004.

Jozsa, Frank P. John, J. Gurthie. *Relocating Teams and Expanding Leagues in Professional Sports.* Westport, Connecticut: Quorum Books, 1999.

Markbreit, Jerry and Alan Steinberg. *Last Call: Memoirs of an NFL Referee.* Chicago: Sports Masters, 2001.

Mitchell, George J. *Report to the Commissioner of Baseball of an Independent Investigation Into the Illegal Use of Steroids and Other Performance Enhancing Substances by Players in Major Baseball*. DLA Piper US LLP. December 13, 2007, accessed March 7, 2017, http://files.mlb.com/mitchrpt.pdf.

Morris, Jeannie. *Brian Piccolo: A Short Season*. Chicago: Bonus Books, 1971.

Moskowitz, Tobias J. and L. Jon Wertheim. *Scorecasting: The Hidden Influences Behind How Sports Are Played and Games Are Won*. New York: Crown Archetype, 2011.

Myers, Lorii. *3 Off the Tee: No Excuses: The Fit Mind-Fit Body Strategy Book, Volume 3*. Barrie, Ontario, Canada: Leda Publishing, 2013.

Nowinski, Christopher. *Head Games: Football's Concussion Crisis from the NFL to Youth Leagues*. Boston: Thought Leaders, LLC, 2011.

Poekel, Charlie. *Babe & the Kid: The Legendary Story of Babe Ruth and Johnny Sylvester*. Charleston: The History Press, 2007.

Poling, Jerry. *After They Were Packers: The Super Bowl XXXI Champs & Other Green Bay Legends*. Madison, WI: Trails Books, 2006.

Ruttman, Larry. *American Jews and America's Game: Voices of a Growing Legacy in Baseball*. Lincoln: University of Nebraska Press, 2013.

Samors, Neal. *Chicago in the Sixties: Remembering a Time of Change*. Chicago: Chicago's Neighborhoods, Inc., 2006.

Sayers, Gale and Al Silverman. *I Am Third: The Inspiration for Brian's Song*, 2nd ed. New York: Penguin Books, 2001.

Sherman, Ed. *Babe Ruth's Called Shot: The Myth and Mystery of Baseball's Greatest Home Run*. Connecticut: Lyons Press, 2014.

Shields, David Lyle Light and Brenda Jo Light Bredemeier. *Character Development and Physical Activity*. Champaign, IL: Human Kinetics Publishers, 1995.

Shorter, Edward. *The Kennedy Family and the Story of Mental Retardation*. Philadelphia: Temple University Press, 2000.

Smith, Dean and Gerald D. Bell with John Kilgo. *The Carolina Way: Leadership Lessons from a Life in Coaching*. New York: The Penguin Press, 2004.

Snyder, Brad. *A Well-Paid Slave: Curt Flood's Fight for Free Agency in Professional Sports*. New York: Viking Penguin, 2006.

Slater, Robert. *Great Jews in Sports*, rev. ed. Queens, NY: Jonathan David Publishers, 2003.

Spatz, Lyle (Editor), *The Team that Forever Changed Baseball and America: The 1947 Brooklyn Dodgers*. Lincoln: University of Nebraska Press, 2012.

Swaine, Rick. *The Black Stars Who Made Baseball Whole: The Jackie Robinson Generation in the Major Leagues, 1947–1959*. Jefferson, NC: McFarland Company, Inc., Publishers, 2006.

Telander, Rick. *Heaven Is a Playground*. Lincoln: University of Nebraska Press, 2009.

Telander, Rick. *The Hundred Yard Lie: The Corruption of College Football and What We Can Do to Stop It*. Champaign, IL: University of Illinois Press, 1996.

Talley, Rick. *The Cubs of '69: Recollections of the Team That Should Have Been*. New York/Chicago: Contemporary Books, 1989.

University of Chicago Press Staff. *The Chicago Manual of Style* (16th Edition). Chicago: The University of Chicago Press, 2010.

Votano, Paul. *Late and Close: A History of Relief Pitching*. Jefferson, North Carolina: McFarland & Company, Inc., Publishers, 2002.

Williams, Pat. *How to be Like Coach Wooden: Life Lessons from Basketball's Greatest Leader*. Deerfield Beach, Florida: Health Communications Inc., 2006.

Wojcik, Pamela Robertson. *Fantasies of Neglect: Imagining the Urban Child in American Film and Fiction*. New Brunswick: Rutgers University Press, 2016.

Wooden, John and Steve Jamison. *The Wisdom of Wooden: My Century On and Off the Court*. New York: McGraw-Hill Education, 2010.

Yates, Donald A. *"Fitzgerald and Football"* in *The Michigan Alumnus Quarterly Review* Vol. LXIV 1957-1958. Ann Arbor: The Alumni Association of the University of Michigan, 1958.

Zaharias, Babe Didrikson. *This Life I've Led: My Autobiography*. New York: A.S. Barnes, 1955.

Zamperini, Louis. *Devil at My Heels: A Heroic Olympian's Astounding Story of Survival as a Japanese POW in World War II*. New York: William Morrow Paperbacks, 2011.

Zweig, Eric and Chris McDonell (Compilers). *Big Book of Sports Quotes*. Ontario, Canada: Firefly Books, 2010.

Magazines/Journals

2013 White Sox Magazine, Vol. 3, ed. 22
Bullpen: The Official Game Program of the Chicago Bulls 2014–2015
Jet Journal of Pearls in Intensive Care Medicine
Profile: Smithsonian National Portrait Gallery News
Sport
Sports Illustrated
Time

Movies

Helgeland, Brian (Director). *42: The Jackie Robinson Story*. Burbank, CA: Warner Brothers, 2013. DVD.

Landesman, Peter (Director). *Concussion*. Culver City, CA: Sony Pictures Home Entertainment, 2016. DVD.

Newspapers

Chicago Jewish News
Chicago Sun-Times
Chicago Tribune
Daily Herald
Evening Independent
Midstream: A Monthly Jewish Review
New York Times
St. Louis Post-Dispatch
Wall Street Journal

Websites (and Blogs)

1869Reds.com (1869 Cincinnati Red Stockings)
AAPRA.org (American Academy for Park & Recreation Administraton)
ABCNews.Go.com
AbeBooks.com
ACLU.org
Acculturated.com
AEISpeakers.com (*American Entertainment International Speakers Bureau*)
AL.com (*Birmingham News*)
AllianceForIntegrity.com
ALSA.org (ALS Association)
Amazon.com
AmericanBar.org (American Bar Association/ABA)
APImages.com
Archive.Boston.com
ArmyNavyGame.com
AskMen.com
Ballotpedia.org (*Ballotpedia: The Encyclopedia of American Politics*)
BaltimoreSun.com
Baseball-Almanac.com
BaseballHall.org and *BaseballHallOfFame.org* (National Baseball Hall of Fame)
BaseballHotCorner.com
BaseballInWartime.com

Baseball-Reference.com
Basketball-Reference.com
BaylorSchool.org
BBC.com
BBHighway.com
BearsHistory.com
BehrmanHouse.com
BeloitDailyNews.com
Bentley.UMich.edu
BigTen.org
BillWalton.com
Biography.com
BleacherReport.com
BleedCubbieBlue.com
Bloomberg.com
BobbyOrr.net
Books.Google.com
BostonGlobe.com
Bowling.com
Brainline.org
BrainyQuote.com
Brandeis.edu
Britannica.com (*Encyclopedia Britannica*)
Brookings.edu (The Brookings Institution)
BrotherlyGame.com
BruinsLegends.blogspot.com
BU.edu (Boston University)
BusinessInsider.com
Bustle.com
CAE.Wisc.edu (Computer–Aided EngineeringUniversity of Wisconsin–Madison)
Cavs.com
CBSNews.com
CBSSports.com
CelticsLife.com
CenturyLinkField.com
ChangingWinds.wordpress.com
Character.org
Chattanoogan.com
ChicagoBaseballMuseum.org
ChicagoBears.com
Chicago.CBSLocal.com
ChicagoMag.com (*Chicago Magazine*)
ChicagoParkDistrict.com
ChicagoReader.com
Chicago.SunTimes.com

ChicagoTribune.com
ChickenSoup.com
Chron.com
  (Houson Chronicle)
Cincinnati.com
Classic.Esquire.com
  (Esquire)
Cleveland.com
ClevelandBrowns.com
ClevelandJewishNews.com
CNN.com
CoachDan.com
  (Dan Venezia)
CoachUp.com
CoachWooden.com
CollegeSportsScholarships.com
Colts.com
ConcordMuseum.org
County.Allegheny.PA.us
Courant.com
  (Hartford Courant)
CSNChicago.com
C-SPAN.org
CSUOhio.edu (Cleveland
  State University)
DailyHerald.com
DallasNews.com
DeadSpin.com
DemocratAndChronicle.com
  (Democrat & Chronicle–
  Part of the USA Network)
DenverBroncos.com
DenverPost.com
DesertNews.com
  (Mojave Desert News)
Dev.RealClearsports.com
DigitalCommons.UNL.edu
  (DigitalCommons @
  University of Nebreska –
  Lincoln)
Dictionary.com
DoubleGSports.com
DrugFreeSport.com
Dummies.com
Ed.gov (U.S. Department
  of Education)
EH.net (The Economic History
  of Major League Baseball)
Encyclopedia.com
EngagedScholarship.CSUOhio.
  edu (Cleveland State Law
  Review)

ERIC.ed.gov (Institute of
  Education Sciences)
ESPN.com
ESPN.Go.com EtymOnLine.com
Facebook.com
FacPub.StJohns.edu
Faculty.SOM.Yale.edu
FIAAA.org (Florida
  Interscholastic Athletic
  Administrators Association)
FiveThirtyEight.com
Forbes.com
Forward.com
FoxBusiness.com
FoxNews.com
FoxSports.com
FoundationCenter.org
FreeP.com (Detroit Free Press)
GazetteExtra.com (Walworth
  County [WI] Today)
GBallMag.com
GCGFinancial.com
Golf.com
GolfDigest.com
GolfHistoryToday.com
GoodReads.com
GotAllYourMarbles.com
GQ.com
Grantland.com
GuideStar.org
GuinnessWorldRecords.com
HangTime.Blogs.NBA.com
HardballTimes.com
Hazlet.SchoolWires.com
HeraldTribune.com
HHOF.com (HockeyHall
  OfFame.com)
HickokSports.com
HighSchoolSports.Syracuse.com
History.com
History.Bulls.com
History.House.gov (U.S. House
  of Representatives: History,
  Art & Archives)
History.Journalism.KU.edu
HistoryNewsNetwork.org
History.State.gov
HistoryVsHollywood.com
Hockey-Reference.com
HoopHall.com (Basketball Hall
  of Fame)

Hoover.Archives.gov
Host.Madison.com
HoustonChronicle.com
HowStuffWorks.com
HuffingtonPost.com
Idiomation.Wordpress.com
IESA.org (Illinois Elementary
  School Association)
IHSA.org (Illinois High School
  Association)
IllinoisCourts.gov
IMDb.com
IncrediblePeople.com
Independent.co.uk
IndyStar.com
InsideHoops.com
InspireMyKids.com
InterviewMagazine.com
ITFTennis.com (International
  Tennis Federation)
JeanneMarieLaskas.com
JesseOwensMemorialPark.com
JewishSports.org
JockBio.com
JNS.org (Jewish News Service)
JPost.com (Jerusalem Post)
Sports.JRank.org
JSOnLine.com (Milwaukee-
  Wisconsin Journal Sentinel)
JustAMarine.BlogSpot.com
Justia.com
KentLaw.iit.edu
Kentucky.com (Lexington
  Herald-Leader)
KevinDurant.com
KUHistory.com
LAGalaxy.com (Los Angeles
  Galaxy official website)
LakelandTimes.com
  (Minocqua, WI)
LandOfBasketball.com
LATimes.com
LaVidaBaseball.com
Law.NYU.edu
LeBronJamesFamily
Foundation.org
LegendsOfHockey.net
LifeScript.com
LinkedIn.com
LiveScience.com
LOC.gov (Library of Congress)

LosAngeles.Dodgers.MLB.com
  (Official Site of the Los
  Angeles Dodgers)
LouGehrig.com
MassLive.com
MathAware.org
MaxPreps.com
MDAnderson.com
MentalFloss.com
MercuryNews.com
  (*San Jose Mercury News*)
Merriam-Webster.com
MHSAA.com (Michigan High
  School Athletic
  Association)
MIAA.net (Massachusetts
  Interscholastic Athletic
  Association)
MiamiHerald.TypePad.com
MIChronicleOnLine.com
  (*Michigan Chronicle*)
Minnesota.PublicRadio.org
MiscBaseball.wordpress.com
MLB.com
MLBCommunity.org
MLBPlayers.com
  (Major League Baseball
  Players Association)
MLBTradeRumors.com
MLive.com
MLSSoccer.com
MothersDayCelebration.com
MWolverine.com
Nature.com
NBA.com
NBCChicago.com
NBCLatino.com
NBCNews.com
NBCSports.com
NCAA.org
NCBI.NLM.NIH.gov (National
  Center for Biotechnology
  Information)
NDInsider.com
NewRepublic.com
*News.MayoMedical
  Laboratories.com*
News.Medill.Northwestern.edu
News.NationalGeographic.com
NewsOK.com
  (*The Oklahoman*)

Newsroom.UCLA.edu
  (*UCLA Today*)
NewYork.Yankees.MLB.com
NFHS.org (National Federation
  of State High School
  Associations)
NFL.com
NFLCommunications.com
*NFLFootballJournal.
  blogspot.com*
NFLPLayerEngagement.com
NHL.com
NIAAA.org (National
  Interscholastic Athletic
  Administrators Association)
NIASHF.org (National
  Italian American Sports
  Hall of Fame)
NJ.com
NMAct.org (New Mexico
  Activities Association)
NoahsArcFoundation.org
NOLA.com (*New Orleans
  Times-Picayune*)
Notre-Dame-Store.com
NPG.SI.edu (National Portrait
  Gallery Smithsonian Institute)
NPR.org (*National Public Radio*)
NPS.gov (US National Park Service)
NWLC.org (National Women's
  Law Center)
NYDailyNews.com
NYFA.edu (New York Film
  Academy)
NYMag.com
NYPost.com
NYTimes.com
NWHerald.com (*Northwest Herald*)
OCRegister.com (*The Orange
  County Register*)
Olympic.org
OregonLive.com
OSU.edu
  (The Ohio State University)
Packers.com
PaleyCenter.org (The Paley
  Center for Media)
Parents.com
Payton34.com
PBA.com
PBS.org

PeeWeeReese.com
People.com
PoetryFoundation.org
Politico.com
Post-Gazette.com
  (*Pittsburgh Post-Gazette*)
PremierSpeakers.com
PressHerald.com
  (*Portland Press Herald*)
ProBasketballWriters.org
ProFootballHOF.com
Pro-Football-Reference.com
ProGolfRefs.com
Prospect.org
ProtectTheBrain.org (*Brain
  Injury Research Institute*)
PsychologyToday.com
PurdueSports.com
RAndA.org
Rangers.NHL.com (*New York
  Rangers official website*)
RealGM.com
RealSimple.com
ReboundMagazine.com
RetroSheet.org
Review.ChicagoBooth.edu
RickTelander.net
RobertFeder.com
RochesterFirst.com
RogerEbert.com
RollingStone.com
RottenTomatoes.com
RugbyFootballHistory.com
RyderCup.com
SABR.org (Society for American
  Baseball Research)
SanDiegoUnionTribune.com
  (San Bernardino)
SBNation.com
SBSun.com
ScientificAmerican.com
ScoutsFocus.com
Seahawks.com
  (Seattle Seahawks)
SeattleTimes.com
SecondCityHockey.com
SFGate.com
Shutterstock.com
SI.com (*Sports Illustrated*)
SixDayWar.org
Slate.com

SmashingInterviews.com

SmithsonianMag.com

SpecialOlympics.org

Spiegel.de

SportingCharts.com

SportingNews.com

SportsCollectorsDigest.com

SportsEngine.com and
  NGIN.com

Sports.JRank.org

SportsNetLA.com

SportsOnEarth.com

Sports-Reference.com

Stack.com

Steelers.com

SteinbergSports.com

StopBullying.gov

Sun-Sentinel.com
  (SunSentinel [Florida])

TeamSpiritInstitute.org

TeamUSA.org

Tennessean.com

Tennis.com

TennisFame.com
  (International
  Tennis Hall of Fame)

TheAtlantic.com

TheConcession.com

TheDailyBeast.com

TheFixIsIn.net

TheFreeLibrary.com

TheGrio.com

TheGuardian.com

TheLLab.com

TheNationalPastime
  Museum.com

ThePlayersTribune.com

ThePostGame.com

TheRoot.com

TheRumpus.net

TheSlate.com

TheStar.com (The Toronto Star)

TheTablet.org

TheUndefeated.com

TheYeshivaWorld.com

ThinkProgress.org

Time.com

TimeForKids.com

TimesFreePress.com
  (Chattanooga Times Free Press)

Today.com (NBC's Today Show)

Today.Duke.edu

TWCNews.com or Spectrum
  LocalNews.com

Twitter.com

UCDMC.UCDavis.edu
  (UC Davis Health)

UCLABruins.com

UConnHuskies.com

UmpireBible.com

UND.com
  (University of Notre Dame)

UPI.com
  (United Press International)

UpRoxx.com (The Culture of Now)

USAToday.com

USATodayHSS.com (USA Today
  High School Sports)

Variety.com

VeryWell.com

WADA-ama.org
  (World Anti-Doping Agency)

WaitButWhy.com

WalterPayton.info

WashingtonPost.com

WBay.com (Green Bay)

WBUR.org (Boston's NPR
  News Station)

WGNRadio.com

WGNtv.com

When-Is.com

WhiteSox.com

Wired.com

Wisconsin.gov

WiseOldSayings.com

WisTCA.org

WNBA.com

WoodenCourse.com

WomensSportsFoundation.org

WordsWithoutBorders.com

WorldBook.BigChalk.com
  (World Book Online)

WorldMap1.com

Writing.UPenn.edu

WSJ.com
  (Wall Street Journal)

WTATennis.com
  (Women's Tennis Association)

YadVaShem.org

YaleDailyNews.com

YogiBerraMuseum.org

YouTube.com

Spiritual/Jewish Books (in Hebrew/Aramaic)

Avot D'Rahbi Natan.

Chadad, Rabbi David. *Maasei Avot ahl Masekhet Avot.* B'ehr Sheva, Israel: Shivuk Sifrei Kodesh, 2005.

Chasida, Rabbi Yisrael Yitzchak. *Otzar Ishei HaTanakh.* (*Encycopeida of Biblical Personalities: As Seen by the Sages of the Talmud and Midrash*). Jerusalem: Reuven Mass, 1999.

Even-Shoshan, Avraham. *The New Dictionary/ HaMilon HehChadash.* Jerusalem: Kiryat Sefer, 1988.

Feinstein, Rabbi Moshe. *Igrot Moshe.* B'nei B'rak: Ohel Yoseph Printers, 1985.

Kehati, Rabbi Pinchas. *Mishnayot M'vuarot.* Jerusalem: Heikhal Shlomo, 1977.

Midrash Rabba.

Midrash Tanchuma.

Mik'raot G'dolot ahl HaTorah.

Mik'raot G'dolot ahl NaKh.

Mirkin, M.A. (Editor), *Midrash Rabba.* Tel-Aviv: Yavneh Publishing House, Ltd., 1987.

Mishna B'rura, Rabbi Yisrael Meir HaKohen.

Mishneh Torah, Rabbi Moses Maimonides.

Otzar Midrashim, Rabbi Yehuda David Eisenstein.

Sefer HaChinukh, Aaron of Barcelona.

Sefer HaTodaah, Rabbi Eliyahu Ki Tov.

Shulchan Arukh, Rabbi Yoseph Karo.

Sifri.

Talmud Bavli (*Babylonian Talmud*).

Talmud Y'rushalmi (*Jerusalem Talmud*).

Torah T'mima, Rabbi Barukh HaLevi Epstein.

Books (in Hebrew/Aramaic and with English Translation/Commentary)

Alcalay, Reuben. *The Complete Hebrew-English Dictionary.* Ramat Gan, Israel: Massada Publishing Co, 1986.

Bulka, Rabbi Dr. Reuven P. *Chapters of the Sages: A Psychological Commentary on Pirkey Avoth.* Northbale, NJ: Jason Aronson Inc., 1993.

Chavel, Rabbi Dr. Charles (Editor). *The Commandments: Sefer Ha-Mitzvoth of Maimonides.* New York: The Soncino Press, 1967.

Fisch, Harold (Editor). *The Jerusalem Bible*, rev. ed. Jerusalem: Koren Publishers Jerusalem, 1997.

Goldwurm, Rabbi Hersh (Editor). *The Schottenstein Editon: Talmud Bavli/The Gemara: The Classic Vilna Edition, with an Annotated, Interpretive Elucidated, as an Aid to Talmud Study,* 73 vols. Brooklyn: Mesorah Publications, 1992.

Herczeg, Rabbi Yisrael Isser Zvi, in collaboration with Rabbi Yaakov Petroff, Rabbi Yoseph Kamenetsky and Rabbi Yaakov Blinder. *The Saperstein Edition: The Torah: With Rashi's Commentary Translated, Annotated, and Elucidated.* Brooklyn: Mesorah Publications, Ltd., 1998.

Jastro, Dr. Marcus. *A Dictionary of the Targumim, the Talmud Babli and Yerushalmi, and the Midrashic Literature.* Ada, MI: Baker Academic, 2005.

Kitov, Rabbi Eliyahu. *The Book of Our Heritage.* Jerusalem: Feldheim Publishers, 1997.

Sachar, Howard M. *A History of the Jews in the Modern World.* New York: Vintage Books/Penguin Random House, 2006.

Sacks, Rabbi Lord Jonathan (Author of Introduction, Translation and Commentary). *The Koren Ani Tefilla Siddur.* Jerusalem: Koren Publishers Jerusalem, 2015.

Scherman, Rabbi Nosson (Translator and Commentor). *The Complete ArtScroll Siddur.* New York: Mesorah Publications, Ltd., 1993.

Scherman, Rabbi Nosson (Editor). *The Stone Edition: The Chumash: The Torah, Haftaros and Five Megillos with a Commentary Anthologized from the Rabbinic Writings.* Brooklyn: Mesorah Publications, Ltd., 1993.

Scherman, Rabbi Nosson (Editor). *The Stone Edition ArtScroll Tanach.* Brooklyn: Mesorah Publications, Ltd., 1996.

Twerski, Rabbi Dr. Abraham J. *Visions of the Fathers: Pirkei Avos with an Insightful and Inspiring Commentary by Rabbi Abraham J. Twerski, M.D.* Brooklyn: Shaar Press, 1999.

Wengrov, Charles (Editor). *Sefer haHinnuch: The Book of [Mitzvah] Education.* Jerusalem/New York: Feldheim Publishers, 1982.

Books (completely or primarily in English)

Bulka, Rabbi Reuven P. *Judaism on Illness and Suffering.* Northvale, NJ: Jason Aronson, Inc., 1998.

Encyclopedia Judaica, 17 vols. Jerusalem: Keter Publishing House Jerusalem, Ltd., 1972.

Foer, Franklin and Marc Tracy, eds. *Jewish Jocks: An Unorthodox Hall of Fame.* New York/Boston: Twelve Books, 2012.

Frank, Anne. *Anne Frank: The Diary of a Young Girl.* New York: Prentice Hall, 1993.

Gordon, Rabbi James M. *Charity and Welfare in Jewish Law and Its Value for the American Legal System.* Unpublished Senior Research Paper. Northwestern University School of Law, 1985.

Grunfeld, Dayan Rabbi Dr. I. *The Jewish Law of Inheritance*. Nanuet, NY: Feldheim Publishers, 1987.

Krohn, Rabbi Pescah. *Echoes of the Maggid*. New York: Mesorah Publications, Ltd., 1999.

Leibowitz, Dr. Nehama (Translated from Hebrew to English by Aryeh Newman.) *Studies in Genesis, Exodus, Leviticus, Numbers and Deuteronomy* (separate volumes). Jerusalem: The World Zionist Organizaiton, Department for Torah Educaton and Culture in the Diaspora, 1980.

Levine, Peter. *Ellis Island to Ebbets Field: Sport and the American Jewish Experience*. New York: Oxford University Press, 1992.

Lieber, Rabbi Moshe. *The Fifth Commandment: Honoring Parents – Laws, Insights, Stories and Ideas*. New York: Mesorah Publications, Ltd., 2000.

Liebergen, Patrick M. (Compiler and Editor). *Singer's Library of Song: A Vocal Anthology of Masterworks and Folk Songs from the Medieval Era Through the Twentieth Century*. Van Nuys, California: Alfred Publishing Co., Inc.

Penslar, Derek J. *Jews and the Military: A History*. Princeton, New Jersey: Princeton University Press, 2013.

Polenberg, Richard. *The World of Benjamin Cardozo: Personal Values and the Judicial Process*. Cambridge, Massachusetts: Harvard University Press, 1999.

Postal, Bernard, Jesse Silver and Roy Silver. *Encyclopedia of Jews in Sports*. Block Publishing Company, 1965.

Raz, Simcha. *A Tzaddik in Our Time: The Life of Rabbi Aryeh Levin*. Nanuet, New York: Feldheim Publishers, 1978.

Resnicoff, Professor Steven H. *Understanding Jewish Law*. Conklin, New York: Matthew Bender, 2012.

Riskin, Rabbi Shlomo. *The Passover Haggadah*. New York: Ktav Publishing House, 1983.

Ruttman, Larry. *American Jews and America's Game: Voices of a Growing Legacy in Baseball*. Lincoln, Nebraska: University of Nebraska Press, 2013.

Sachar, Howard M. *A History of the Jews in the Modern World*. New York: Vintage Books, 2005.

Siegman, Joseph. *Jewish Sports Legends*. Washington, D.C.: Brassey's Inc., 1997.

Silber, Rabbi Yitzchok Isaac. *The Code of Jewish Conduct, Hilchos BeinAdom L'chaveiro: Laws of Interpersonal Relationships, file:///C:/Users/J/Downloads/Code%20of%20Jewish%20conduct%20Mishpete%20Hashalom%20complete.pdf*.

Slater, Robert. *Great Jews in Sports*. Middle Village, NY: Jonathan David Publishers, Inc., 1983.

Telushkin, Rabbi Joseph. *Jewish Literacy: The Most Important Things to Know About the Jewish Religion, Its People, and Its History*. New York: William Morrow, 1991.

Telushkin, Rabbi Joseph. *Jewish Wisdom: Ethical, Spiritual, and Historical Lessons from the Great Works and Thinkers*. New York: William Morrow, 1994.

Wisniewski, David. *Golem*. New York: Clarion Books, 1996.

Journals and Magazines

Journal of Halacha & Contemporary Society
Moment
The Decalogue Journal

Newspapers

Chicago Jewish News
International Jerusalem Post

Websites

Aish.com
AishDas.org
AllAboutJerusalem.com
AmericanThinker.com
AmericasLibrary.gov
AnneFrank.org
BaltimoreSun.com
Baseball-Reference.com
Beerot.co.il (B'eirot Yitzchak)
Beinenu.com
Biography.com
BIU.ac.il (Bar-Ilan University)
BKNW.org (Beis Haknesses of North Woodmere)
BostonGlobe.com
Brandeis.edu
Britannica.com (Encyclopedia Britannica)
Bucknell.edu (Bucknell University)
BusinessHalacha.com (Business Halacha Institute)
CBSNews.com
CBSSports.com
Chabad.org

ChicagoBaseballMuseum.org
ChicagoTribune.com
CIA.gov
Columbia.edu
Congress.gov
ConstitutionCenter.org
CSLewis.org
Daat.ac.il
DaatTorah.blogspot.com
DeathOfDoctrine.com
ESPN.com
EuroBasket.com
Faculty.Georgetown.edu
Forward.com
Georgetown.edu
GpoPhoto.gov.il
   (The National Photo
   Collection)
Haaretz.com
History.com
History.State.gov
HuffingtonPost.com
JewishBaseballNews.com
JewishEncyclopedia.com
JewishHistory.org
JewishJournal.com
JewishWeek.TimesOfIsrael.com
JewishMag.com
   (Jewish Magazine)
JewishPress.com
History.com
JLaw.com (Jewish Law)
JSpace.com
JStor.org
JTA.org (Jewish
   Telegraphic Agency)
JewishTreats.org
JewishVirtualLibrary.org
Justice.gov.il (Israel Ministry
   of Justice)
JWA.org
   (Jewish Women's Archive)
JWeekly.com
Kotar.co.il
Lookstein.org (Lookstein
   Center for Jewish Education
   of Bar Ilan University)
Metapedia.org
MoralHeroes.org
MorashaSyllabus.com

MyJewishLearning.com
MythsandFacts.org
NBPA.com (National Basketball
   Players Association)
NCAA.com
Nechama.org.il
Newsweek.com
NewYorker.com
NJOP.org (National Jewish
   Outreach Program)
NLEResources.com (The
   Global Resource for Jewish
   Educators and Outreach
   Professionals)
NobelPrize.org
NOVAonline.nvcc.edu
NPR.org
NYCourts.gov
NYTimes.com
Olamot.net
OskarSchindler.dk
OU.org
PBS.org
People.com
RabbiSacks.org
RavKookTorah.org
SacBee.com
Salk.edu
Scholarship.Law.
   Marquette.edu
SeeTheHolyLand.net
Sefaria.org
Senate.gov
SFGate.com
SI.com
Sites.Google.com/site/
   CvodHadam/home/hqdmh
   ("K'vod HaAdahm B'Yahadut")
SportsWorld.NBCSports.com
StandWithUs.com
TamirGoodman.com
TabletMag.com
TheGuardian.com
TheJewishWeek.com
ThinkProgress.org
TimesofIsrael.com
Torah.org
Towson.edu
UCSB.edu (University of
   California Santa Barbara)

USATodayHSS.com
   (USA Today High
   School Sports)
USHMM.org (United States
   Holocaust Memorial
   Museum)
USNews.com
WashingtonJewishWeek.com
WashingtonPost.com
Writing.UPenn.edu
WSJ.com
   (Wall Street Journal)
YadVaShem.org
YU.edu (Yeshiva University)
YUTorah.org
Zadikim.org
Zissil.com